D1497917

DICTIONARY OF AMERICAN FAMILY NAMES

DICTIONARY OF AMERICAN FAMILY NAMES

ELSDON C. SMITH

Author of *The Story of Our Names*

HARPER & ROW PUBLISHERS

New York

DICTIONARY OF AMERICAN FAMILY NAMES

Printed in the United States of America

 For information address
Harper & Row, Publishers, Incorporated,
49 East 33rd Street, New York 16, N. Y.

C-Q

Library of Congress catalog card number: 56-8766

To My Wife

CLARE

CONTENTS

PREFACE

In this vast melting pot of the world, which we call the United States of America, live the peoples of many lands. Here, side by side, they dwell, bound together by similar ideals, blood ties, common interests and enjoyment of the American way of life. Each family carries a distinctive label, a gift from medieval times, allied with its own identity and never forgotten—the family name. Since it has been a commonplace, in the possession of the family for generations, even for many centuries, it is taken for granted. Now and then one pauses to wonder how that particular family name came to identify one's ancestors.

To answer that question is the purpose of this dictionary. Some rare names originated as a result of particular actions or circumstances, the exact nature and origin of which are now probably forever lost. Others can be investigated and their origin discovered, especially the common ones that arose in many different places at about the same time. All of the common names in this country, with some of their variant forms, are here included. Many of the names have taken on a flavor or tinge that is American, the exact form not being found elsewhere, although they have been identified by the country or countries of origin.

A dictionary of this type, involving, as it does, many diverse languages and dialects, not only as spoken at the present time, but including forms used in medieval times, cannot be compiled without assistance and advice from many scholars learned in onomastics.

The American Name Society was organized some years ago to promote the study of names, and this organization has brought together practically all the scholars in this country interested in onomatology. The membership of this Society has been the principal source from which advice could be sought in connection with the many problems that arose in regard to particular family names.

With great pleasure the author therefore acknowledges his indebtedness to the following very able and learned scholars: Samuel H. Abramson, Timothy M. Bishop, Samuel L. Brown, Albert J. Carnoy, Charles Collins, Joseph N. Corcoran, Jack Autrey Dabbs, Geart B. Droege, Gösta Frantzen, Peter Fu, Joseph G. Fucilla,

Demetrius J. Georgacas, Erwin G. Gudde, E. Gustav Johnson, Ellen Johnson, Aneale L. Kushmar, J. J. Lamberts, Werner F. Leopold, Alexander McQueen, Max Markrich, P. J. Meertens, James A. Morrison, Merle Morrison, Jens Nyholm, Ernst Pulgram, J. B. Rudnyćkyj, Alfred Senn, Mary Florence Steiner, John P. Sydoruk, and Gutierre Tibón.

However, none of the errors can be charged against any of these erudite and competent scholars. Let's face it: the instances of bad judgment and errors are due entirely to the ignorance of the author.

Much of the completeness and accuracy of the work can be credited to the careful help and support from Clare I. Smith, my wife, who spent countless hours, days and weeks in studies of the relative frequency of American family names, and in checking and cross-checking for accuracy and completeness in the explanations. Without her steady help and encouragement this work would have taken many months longer.

To list the works consulted would serve little purpose here, since works in English on personal names are listed in *Personal Names: A Bibliography,* compiled by the author and published by the New York Public Library in 1952. Many later works have been listed by the author in bibliographies published by *Names, Journal of the American Name Society.* A select list of the more important works on personal names has been listed in Chapter XIV of *The Story of Our Names,* by the present author, published by Harper & Brothers in 1950. Of course, various works on personal names in other languages have been consulted as well as numerous standard reference works.

ELSDON C. SMITH

INTRODUCTION

After the Crusades in Europe, people began, perhaps unconsciously, to feel the need of a family name, or at least a name in addition to the simple one that had been possessed from birth. The nobles and upper classes, especially those who went on the Crusades, observed the prestige and practical value of an added name and were quick to take a surname, usually the name of the lands they owned. When the Crusaders returned from the wars, the upper classes who had stayed at home soon followed suit.

When the clerks who kept the records in the manors and on the feudal lands of the nobles and the great landowners noted the payment of fines and amercements by the vassals, they needed an additional description in order to distinguish one Robert or Leofric from another. The inclination to ridicule or compliment a neighbor or acquaintance by applying a nickname contributed to the rise of surnames.

It would do no good for the lord's clerk to ask the peasant what additional name he possessed. He didn't have any other name and hadn't thought about the matter. Therefore, when the clerk noted the vassal's name in the manor records he added, of his own initiative, a brief description. It was likely that the vassal was not known among his neighbors by the description put down by the scribe. The very earliest bynames were not names by which those so described were known, except in isolated instances.

The early forms of most descriptive bynames were with prepositions, as *atte Hill* (at the hill), *on Mylatune* (from Milton), *de Bedeford* (from Bedford), *of Boclande* (of Buckland), *buta Port* (outside the gate), *del Boys* (at the wood), *Cole sunu* (son of Cole), *filius Alann* (son of Allan), and *the Clerec* (the clerk or clergyman). Early documents were written in Latin in many countries and the names took Latin forms although the man would be known generally by the descriptive word in the common tongue, and so the family names are, in England, for example, English and not Latin. English surnames have generally dropped the prepositions, except a few names like *Atterbury, Bywater* and *Underwood.* Many French and Italian names have retained the preposition or article, as *Dupont* and *Lo Bello.*

Surnames are not just words or sounds. They originated as descriptions of the person for reasons of better identification. These early additional names were bynames and not family names. They described one individual and not his whole family.

A byname, that is, a name in addition to the Christian name and not necessarily a family name, was at first not hereditary. As long as it was descriptive of the person to whom it was applied, it was not handed down from father to son, although in some cases the same name might be borne by both father and son, as when both had red hair or both followed the same occupation. It was only gradually, over several centuries, that bynames or surnames became hereditary family names. Just as a nickname need be appropriate only for an instant, a byname which became a family name need be descriptive only for a short time.

In England, by the end of the fourteenth century, surnames were generally hereditary; in France the process evolved a little earlier and in Germany a little later. In Italy the patricians of Venice adopted an hereditary surname system during the tenth and eleventh centuries, and they were the first in Europe. On the other hand, many family names became hereditary in very recent times in Norway, Sweden, Turkey, the mountainous districts of Wales and Scotland and among the Germanic and Slavic Jews.

Names first became hereditary, in most countries, among the nobles and landowners. Since so many of their names were the names of the lands they held, when the son inherited the land it was only natural that he inherit the name. Among the lower classes, since the son generally learned from, and followed, the trade of his father, the same occupational name was applied, not because it was inherited, but because it applied to the son as well as the father. The occupational name could be said to be inherited only when the son followed another trade but was known by the same surname as the father.

Even today if one had to identify another whose name was not known, it would likely be done in one of four ways: (1) the place where the man now lived or had previously lived would be mentioned, as at the sign of the bell, or by the hill or stream, or from the manor of Newton; or (2) by the man's occupation, as the smith or the carter; or (3) by referring to the father's name, as the son of John or Rob; or (4) by noting the man's most prominent characteristic, as short, fat, red (hair), or crooked mouth.

Practically all of the European family names were thus derived in one or another of the following four ways:

I. From the man's place of residence, either present or past;
II. From the man's occupation;
III. From the father's name;
IV. From a descriptive nickname.

From the man's place of residence.

Almost every city, town or village extant in the Middle Ages has served to name one or more families. While a man lived in the town or village he would not be known by its name, as that would be no means of identification—all in the village would then be so named. But when a man left his birthplace or village where he had been known, and went elsewhere, people would likely refer to him by the name of his former residence or by the name of the land which he owned. In many cases, the surname is the form of the place name current at the time the surname arose, and thus not easily recognizable on modern maps. In other cases, the place name which gave rise to the family name cannot be found on maps because the place no longer exists. It is curious to note, however, that the spelling of the surname changed along with the spelling of the town name in most cases.

Some had the name of a manor or village because they were lords of that manor or village and owned it. However, of people today who have a place name as a surname, a very small minority descended from the lord of that manor. The majority descended from vassals or freemen who once lived in the village or manor.

One might acquire a place name as a surname by living at or near the place. This is particularly true of topographical features. When people lived close to the soil, as they did in the Middle Ages, they were acutely conscious of every local variation in landscape and countryside. Every field or plot of land was identified in normal conversation by a descriptive term. If a man lived on, or near, a hill or mountain, he might receive the word as a family name. Every country had hills and mountains and living on, or near, them gave many people names, as Mr. *Maki,* from Finland, Mr. *Dumont* and Mr. *Depew,* from France, Mr. *Zola,* from Italy, Mr. *Jurek,* from Poland, Mr. *Kopecky,* from Czechoslovakia, and the ubiquitous Mr. *Hill.*

Dwelling at, or near, a lake, brook or river would distinguish one from others who lived further from the water, and such names were quite common in almost every country. Lakes gave rise to *Jarvi* (Finland), *Kuhl* (Germany), *Loch* (Scotland), and *Pond, Pool, Leake, Lynn* and *Lake* (England), while streams produced *Strom* (Sweden), *Potocki* (Poland), *Joki* (Finland), *Rio* and *Rivera* (Spain), *Klink* (Holland and Germany), and *Brooks* and *Rivers* (England), to list only a few of the most common names. Many other names include a suffix after the word to designate the man who lived at or near the lake or stream.

Woods, stones, fields, plains, swamps, enclosures or fenced-in places and trees are natural objects in all the old world countries and have served to name the people living on, in or near them. Fords were common at a time when there were few bridges. Many of these names that appear to be from a topographical term are really from a definite town, village or field name that cannot be identified at the present time. Today we live in cities and towns where streets are named and houses are numbered so we have little occasion to use topographical terms.

When a family name derives from the name of a town where the original bearer once resided, a brief explanation or translation of the town name is given in parentheses wherever possible. When more than one meaning of a place name is given, the reason often is that there are several villages with exactly the same name with reference to present-day spelling, although they were derived in different ways. For example, *Broughton* is a very common English place name. Certain villages of that name in Buckinghamshire, Cumberland, Derbyshire, Huntingdonshire, Lancashire, Leicestershire, Nottinghamshire, Oxfordshire, Wiltshire, Warwickshire, Worcestershire and Yorkshire referred to "a homestead on a brook," while other villages named Broughton, in Lancashire, Lincolnshire, Northamptonshire, Shropshire, Staffordshire and Sussex, designated "a homestead by a fortified place," and Broughton, in Hampshire and Lincolnshire, originally meant "a homestead on a hill or barrow." Many place names in Europe are of great antiquity; the meanings are so obscure that it would serve little purpose to give them without a lengthy discussion of the reasons for accepting that explanation.

To ascertain properly the meaning of the different elements in a name is not always easy. This is especially true of the common elements and more particularly true of those which make up place names, such as the English *ham, thorp, wic* and *worth*. Take the simple element *hope,* found in so many place names which have been taken as family names. It meant, among other meanings, "a piece of enclosed land in the midst of fens," "a small, enclosed valley, a blind valley," "a valley." Take again, for example, the Old English *leah,* generally found as *-ley,* a terminal element in a great many English place names and consequently an element in numerous family names. It meant "an open place in a wood, a glade, a spot where grass grew," "meadow or pasture land," "open, arable land," or "a wood, grove or forest," some of these definitions being in direct apposition. In some instances the exact meaning can be ascertained, in others it can only be guessed. The most common English place name element is *-ton,* meaning "an enclosure," "a homestead," "a village," "a town," at various times and in different parts of England. Similar difficulties occur in names from languages other than English. Most elements now meaning town or city started out meaning "a place or a settlement," often a place where only one family resided.

An important source of family names arises from residence in a house or inn identified by a signboard. In some countries, in very early times, inns and public houses were required by law to display a sign. Since few people could read, pictorial signs, rather than the written signs we have today, were the almost invariable rule. Even the early Greeks and Romans identified their public places by distinctive signs. One public house might display the picture of a white horse, another a goblet, while another might have a bush over its door. One of the commonest was a bell; others were ball, cock and swan. Animals, birds and fishes of all kinds were popular. Some of these signs were wooden or stone images, others were merely painted pictures. In later times more elaborate signs were common, and in London there were the *Angel and Glove,* the *Three Kings, Adam and Eve,* the *Whistling Oyster* and many others.

When a man lived or worked in a building identified by a pictorial sign it was only natural to refer to him by reference to his distinctive place of residence. In medieval times most people also lived where they worked. There can be little doubt that the ancient signboards provide explanation of many otherwise inexplicable family names, but the direct evidence is scanty because of the disappearance of the very early signboards. Every conceivable object, both animate and inanimate, became the subject of signboards in various countries, and influenced family names.

With regard to family names from signboards a note of caution is necessary. In later times many tradespeople adopted punning signs which helped the customers to remember their names, although such signs may have had little to do with the derivation of their names. Some went to extremes. Thus, in England, Mr. Chester exhibited a chest with a star on it; Mr. Lionel had a lion with *L* on its head; John Handcock used a hand and a cock, while John Drinkwater imitated his name with a fountain. In other European countries the same practice prevailed. Tavern, inn and shop signs continued after house signs fell into disuse.

From the man's occupation.

To describe one by reference to his occupation or profession is most natural. The most common occupational surnames are not necessarily those of the occupations followed by the most men in the Middle Ages. Where everybody was a fisherman or where everybody tilled the soil, the occupation would not serve to describe the bearer. If the fisherman moved inland or the tiller of the soil worked among sheep raisers, their occupation would become a means of identification to set them apart from others in the neighborhood.

Most of the occupations or professions reflected in our family names are those known in the small villages in Europe, or those followed in a king's, or important noble's, household, or in some large religious house or monastery. During the Middle Ages much of Europe was composed of small villages. Even the larger cities would be regarded as comparatively small today. Every village, no matter how small, would need the services of one who could work and fashion objects out of iron or other metals and thus the smith is found in every country. Bulgaria surnames him *Kovac,* the Danes use *Smed,* the Hungarians say *Kovars,* the French call him *Lefevre* and *Faure,* the Germans say *Schmidt* or *Smidt,* in Italy it is *Ferraro,* the Russians refer to *Kuznetzov,* and the Poles to *Kowal.*

Every village required the services of a *Carpenter* to build houses of wood and of a *Miller* to grind the grain. The *Bakers* and *Cooks* prepared the bread from the ground grain. *Taylors* made the clothing while the *Shoemakers* shod the people. Where the inhabitants all tilled the soil, they needed men to take care of the animals. The *Shepherds* tended the sheep. *Haywards* saw that fences or hedges were kept in repair to keep the animals from the growing crops. The *Bailiff* and the *Steward* had charge of the lord's affairs, and the *Parker* tended the lord's parks. All these common occupations and many others are repeated in the family nomenclature of every country.

Priests were always present in large numbers to nurture the religious life of the people. The clergy were not all required to lead a celibate life. The minor clergy had privileges not possessed by the common man. As the clergy were about the only ones with any education, when one desired to prove that he was a member of the clergy, about all he needed to do was to prove that he could read. In the case of one accused of crime the status of clergy was important. The clergy were tried in the church courts, which were more lenient than the judges in the secular courts, so that when one who could read was charged with a crime, he could plead "benefit of clergy," and prove it by reading the passage pointed out to him in the Bible and thus be tried in the less severe clerical courts. All this stimulated the origin of surnames referring to the many religious offices.

Occupations which were looked up to and respected were more likely to produce permanent family names than those which called attention to servile status. The *Stewards*, *Sargents* and *Franklins* surnamed many more people in proportion to their numbers than the *Vassals* or *Cotters*.

From the father's name.

The patronymical name, that is, the surname derived from the name of the father is very common in all countries, and each common given name takes many forms in all countries. As children were growing up, it was natural to refer to them by the name of their paternal parent. It is easy to ascertain what Christian names and what forms of them were popular during the surname period by examining the family names derived from them. In some cases where the mother came from a more important family, or was a widow, the children might acquire their mother's name. Among Jews it was common practice to take the name of the mother, and, in a few cases, of one's wife. A boy apprenticed to learn a trade who lived with the master's family often was known by the forename or surname of the master rather than that of his father, he having grown to manhood and having become known to others in association with his master rather than his parents.

Some family names derived from the father's name use exactly the same form as the father's forename, such as *George* and *Thomas*. Many German names follow this principle. But the greater number in the western countries have some patronymical ending or beginning. With English names it is the termination *-son*. Other endings, indicating "son" are the Danish and Norwegian *-sen,* the Armenian *-ian,* the Finnish *-nen,* the Greek *-pulos,* the Polish *-wiecz* and the Spanish *-ez.* Prefixes denoting "son" are the Scotch and Irish *Mac-,* the Norman *Fitz-* and the Welsh *Ap-*. The Irish *O'* means "grandson." Many of these prefixes have been dropped, especially among the Irish. In this dictionary, names which originally had the prefix are explained as "the son of . . ." or "grandson of . . ."

Other important terminations of family names are the diminutive endings. These are particularly numerous among the French, German, Irish, Italian and Spanish names. Children and older people were often referred to by hypocoristic forms, that is, an endearing or shortened form of the Christian name, such as *Dick* for Richard or *Clem* for Clement, described in the dictionary as "pet names." They are the accented syllable and may be the first part of the name as *Abe* from Abraham or *Dan* from Daniel; the middle part, as *Hans* from Johannes and *Zeke* from Ezekiel; or the last part, as *Mass* from Thomas or *Zander* and *Sander* from Alexander.

European family names which embody a Christian name include all the important Bible names in their different national forms. As an example, John, in its various national forms, produces common surnames in all countries. There are *Johnson* and *Jackson* in England, *Johns* and *Jones* in Wales, *Jensen, Jansen* and *Hansen* in Denmark, *Jonsson* and *Johanson* in Sweden, *Janowicz* in Poland, *Ivanov* in Russia and Bulgaria, *Ianson* in Scotland, *Janosfi,* in Hungary, *Jantzen* in Holland, and *MacEoin* in Ireland, all referring to the son of John. *Peter, Paul, James, Simon, Michael* and *Thomas,* in their various national forms, are also exceedingly common in every country where the Bible is known.

A brief translation or explanation of the personal name from which the family name arose is generally given in parentheses. Many names which appear to be from common words are really rare old forenames which have dropped from ordinary usage. *Gold,* for example, is from the Old English *Gold* or *Golda,* a not uncommon early personal name.

It will be noted that many surnames are from the old Teutonic names, most of which are dithematic in form, that is, they consist of two elements; and translations, separated by a comma, of the two elements only are given. Certain name-themes were in use, and almost any two of them could be combined to make a name with little or no attention being given to the meaning of the combined name. Thus *William,* from *vilja* "resolution" and *helma* "helmet," means "resolution, helmet" and not "the resolute helmet" or "helmet of resolution." There is no relationship between the two elements; they are merely combined to make a new concept, a man's name. *Robert* is from two name-themes, *hrode* meaning "fame," and *beorht* meaning "bright," and there is no semantic connection between the two elements. Many name-themes are found either at the beginning or end of the name. There is *Wulfgar* and *Garulf,* and there is *Wulfsige* and *Sigewulf.* "Wolf" is a very common name-theme. Some name-themes are found usually at the beginning, others only at the end.

From a descriptive nickname.

If a man were unusually tall, or short, or fat, or slim, or slow, or fast, or long-legged, the fact would be observed and he would be nicknamed accordingly. Today, even strangers will quickly call a red-haired man "Red." Such a descriptive nickname would be added to his forename and might become a surname. *Red,* under its various forms, is a common family name in many countries. *Reid, Reed* and *Read* are very common in England where also are found *Ruff, Russ, Russel,* and *Ruddy.* In France it would be *Rousseau, Rouse,* or *Larouse,* in Italy, *Purpura* and *Rossi,* the Czecho-Slovakians would call him *Cervenka* or *Cerveny,* the Hungarians say *Voros,* the Germans, *Roth,* the Grecian form would be *Cokinos* or *Pyrrhos,* and the Irish *Flynn.*

Names calling attention to light or dark complexion are common throughout the world. Light complexion is designated by words meaning white or pale. Thus we find *Bianco* (Italy), *Le Blanc* (France), *Labno* (Poland), *Lichter* (Germany and Holland), *Weiss* (Germany), *Bialas* (Poland), *Bily* and *Bilek* (Czecho-Slovakia), and, of course, *White* and *Light* (England). Dark-complexioned people are named by words meaning brown, dark or black. Thus, *Brown,* and *Brun* and *Braun* come from England, France and Germany, respectively. Mr. *Black* is well known; Mr. *Schwartz* comes from Germany, Mr. *Morin* from France, Messrs. *Karas, Karras* and *Melas* speak Greek, Mr. *Fekete* is a Hungarian, Mr. *Cherney* hails from Czecho-Slovakia, while the Russians would call him *Chernoff* and the Hebrews, *Pincus;* Mr. *Fosco* comes from Italy, and Mr. *Czernik* from Poland, to name only a few who end up in America.

Small or short men are so named everywhere. Italy calls them

Basso or *Curcio*. Germany refers to them as *Klein, Kurtz, Stutz* and *Wenig*. The Poles say *Niziolek* and the Hungarians mention *Kiss*. In France it is *Lacour*. Russia names them *Malek,* and Poland knows them as *Malek* and *Malecki,* while in Lithuania it is *Mazeika* and in Czecho-Slovakia *Maly*. Besides *Small* and *Short,* England has named many of them *Litt* and *Lytle,* while the Scotch form is *Smail*. Tall or big men, likewise, stand out throughout the world. There is *Le Grand* and *Grande* from France; and *Nagy* from Hungary. It is *Longo* in Italy, *Groot* from Holland, *Feltz, Hoch, Homan,* and *Lang* in Germany, *Large, Long* and *Lang,* as well as *Longfellow* in England. The fat man is often distinguished from the large man. Germany calls him *Dick, Gross* and *Groth,* France says *Gras*. In Ukraine it is *Waskey*. The absence of "Fat" or a synonym of that word as a very common name in England draws attention to the gaunt bodies of the English.

Among some peoples the more opprobrious nicknames seem to be accepted with equanimity. One might be called Thief, Cuckold or Bastard. Other names referring to sex and parts of the body are not uncommon, as proved by early records. Among the English and most Americans this type of surname has all but disappeared. Such nicknames tend to be altered into inoffensive or meaningless words. Indeed, many milder nicknames, once so common, have gone into the discard.

Family names originating from nicknames can easily be mistaken for names in other classifications. A man who tilled the soil for a livelihood might make his own shoes in the evening and might thus receive the nickname of *Shoemaker,* though that was not his occupation. He might have made only one pair of shoes in his lifetime. Another might be nicknamed with a place name because he had once made a trip to that place. One who made a trip to Paris and bored others by continually talking about it might be so nicknamed. *Palmer* was the palm-bearing pilgrim who had returned from the Holy Land. A man might be referred to as *Hansen* merely from some close relationship with an older man named *Hans,* although not related to him. There is a semantic relationship between topographical terms and bodily shape; a short, lumpish person, for example, might be referred to as a hillock or mound, a tall, thin man, or one with a pointed head, might be likened to a pointed hill. Indeed, any word could be used as a nickname and might become a surname.

Animal names are found as common surnames in all European

countries. Every familiar animal, bird or fish has entered into some family name. The bear was the king of beasts in the north of Europe and has been much used in the formation of names. Such names are derived from a nickname applied by a man's neighbors, from some real or fancied resemblance to the animal. One noted for speed or an awkward stride might be called *Hare, Haas* or *Cooney.* A cunning or crafty person might be called *Fox, Fuchs, Voss, Todd, Liska, Liss, Volpe, Colfax* or some other name, depending on the language or dialect spoken where he lived; a dirty or filthy person, *Hogg;* a vain man, *Poe;* an excellent swimmer, *Fish.* Color, voice, temperament and bodily shape tend to originate these animal nicknames. A dark man might be called *Crow,* one with a pleasant voice might be likened to a *Lark,* the quiet man to a *Dove* and the long-legged man would call to mind a *Crane, Heron* or *Stork.*

Another source of animal names is the house, shop or inn signs previously explained. However, all of these names must be carefully examined as the origin may be some word corrupted into the name of a familiar animal. *Badger,* for example, generally does not refer to the animal, but is one who buys commodities and transports them in a bag elsewhere for sale, or who comes from Badger, in Shropshire. Mr. *Beaver,* in many cases, came from Beauvoir, in France. Many animal surnames were first applied as forenames and are thus patronymics. One reason for the frequency of names of animals is that they were popular and common terms among the people of all parts of Europe, and since they entered into numerous dialects, we have many different names for each familiar animal, bird or fish.

These four classes of names explain the overwhelming majority of family names of Europe. Indeed, one should say that practically all surnames (except those few consciously adopted) belong to one or another of these four classes. Names in European countries are uniform in their meanings. The difference is only in the language from which they are derived. This uniformity in Europe in regard to the origin of family names might be stressed by considering the compound name, *Drinkwater,* an English name, not at all unknown. In France, the same name arose and the French spelled it *Boileau.* The Italians observed the phenomena and labeled the man *Bevilacqua.* Among the Germans the name is rather rare, but some do bear the name of *Trinkwasser,* while *Waterdrinker* is a Dutch version.

In some countries one class of names is emphasized more than others. Among the Welsh, Scotch, Irish, Danes, Swedes and Norwegians, patronymical names (surnames derived from the fathers' names) predominate, and they are very popular among the Germans and Poles; many descriptive nicknames are found among the Italians and Irish; place names are common with the English and Germans.

Corruption of family names.

Before spelling became frozen by the universal use of dictionaries and the spread of education, family names were in a constant state of flux in all countries. Names like the Scotch *Ogilvie,* the German *Baer* and the Irish *Shaughnessy,* have almost an infinite number of forms and spellings. The component parts of a name may change in form. For example, the ubiquitous *-ham* may be altered to *-am, -um, -om, -man, -nam, -num, -son* and *-hem.* As the languages and dialects changed in spelling, so did many of the names. Some retained archaic spellings, however, and thus their simple meaning became lost to the person not learned in onomatology. Various laws in the different European countries, particularly military rules and regulations, have, in this century, tended to restrict the alteration of family names.

As surnames have undergone various corruptions and changes in the countries where they arose, it is not surprising that this process of corruption and change was greatly accelerated when brought to America. For the unlettered pioneer, names of all nationalities took on a roughly phonetic spelling. There was, and still is, a strong propensity to alter an unfamiliar name into a familiar name or word with a similar sound. The Dutch *Roggenfelder* became the American *Rockefeller;* the German *Dietz* became *Deeds* in America. The number of alterations of this kind is endless. Many names that appear to be English are really derived from other tongues. The longer, more awkward or unpronounceable ones are shortened and simplified, generally with the idea of making them more like English names or at least easier on the eye and ear familiar with the English tongue. Some are deliberately translated into the more popular names. Thus, people of other nationalities than the ones mentioned in this dictionary can be found for almost every name. Many English *Millers* are really German *Muellers;* many English *Smiths* are really German *Schmidts.*

In numerous instances the spelling of foreign names is altered to make their pronunciation more agreeable to American ears.

Even among common English names this principle produces mutation. The terminal *-s* in many cases has no meaning other than to give a certain ease in enunciation, as *Stubbs* and *Brooks*. In other names, such as the Welsh *Edwards* and *Williams,* the final *-s* definitely designates the patronymic; in some cases it merely indicates the possessive and in others the plural, while in still others it is only the remaining evidence of an old case ending. Names without the terminal *-s* exist alongside of those where it has been added. In some instances the form with the final *-s* is more common than without it, while in other names the opposite is true. Another common alteration brought about by pronunciation is the medial *p,* as in *Thompson* and *Simpson.* The common *-sson* termination of Swedish patronymical names commonly drops one *s* in this country, *Petersson* quickly becomes *Peterson.* Many names have a terminal *-e* or *-d* or *-t,* or not, according to the fancy of present or past bearers. There are many other common corruptions and substitutions of consonants. It would take a large book to explain all of them. Each vowel may change to any other vowel. Variations in names tend to follow certain definite rules and many difficult names can be explained after the correct principle is applied.

Nationality.

In many cases, designating the proper nationality has presented difficulties. The nationality, or nationalities, given after each name merely designates the country from which most of the persons bearing that name came, and is not meant in any way to denote the language from which the word or root giving rise to the name comes. Many strictly English surnames are derived from French words or places. Many French and Italian names come from Teutonic words.

Separating nationalities within a family of languages poses problems. In the Scandinavian countries many names are common to two or more countries. Thus *Nelson* and *Larson* are found commonly in both Norway and Sweden. The Celtic countries have names popular in all of them. It has been impractical to attempt to distinguish carefully between the various Soviet Socialist Republics. The Ukrainians have been identified separately, but the Byelorussians, or White Russians, have generally been included under Russians. The Slavic countries have many names in common. The Teutonic languages have provided family names which have the same form and meaning in different countries, but are more common in some nations than in others. The Romance countries have presented fewer difficulties than most of the language families.

In designating nationality the troublesome question arises as to how long a name must be resident in a country to be considered native to that country. A French name that came over to England with the Conqueror, in 1066, and has resided ever since then in England, can surely be considered an English name, especially if the name, even though French in appearance, is not common in that form in France. Roger de Beaumont, for example, is listed in *Domesday Book* (1086) as one of the Dorsetshire landowners; he took his name from Beaumont in Normandy, and the name has become common in England and the United States.

But what about the French Huguenots who went to England, Switzerland and Germany during the seventeenth century? No hard and fast rule can be set up, especially in those cases where it is difficult to find out just how long a name has been current in a country. Consistency is neither possible nor always desirable when dealing with all languages and dialects in each language, as well as archaic terms and provincial usage. To some extent the classification is arbitrary. A name may have been a rare name in a country for hundreds of years until its numbers were bolstered by another name, exactly the same in spelling but entirely different in origin. The nationality given would then be that of the later arrival.

Names may have been altered by being resident for a time in another country, but still may not have attained the nationality of that country through which it came. For example, a Polish name may have emigrated to Germany, and in the course of a hundred years the name may have been altered to look like a German name. However, upon becoming current in the United States, it might still be a Polish name and indicate Polish nationality. Thus *Bieschke* came to the United States from Poland by way of Germany. Some of the difficulties attendant upon designating nationality could have been avoided by merely noting the language from which the name was derived. However, this would not have satisfied many who wished to learn about their names and their national origin. To say that a name resident in England since the Conquest was derived from Erse, Gaelic, Breton, Cornish, Swedish, Norwegian, Icelandic, French, Dutch, Old High German or some other language, would not tell the bearer much. It might also be traced back to the Latin, Greek, Hebrew or Sanskrit, but that would be the work of the philologist, not the onomatologist.

The same name with the same spelling may be derived independently from two or more different languages and have entirely different explanations which are sometimes given under one entry. For example, the name *Brody,* sometimes spelled *Brodie,* is found in Ireland, Scotland, Germany and Russia. In Ireland it was originally *MacBruaideadha,* that is, the son of Bruaideadh (fragment, or morsel). The Scotch derived it from the barony of Brodie, in Moray, meaning a muddy place, while in Germany it referred to a man with a large or unusual beard. The Russians with that name came from Brody, in Russia. In the dictionary variant forms of the name may also be given, and the explanations may not apply equally to all forms. Thus among the Germans and Russians the form is usually *Brody* and not *Brodie.* This is an incongruity that must be accepted because of limitations of space. Whether names are grouped together or separated depends to some extent on the degree of difference in meaning and the importance of the different forms from the point of view of numbers.

Names from one language frequently spill over into another language, especially into the language current in the country where the bearer lives. If a dozen people in America have a name marked as German, for example, one can be very sure that at least one or two among them will not be a German. He may be a Frenchman, Belgian, Russian or Pole, whose name originally was so near to the German name in spelling or sound that it gradually changed to the German form. If a dozen people have a common English name, possibly three of them are of a nationality other than English, whose names have gradually adapted themselves in this country to a familiar English form. Part of them may have deliberately altered them to the English form. When two or more nationalities have substantially contributed to a certain name, more than one nationality has been credited even though in one of them there has been a slight change. Diligent search might even turn up a dozen origins for a single name; only the more important ones are listed in this dictionary because of space limitations.

Jewish names.

Jewish family names have presented unusual problems since many of them are of comparatively recent origin and artificial in nature due to their conscious adoption. In Europe, particularly outside of Spain and Portugal, many Jews did not have surnames until compelled to assume them by laws promulgated in the latter part of the eighteenth and early part of the nineteenth centuries. While a great many Jews accepted as surnames the names of the cities or villages where they were born or from whence they came and others were known or identified by the name of their father, it is clear that some knowingly adopted unusual or fanciful names. The only explanation that can be given of names like *Rosenblum* and *Greenblatt* is a translation into English. Jews living in crowded, airless and sunless ghettos frequently adopted names which alluded to green woods and fields. Some who were slow in accepting a surname were arbitrarily assigned names by the governing authorities. Some of these were of a ridiculous or startling nature. However, most of these odd and unusual names were quickly dropped or altered, especially upon arrival in the United States.

No attempt has been made to identify Jewish family names as such. Some names are borne only by Jews, others are borne by both Jews and Gentiles. Assigning nationalities to some of these Jewish names has brought forth complications. However, all of these Jewish names have been identified by nationality except a few, such as *Cohen* and *Levy,* which have been designated merely as Hebrew. It must be remembered, however, that many Eastern European Jews, upon coming to the United States, adopted German family names because at that time the German Jewish names were the aristocratic names among the Jews.

A curious practice found among the Jews has been that of adopting surnames formed from abbreviations or contractions of a man's own name added to the Hebrew titles and names of his father, or of the father's Hebrew names. Descendants of Ben Rabbi Judah Lowe became *Brill;* Rabbi David, the Hazan, produced *Bardah;* Sabbatai Cohen originated the surname *Schach.* Sheliah Tzibbur (minister of the congregation) gave rise to the name *Schatz,* while Segan Leviyyah, literally "assistant of the Leviteship," became *Segal, Segel* and the like.

Jews have assimilated their Jewish names with non-Jewish names current in the countries where they lived. They change to a similar-sounding name, generally one beginning with the same initial as their Jewish name. *Rabbin* becomes *Robin* and *Rabbinowitch* becomes *Robinson.* Other names are loosely translated into names current among the non-Jewish majority.

Mortal man is forever reaching for better things, and toward what he views as noble, genteel or aristocratic; and certain names, from time to time, are regarded as socially acceptable and others as plebeian. Names in Poland terminating in *-ski* were held in high esteem; a larger proportion of Poles in America bear such names than in Poland! If a degree of prestige can be obtained by the use of such a name, the element could be easily attached to occupy one's time while crossing the ocean. Certain farm names carried prestige among Norwegians, and what was to prevent them from adopting such names upon emigrating to America? In the same way many Swedes looked back and adopted the distinctive soldier name of a grandfather.

These soldier names in Sweden were an unusual feature of their permanent family names. When a young man of the peasant class was inducted into the army, he frequently adopted another name for use during his military career. Perhaps his family name was too common to identify him properly when associated with many others. These soldier names were usually of one syllable, a common Swedish word, as *Alm* (oak), *Bjork* (birch), *Hjelm* (helmet), *Quist* (twig), *Rask* (quick) or *Varg* (wolf) and the like, and might be changed when the soldier was assigned to another post. When the soldier returned to civilian life he usually discarded his soldier name and re-assumed his old family name. The soldier name was perpetuated as an hereditary family name when it was adopted by the soldier's descendants.

Common in many European countries was the custom, after one graduated from a university, to adopt a new surname, usually a translation into a Greek or Latin form of a word, or name, bearing some relationship to the bearer. If the name of one's old home was *Skog* (forest), he might adopt *Sylvander;* if the patronymic was *Karlsson,* it might be altered to *Carolus.* Linnaeus, the Swedish botanist, Latinized his original surname, *von Linné,* after he had completed his formal education. Philipp Schwarzert, the German scholar, made a translation to *Melanchthon.* Wilhelm Holtzmann, the sixteenth-century classical scholar, translated his surname to *Xylander.*

In all countries very few people have consciously selected their family names. They have merely acquiesced, generally unconsciously, in a name by which they have become known. Even those who deliberately change their name are strongly influenced by the name they seek to discard. Most of the people who change their name merely shorten the name they bear, alter its spelling to simplify it, or translate it into the language current in the place where they live. Few deliberately choose an entirely different name unless adopted into another family.

Among some of the early Swedes and Norwegians the surname changed with each generation. Thus Lars the son of Swen Olesson was not Lars Olesson but Lars Swensson, and his son would bear the surname of Larsson.

To get away from the ordinary patronymical name in Sweden the government encouraged its citizens to adopt nature names, that is, names composed of two elements, usually words for trees, plants, flowers or topographical terms, without regard to meanings, and without any, or very little, relationship to the person adopting the name. Therefore, in this dictionary, such Swedish names as *Bergstrom, Almquist, Sandstrom* and *Stromkvist* can only be translated into English.

Because of the extreme age of some of the Chinese family names, only a translation has been attempted in most instances. The Chinese were the first to have hereditary family names, having had them for more than two thousand years. As the Chinese family names were greatly limited in number, the Chinese have more of the common names than their numbers in this country would seem to warrant.

Scotch and Irish names beginning with *Mac* are spelled *Mac* or *Mc* in accordance with the spelling under which the greater number of any particular name are found, but they are all listed together as if spelled *Mac*. Both Irish and Scotch purists complain that the contraction to *Mc* is "wrong." In America, however, most people contract the prefix to *Mc,* the tendency being slightly stronger among the Irish. Most Irish names may take the *O'* prefix meaning "grandson." With respect to capitals in the middle of names, there is no uniformity, the prevailing practice as to a particular name is followed in this dictionary. There is usually little or no difference in nationality or meaning whether the name appears as *Du Pre* or *Dupre.*

In Italy, names beginning with a preposition or article are always written with a space between the two words, as *De Leo, La Guardia* and *Dal Santo.* The American custom of closing the space is probably due to the influence of the Gaelic *Mac* names, which are usually written without any space between the prefix and the name. In this dictionary all names are entered in the form in which they are current in America.

French and Italian names, especially the latter, besides many

German and some Slavic names, are notable for the decapitation of the baptismal names. Thus the French reduce *Thomas* to *Massie, Masset, Massin, Masson* and the like, while the Germans use *Mass,* and the Italians, *Massa* and *Masso.* Various names beginning with *Cob-* and *Kob-* are aphetic forms of *Jacob* or *Jakob.* The Italian *Como* is from *Giacomo* (James), while *Zola* and *Cozzi* are from *Franzola* and *Francescozzi,* respectively.

In this *Dictionary of American Family Names* all the common surnames found in the United States are included. American family names consist of the family names of the entire world, with the European names predominating since most of the American population are descended from European nationals. Counts have been made in many large city, telephone and other directories to insure the inclusion of the most common names in the United States. Where several forms of a name are given, the most common form is given first, except possibly in a few dozen cases where two forms were so close together in point of number that it could not be known for sure which form was in most common use. In addition, the family names of many famous Americans are explained as well as some with curious or interesting names. People with odd or unusual names are prone to alter them and thus avoid the constant comment about them.

Whether a name is given as a main entry or as a variant of another name depends on how many people bear the name in America and also how far away it is, alphabetically, from the more popular name. *I* and *y* are both found, yet *Bird* is not given as a variant of *Byrd,* the more common form, as they are too far apart in the alphabet. This does not apply to *Jacobi* and *Jacoby,* and they are grouped together. *Harrison,* a very common name, is given with *Harris,* the more common one, because it would otherwise come next in alphabetical order and the explanation is the same. *Johns,* on the other hand, is separate from *Johnson* because of difference in nationality. Famous names are given more attention than their numbers warrant.

When variants of the names are listed, it must be understood that, in general, the explanations refer principally to the first form. There may, of course, be other minor explanations for some of the variants. This method was adopted in order to provide as much information as possible in the limited space available. A complete discussion of a name and its variants and cross-explanations would consume several pages for almost every entry and much would be repetitious.

Attention in this dictionary is given to the way in which the family name originated, and its meaning from an onomastic viewpoint. The philologist and the linguist are interested only in the word root, or stem, from which a name is derived, while many people are interested in the way their family name developed into its present form. Besides the exact word which formed the name, the customs and habits of many peoples must be studied. Without a feeling for the origin of family names and an understanding of how they gradually arose in various countries, the philologists are sometimes led astray in suggesting that a name is derived from a certain word or root when an understanding of the process by which names originated would cause them to reject that word and search further. A word meaning the same in another language may not be defined in exactly the same way since the root word may have affected the name differently in the other language. To be absolutely sure of the meaning and derivation of any particular family name, it would have to be traced genealogically back to its origin and the circumstances of the origin studied. This is impossible, of course, but we know that the large majority of the common names, as contained herein, arose exactly in the way explained in the dictionary.

In arriving at an explanation of a surname, it must be remembered that the meaning of the word or stem from which the surname is derived is not the dictionary meaning at the present day, but the meaning of the word at the time and in the place where the family name came ino existence. Over the years words sometimes change radically in meaning; sometimes they change only slightly. *Seeley* once referred to the happy or prosperous one, then, the good, simple, innocent man. The word later changed in meaning to the silly, foolish or stupid person. As a surname it carried, chiefly, the earlier and more felicitous connotations. Thus the meaning of the surname is different from the meaning of the word today.

In the Middle Ages a word may have had different meanings or different shades of meanings in different parts of the country. At a time when dictionaries were scarce or non-existent, words were often used with little regard for the finer shades of meaning. For this reason, it will be found that in the following list an element in a name may be defined with one meaning or shade of meaning in one name and with a different meaning in another name.

Too much emphasis cannot be placed on the fact that a family name may have more than one origin, although only the most important ones are listed in this dictionary. Many names are common simply because they are derived from several different sources. *Barnes* designates the dweller near the barn or grain-storage building in some instances, while in others it is the bairn, or child, or young person of a prominent family; some with the name are descendants of Beorn (nobleman) or of Barn, a pet form of Barnabas (son of prophecy), while still others came from Barnes, the name of villages in both England and Scotland. Infrequently, it is also the Polish shortening from Bernhard and a German pet form for Berinhard. All of these origins combine to make the name very common. Indeed, most of the very common names are common because they owe their existence to several different origins. In this dictionary different derivations or origins have been separated by semicolons. Because of the limitations of space, only the more important derivations are included.

In this book the diacritical marks of the various languages are disregarded because they are not customarily used in American family names. A true "American" name does not have an accent, a tilde, an umlaut, a circumflex, a cedilla or any of the numerous other signs or marks used in the various languages. Americans just refuse to take the time to add such marks, and the foreigner soon ceases to insist upon it and he, himself, ignores the diacritical mark.

This is not a failure to recognize the difficulty in explaining many European names. For example, there is the Finnish *Saari,* designating a "dweller on an island," and the Finnish *Sääri,* meaning "dweller on, or near, a ridge." When Mr. Sääri comes to America and quickly drops the diacritical marks, one cannot later be sure of the meaning of his name. However, this difficulty is always present in any other name that has more than one origin. Names that come from languages using other than the Latin alphabet present their difficulties; not all have used the same system of transliteration.

For a more complete discussion of personal names see the author's *The Story of Our Names* published by Harper & Brothers in 1950.

LIST OF ABBREVIATIONS

Arab.	Arabian
Arm.	Armenian
Bel.	Belgian
Bulg.	Bulgarian
Chin.	Chinese
Cz.-Sl.	Czecho-Slovakian
Dan.	Danish
dim.	diminutive
Du.	Dutch
Eng.	English
Finn.	Finnish
Fr.	French
Ger.	German
Gr.	Greek
Heb.	Hebrew
Hun.	Hungarian
Ice.	Icelandic
i.e.	that is
Ir.	Irish
It.	Italian
Jap.	Japanese
Lith.	Lithuanian
Nor.	Norwegian
Pol.	Polish
Port.	Portuguese
q.v.	which see
Rom.	Romanian
Rus.	Russian

ABBREVIATIONS

Scot.	Scottish
Sp.	Spanish
Sw.	Swedish
Swis.	Swiss
Syr.	Syrian
Wel.	Welsh
Ukr.	Ukrainian
Yu.-Sl.	Yugoslavian

Different origins are separated by a semicolon. The first form listed is the most common.

DICTIONARY OF AMERICAN FAMILY NAMES

Aagaard, Aagard (*Nor.*) Dweller in the yard by the river.

Aaron, Aaronson, Aarons (*Eng.*) Descendant of Aaron (lofty mountain).

Aarsen (*Du.*) The son of Arthur (valorous, noble or bear man).

Abbate, Abate (*It.*) One who was a member of an abbot's entourage.

Abbey, Abbie (*Scot.*) Variants of Abbott, q.v.

Abbott, Abbot (*Eng.*) A member of an abbot's entourage; sometimes the lay abbot of a monastery who inherited his office; son of little Abb, a pet form of Abraham (father of multitudes); descendant of Abet or Abot, pet forms for Abel (breath or vanity).

Abdullah, Abdallah (*Arab.*) The servant of God.

Abel, Abell (*Eng.*) Descendant of Abel (breath or vanity).

Abelson (*Eng.*) The son of Abel (breath or vanity).

Abercrombie, Abercromby (*Scot.*) One who came from the barony of Abercrombie (crooked marsh), in Fife.

Abernathy, Abernethy (*Scot.*) One who came from Abernethy (at the narrow opening), in Perthshire.

Abraham, Abrahams, Abrahamson (*Eng., Sw.*) Descendant of Abraham (father of multitudes).

Abrams, Abram, Abramson (*Eng.*) Descendant of Abram (high father).

Abt (*Ger.*) A member of an abbot's entourage; sometimes the lay abbot of a monastery who inherited his office.

Acheson, Aitchison (*Eng.*) The son of Ache (sword), or of Adam (red earth).

Achilles (*Ger.*) Descendant of Achilles (without lips).

Acker (*Eng.*) One who lived on a homestead of one acre.

Ackerman, Ackermann, Acreman (*Ger., Eng.*) One who plowed the lord's land and tended his plow teams.

Ackroyd (*Eng.*) Dweller at the oak clearing.

Acland, Ackland (*Eng.*) One who came from Acland (Acca's lane), in Devonshire.

Acorn (*Ger.*) One who came from Eichhorn (place where squirrels abound), in Germany; dweller at the sign of the squirrel; dweller at the forest corner.

Acton (*Eng.*) One who came from Acton (homestead by the oaks, or, in some cases, Aca's homestead), the name of many places in England.

Adair (*Scot., Ir.*) Descendant of Edzear or Edgar (rich, spear); dweller near the oak-tree ford; grandson of Daire, an old Irish name.

Adamczyk (*Pol.*) The son of Adam (red earth).

Adamek, Adamik (*Cz.-Sl.*) Descendant of little Adam (red earth).

Adamowicz (*Pol.*) The son of Adam (red earth).

Adamowski, Adamoski (*Pol.*) One who came from Adamowo (Adam's village), in Poland.

Adams, Adamson, Addams, Adam (*Wel., Eng.*) The son of Adam (red earth).

Adamski (*Pol.*) The son of Adam (red earth).

Adcock (*Eng.*) Descendant of little Ad, a pet form of Adam (red earth).

Addington (*Eng.*) One who came from Addington (the village of Eadda's people), the name of several places in England.

Addison, Addis, Addie (*Eng., Scot., Wel.*) The son of Addie, a pet form of Adam (red earth); the son of Ada or Adda (noble cheer).

Adelman, Adelmann (*Eng., Ger.*) The servant of Adal or Edel (noble).

Adler (*Ger.*) Dweller at the sign of the eagle.

Adolph, Adolf, Adolfson, Adolphson (*Ger., Eng.*) Descendant of Adolf or Athalwolf (noble, wolf).

Affleck (*Scot.*) One who came from the barony of Auchinleck (field of the flat stone), in Ayrshire, or from Affleck in Angus.

Agassiz, Agassie (*Swis.*) Dweller at the sign of the magpie.

Agnew (*Eng.*) Dweller at the sign of the lamb.

Ahern, Ahearn, Aherne (*Ir.*) Grandson of Eachthighearna (horse owner).

Ahrens (*Du.*) Dweller at the sign of the eagle.

Aiken, Aikens, Aikin (*Eng.*) Descendant of little Ad, a pet form of Adam; descendant of Acen (oaken).

Ainsley, Ainslie (*Eng., Scot.*) One who came from Annesley (An's wood), in Nottinghamshire, or from Ansley (wood with a hermitage), in Warwickshire.

Ainsworth (*Eng.*) One who came from Ainsworth (Aegen's homestead), in Lancashire.

Airth (*Scot.*) One who came from the barony of Airth (level green among hills), in Stirlingshire.

Aitken, Aitkins (*Eng., Scot.*) Descendant of little Ad, a pet form of Adam (red earth).

Akerman (*Eng.*) One who plowed the lord's land and tended his plow teams.

Akers, Aker (*Eng.*) One who lived in the field; one who farmed one acre.

Akins, Akin (*Eng., Scot.*) Variants of Aiken, q.v.; dweller near Akin, a strait in Scotland named after King Hakon of Norway.

Albano (*It.*) One who came from Albano (white), in Italy.

Albee, Allbee, Alby (*Eng.*) One who came from Alby (Ali's homestead), in Norfolk.

Albers, Alber (*Ger.*) Descendant of Albert (noble, bright).

Albert, Alberts, Albertson (*Eng.*) The descendant, or son, of Albert (noble, bright).

Albrecht, Albright (*Ger.*) Descendant of Albrecht (noble, bright).

Alcock, Alcox (*Eng.*) Descendant, or son, of little Al, a pet form of Alan or Allen.

Alcott (*Eng.*) Dweller in the old cottage; descendant of Alcot or Algot (noble, god).

Alden, Aldine, Aldin (*Eng.*) Descendant of Aldwin (old friend).

Alderman (*Eng.*) One who was a city officer or magistrate; governor of a guild.

Aldred (*Eng.*) Descendant of Aldred (old, counsel).

Aldrich (*Eng.*) Descendant of Alderich (noble, ruler); sometimes a variant of Aldridge, q.v.

Aldridge (*Eng.*) One who came from Aldridge (village among alders), in Staffordshire.

Alex (*Eng.*) Descendant of Alex, a pet form of Alexander (helper of mankind).

Alexander (*Scot., Eng.*) Descendant of Alexander (helper of mankind).

Alford (*Eng.*) One who came from Alford (the alder ford, or the ford of Ealdgyth), villages in Lincolnshire and Somerset.

Alfred, Alfredson (*Eng.*) Descendant of Alfred (elf, counsel).

Alger, Algar (*Eng.*) Descendant of Aldgar (old, spear), or Athelgar (noble, spear), or Aelfgar (elf, spear).

Allard (*Eng.*) Descendant of Alard (noble, hard).

Allardyce, Allardice (*Scot.*) One who came from the barony of Allardyce, in Kincardineshire.

Alegretti (*It.*) The happy, gay person.

Allen, Allan, Alan (*Eng., Scot.*) Descendant of Alan (a very old name of obscure origin); dweller near the Allen (green plain), the name of rivers in Cornwall, Dorset, Northumberland and Stirlingshire.

Alley, Allie (*Eng.*) Dweller at a narrow passage; descendant of little Al, a pet form of Alan or Alexander, q.v.

Alleyne, Allain, Allyn (*Eng.*) Descendant of Alleyne, early form of Allen, q.v.

Allison, Alison (*Scot., Eng.*) The son of Ellis (God is salvation); corruption of Allanson, q.v.; the son of Alis, a short form of Alister or Alexander (helper of mankind); the son of Alice (noble cheer), occasionally a masculine name.

Allman, Alleman, Allemang (*Eng., Fr.*) One who came from Alemaigne (all men), Germany; a name generally applied to anyone from the Baltic States or from Holland.

Alm (*Sw.*) Elm.

Almquist, Almkuist (*Sw.*) Elm twig.

Almy (*Eng.*) Dweller at the elm island.

Alpert, Alport, Allport (*Eng.*) One who came from Alport (old town), in Derbyshire.

Alston (*Eng.*) One who came from Alston (the village of one whose name began with Al), the name of several places in England.

Alt (*Ger.*) One who was older than another with whom he was associated; descendant of Aldo, a pet form of names beginning with Alt (old), as Aldhard, Altraban, and Alderich.

Alter (*Ger.*) The old man; descendant of Althar (old, army); dweller at, or near, a poplar tree.

Altergott (*Ger.*) A nickname, the old god.

Altman, Altmann (*Ger.*) The old servant; descendant of Aldman (old, man).

Alton, Alten, Altone (*Eng.*) One who came from Alton (the old village, or the village at the source of the river), the name of several places in England.

Alvarez, Alvaroz (*Sp.*) The son of Alva (white).

Alvord, Alward (*Eng.*) Variants of Alford, q.v.

Amato (*It.*) Descendant of Amato (beloved).

Amberg (*Dan.*) Dweller on, or near, a large hill or mountain.

Ambrose (*Eng.*) Descendant of Ambrose (immortal).

Ames, Amis (*Eng.*) The son of Ame or Amis (friend); descendant of Ame, a pet form of Amery (work, rule); variants of Eames, q.v.

Amirault, Amerault (*Fr.*) The highest ranking naval officer, a surname sometimes applied in derision.

Amory, Amery (*Eng.*) Descendant of Amery (work, rule).

Amos (*Eng.*) Descendant of Amos (burden-bearer); a variant of Ames, q.v.

Amundsen, Amundson (*Nor., Ice.*) The son of Amund (protector, forever).

Andersen, Anders (*Nor., Dan.*) The son of Andrew (man).

Anderson, Andrews, Andrew (*Eng., Scot.*) The son of Andrew (man).

Andersson, Anders (*Sw.*) The son of Andrew (man).

Andre, Andres (*Fr.*) Descendant of Andre (man).

Andresen (*Nor.*) The son of Andre (man).

Andrzejewski (*Pol.*) The son of Andrzej (man).

Angel, Angell (*Eng.*) One who acted as a religious messenger or as a messenger from God; a nickname for an angelic person; descendant of Angel, a man's name in England; variants of Angle, q.v.

Angelo, Angeli, Angele (*It.*) Descendant of Angelo (an angel).

Angle (*Eng.*) Dweller at, or near, the angle or corner.

Angus (*Scot.*) Descendant of Angus (one choice); one who came from the district of Angus (said to be named after Angus, king of the Picts), the ancient name of Forfarshire.

Annis (*Eng.*) The son of Annis, the popular pronunciation of Agnes (pure), one of the commonest feminine names in the twelfth to sixeeenth centuries.

Anstruther (*Scot.*) One who came from Anstruther (marshy meadow), in Fife.

Antanaitis, Antanavic (*Lith.*) The son of Antan (inestimable).

Anthony (*Wel.*) Descendant of Anthony (inestimable).

Anton (*Ger.*) Descendant of Anton (inestimable).

Antonelli, Antonello, Antonellis (*It.*) Descendant of little Anton (inestimable).

Antonescu (*Rom.*) Descendant, or follower, of Anton (inestimable).

Antonopoulos, Antonopulos (*Gr.*) The son of Antonos (inestimable).

Apfelberg (*Ger.*) One who came from Eifelberg (chain of mountains), in Germany.

Appel, Appell, Apple, Apfel (*Ger., Eng., Du.*) Dweller near an apple tree.

Applebaum, Appelbaum, Apfelbaum (*Ger.*) Dweller near an apple tree.

Appleby (*Eng.*) One who came from Appleby (homestead where apples grew), the name of several places in England.

Applegate (*Eng.*) Dweller at the gate or entrance to the apple orchard.

Appleton (*Eng.*) One who came from Appleton (place where apples grew), the name of various places in England.

Applewhite (*Eng.*) One who came from Applethwaite (clearing where apples grew), the name of places in Cumberland and Westmorland.

Appleyard (*Eng.*) Dweller at the apple orchard.

Arbuckle (*Scot.*) One who came from Arbuckle (height of the shepherd), in Scotland.

Arcaro, Arcara, Arcari (*It.*) One who made bows, i.e., weapons.

Archer (*Eng.*) A fighting man armed with bow and arrows.

Archibald, Archie (*Eng., Scot.*) Descendant of Archibald (simple, bold). Archie is the pet form.

Ard, Aird (*Scot.*) One who came from the Aird, a district in the Vale of Beauly, in Scotland.

Arden (*Eng.*) One who came from Arden (dwelling house), the name of several places in England.

Arends, Arend (*Ger., Du.*) Descendant of Arend (eagle, rule).

Arendt (*Nor.*) Descendant of Arend (eagle, rule).

Arenson, Arens (*Nor.*) The son of Aren (eagle, rule).

Arenz, Arentz (*Dan.*) Descendant of Arenz (eagle, rule).

Argos (*Ger.*) The light-complexioned or white-haired man.

Arkin (*Nor.*) Descendant of little Arke or Erke (ever king).

Armbruster, Armbrust (*Ger.*) Fighter armed with a crossbow; one who made and sold crossbows.

Armitage (*Eng.*) Dweller at, or near, the habitation of a hermit.

Armour, Armor (*Eng.*) One who made defensive armor for the body.

Armstead, Armistead (*Eng.*) Dweller at the hermit's dairy farm.

Armstrong (*Eng., Scot.*) The strong-armed man.

Arndt, Arndtsen (*Dan.*) Descendant of Arndt (eagle, rule).

Arneson, Arnesen, Arnesson (*Nor., Dan.*) The son of Arne (eagle).

Arnett, Arney, Arnet, Arnette (*Eng.*) Descendant of little Arnold (eagle, rule).

Arnold, Arnolde (*Eng.*) Descendant of Arnold (eagle, rule).

Aronson, Arons, Aron (*Sw.*) The son, or descendant, of Aron (lofty mountain).

Arquilla (*Sp.*) One who operated a kiln.

Arrington (*Eng.*) One who came from Arrington (the homestead of Erna's people), a village in Cambridgeshire.

Arrowsmith, Arrasmith (*Eng.*) One who made arrows, especially arrowheads.

Arsenault, Arseneau, Arceneaux (*Fr.*) One who had charge of the arsenal where weapons were stored.

Arthur (*Eng.*) Descendant of Arthur (Thor's eagle).

Arvia, Arvio (*It.*) Dweller on, or near, the plowed land.

Arvidson, Arvidsson (*Sw.*) The son of Arvid (man of the people).

Aschenbrenner, Aschenbrener (*Ger., Eng.*) One who made potash, an ash-burner.

Ascher, Asher (*Ger.*) Dweller near an ash tree; descendant of Ascher (ash, army); one who came from Asch, in Germany.

Ash, Ashe (*Eng.*) One who lived near the ash tree.

Ashburn, Ashburne (*Eng.*) Dweller near the Ashburn (ash-tree brook), a river in Sussex.

Ashby (*Eng.*) One who came from Ashby (the village where ash trees grew), the name of various places in England.

Ashcraft, Ashcroft (*Eng.*) Dweller on the small field where ash trees grew.

Asher (*Eng.*) Descendant of Asher (spear, army).

Ashford (*Eng.*) One who came from Ashford (the ford where ash trees grew), the name of various places in England.

Ashley (*Eng.*) One who came from Ashley (the wood where ash trees grew), the name of various places in England.

Ashton (*Eng.*) One who came from Ashton (the village or homestead where ash trees grew), the name of various places in England.

Askew (*Eng.*) One who came from Aiskew (oak wood), in Yorkshire.

Aspinwall, Aspinall, Aspenwall (*Eng.*) Dweller near the aspen tree, stream or spring.

Asquith (*Eng.*) One who came from Askwith (ash wood), in Yorkshire.

Aston, Astin, Astone (*Eng.*) One who came from Aston (the village to the east), the name of many places in England.

Astor (*Eng.*) Descendant of Easter (name given to a child born at Eastertide).

Asztalos (*Hun.*) The worker in wood, a carpenter.

Atherton (*Eng.*) One who came from Atherton (Ethelhere's homestead), in Lancashire.

Atkins, Atkinson, Atkin (*Eng.*) The son of little Ad, a pet form of Adam (red earth).

Atlas, Atlass (*Eng.*) Descendant of Edel or Eidel (noble), corrupted through Edlin and Eidles which became Atlas.

Attridge (*Eng.*) Dweller at, or near, a ridge or range of hills.

Atwater, Attwater (*Eng.*) Dweller at a stream or lake.

Atwell, Atwill, Attwell (*Eng.*) Dweller at a well, spring or stream.

Atwood, Attwood (*Eng.*) Dweller at, or near, a wood.

Aucoin (*Fr.*) Descendant of Alcuin (temple, friend).

Audubon (*Fr.*) Literally French for "of the good," probably a shortened form of a longer name or description.

Auer (*Ger.*) Dweller in, or near, a marsh; dweller at the sign of the bison.

Auerbach (*Ger.*) One who came from Auerbach, in Germany.

Auger, Auge (*Fr.*) Descendant of Adalgar (noble, spear).

Augustine, August, Augustin, Augustyn (*Eng.*) Descendant of Augustine (majestic).

Auld, Ault (*Scot.*) Descendant of Ealda (old); the elderly person.

Austin, Austen (*Eng., Scot.*) Descendant of Austin, a variant of Augustine (majestic).

Autry, Autrey (*Fr.*) Descendant of Aldric (old, powerful).

Averill (*Eng.*) Descendant of Averil (boar, battle); one who came from Haverhill (hill where oats were grown), in Suffolk.

Avery (*Eng.*) Descendant of Aelfric (elf, ruler) or Everard (wild, boar); one who came from Evreux, in France.

Axelrod, Axelrood (*Eng.*) Dweller at the clearing by the ash trees; one who made wheel axles.

Axelson, Axell, Axel (*Sw.*) The son of Axel (divine reward).

Ayers, Ayer (*Eng.*) Descendant of the heir, i.e., the person in whom the fee of the real property of an intestate is vested at his death.

Aylward (*Eng.*) Descendant of Aylward (noble, guardian).

Babb, Babbe, Babbs (*Eng.*) Descendant of Babba (baby?), or of Babb, a pet form of Barbara (stranger), or of Bab, a pet form of Baptist (baptizer).

Babbitt (*Eng.*) Descendant of little Babb or Babba. *See* Babb.

Babcock (*Eng.*) The son of Babb or Bab. *See* Babb.

Babiarz (*Pol.*) One who likes women.

Babson (*Eng.*) The son of Babb or Babba. *See* Babb.

Bach, Bache (*Ger., Eng.*) Dweller in the stream valley; one who came from Bache (valley of a stream), the name of several places in England.

Bachelor, Bachelder, Batchelder (*Eng.*) The holder, or tenant, of a small farm; an officer or servant who has care of the door in a large household; the young person, or young knight.

Bachman, Bachmann (*Ger.*) Dweller at, or near, a brook or stream.

Bachrach (*Ger.*) One who came from Bacharach, in Germany.

Back, Backe (*Eng.*) Dweller by a brook; variants of Bach, q.v.

Backhaus (*Ger.*) The man who lived near, or who worked in, the bakehouse.

Backman, Backmann (*Ger.*) Dweller at, or near, a brook or stream.

Backus (*Eng.*) Dweller in, or near, the bakehouse.

Bacon (*Eng.*) A swineherd or peasant, from the nickname, Bacon; a bacon or lard dealer; dweller at the sign of the pig, at a time when bacon meant the live pig.

Bader (*Ger.*) One who practiced surgery, a barber surgeon; one who came from Baden, in Germany; descendant of Bathari (combat, army).

Badger, Bagger (*Eng.*) One who buys grain and other commodities and carries them elsewhere in a bag to sell; one who came from Badger (Bacga's shore), in Shropshire.

Baer, Barr, Behr, Bear, Bahr, Baeha (*Ger., Eng.*) Dweller at the sign of the bear; one thought to possess bearlike qualities. The bear was the king of beasts in the north of Europe.

Baggett, Baggott, Baggot (*Eng.*) Descendant of little Baga or Bacga (the fat one).

Baggs, Bagge, Bagg (*Eng.*) Descendant of Baga or Bacga (the fat one).

Bagley (*Eng.*) One who came from Bagley (the rams' or pigs' woodland), the name of various places in England.

Bagwell, Bagwill (*Eng.*) One who came from Bagnall (Baga's wood), in Staffordshire.

Bahnson, Bahnsen (*Ger.*) Descendant of Panno, a pet form of names beginning with Ban (precept), as Banager and Banhart.

Baier, Bair (*Ger.*) One who came from Bavaria.

Bailey, Baillie, Bailie, Baily (*Eng., Scot.*) One charged with public administrative authority in a certain district by the king or a lord; one who acted as agent for the lord in the management of the affairs of the manor; one who came from Bailey (clearing where berries grew), in Lancashire.

Bailly, Bally, Bayle (*Fr.*) Variants of Bailey, q.v.

Bain, Baine (*Eng.*) Dweller near the Bain (straight), the name of rivers in Lincolnshire and Yorkshire.

Bainbridge (*Eng.*) One who came from Bainbridge (bridge on the Bain, i.e., straight, river), in Yorkshire.

Baines, Baynes, Banes (*Scot.*) The fair or light-complexioned man.

Baird (*Scot.*) Descendant of the poet or bard; one who came from Bard, in Scotland.

Bak (*Eng.*) Dweller by a brook.

Baker, Baxter (*Eng., Wel.*) One who made bread.

Bakke, Bakken (*Nor.*) Dweller at, or near, a hill.

Balance, Ballance (*Eng.*) Dweller at the sign of the balance, usually designating a scale maker.

Balch (*Eng.*) The bald man.

Balcom (*Eng.*) One who came from Balcombe (Baegloc's hollow), in Sussex.

Baldwin (*Eng.*) Descendant of Baldwin (bold, friend).

Balfour (*Scot.*) One who came from Balfour (village by pasture land), in Fifeshire.

Ball, Balle, Baller (*Eng.*) Descendant of Baldwin (bold, friend); dweller at the sign of the ball; the bald-headed man.

Ballantine, Ballantyne (*Scot.*) One who came from Ballindean (village by the hill), in Fifeshire.

Ballard (*Eng.*) The bald-headed man.

Ballou (*Fr.*) One who came from Bellou, in France.

Balogh (*Hun.*) One who shod horses.

Balsamo (*It.*) One who made and sold balm, or perfumes and ointments.

Balzer, Balthazar, Balthaser (*Ger.*) Descendant of Balthasar (Bel has formed a king).

Bamberger, Bamberg (*Ger.*) One who came from Bamberg (Bab's hill), in Bavaria.

Bambrick (*Eng.*) Dweller at a footbridge, i.e., a single log across a stream.

Bambury (*Eng.*) One who came from Bamborough or Bamburgh (Bebbe's fort), in Northumberland; one who came from Banbury (Bana's fort), in Oxfordshire.

Bamford (*Eng.*) One who came from Bamford (ford with a footbridge), the name of places in Derbyshire and Lancashire.

Banas (*Hun.*) The lord, or head, of the household; the lord's servant; nickname given to one assuming superior rank.

Bancroft (*Eng.*) Dweller at an enclosure, or yard, where beans grew.

Banfield (*Eng.*) Dweller at a field where beans grew.

Bangs, Bang (*Eng.*) Dweller near a mound or embankment.

Bankhead (*Scot.*) One who came from Bankhead (end of the ridge), the name of several small places in Scotland.

Banks, Bank, Banker (*Eng.*) Dweller near a mound or embankment.

Bannister, Banister (*Eng.*) One who made and sold baskets; one who fought with a crossbow.

Bannon (*Ir.*) Grandson of Banain (little white one).

Baran (*Eng., Pol.*) Variant of Baron, q.v.; descendant of Baran (ram).

Baranowski (*Pol.*) One who came from Barano(w) or Baranowice (Baran's settlement), in Poland.

Baranski (*Pol.*) The son of Baran (ram).

Barber, Barbour (*Eng.*) .The hairdresser; one who practiced surgery, i.e., acted as a bloodletter.

Barclay, Barkley (*Eng.*) Variants of Berkeley, q.v.

Bard, Bart (*Eng.*) Descendant of Bard or Bart, pet forms of Bartholomew (son of Talmai, furrow); descendant of the poet or bard.

Barden, Bardon, Bardin (*Eng.*) One who came from Barden (valley where barley grew), in Yorkshire.

Barfield, Barefield (*Eng.*) One who came from Bardfield (border field), in Essex.

Barger, Bargar (*Eng.*) One who worked on a small boat or small sailing vessel, a sailor.

Barham (*Eng.*) One who came from Barham (homestead on the hill), the name of several places in England.

Barker (*Eng.*) One who prepared leather with bark, a tanner.

Barkhouse, Barkus (*Eng.*) Dweller in a house made of birch wood; dweller near the building where bark was stored for tanning purposes.

Barkin (*Eng.*) One who came from Barking (Berica's people), in Essex.

Barksdale, Barksdalle (*Eng.*) One who lived at, or near, the valley of the birch trees.

Barlow (*Eng.*) One who came from Barlow (barley hill or clearing), the name of places in Derbyshire and Lancashire.

Barnaby (*Eng.*) One who came from Barnaby (Beornwald's homestead), in Yorkshire.

Barnard (*Eng.*) Descendant of Bernard (bear, firm).

Barnas (*Pol.*) Descendant of Bernhard (bear, firm), or of Barnutz and Barnitzki; a name made up by prefixing Bar (son) to the initials of the father's name.

Barnes, Barns (*Eng., Scot.*) Dweller near the barn, or grain storage building; the bairn or child, often a young person of a prominent family; descendant of Beorn (nobleman); one who came from Barnes in Surrey and Aberdeenshire; (descendant of Barn, a pet form of Barnabas (son of prophecy).

Barnett, Barnette, Barnet (*Eng.*) Descendant of little Bernard (bear, hard).

Barney (*Ir.*) Descendant of Barney, a pet form of Barnabas (son of prophecy).

Barnhart, Barnhardt, Barnhard (*Ger.*) Descendant of Berinhard (bear, strong).

Barnhill (*Eng.*) One who came from Barnhill (Beorn's hill), in Yorkshire.

Barnicle (*Eng.*) One who came from Barnacle (barn slope), in Warwickshire.

Barnum (*Eng.*) Variant of Barham, q.v.

Baron, Barron, Barone (*Scot., Ir.*) The landowner who held his land of the king; one who fomented strife; descendant of Baron (baron).

Barr, Barre (*Scot.*) One who came from Barr (height), in Ayrshire and Renfrewshire; dweller at the top of the hill.

Barrett, Barrette (*Eng.*) Descendant of Barret (bear, rule).

Barrington (*Eng.*) One who came from Barrington (the homestead of Bara's or Beorn's people), the name of several places in England.

Barrow, Barrows (*Eng.*) One who came from Barrow (wood, or hill), the name of many places in England.

Barry, Barrie (*Scot., Ir.*) One who came from Barry (height on the isle), in Angus; one who was diligent; descendant of Barry (spear).

Barrymore (*Eng.*) Dweller at the woodland marsh.

Barstow (*Eng.*) Dweller at, or near, the place where grain was stored.

Barta, Bartos (*Cz.-Sl.*) Descendant of Bartos, a pet form of Bartholomew (son of Talmai, furrow).

Bartels, Bartel, Bartell (*Eng.*) Descendant of little Bart, a pet form of Bartholomew (son of Talmai, furrow).

Barth (*Ger., Eng.*) The man with the beard; descendant of Barth, a pet abbreviation of Bartholomew (son of Talmai, furrow).

Barthold, Barthol (*Ger.*) Descendant of Berchtwald (bright, forest).

Bartholomew, Bartholomay, Bartholomae, Bartholmey (*Eng.*) Descendant of Bartholomew (son of Talmai, furrow).

Bartlett, Bartle, Bartlet (*Eng.*) Descendant of little Bart, a pet form of Bartholomew (son of Talmai, furrow).

Bartley (*Eng.*) One who came from Bartley (birch wood), the name of places in Hampshire and Warwickshire.

Barto, Bartok (*Hun.*) Descendant of Bart, a pet form of Bartholomew (son of Talmai, furrow).

Barton (*Eng.*) One who came from Barton (grain farm), the name of various places in England.

Bartz, Barz (*Ger.*) Dweller at the sign of the bear; one with some bearlike characteristic; descendant of Barz or Bartz, a pet form of names beginning with Bar (bear), as Berulf, Berowin and Bernhelm; dweller near tree stumps.

Baruch, Baruck (*Ger.*) Descendant of Baruch (blessed).

Barwick, Barwig (*Eng., Ger.*) One who came from Barwick (barley farm), in Norfolk; descendant of Beriwick (bear, farm).

Bascom, Bascomb (*Eng.*) One who came from Boscombe (box-tree valley), in Wiltshire.

Basile, Basil (*Eng., It.*) Descendant of Basil or Basilio (king).

Basket, Baskette (*Fr.*) Descendant of little Basque (man).

Baskin (*Eng.*) Descendant of little Bass or Bassa (short).

Bass, Basse (*Eng.*) The short or fat person; descendant of Bass (short).

Bassett, Bassette, Basset (*Eng., Fr.*) Descendant of little Bass or Bassa (short); the short man.

Bassler, Basler (*Ger., Swis.*) One who came from Basel, in Switzerland.

Basso (*It.*) The small, short man; dweller on the low land; descendant of Basso, a pet form of Giacobasso (the supplanter).

Bastian, Bastien (*Du., Eng., Fr.*) Descendant of Bastian, a pet form of Sebastian (venerable).

Batchelor, Batcheller (*Scot.*) The holder, or tenant, of a small farm; an officer or servant who has care of the door.

Bateman, Batman (*Eng.*) The servant of Bate, a pet form of Bartholomew (son of Talmai, furrow); the man who baited bears kept for amusement.

Bates, Bate, Batts, Batt, Bat (*Eng.*) The son of Bate, a pet form of Bartholomew (son of Talmai, furrow); one of stout, heavy appearance.

Bateson, Batson (*Eng.*) The son of Bate, a pet form of Bartholomew (son of Talmai, furrow).

Bath (*Eng.*) One who came from Bath (referring to the Roman baths), in Somerset.

Battaglia (*It.*) A combatant, one engaged in war.

Battista (*It.*) Descendant of Battista (Baptist), from St. John the Baptist.

Battle, Battles (*Eng.*) One who came from Battle (named after the battle of Hastings), in England; descendant of Bartle, a pet form of Bartholomew (son of Talmai, furrow).

Batty, Baty, Battie, Battey (*Eng.*) Descendant of Batt, a pet form of Bartholomew (son of Talmai, furrow).

Bauer, Baur (*Ger.*) One who tilled the land, a farmer.

Baum, Baumel, Baumer, Baumler (*Ger.*) Dweller near a tree; dweller at the barrier placed across roads by the toll collector.

Baumann, Bauman, Baughman (*Ger.*) One who tilled the land, a farmer.

Baumgartner, Baumgart (*Ger.*) The tree gardener, nurseryman or orchard-grower.

Bay (*Eng.*) One with reddish-brown hair; dweller near a bay or pool.

Bayer, Bayr (*Ger.*) One who came from Bavaria, in Germany.

Baylie, Bayley, Bayly (*Eng.*) Variants of Bailey, q.v.

Bayliss, Bayless, Bayles, Baylis (*Eng.*) The son of the bailiff. *See* Bailey.

Beach (*Eng.*) Dweller at, or near, a beach tree or brook.

Beadell, Beadle, Beadles (*Eng.*) The crier, or usher, in a court; town crier; a constable.

Beal, Beale, Beall, Beals (*Eng.*) One who came from Beal (bee hill, or Beaga's corner), the name of places in Northumberland and Yorkshire.

Beam (*Eng.*) One who lived by a tree; dweller at the footbridge.

Bean, Beane, Beans (*Eng., Scot.*) Descendant of Ben, a pet form of Benjamin (son of my right hand), or of Benedict (blessed); the light-complexioned man.

Beard (*Eng.*) One who came from Beard (bank), in Derbyshire; one who had an unusually hairy chin.

Beardsley, Bardsley (*Eng.*) One who came from Bardsley (Beornred's wood), in Lancashire.

Bearse, Bearce (*Wel.*) The son of Piers (rock).

Beasley, Beesley (*Eng.*) Dweller in, or near, the meadow or wood where bees were found.

Beaton, Beton (*Scot., Eng.*) Descendant of little Bate, a pet form of Bartholomew (son of Talmai, furrow), or of Bete or Beat, pet forms of Beatrice and Beatrix (she who blesses).

Beatrice (*It.*) Descendant of Beatrice (she who blesses).

Beatty, Beattie, Beaty (*Scot., Eng.*) Descendant of little Bate or Baty, pet forms of Bartholomew (son of Talmai, furrow), or of Bete or Beat, pet forms of Beatrice and Beatrix (she who blesses).

Beauchamp (*Fr.*) One who came from Beauchamp (beautiful field), in France.

Beaudoin (*Fr.*) Descendant of Baudouin or Baldavin (bold, friend).

Beaumont (*Eng., Fr.*) One who came from Beaumont (beautiful mountain), the name of five places in Normandy, as well as several places in England.

Beaupre (*Fr.*) Dweller in, or near, the beautiful meadow.

Beauregard (*Fr.*) The handsome or good-looking man, a name sometimes applied in an ironical manner; one who came from Beauregard (beautiful place), the name of several places in France.

Beaver, Beavers (*Eng.*) Dweller at the sign of the beaver; one who came from Beauvoir (fair view), in western France.

Bebb (*Wel.*) Descendant of Bebb; descendant of Babb, a pet form of Barbara (the stranger).

Bechtel, Bechtell (*Ger.*) Descendant of Betto, a pet form of names beginning with Bercht (bright or famous), as Berhtari, Berahtram and Berhtolf.

Bechtold, Bechtolt (*Ger.*) Descendant of Berchtwald (bright, forest).

Beck, Bech (*Nor., Eng., Ger., Sw., Ice.*) Dweller at, or near, the brook or stream; brook.

Becker (*Eng., Ger.*) Dweller at a brook; one who made bread.

Beckett, Becket, Beckette (*Eng.*) Dweller at the head of the stream; one who came from Beckett (bee, or Bicca's, cottage), the name of places in Berkshire and Devonshire.

Beckham, Beckum (*Eng.*) One who came from Beckham (Becca's homestead), in Norfolk.

Beckley (*Eng.*) One who came from Beckley (Beocca's meadow).

Beckman, Beckmann (*Eng., Ger.*) Dweller at a brook; one who made bread.

Beckwith (*Eng.*) One who came from Beckwith (beech wood), in Yorkshire.

Bedell (*Eng.*) The crier, or usher, in a court; town crier; a constable.

Bedford (*Eng.*) One who came from Bedford (Beda's ford), in Bedfordshire.

Bednarczyk (*Pol., Cz.-Sl.*) Little son of the maker of casks and barrels.

Bednarek, Bednarik (*Pol., Cz.-Sl.*) Son of the cooper, or maker of casks and barrels.

Bednarski (*Pol.*) One who made casks or barrels, a cooper.

Bednarz, Bednar (*Pol., Cz.-Sl.*) One who made and sold casks and barrels, a cooper.

Beebe, Beeby (*Eng.*) Dweller at the bee farm or apiary.

Beecham, Beacham (*Eng.*) One who came from Beechamwell, originally Bicham (Bicca's homestead), in Norfolk; a corruption of Beauchamp, q.v.

Beecher, Beech (*Eng.*) Dweller at, or near, a beech tree.

Beekman (*Du.*) Dweller at, or near, the brook or stream.

Beeler, Bieler (*Ger.*) Dweller on, or near, a hill.

Been, Beene, Beenes (*Eng.*) Descendant of Been or Ben, pet forms of Benjamin (son of my right hand).

Beers, Beer (*Eng.*) Dweller at, or in, the wood or grove.

Beetle (*Eng.*) One who came from Beetley (wood where wooden mallets were obtained), in Norfolk.

Beggs, Begg (*Scot.*) Descendant of Begg (little).

Begley (*Ir., Eng.*) Grandson of the little poet; a variant of Beckley, q.v.

Behm, Behmer (*Ger.*) One who came from Bohemia (home of the Boii).

Behnke (*Ger.*) Dweller at the sign of the little bear.

Behr (*Ger.*) One who lived at the sign of the bear; one with some characteristic of the bear; descendant of Bero, a pet form of names beginning with Bar (bear), as Beroward, Beriwick and Berulf.

Behrens, Behrendt, Behrends, Behrend, Behrent (*Ger.*) Dweller at the sign of the bear.

Beilfuss, Beilfus (*Ger.*) Descendant of Bilifuns (sword, quick).

Belanger, Bellanger (*Fr.*) One who came from beautiful Anger (ancient name combining *Ans,* a divinity and *gari,* (spear); one who came from Angre or Angres, in France; variants of Boulanger, q.v.

Belcher (*Eng., Fr.*) Descendant of the beautiful, beloved person; the patriarch or elderly man of the family.

Belden, Belding (*Eng.*) Dweller at, or near, a beautiful hill.

Belford (*Eng.*) One who came from Belford, in Northumberland.

Bell, Belle (*Eng.*) Dweller at the sign of the bell; the handsome one; descendant of Bel, a pet form of Isabel (oath to Baal).

Bellamy (*Fr.*) The beautiful friend, an epithet often applied ironically.

Beller (*Eng.*) One who made and sold bells.

Bellinger, Belling (*Ger.*) One who came from Bellingen, the name of two places in Germany.

Bellis (*Wel.*) The son of Elias (Jehovah is my God), or Elisha (God of Salvation); also sometimes from the old Welsh *Elissed* or *Helised* (charitable, benevolent).

Belliveau (*Fr.*) Dweller in a beautiful valley.

Bellman, Belman (*Eng.*) One employed to go around the streets of a town with a bell to make public announcements, a town crier.

Bellmonte, Belmont (*Fr.*) One who came from Belmont (fair hill), the name of various lordships in France.

Bellows, Bellew (*Eng.*) One who came from Bellou or Belleau (fair water), in France.

Beman, Beeman, Beaman (*Eng.*) One who kept bees.

Bemis, Bemiss (*Eng.*) One who came from Beaumetz, in Normandy.

Bench, Benche (*Eng.*) One who lived at the ledge or terrace.

Benda (*Ger.*) Descendant of Benda, a pet form of Benedictus (blessed).

Bender (*Ger.*) One who made casks, a cooper.

Bendix, Benedix (*Eng.*) Descendant of Benedict (blessed).

Benedetto, Benedetti (*It.*) Descendant of Benedetto (blessed).

Benedict, Benedick (*Eng.*) Descendant of Benedict (blessed).

Benes (*Cz.-Sl.*) Descendant of Benes, a form of Benedict (blessed).

Benfield (*Eng.*) Dweller in, or near, a field, where beans were grown; one who came from Binfield (bent grass field), in Berkshire.

Bengston (*Eng.*) One who came from Bynna's homestead; one who came from Bensington (the village of the Benesingas), in Oxfordshire.

Benjamin (*Eng.*) Descendant of Benjamin (son of my right hand).

Benner (*Eng.*) One who grew and sold beans; one who made baskets.

Bennett, Bennet (*Eng.*) Descendant of Bennet or Benedict (blessed).

Benoit (*Fr.*) Descendant of Benoit (blessed).

Benson, Bensen (*Eng., Dan.*) One who came from Benson (Benesa's homestead), in Oxfordshire; the son of Ben, a pet form of Benedict (blessed), or of Benjamin (son of my right hand).

Bent, Bente (*Eng.*) Dweller at an unenclosed pasture, moor or heath; dweller where bent grass grew.

Bentley, Bently (*Eng.*) One who came from Bentley (clearing overgrown with bent grass), the name of many places in England.

Benton (*Eng.*) One who came from Benton (place where bent grass grew), in Northumberland.

Benz, Bentz (*Ger.*) Dweller at the sign of the little bear; descendant of Benz, a pet form of Benedictus (blessed); one who came from Benz, in Germany.

Bercher (*Eng.*) Dweller at a birch tree or birch grove; one who had the care of sheep, a shepherd.

Bercovitz, Bercovitch (*Pol.*) The son of Berko, a pet form of Baruch (blessed).

Beresford (*Eng.*) One who came from Barford (barley ford, perhaps ford used at the time of harvest), the name of several places in England.

Bereskin, Beroskin (*Ukr.*) A corruption of Berozski, dweller near a birch tree.

Berg (*Nor., Sw., Dan.*) Dweller near the hill or mountain. See also Burg.

Berge (*Nor.*) Dweller at, or near, a rocky mountain.

Bergen, Bergan (*Nor.*) Dweller on the mountain.

Berger, Bergeret, Bergeron (*Fr., Ger.*) One who took care of a flock, a shepherd; dweller on, or near, a mountain.

Berggren, Bergren (*Sw.*) Mountain branch.

Berglund (*Sw.*) Mountain grove.

Bergman, Bergmann (*Ger.*) Dweller in the mountains.

Bergquist, Berquist (*Sw.*) Mountain twig.

Bergstresser, Bergstrasser (*Ger.*) Dweller on a mountain road.

Bergstrom (*Sw.*) Mountain stream.

Berkley, Berkeley (*Eng.*) One who came from Berkeley (birch wood), in Gloucestershire, or Berkley, in Somerset; dweller in, or near, a birch wood.

Berkowitz, Berkovitz, Berkowicz (*Pol., Ukr.*) The son of Berek or Berko, pet forms of Baruch (blessed).

Berkson (*Eng., Ger.*) The son of Berk, a pet form of Baruch (blessed); the son of Baer or Ber (bear).

Berland, Berlander (*Ger., Eng.*) Dweller on, or near, the field where barley was grown; one who came from Berland (bear land), in Norway.

Berlin, Berliner, Berlinger (*Ger.*) One who came from Berlin (uncultivated field), in Germany; descendant of Ber or Berl (bear).

Berman (*Eng., Ger.*) One who owned a bear and led it about for public exhibition of its tricks; descendant of Berman (bear, man).

Bernard (*Fr., Eng.*) Descendant of Bernard (bear, firm).

Bernberg (*Ger.*) One who came from Bernburg (bear mountain), in Germany.

Berndt, Bernd (*Ger.*) Descendant of Berndt (bear, firm).

Berner (*Eng., Swis.*) One who burned brick or charcoal; a keeper of hounds; one who came from Bern (place where bears abounded), in Switzerland.

Bernhardt, Bernhard (*Ger.*) Descendant of Berinhard (bear, brave).

Bernier (*Fr., Eng.*) A keeper of hounds; descendant of Bernard (bear, firm).

Berns, Bern, Bernes (*Eng., Swis., Ger.*) One who came from Bernes (bear), in Normandy, or from Bern (place where bears abounded), a city and canton in Switzerland, or from Bern, in Germany.

Bernstein, Bernstine (*Ger.*) One who who came from Bernstein (amber), now in Poland.

Berra (*It.*) Dweller in a hut or hovel.

Berry, Berryman (*Eng.*) Dweller at, or near, a hill; dweller at, or near, a stronghold or fortified place.

Bertram (*Eng.*) Descendant of Bertram (bright, raven).

Bertrand, Bertran (*Fr.*) Descendant of Bertrand (bright, raven).

Bertucci (*It.*) Descendant of little Berto (bright), a pet form of names so ending, such as Alberto.

Berube (*Fr.*) Dweller on, or near, marshy land.

Besser, Besserer (*Dan., Ger.*) One who came from Besser (better place), in Denmark; one who collected fines.

Bessie, Besse, Bess (*Fr.*) Dweller near, or in, a birch-tree grove.

Best (*Eng.*) Dweller at the sign of the beast; one with the qualities of a beast, probably not in an uncomplimentary sense.

Betts, Betz (*Eng., Ger.*) Descendant of Beatrice (one who blesses); descendant of Bezzo, a pet form of names beginning with Baer (bear), Bercht (shining, or famous), or Bad (fight).

Bevan, Bevans (*Wel.*) The son of Evan (young warrior).

Beveridge (*Eng.*) Dweller at a farm, or ridge, frequented by beavers; one who came from Besser (better place), in in Dorsetshire.

Beverley, Beverly (*Eng.*) One who came from Beverley (beaver stream), in Yorkshire.

Bevilacqua (*It.*) One known as a teetotaler, i.e., one who drank water.

Bey (*Eng.*) Dweller at the curve, or bend, in the river.

Beyer, Beier (*Ger., Du.*) One who came from Bavaria, in Germany.

Beynon (*Wel.*) The son of Eynon or Einion (anvil).

Bialas, Bialy (*Pol.*) The light-complexioned or white-haired man.

Bialek (*Pol.*) The small, light-complexioned or white-haired man.

Bianco, Bianchi (*It.*) The light-complexioned or white-haired man.

Bickford, Beckford (*Eng.*) One who came from Bickford (Bica's ford), a village in Staffordshire, or Beckford (Becca's ford), in Gloucestershire.

Bickham, Bickhem (*Eng.*) Variants of Beckham, *q.v.*

Bickley, Bickle (*Eng.*) One who came from Bickley (Bicca's homestead), the name of several places in England.

Biddle (*Eng.*) A variant of Bedell, *q.v.*

Bidwell, Bidwill (*Eng.*) One who came from Bidwell (stream in a valley), in Bedfordshire.

Bieber (*Ger.*) One who came from Bieber (beaver's place), in Germany.

Biedenweg (*Ger.*) One who lived "by the way" or street.

Biedermann, Biederman (*Ger.*) The upright, honest servant or vassal.

Biel, Biehl, Biehler (*Ger.*) One who came from Buhl or Buhler (small hill), in Germany.

Bielski (*Pol.*) One who came from Bielsk (white), in Poland.

Biernat (*Ger.*) Descendant of Berinhard (bear, brave).

Bieschke (*Pol.*) Descendant of little Piotr (rock).

Bigelow, Biglow (*Eng.*) Dweller on, or near, the barley hill; one who came from Baguley (ram's woodland), the name of several places in England.

Biggers, Bigger, Biggar (*Eng., Scot.*) One who buys, a purchaser; one who came from Biggar (barley field), in Lanarkshire.

Biggs, Bigg, Bigges (*Wel., Eng.*) The large, tall, bulky or proud man; the mighty, powerful man; descendant of Bicca (thick or big).

Bigley (*Ir.*) A variant of Begley, *q.v.*

Bigott, Bigot (*Eng., Fr.*) Nickname given to one by reason of the excessive use of the oath, "by God"; a hypercritical or intolerant person.

Bilek, Bilko (*Cz.-Sl.*) The light-complexioned or white-haired man.

Bill, Bille (*Ger., Eng.*) Descendant of Bilo, a pet form of names beginning with Bil (sword), as Bilihar and Biligarda; descendant of Bil (sword). Not from Bill, a relatively late pet form of William.

Biller (*Eng.*) One who made bills, weapons consisting of a long staff terminating in a hook-shaped blade.

Billings, Billing (*Eng.*) One who came from Billing (Billa's people), in Northamptonshire, or from Billinge (sword), in Lancashire.

Billingsley, Billingslea, Billingsly (*Eng.*) One who came from Billingsley (Bylga's glade), in Shropshire.

Billy, Billie (*Scot.*) One who came from Billie or Bellie (village, farm), in Scotland.

Bily (*Cz.-Sl.*) The light-complexioned or white-haired man.

Binder (*Eng.*) One who binds, a bookbinder; one who binds sheaves behind the reapers.

Bingham (*Eng.*) One who came from Bingham (Bynna's estate), in Nottinghamshire.

Birch, Bircher, Birchet (*Eng.*) Dweller at, or near, the birch tree or birch-tree grove.

Bird (*Eng.*) Dweller at the sign of the bird; one with birdlike characteristics.

Birmingham (*Eng.*) One who came from Birmingham (the homestead of Beornmund's people), a city in Warwickshire.

Birnbaum, Bernbaum, Bernbom (*Ger.*) Dweller near the pear tree; one who came from Birnbaum, now in Poland.

Bisbee (*Eng.*) One who came from Beesby (Besy's homestead), in Lincolnshire.

Bischoff, Bischof, Bishoff, Bischoffer (*Ger.*) Member of a bishop's entourage or household; one who came from Bischof, in Germany; one playing the part of a bishop in play or pageant.

Bishop, Bishopp (*Eng.*) A member of a bishop's entourage; descendant of Biscop (bishop).

Bissett, Bissette (*Eng., Scot.*) The little brown or dark-complexioned man.

Bittner (*Ger.*) One who made casks or barrels, a cooper.

Bixby (*Eng.*) One who came from Bigby (Bekki's homestead), in Lincolnshire.

Bjork (*Sw.*) Birch.

Bjorklund (*Sw.*) Birch grove.

Bjornson, Bjornsen (*Nor.*) The son of Bjorn (bear).

Black (*Eng.*) One with a dark or swarthy complexion; descendant of Blaec or Blac (black or pale). Note:

Old English *blaec* is black, whereas Old English *blac* is white or pale, and the two words are inextricably confused in names.

Blackburn (*Eng., Scot.*) One who came from Blackburn (dark-colored stream), a town in Lancashire, or from Blackburn, the name of several places in Scotland. *See* note under Black.

Blackledge, Blacklidge (*Eng.*) Dweller at a black pool.

Blackman, Blackmon (*Eng.*) Descendant of Blaecman or Blacman (dark man), a not uncommon Early English name. *See* note under Black.

Blackstone (*Eng., Scot.*) The man from Blackstone (black boundary stone), the name of several places in both England and Scotland; descendant of Blaecstan (black stone). *See* note under Black.

Blackwell (*Eng.*) Dweller at, or near, the dark stream. *See* note under Black.

Blackwood (*Scot.*) The man from Blackwood (dark wood), the name of lands in Lanarkshire and Dumfriesshire.

Blaha (*Cz.-Sl.*) The blithesome or happy person.

Blaine, Blain (*Scot.*) The son of the disciple of Blaan or Blane (the lean), an early Scottish saint.

Blair (*Scot.*) Dweller on a plain; one who came from Blair (plain), the name of several places in Scotland.

Blaisdell (*Eng.*) One who came from Bleasdale (bare spot on a hillside), in Lancashire.

Odell, O'Dell, Odel (*Eng.*) One who came from Odell (wood hill), in Bedfordshire. The place was also called Woodhill.

Blake (*Eng.*) One with a swarthy complexion; descendant of Blaec, meaning either black or pale. *See* note under Black.

Blakemore (*Eng.*) One who came from Blackmore (black wasteland), the name of several places in England.

Blakeslee, Blakesley (*Eng.*) One who came from Blakesley (wood of the black wolf), in Northamptonshire.

Blakly, Blakely, Blakeley (*Eng.*) One who came from Blackley (the black wood or clearing), in Lancashire.

Blanc, Blanchet, Blanchon (*Fr.*) The light-complexioned or white-haired man.

Blanchard, Blancard (*Fr., Eng.*) Descendant of Blanchard (white, hard); dweller at the sign of the blanchard (white horse); the light-complexioned or white-haired man.

Bland (*Eng.*) One who came from Bland, in Yorkshire; the light-complexioned man.

Blandford (*Eng.*) One who came from Blandford (ford where gudgeons abound), in Dorset.

Blank, Blanks, Blanke (*Eng.*) One with a fair or light complexion; one who had white hair.

Blankenship, Blankensop (*Eng.*) One who came from Blenkinsopp (top valley), in Northumberland.

Blatchford (*Eng.*) One who came from Blackford (black ford), in Somerset.

Blatt (*Ger.*) Leaf.

Blau (*Ger., Du.*) One who was light-complexioned or blond; one wearing some article colored blue.

Blauvelt (*Du.*) One who lived at, or near, the blue field, referring to the flax field.

Blaylock, Blalock (*Eng.*) One who had lead-colored hair.

Blazek (*Cz.-Sl., Pol.*) Descendant of Blazek, a pet form of Blasius (babbler).

Blechman (*Ger.*) One who worked with tin, a tinsmith.

Bledsoe (*Eng.*) One who came from Bletsoe (Blaecci's hill), in Bedfordshire.

Bleecker, Bleeker (*Du.*) One who bleached cloth, a fuller.

Blennerhassett (*Eng.*) One who came from Blennerhasset (hay hut on a hill), in Cumberland.

Blessing (*Eng.*) One who took the personified part of "blessing" in the morality plays.

Blessington (*Eng.*) One who came from Bletchingdon (Blecces' hill), in Oxfordshire.

Bliss (*Eng.*) One with a blithesome or happy disposition.

Blitsstein, Blitzstein (*Ger.*) Lightning stone.

Bloch, Block (*Ger., Eng.*) one who lived at the sign of the block or cube; the short, stumpy, or stupid man.

Bloden (*Eng., Ger.*) One who came from Blaydon (blue hill), in Durham; dweller near a flowering thorn tree.

Blodgett (*Wel.*) The son of little Lloyd (gray).

Blomberg, Bloomberg (*Sw.*) Flower mountain.

Blomgren, Bloomgren (*Sw.*) Flower branch.

Blomquist, Bloomquist (*Sw.*) Flower twig.

Blood (*Wel.*) The son of Lloyd (gray).

Bloom, Blom (*Sw.*) Flower.

Blount, Blunt (*Eng.*) The fair or light-complexioned man.

Blowers, Blower (*Eng.*) The bellows-blower who helped the smith at the forge.

Blue (*Eng.*) One with a livid complexion; one who dressed in blue.

Blum, Blume (*Ger.*) Flower.

Blumberg (*Ger.*) One who came from Blumberg (flower mountain), the name of two places in Germany.

Blumenthal (*Ger*). One who came from Blumenthal (flower valley), the name of seven towns in Germany.

Blyth, Blythe (*Eng.*) One who came from Blyth (gentle or merry), in Nottinghamshire; dweller near the Blyth or Blythe rivers in England; one with a gay or pleasant disposition.

Board, Bord (*Eng.*) Dweller at a cottage or small farm.

Boardman (*Eng.*) One who hewed boards; dweller at a small farm.

Bobb, Bobbe (*Eng.*) Descendant of Bobba (a lall name).

Bobbitt, Bobbett (*Fr.*) A haughty person who made a show of pomp; one who stammered or stuttered.

Bober (*Cz.-Sl.*) Dweller at the sign of the beaver; one with the characteristics of a beaver.

Boccaccio (*It.*) One with an ugly mouth.

Bochenek (*Pol.*) Dweller at the sign of the loaf of bread.

Bock (*Ger.*) Dweller at the sign of the buck; one thought to have some of the qualities of a male goat; descendant of Burgio, a pet form of names commencing with Burg (stronghold), as Burghard and Burgoald.

Bode (*Du., Ger.*) An officer of the court, town crier or constable; descendant of Bode, a pet form of names beginning with Bod (messenger), as Bodewig and Butulf.

Bodfish (*Eng.*) Dweller at the sign of the flat fish; seller of flat fish, such as the halibut.

Bodkin, Bodkins (*Eng.*) Descendant of little Baud, a pet form of Baldwin (bold, friend).

Body (*Hun.*) One who came from Bod (meadow), in Hungary.

Boe (*Nor.*) One who lived on a farm.

Boehm, Boehme, Boehmer (*Ger.*) One who came from Bohemia (home of the Boii).

Boer (*Du.*) One who tilled the land, a farmer.

Boersma, Boerema (*Du.*) Descendant, or servant, of the farmer.

Boettcher, Boettger, Boetticher, Boettiger (*Ger.*) One who made, or sold, barrels or casks, a cooper.

Bogan, Boggan (*Ir.*) Grandson of Bogan (dim. of soft or tender).

Bogard, Bogaart, Bogaert (*Du.*) One who tended an orchard.

Boggs, Bogg, Boggis, Bogges (*Eng.*) Dweller at, or near, a bog or marsh.

Bogue, Boag (*Scot., Eng.*) One who came from Bogue (soft, moist), in Kirkcudbrightshire; descendant of Boge or Boga (bow).

Bohac (*Cz.-Sl.*) The rich man.

Bohl, Bohle, Bohling, Bohlig, Bohlmann, Bohlman (*Ger.*) The bold, or brave, man; one who came from Bohl, in Germany.

Bohmann, Bohman, Bohm (*Ger.*) One who came from Bohemia (home of the Boii).

Bohn (*Ger.*) Descendant of Bono, a pet form of names beginning with Bon (demand), as Bonard and Bonuald.

Bohren, Bohrer (*Ger.*) Dweller in, or near, the pine woods.

Boileau, Boilleau, Boileve (*Fr.*) One who drank water, an early nickname for a teetotaler.

Bois, Boys, Boyes (*Fr.*) Dweller near, or in, a wood.

Boit (*Fr.*) One who made and sold boxes.

Boland, Bolan, Bowland, Bowlan (*Eng.*) One who came from Bowland (land by the bend of the river), in Lancashire.

Bolden (*Eng.*) One who came from Boldon (hill with a homestead), in Durham.

Boldt, Bolt, Bold, Bolte (*Ger., Eng., Scot.*) Descendant of Baldo, a pet form of names beginning with Bald (bold or daring), as Baldhart, Baldher and Baldawin; the bold or fierce man; dweller at a hall or mansion; a short, heavy man; one who came from Bold (dwelling), in Peeblesshire.

Boles, Bole (*Eng.*) One who came from Bole (tree trunk), in Nottinghamshire, or Bolas (wood where bows were obtained), in Shropshire; dweller at the sign of the bull; one with bullish characteristics.

Bolger, Bolgar (*Eng., Ir.*) One who made leather wallets or bags; the light-complexioned man.

Bolin, Bolen, Bollin (*Eng.*) Dweller near the Bollin River in Cheshire.

Boller (*Eng.*) One who made or sold bowls.

Bollinger, Bolling (*Ger., Swis.*) One who came from Bollingen, on Lake Zurich in Switzerland.

Bolotin (*Rus.*) Dweller on, or near, a marsh.

Bolster (*Eng.*) One who sifted meal; one who made bolts or arrows.

Bolton, Boltin (*Eng., Scot.*) One who came from Bolton (dwelling, enclosure), the name of various places in England and one in Scotland. In some instances it referred to one in the village proper in contradistinction to the outlying parts.

Bond, Bonde, Bonds (*Eng., Ice.*) A householder or a tiller of the soil; a peasant proprietor.

Bondi (*It.*) "Good day," perhaps a nickname of one who habitually used this salutation.

Bonelli, Bonello (*It.*) The small, good man.

Bonfiglio, Bonfilio, Bonfigli (*It.*) The good child.

Bonk (*Pol.*) One having the characteristics of a horsefly.

Bonnell (*Scot., Ger.*) One who came from Bonhill (house by the stream), in Scotland; descendant of Bono, a pet form of names beginning with Bon (demand), as Bonard and Bonuald.

Bonner (*Eng.*) The kind, gentle person.

Bonnet, Bonnett, Bonnette (*Fr.*) Descendant of Bonet (the good); one who made and sold hats.

Bonney, Bonny (*Eng.*) The good, kind person.

Bono, Buono (*It.*) The good, generally a shortened form of some compound name.

Bonomo, Bonomi, Buonomo (*It.*) The good man, or good-natured fellow; a simpleton.

Boodberg (*Sw.*) Booth mountain.

Booker (*Eng.*) One who copied books; dweller at, or near, a beech tree.

Boone, Boon, Bowne (*Eng.*) One who came from Bohon, in France.

Booth (*Eng.*) Dweller at a hut or stall.

Boothby (*Eng.*) One who came from Boothby (village with huts or stalls), in Lincolnshire.

Booz, Booze, Boozer, Boos (*Du., Eng.*) The angry or cross man; descendant of Boaz (in him is strength); dweller near the cattle stall.

Borchardt, Borchert, Borchering (*Ger.*) Descendant of Burghard (castle, strong).

Borden (*Eng.*) One who came from Borden (swine pasture hill), in Kent.

Borders, Bordner, Border (*Eng.*) One who held a cottage in the English manor, at his lord's pleasure, for which he rendered menial service.

Borg, Borge (*Sw., Nor., Ger.*) Dweller in, or near, a fortified castle; one who came from Borg (stronghold), the name of several places in Germany.

Borgardt, Borgard, Borgert (*Ger.*) Descendant of Burghard (castle, strong).

Borgman (*Ger., Du.*) One who borrows or lends money or goods; descendant of Burgman (castle, man).

Boris (*Hun.*) Descendant of Boris (stranger).

Bork (*Pol.*) An abbreviated form of Borowski, q.v.

Born, Borne (*Eng., Ger.*) Dweller at the brook or spring.

Bornstein (*Ger.*) Dweller near a stony spring.

Borowski, Borkowski (*Pol.*) Dweller in a small wood.

Borrows, Borroughs (*Eng.*) Dweller in, or near, a stronghold or fortified place; dweller on, or near, a hill.

Borst (*Ger.*) One who had bristly hair.

Borucki (*Pol.*) One who came from Boruty (Boruta's place), a village in Poland.

Bos, Bose (*Du., Ger.*) Dweller in, or near, the woods; the quarrelsome man.

Bosco (*It.*) Dweller in, or near, a woods.

Bosley (*Eng.*) One who came from Bosley (Bosa's wood), in Cheshire.

Boss, Bosse (*Eng.*) Dweller at a wood; a fat person.

Boston (*Eng.*) One who came from Boston (St. Botulf's stone), a village in Lincolnshire.

Bostwick, Bostock (*Eng.*) One who came from Bostock (Bota's cell), in Cheshire.

Boswell (*Eng.*) One who came from Bosville (wood town), a village in Normandy.

Bosworth (*Eng.*) One who came from Bosworth (Bar's or Bosa's homestead), in Leicestershire.

Both, Bothe (*Eng.*) Variants of Booth, q.v.

Bothfield, Bothfeld (*Eng.*) Dweller in the hut in the open field.

Bothwell (*Scot.*) One who came from Bothwell (booth by the fish pool), in Lanarkshire.

Botsford (*Eng.*) One who came from Bottesford (house by the river crossing), the name of places in Leicestershire and Lincolnshire.

Bottom, Bottome, Bottoms, Bottum (*Eng.*) Dweller in the valley.

Boucher, Bouchier, Boucharin (*Fr.*) One who cut and sold meats, a butcher.

Boudreau (*Fr.*) Descendant of Boudon (armed messenger).

Boulanger (*Fr.*) One who made bread, a baker.

Bourke, Bourk (*Ir.*) Dweller at, or near, a stronghold or fortified place.

Bourne, Bourn (*Eng.*) Dweller near the brook or stream.

Bouvier, Bouyer (*Fr.*) One who took care of cattle.

Bowden (*Eng., Scot.*) One who came from Bowden (Bucge's pasture), the name of several places in England, or from Bowden (house on the hill), in Scotland.

Bowditch, Bowdish (*Eng.*) One who came from Bowditch (arched bridge ditch), in Dorsetshire.

Bowdoin (*Fr.*) A partially Englished variant of Beaudoin, q.v.

Bowen (*Wel.*) The son of Owen, Welsh form of Eugene (wellborn).

Bowers, Bower (*Eng., Scot.*) Dweller in a cottage or chamber; one who came from Bower (house), in Peeblesshire; one who built houses; one who made and sold bows.

Bowes, Bowe (*Eng.*) One who came from Bowes (bows, probably referring to an arched bridge), in Yorkshire; descendant of Boga (bow).

Bowie (*Ir., Scot.*) Grandson of little Buadhach or Buagh (victorious); one who had yellow or fair hair.

Bowker (*Eng.*) A variant of Booker, q.v.; one who had charge of money.

Bowles, Bowler, Boles, Boler (*Eng.*) One who made or sold concave vessels or bowls.

Bowman (*Eng., Scot.*) A fighting man armed with a bow; one who made bows; the servant in charge of the cattle.

Bowser (*Fr.*) One who made and sold purses.

Bowyer (*Eng.*) One who made or sold bows.

Box (*Eng.*) Dweller near the box tree.

Boyce, Boece (*Fr.*) Dweller near, or in, a wood.

Boyd (*Ir., Eng.*) One who had yellow hair; dweller by the Boyd River, in Gloucestershire.

Boyer (*Eng., Fr.*) One who made and sold bows; one who took care of, or drove, cattle.

Boylan, Boyland (*Eng.*) One who came from Boyland (Boia's grove), in Norfolk.

Boyle, Boyles, Boyell, Boyll, Boyl (*Ir., Scot.*) Grandson of Baoigheall (vain pledge); one who came from Beauville, the name of two places in France.

Boynton (*Eng.*) One who came from Boynton (village of Bofa's people), in Yorkshire.

Braband, Brabant, Brabandt (*Du.*) One who came from Brabant (the plowed district), in Holland.

Brach, Brack, Bracke, Brachman (*Ger.*) Dweller on, or near, the fallow land.

Bracken, Brackin (*Eng.*) One who came from Bracken (fern), in Yorkshire.

Brackett (*Eng.*) Dweller at the sign of the little hunting dog.

Bradbury, Bradberry (*Eng.*) One who came from Bradbury (fort built of boards), in Durham.

Braddock (*Eng.*) One who came from Braddock or Broadoak (broad oak), the name of a village in Cornwall.

Braden, Braddan (*Eng.*) One who came from Bradden (broad valley), in Northamptonshire, or Bradon or Braydon, in Somerset and Wiltshire, respectively.

Bradford (*Eng.*) One who came from Bradford (wide ford), the name of various places in England.

Bradley (*Eng.*) One who came from Bradley (wide meadow), the name of many places in England.

Bradshaw (*Eng.*) One who came from Bradshaw (extensive grove), in Derbyshire; dweller in, or near, the big woods.

Bradtke, Bratke (*Cz.-Sl., Ger.*) Descendant of the little brother; descendant of Brado (of obscure origin); dweller at the sign of the little bear.

Bradwell (*Eng.*) One who came from Bradwell or Broadwell (wide stream), the names of several places in England.

Brady (*Ir.*) The son of Bradach (spirited).

Bragg, Braggs (*Eng.*) Descendant of Brego (chief).

Brainerd, Brainard (*Eng.*) Descendant of Brandhard (sword, hard).

Braithwaite, Brathwaite, Breathwaite (*Eng.*) One who came from Braithwaite (broad clearing), the name of places in Cumberland and Yorkshire.

Bramhall (*Eng.*) One who came from Bramhall (broom corner), in Cheshire.

Bramson (*Ger.*) The son of Bram, a shortened form of Abraham (father of multitudes).

Branch, Branche (*Eng., Fr.*) One who came from Branche (bow), in Normandy; descendant of Branca or Brancher (ruler), names of two early saints; a name referring to the "day of branches," i.e., Palm Sunday.

Brandeis (*Ger., Cz.-Sl.*) Dweller on a burned clearing; one who came from Brandeis, the name of three places in Bohemia.

Brandenburg, Brandenburger (*Ger.*) One who came from Brandenburg, a district in northern Germany.

Brandon (*Eng.*) One who came from Brandon (broom hill), the name of several villages in England.

Brandt, Brand, Brant (*Ger., Eng.*) Dweller on a farm cleared by burning; dweller near the Brant (steep), a river in Lincolnshire.

Branham, Brannam (*Eng.*) One who came from Brantham (Branta's homestead), in Suffolk.

Brannigan, Branigan (*Ir.*) Grandson of little Bran (raven).

Branscomb, Branscombe, Branscom (*Eng.*) One who came from Branscombe (Branoc's valley), in Devonshire.

Bransfield (*Eng.*) One who came from Bramfield (steep field, or Brant's field), in Hertfordshire.

Branson (*Eng.*) The son of Brand (sword).

Brantley, Brantly (*Eng.*) One who lived at, or near, the meadow where broom grew; one who came from Bramley (clearing overgrown with broom), the name of various places in England.

Brauer, Brower (*Ger., Du.*) One who brewed beer.

Braun, Brauneis, Braune (*Ger.*) The dark-complexioned man.

Braverman (*Ger.*) The brave or courageous man.

Brawley (*Scot.*) Dweller on the broad meadow.

Braxton (*Eng.*) One who lived at, or near, Bracca's boundary mark.

Bray (*Eng.*) One who came from Bray (brow of a hill), the name of places in Berkshire and Devonshire; one who came from Bray, the name of several places in France; the brave man.

Brazelton (*Eng.*) Dweller at a place where sulphate of iron, or a red dyewood, was worked.

Brazier, Brasier (*Eng.*) One who worked in brass.

Breckenridge, Breckinridge (*Scot.*) Dweller at the fern ridge or hill; one who came from the lands of Brackenrig (ridge overgrown with bracken), in Lanarkshire.

Breed, Breede, Brede (*Eng.*) One who came from Brede (flat expanse), in Sussex; dweller on the plain.

Breen (*Ir.*) Grandson of Braon (sorrow); variant of O'Brien, q.v.

Breese, Breeze (*Wel.*) The son of Rhys (ardor, a rush).

Breger, Bregar, Bregger (*Ger.*) Dweller on the bank of a river; one who begs for alms.

Breitenbach, Breidenbach (*Swis., Ger.*) One who came from Breitenbach (settlement by a wide brook), in Switzerland; dweller near a wide stream; one with a big stomach.

Brelsford (*Eng.*) One who came from Brailesford (burial place by the ford), in Derbyshire.

Bremer, Bremen (*Ger.*) One who came from Bremen (by the seashore), in Germany.

Brennan, Brennen (*Ir.*) Grandson of little Bran (raven).

Brenner (*Eng.*) One who burned brick or charcoal, a burner.

Brent (*Eng.*) One who came from Brent (high place), in Devonshire; dweller near the Brent River in Middlesex.

Brenton (*Eng.*) One who came from Brinton (Bryni's homestead), in Norfolk.

Bresnahan, Bresnihan (*Ir.*) Variants of Brosnahan, q.v.

Bressler, Bresler, Breslau, Breslauer (*Ger.*) One who came from Breslau (named after King Vratislaw), in Germany, now Wroclaw in Poland.

Breton (*Eng.*) One who came from Bretton (newly cultivated enclosure), the name of places in Derbyshire and Yorkshire.

Brett (*Fr., Ger.*) One who came from Brette, the name of two places in France; one who came from Bretagne, or Brittany, in France; descendant of Briddo (bridle).

Bretz (*Ger.*) Descendant of Briddo (bridle).

Brewer, Brewster (*Eng.*) One who brewed beer or ale.

Breyer, Breier, Breuer (*Ger.*) One who brewed beer; one who came from Brey, in Germany.

Brice (*Wel.*) The son of Rhys (ardor, a rush).

Brickett (*Eng.*) One who came from Bricett (place infested by horseflies), in Suffolk.

Brickley (*Eng.*) Dweller at, or on, the meadow newly broken up for cultivation.

Brickman (*Eng.*) Dweller near a bridge; dweller on a heath or on fallow land.

Bridgeforth, Bridgeford, Bridgforth (*Eng.*) One who came from Bridgford (ford with a footbridge), the name of several places in England.

Bridgeman, Bridgman, Briggeman (*Eng.*) The keeper of a bridge; dweller near a bridge.

Bridges, Bridge (*Eng.*) Dweller at, or near, a bridge.

Bridgewater (*Eng.*) One who came from Bridgwater (the bridge), in Somerset.

Brierly (*Eng.*) One who came from Brierly (glade where briars grew), in Yorkshire.

Briggs, Brigg (*Scot., Eng.*) Dweller near a bridge.

Brigham (*Eng.*) One who came from Brigham (homestead by the bridge), the name of places in Cumberland and Yorkshire.

Bright, Breit, Brite (*Eng., Ger.*) Descendant of Beorht (bright); the big, broad man.

Brill, Brille (*Eng., Du., Ger.*) One who came from Brill (hill), in Buckinghamshire; one who came from The Brille, in Holland; one who made, or wore, spectacles; one who came from Brill, the name of four places in Germany; an abbreviation of Ben Rabbi Judah Lowe.

Brink (*Eng.*) Dweller at the edge or slope of a hill.

Brinkman, Brink, Brinkmann, Brinker (*Ger., Du.*) Dweller on, or near, the grassy hill.

Briscoe, Brisco (*Eng.*) One who came from Briscoe (birch wood), the name of places in Cumberland and Yorkshire.

Bristol, Bristow, Bristle (*Eng.*) One who came from Bristol (the site of the bridge), in Gloucestershire.

Britt (*Eng.*) One who came from Brit (the port or borough belonging to Bredy), in Dorset. *See also* Brett.

Britton, Brittain, Briton (*Eng.*) One who came from Brittany (figure picture), a region in France.

Broadfoot (*Scot.*) One who came from Bradfute (foot of hill place), a lost place name formerly either in Ayrshire or Dumfriesshire.

Broadford (*Eng.*) Dweller near a wide stream crossing.

Broadhead, Brodhead (*Eng.*) One who had a big head; dweller at the wide headland.

Broberg (*Sw.*) Bridge mountain.

Brock, Brocker, Brocks (*Eng.*) Dweller on the newly cleared and enclosed land; dweller near the stream or marsh land; dweller at the sign of the badger; one who lived near the Brock River, in Lancashire.

Brockman, Brockmann (*Eng.*) Dweller at a brook.

Brod, Broda (*Pol., Ger.*) One who had an unusual beard; one who came from Broda, in Mecklenburg.

Broderick (*Wel.*) The son of Rhodri (circle, ruler), or Roderick (famous ruler).

Brodny (*Rus.*) One who lived near a shallow stream crossing.

Brodsky (*Rus.*) One with an unusual beard.

Brody, Brodie (*Ir., Scot., Ger., Rus.*) The son of Bruaideadh (fragment); one who came from the barony of Brodie (muddy place), in Moray; one who had an unusual beard; one who came from Brody, in Russia.

Broemel (*Eng., Ger.*) One who came from Bremhill (bramble hill), in Wiltshire; dweller near a bramble or blackberry bush; descendant of Broemel, a variant of Brumo, a pet form of names beginning with Brun (brown), as Brunold and Brunomund.

Brogan (*Ir.*) Grandson of little Brog (sorrowful).

Broker, Brooker (*Eng.*) One who sells goods, a retailer; one who lived at the brook or stream.

Bromberg (*Ger.*) Dweller on a brown mountain; one who came from Bromberg (brown mountain), in Austria.

Bromfield, Broomfield (*Eng.*) One who came from Bromfield or Broomfield (broom-covered field), the names of several places in England.

Bromley (*Eng.*) One who came from Bromley (clearing where broom grew), the name of several places in England.

Broms, Brom, Brome (*Eng.*) One who came from Brome, Broom or Broome (place where broom grew), the names of several places in England; dweller near where broom grew.

Bronson, Brons (*Eng.*) The son of Brun (brown).

Bronstein, Bronston, Bronstine (*Ger.*) Dweller near a brown stone, usually a boundary mark.

Brooks, Brookes, Brook, Brookman, Brooke (*Eng.*) Dweller near the spring or brook, sometimes marsh.

Broome, Broom, Broomes (*Eng.*) One who came from Broome or Broom (place where broom grew), the names of several places in England.

Brophy (*Ir.*) Grandson of Brogh or Broha (origin obscure).

Brosnan, Brosnahan, Brosnihan (*Ir.*) One who came from Brosna in Kerry; dweller near the Brosna River.

Brothers (*Eng.*) Descendant of a lay brother, a member of a men's religious order preparing for holy orders; descendant of Brother (brother).

Broughton (*Eng.*) One who came from Broughton (homestead on a brook, homestead by a fortified place, or homestead by a hill or barrow), the name of many places in England.

Brouillet, Brouillette, Brouillete (*Fr.*) Dweller in, or near, a small, swampy wood; one who came from Breuil (swampy wood), in France.

Browder (*Ir.*) Grandson of Bruadar (brother).

Brower, Brouwer, Browar (*Du.*) One who brewed beer, a brewer.

Brown, Browne, Broun (*Eng., Scot.*) One with a dark complexion; descendant of Brun (brown).

Brownell (*Eng.*) Descendant of little Brun (brown).

Brownfield (*Scot.*) One who came from Brounfield (Brun's field), in Scotland.

Browning (*Eng.*) The son of Brun (brown); descendant of Bruning (brown, friend).

Brownlee, Brownley, Brownlie (*Eng.*) Dweller at the brown meadow.

Brownlow (*Eng.*) Dweller at the brown hill or burial mound.

Brownstein (*Ger.*) Dweller near a brown stone, usually a boundary mark.

Bruce, Bruse (*Scot.*) One who came from Braose (now Brieuse), in Normandy.

Bruckner, Brucker, Bruck (*Ger.*) Dweller at, or near, a bridge.

Bruhn (*Ger.*) The dark-complexioned man.

Brumfield (*Eng.*) One who came from Broomfield or Bromfield (broom-covered field), the names of various places in England.

Brundage (*Eng.*) One who came from Brundish (Edisc on the stream), in Suffolk, or from Brownedge (brown hill), in Lancashire.

Brunke, Brunk (*Ger.*) Descendant of little Brun (brown), or of Bruno, a pet form of names beginning with Brun (brown), as Brunwig and Brunolf.

Brunner, Bruner (*Ger.*) One who dug wells.

Bruno (*Ger.*) Descendant of Bruno (brown). Bruno is also a pet form of names beginning with Brun (brown), as Brunrat and Brunwart.

Bruns, Brune, Brun (*Ger., Fr., Eng.*) Descendant of Brun (brown).

Brunsdale (*Eng.*) Dweller at Brun's valley.

Brunson (*Nor., Eng.*) The son of Brun (brown).

Brunswick (*Ger.*) One who came from Brunschweig (Bruno's country), a city and former state in Germany.

Brush (*Eng.*) Dweller in, or near, broom or heather.

Bryant, Bryan, Brien (*Ir.*) Descendant of Bryan (hill).

Bryson (*Eng.*) The son of Bryce (speedy).

Brzezinski, Brzozowski (*Pol.*) Dweller near a birch tree.

Buchanan (*Scot.*) One who came from Both-Chanain (the Canon's seat), in Stirlingshire.

Buchbinder (*Ger.*) One who bound books.

Bucher, Bucker (*Ger.*) One who copied books.

Buchholz, Buchholtz, Bucholz, Buckholtz (*Ger.*) Dweller in, or near, a beech grove.

Buchler (*Ger.*) One who pressed oil from beechnuts; one who came from Buchel, in Germany.

Buchman, Buchmann (*Ger.*) Dweller at, or near, the beech trees.

Buchwald, Buchwalder (*Ger.*) One who lived near the beech wood; one who came from Buchwald (beech wood), in Germany.

Buck, Bucke (*Eng.*) Dweller at the sign of the male deer.

Buckingham (*Eng.*) One who came from Buckingham (the homestead of Bucca's people), in Buckinghamshire.

Buckland (*Eng.*) One who came from Buckland (land held by charter), the name of many places in the south of England.

Buckles, Bucknell (*Eng.*) One who came from Bucknall (Bucca's corner), or from Bucknell (Bucca's hill), each the name of two villages in England.

Buckley, Buckle, Buckly (*Eng.*) One who came from Bulkeley (bullock pasture), in Cheshire.

Buckner (*Ger.*) Dweller at, or near, a beech tree; descendant of Burghar (stronghold, army).

Buda (*Hun.*) One who came from Buda (Buda's town), in Hungary.

Budd, Bud (*Eng.*) Descendant of Buda (messenger), or of Bud, a pet form of Baldwin (bold, friend) and of Botolf (command, wolf); the foolish, stupid man.

Budz (*Pol.*) Descendant of Budz, a pet form of Budzimir or Budzislaw (awaken); one who came from Budzyn (the huts), in Poland.

Budzinski, Budzynski (*Pol.*) One who came from Budzyn (the huts), in Poland.

Buehler, Buhl, Buehl, Buhler (*Ger.*) One who lived on, or near, a hill.

Buell (*Eng.*) One who came from Bueil, in France.

Buelow, Bulow (*Ger.*) One who came from Buelow, in Mecklenburg.

Buerger, Buerker (*Ger.*) Dweller in a town; descendant of Burghar (stronghold, army).

Buettner, Buttner (*Ger.*) One who made and sold casks, a cooper.

Buford, Bueford (*Eng.*) One who came from Beeford (ford at which bees were found), in Yorkshire.

Bugg, Buggs, Bugge (*Eng., Ger.*) Descendant of Buga or Bugga (to stoop); descendant of Burgio, a pet form of names beginning with Burg (castle), as Burgmar and Burcward.

Buggie, Buggy, Bugay, Bugee (*Eng.*) Descendant of Buga or Bugga (to stoop); one who came from Bugey, in France.

Buick, Buyck (*Du.*) One who had a large stomach or paunch.

Bukowski (*Pol.*) Dweller near a beech tree; one who came from Bukow(o), the name of many places in Poland, Ukraine and Byelorussia.

Bulganin (*Rus.*) One whose actions gave rise to scandal.

Bulger (*Eng., Ir.*) One who made leather wallets or bags; the light-complexioned man.

Bull (*Eng.*) Dweller at the sign of the bull; one thought to possess some characteristic of a bull.

Bullard (*Eng.*) One who kept, or tended, bulls.

Bullitt (*Eng.*) Dweller at the sign of the bull's head; one with a bull-shaped head.

Bullock, Bullocks (*Eng.*) Dweller at the sign of the young bull; one with some quality of a young bull.

Bumgardner (*Ger.*) Variant of Baumgartner, q.v.

Bumstead, Bumsted (*Eng.*) One who came from Bumpstead (reedy place), in Essex.

Bunch, Bunce, Bunche (*Eng.*) Descendant of Bunn (good).

Bundy, Bunde (*Eng.*) Descendant of Bondig (householder or free man).

Bunker (*Fr.*) The good-hearted man; one who came from Boncourt (good farm), in France.

Bunting (*Eng.*) Descendant of Bunting (the good little pet), a term of endearment for children; dweller at the sign of the bunting (finch).

Bunyan (*Wel.*) The son of Einion (anvil), or of Eniawn (upright).

Burbank (*Eng.*) Dweller at the cottage on the mound or embankment.

Burch, Burcher (*Eng.*) Dweller at the birch tree or grove.

Burchett, Burchette (*Eng.*) Descendant of little Burchard (castle, firm); dweller at the head or end of the birch grove.

Burchill, Burchell (*Eng.*) Dweller at, or on, the hill of birch trees.

Burda (*Cz.-Sl., Pol.*) The brawling or pugnacious man.

Burden, Burdon (*Eng.*) One who came from Burdon (valley with a cow barn, or hill with a fort), the name of several places in England.

Burdett, Burditt (*Eng., Fr.*) Descendant of Bordet (little shield); dweller near the border; dweller on a rented farm.

Burdick, Burdette, Burdett, Burditt (*Eng.*) Descendant of little Borda (shield); one who came from Bourdic, the name of two places in France.

Burg, Burge, Burgh (*Eng.*) Dweller at the fort or fortified place. *See also* Berg.

Burger (*Ger., Du.*) One who came from Burg (fort or stronghold), the name of places in Germany and Switzerland; variant of Buerger, q.v.

Burgess, Burges, Burgis (*Eng.*) A citizen or freeman of a borough who owed special duties to the king and had certain privileges.

Burgoyne (*Eng.*) One who came from Burgundy (dwellers in fortified places), a region mostly in France.

Burian (*Ukr.*) Dweller among, or near, weeds.

Burke, Burk, Berk, Birk, Berke (*Ir.*) Dweller at, or near, the burgh or stronghold.

Burkhardt, Burkhart, Burchardt, Burckard, Burghart, Burghardt (*Ger.*) One who lived in a strong castle or fortress.

Burks, Burkes (*Eng., Ir.*) Dweller at, or near, the stronghold or fortified place.

Burleigh, Burley (*Eng.*) One who came from Burley (wood belonging to a fort), the name of several places in England.

Burlingame (*Eng.*) One who came from Burlingham (the village of Baerla's people), in Norfolk.

Burman, Burmann (*Eng.*) Dweller in a cottage; servant of the peasant.

Burmeister, Burmester (*Ger.*) One who tilled the land, a farmer.

Burnell (*Fr.*) The dark or brown-complexioned man.

Burnett, Burnette (*Eng.*) One who came from Burnett (place cleared by burning), in Somerset; the small, brown-complexioned one.

Burnham, Burnam (*Eng.*) One who came from Burnham (estate on a stream), the name of various places in England.

Burns, Burnes (*Eng.*) Dweller at a brook.

Burnside (*Eng.*) One who came from Burnside (Brunwulf's headland), in Westmorland.

Burnstein, Burnstine (*Ger.*) Amber.

Burr (*Eng.*) One who came from, or worked at, the fortress.

Burrage (*Eng.*) Descendant of Burgric (castle, rule).

Burrell, Burrel, Burrill (*Eng.*) One who came from Burrill (hill of the fort), in the North Riding of Yorkshire; one who made, or wore, burel, a coarse, brown woolen cloth.

Burris, Burress, Burres (*Eng.*) Dweller near a stronghold or fortified place; a corruption of Burrows, q.v.

Burrows, Burroughs (*Eng.*) One who came from Burrow or Burroughs (fort or hill), the names of several villages in England; dweller near a stronghold or fortified place.

Burt, Burtt (*Eng.*) Descendant of Bert (bright).

Burton, Burtin (*Eng.*) One who came from Burton (village by a fort, or fortified manor), the name of many villages in England.

Busby, Busbey (*Eng., Scot.*) One who came from Busby (shrub homestead), in Yorkshire; one who came from the lands of Busby (bush village), in Renfrewshire.

Bush, Busch, Busche (*Eng., Ger.*) Dweller at the sign of the bush (usually a wine merchant); one who dwelt near a bush.

Bushell, Bushelle (*Eng.*) Dweller at the slope or corner overgrown with bushes; variant of Bussell, q.v.

Busse, Buss (*Fr., Eng., Ger.*) One who came from Bus (wood), in France; dweller at a wood or thicket; descendant of Burgio, a pet form of names beginning with Burg (place of protection), as Burghard and Burgmar.

Bussell (*Eng.*) Dweller at, or near, a thicket or small wood; one who came from Boissel (small wood), in France.

Bussey, Bussie (*Eng.*) One who came from Bussy or Boissy (little wood), in Normandy; dweller at a small wood; one who came from Bushey (a thicket), in Hertfordshire.

Buswell (*Eng.*) A variant of Boswell, q.v.

Butcher (*Eng.*) One who cut and sold meat.

Butkus (*Lith.*) Descendant of Butkintas.

Butler, Buttler (*Eng.*) One who made, or had charge of, bottles; one in charge of the butts or casks of wine.

Butterfield (*Eng.*) Dweller in, or near, a good pasture providing food for cows.

Butters (*Eng.*) Descendant of Botthar or Bothere (messenger, army).

Butterworth (*Eng.*) One who came from Butterworth (butter farm), in Lancashire.

Button (*Eng.*) One who came from Bitton (homestead on Boyd River), in Gloucestershire.

Buttrick, Butterick (*Eng.*) One who came from Butterwick (butter farm), the name of several places in England.

Butts, Butz (*Ger.*) One who oversees and gives commands; descendant of Bucco, a pet form of names beginning with Burg (castle), as Burghard, Burghar and Burcward.

Buxton (*Eng.*) One who came from Buxton (rocking stone), in Derbyshire.

Buzzell, Buzzelli (*It.*) Descendant of Buzzelli, a pet form of Giacobuzzi (the supplanter).

Byczek (*Pol.*) One who took care of young bulls.

Byers, Byer (*Eng.*) Dweller near a cattle shed; dweller at a land corner; one who purchased merchandise to sell to others.

Byrd (*Eng.*) Dweller at the sign of the bird; one with birdlike characteristics.

Byrne, Byrnes (*Ir.*) Grandson of Bran (raven), or of Biorn or Bjorn (bear).

Byron, Byram, Byrum (*Eng.*) Descendant of Byron (from the cottage); one who came from Byram (tumulus or cowshed), in Yorkshire.

Bysshe (*Eng.*) Dweller at the thicket or brushwood.

Cabot (*Fr.*) One with a small head; dweller at the sign of the miller's thumb, a fresh-water fish.

Cadigan, Cadogan (*Ir.*) Grandson of little Ceadach (possessing hundreds).

Cady (*Scot.*) Descendant of little Cadda (battle).

Cage (*Eng.*) Dweller near, or worker at, a prison.

Cahill, Cahall (*Ir.*) Grandson of Cathal (battle powerful).

Cahn (*Ger.*) Variant of Cohen, q.v.

Cain, Caine (*Ir., Eng.*) Descendant of Cathan (warrior); one who came from Caen, in France; descendant of Cana (of mature judgment).

Caird (*Scot.*) A craftsman; a traveling tinker who repaired pots and kettles.

Cairns (*Eng., Scot.*) Dweller near a rocky place or natural pile of rocks; one who came from Cairns (rocky place), in Midlothian.

Cairo, Caire (*It.*) One who came from Cairo (victorious), in Italy; perhaps, in a few cases, one who came from Cairo (victorious), in Egypt.

Calabrese (*It.*) One who came from Calabrese, in Italy.

Calder (*Eng.*) One who lived near the Calder (violent stream), the name of several rivers in England.

Calderon (*Sp.*) One who made and sold large kettles or boilers.

Calderone, Caldrone (*It.*) Same as Calderon, q.v.

Calderwood (*Eng.*) Dweller at the wood by the Calder (violent stream), the name of several rivers in England.

Caldwell, Colwell (*Eng.*) One who came from Caldwell (cold stream), in Yorkshire.

Calhoun, Calhoon, Calhoune (*Ir., Scot.*) Grandson of Cathluan (battle hero, or battle joyful); contraction of Colquhoun, q.v.

Caliendo (*It.*) One with some characteristic of a lark.

Calkins, Calkin (*Eng.*) Descendant of little Cal, a pet form of Caleb (dog).

Call (*Scot., Ir.*) Descendant of Cathal (battle mighty).

Callahan, Callaghan (*Ir.*) Grandson of little Ceallach (contention).

Callan, Callen (*Ir.*) Grandson of little Cathal (battle mighty).

Calloway, Callaway (*Eng.*) Descendant of Calewa (bald); one who came from Galloway (stranger Gael), in Scotland.

Calvert (*Eng.*) One who tended calves, a calfherd.

Calvin (*Eng.*) Descendant of Calvin (bald).

Cameron (*Scot.*) The man with a crooked or wry nose; one who came from Cameron (crooked hill), the name of three places in Scotland.

Camp (*Eng.*) Dweller in, or near, a field.

Campagna (*It.*) Dweller in, or near, a field or meadow.

Campana (*It.*) One who was deaf; dweller near the bell, or at the sign of the bell.

Campanella, Campanino (*It.*) One who lived near the bells, or belfry; one who lived at the sign of the bell.

Campbell (*Scot.*) One with a wry mouth, or, perhaps, arched lips. It has been suggested that the epithet was applied by neighboring clans on account of moral, rather than physical, defects.

Campo (*It., Sp.*) Dweller in, or near, a field.

Canfield (*Eng.*) One who came from Canfield (Cana's field), in Essex.

Cann, Can (*Eng.*) One who came from Cann (deep valley), in Dorset.

Cannell (*Eng.*) A Manx form of Connell, q.v.

Canning (*Eng.*) One who came from Cannings (Cana's people), in Wiltshire; a corruption of Cannon, q.v.

Cannon, Canon, Canning (*Eng., Ir.*) A clergyman on the staff of a cathedral or important church; a member of a canon's entourage; descendant of the wolf cub.

Cantor, Cantore (*Eng., It.*) The soloist who sang liturgical music in the synagogue; one who leads the singing in a cathedral.

Cantrell, Cantrall (*Fr., Eng.*) One who likes to sing; the little singer.

Canty (*Ir.*) Descendant of Encantie (satirist).

Capehart (*Ger.*) Variant of Gebhardt, q.v.

Capek (*Cz.-Sl.*) Dweller at the sign of the little stork; one thought to possess the qualities of a little stork.

Caplan, Caplin (*Ger., Pol.*) An Anglicization of Kaplan, q.v.

Capra, Capri, Caprio (*It.*) Dweller at the sign of the goat.

Caputo, Capone, Caponi (*It.*) One with a large or unusual head; one who was stubborn or dull-witted.

Carberry, Carbery (*Ir.*) Grandson of Cairbre (charioteer).

Carbone, Carboni (*It.*) One who mined coal or burned charcoal.

Card, Carde (*Eng., Fr.*) One who cards or combs wool.

Cardella, Cardelli, Cardello (*It.*) Dweller at the sign of the goldfinch.

Cardozo, Cardoso (*Sp., Port.*) One who came from Cardoso (place where thistles grew), in Spain.

Carew (*Eng.*) One who came from Carew (fort), in Pembrokeshire.

Carey, Cary (*Ir.*) Grandson of the dark-complexioned man.

Carl, Carle (*Eng.*) The husbandman or countryman; descendant of Carl (man).

Carlin, Carlan (*Ir., Fr.*) Descendant of Caireallan; descendant of little Carl (man).

Carlisle, Carlyle (*Eng.*) One who came from Carlisle (wall of the god Lugus), in Cumberland.

Carlow, Carlough (*Scot.*) One who came from Carlowrie (speaking rock), in Scotland.

Carlson, Carlsen (*Nor., Sw., Dan.*) The son of Carl (man).

Carlton, Carleton (*Eng.*) One who came from Carleton (the village of the free men), the name of many places in England.

Carmichael, Carmichel, Carmickle (*Scot.*) One who came from Carmichael (castle of St. Michael), in Lanarkshire.

Carmody (*Ir.*) Grandson of Cearmaid (black hunting dog).

Carnegie (*Scot*) One who lived in the lands of Carryneggy, in Angus.

Carnes, Carne (*Eng.*) Dweller near a natural pile of rocks; one who came from Carn, the name of various small places in Cornwall.

Carney, Carny (*Ir.*) Grandson of Cearnach (victorious).

Carnoy (*Fr., Bel.*) One who came from Carnoy (forest of hornbeam trees), the name of places in Belgium and France.

Carollo (*It.*) Descendant of little Carlo (manly).

Caron (*Eng., Fr.*) One who came from Cairon, the name of two places in France; one who made and sold wheels, a wheelwright.

Carone, Caronia (*It.*) Descendant of the youngest child.

Carpenter, Carpentier (*Eng., Fr.*) One who worked with wood.

Carr (*Eng., Ir., Scot.*) Dweller at, or near, a rock or marsh, or an enclosed place; grandson of Carra (spear).

Carrier (*Fr.*) One who worked in a quarry.

Carrington (*Eng.*) One who came from Carrington (the homestead of Curra's people), the name of villages in Cheshire and Lincolnshire.

Carroll, Carol (*Ir.*) Grandson of Cearbhall (stag).

Carson (*Scot.*) Dweller in, or near, a marsh.

Carter, Cartter (*Eng.*) One who drove a cart.

Cartwright (*Eng.*) One who made carts, usually small two-wheeled vehicles.

Caruso (*It.*) One with shorn or close-cut hair; one who worked in the sulphur pits.

Carver (*Eng.*) The wood carver, or cutter.

Cascio (*It.*) Descendant of Cassius (vain).

Case (*Eng.*) One who came from Case, in France; dweller at a manorial farm.

Casey (*Ir.*) Grandson of Catharach (vigilant, or watchful).

Cash (*Eng.*) An English variant of Cass, q.v.

Cashin, Cashen (*Ir.*) Grandson of Casan (little, curly-haired one).

Cashman (*Ir., Eng.*) Grandson of Casan (little, curly-haired one); an officer whose duty was to make arrests.

Casper (*Ger., Eng.*) Descendant of Caspar or Kaspar (master of the treasure).

Cass (*Fr., Eng.*) Dweller at, or near, an oak tree or forest, or at a hedged enclosure; one who made and sold copper pots; the son of Cass, a pet form of Cassandra (helper of men).

Cassidy, Cassiday (*Ir.*) Grandson of Caiside (curly-headed).

Castillo (*Sp.*) Dweller in, or near, a castle.

Castle (*Eng.*) Dweller in, or near, the large fortified building; worker in the castle.

Castro (*Sp., Port.*) One who lived at, or near, the castle or fortress; one who came from Castro (fortress), in Spain.

Caswell (*Eng.*) One who came from Caswell (spring or stream where water cress grew), the name of several places in England.

Catalano, Catalani (*It.*) One who came from Catalan, in Spain.

Cates, Cate (*Eng.*) The son of Cate, a pet form of Cato (cautious); one who had charge of provisions.

Catlin (*Fr.*) Descendant of little Catherine (pure).

Catron (*Fr.*) Descendant of Catron, a pet form of Catherine (pure).

Caulfield (*Scot., Eng.*) One who came from Cauldfield (cold field), in Dumfriesshire; dweller at a cabbage field, or at a cold or bleak field.

Cavanaugh, Cavanagh (*Ir.*) Grandson of little Caomh (comely) or Caomhan, the names of fifteen Irish saints.

Cawley (*Eng.*) One who came from Caughley (jackdaw wood meadow), in Shropshire.

Cella (*It.*) Dweller in a cell, probably in some religious house.

Cerf (*Fr.*) Dweller at the sign of the hart.

Cermak (*Cz.-Sl.*) One with the qualities of a robin; dweller at the sign of the robin.

Cerny (*Cz.-Sl.*) One with a swarthy complexion, black.

Cervenka (*Cz.-Sl.*) The ruddy or red-haired man.

Cerveny (*Cz.-Sl.*) The red-haired or ruddy man.

Cesario, Cesare, Cesaro (*It.*) Descendant of Cesario (the hairy one); dweller at, or near, a fruit grove or flower garden.

Chadwick (*Eng.*) One who came from Chadwick (Ceadda's farm), the name of places in Lancashire and Warwickshire.

Chait, Chaitkin, Chaitlen (*Heb.*) One who made outer garments, a tailor.

Chalmers (*Scot.*) Officer in charge of the private household of a king or nobleman; one who served as a chamber attendant.

Chamberlain, Chamberlin (*Eng., Fr.*) The officer in charge of the private household of a king or important nobleman.

Chambers (*Eng.*) The officer in charge of the private household of a king or important nobleman.

Champagne (*Fr.*) One who came from the Champagne (level country), a region in France.

Champion (*Eng.*) One who engaged in combat, a champion.

Chan (*Chin.*) Old.

Chancellor (*Eng., Scot.*) One who held the office of chancellor, an official who kept registers of an order of knighthood, or an ecclesiastical judge; one who was an official secretary.

Chandler (*Eng.*) One who made or sold candles and small wax images for ecclesiastical offerings.

Chaney (*Eng.*) A variant of Cheney, q.v.

Chang (*Chin.*) Draw-bow; open; mountain.

Chapin (*Fr.*) One who made and sold low shoes.

Chaplin (*Eng.*) A clergyman who has a chapel, a chaplain.

Chapman, Chipman, Chepman (*Eng.*) The merchant or tradesman, a peddler.

Chappell, Chapel, Chapple, Chapell (*Eng.*) Dweller near a chapel or sanctuary.

Charles (*Eng.*) Descendant of Charles (man); one who came from Charles (rock palace), in Devonshire.

Charley (*Eng.*) One who came from Charley (rock woods), in Leicestershire.

Charlton, Charleston (*Eng.*) One who came from Charlton (village of the free peasants), the name of many places in England.

Chartier (*Fr.*) One who drove a cart, a carter.

Chase, Chace (*Eng.*) Dweller at the hunting ground or woods.

Chatfield (*Eng.*) One who came from Catfield (field frequented by wild cats), in Norfolk.

Chatham (*Eng.*) One who came from Chatham (homestead by a forest), in Essex.

Chatman (*Eng.*) A variant of Chapman, q.v.

Chaucer (*Eng.*) One who made, or sold, pantaloons or tight coverings for the legs and feet.

Chauncy, Chauncey (*Eng.*) One who came from Chancey or Chancay, in France.

Chavez (*Sp.*) Descendant of Isabel (oath to Baal), a Spanish male name.

Cheatham, Cheetham, Cheathem, Cheetam, Cheatum (*Eng.*) One who came from Cheetham (homestead by a forest), in Lancashire.

Cheek, Cheeks, Cheke (*Eng.*) One with a prominent jaw; a pet name of endearment meaning chick or little chicken.

Cheever, Cheevers (*Eng.*) Dweller at the sign of the goat; one who cared for goats.

Cheney, Cheyne (*Eng.*) One who came from Quesney, Cheney, or Chenay (oak grove), in France; dweller near the chain, or barrier, used to close a street at night.

Cherney (*Cz.-Sl.*) The dark-complexioned man.

Chernoff (*Rus.*) The dark-complexioned person.

Cherry, Cherrie, Cherrey (*Eng.*) Dweller at, or near, a cherry tree; a beloved person.

Chesley (*Eng.*) One who came from Chearsley (Ceolred's meadow), in Buckingham.

Chester (*Eng.*) One who came from Chester (walled town), the name of several places in England; dweller near an old Roman fort.

Chevalier, Chevallier (*Fr.*) One who acted as a military servant to the king, a knight; one who held his land of the king in exchange for military service.

Chevallo (*It.*) Nickname given because of some horselike quality; dweller at the sign of the horse.

Chew (*Eng., Chin.*) One who came from Chew (river of the chickens); dweller near the river Chew, in England; one who came from Chew, a province in China.

Chiappetta, Chiappetti, Chiapetta (*It.*) Descendant of little Ciapo, a pet form of Giacomo (the supplanter).

Chick (*Eng.*) A pet name of endearment from the chicken; dweller at the sign of the chick.

Chiesa (*It.*) Dweller near a church.

Childers, Childer (*Eng.*) Of obscure origin, but possibly a descendant of

Chilbert (cauldron, bright); or possibly referring to one who has had a child; might be a contraction of childer-house, and thus designate one who operated such a place.

Childress (*Eng.*) A variant of Childers, q.v.

Childs, Child, Childe (*Eng.*) An attendant, a young man or young knight, sometimes the youngest son; descendant of Cilda (child).

Chin (*Chin.*) From the dynasty of that name.

Chionis, Chionos (*Gr.*) One who came from Chios (snow), an island, also chief town, in the Aegean Sea.

Chisholm, Chisholme, Chisolm (*Scot.*) The occupant of the estate of Cheseholm (meadow where cheese is made), in Roxburghshire.

Chmiel (*Pol.*) One who grew hops.

Chmielewski (*Pol.*) The son of the hop grower.

Choate, Choat (*Eng.*) The fat or chubby person.

Christ, Chrest (*Eng.*) Descendant of Christ, a pet form of Christian (follower of Christ), or of Christopher (Christ-bearer).

Christensen, Christenson (*Dan.*) The son of Christian (follower of Christ).

Christian (*Eng.*) Descendant of Christian (follower of Christ).

Christiano, Christiani (*It., Port., Sp.*) Descendant of Christiano (follower of Christ).

Christiansen, Christianson (*Nor.*) The son of Christian (follower of Christ).

Christie, Christy (*Scot., Eng.*) Descendant of Christie or Christy, pet forms of Christian (follower of Christ) and Christopher (Christ-bearer).

Christman, Christmann, Chrisman (*Ger.*) Descendant of Christianus (follower of Christ).

Christmas (*Eng.*) Descendant of Christmas, a name given to a child born on that day.

Christopher (*Eng.*) Descendant of Christopher (Christ-bearer); dweller at the sign of St. Christopher.

Christophersen, Christoffersen (*Dan., Sw.*) The son of Christopher (Christ-bearer).

Christopherson (*Eng.*) The son of Christopher (Christ-bearer).

Chubaty (*Ukr.*) One with a prominent tuft.

Chudak (*Cz.-Sl.*) A poor man, one who owned little in material goods.

Church (*Eng.*) Dweller near a building used for Christian worship.

Churchill, Churchull (*Eng.*) Dweller on, or near, the church hill; one who came from Churchill (church hill), the name of several places in England.

Chute (*Eng.*) One who came from Chute (forest), in Wiltshire.

Ciccolo, Ciccola (*It.*) Descendant of Cicco, a pet form of Francisco (the free).

Ciccone (*It.*) Descendant of big Cicco, a pet form of Francisco (the free).

Cicero (*It.*) Descendant of Cicero (chick pea or vetch).

Cichon, Cichy (*Pol.*) The quiet, or calm, person.

Cieslak, Ciesla (*Pol.*) The worker in wood, a carpenter.

Cimino (*It.*) One who grew cumin or caraway, a plant of the carrot family; dweller near where cumin or caraway grew.

Ciszewski (*Pol.*) One who came from Ciszewo, in Poland; the quiet man.

Citron (*Fr.*) One who raised and sold lemons.

Claesson, Claessens, Claeson (*Sw., Nor.*) The son of Claes, a pet form of Nikolaus (people, victory).

Clagett, Claggett (*Eng.*) One who came from Claygate (entrance to the clayey district), in Surrey.

Clair, Claire (*Eng., Fr.*) Descendant of Clair (illustrious), a man's name; the light-complexioned man; one who came from Clare (clayey slope), the name of several places in England; one who came from St. Clare or St. Clair, the name of various places in France.

Clancy, Clancey (*Ir.*) The son of Flannchadh (ruddy warrior).

Clapp (*Eng.*) Descendant of Clapa (chatter).

Clare (*Ir.*) One who came from Clare (plain, or flat piece of land), the name of several villages and a county, in Ireland.

Clark, Clarke, (*Eng.*) A clergyman, scholar, scribe or recorder (British pronunciation of clerk).

Clasby (*Eng.*) One who came from Cleasby (Klepp's homestead), in Yorkshire.

Clason, Clayson, Classon (*Scot., Eng.*) The son of Clas, a pet form of Nicholas (people, victory).

Class (*Eng.*) Descendant of Clas, a pet form of Nicholas (people, victory).

Classen, Clasen, Claassen (*Sw., Nor.*) The son of Clas, a pet form of Nicholas (people, victory).

Clausen, Claussen, Clauson (*Nor., Eng.*) The son of Claus, a pet form of Nicholas (people, victory).

Claxton (*Eng.*) One who came from Claxton (Clac's homestead), the name of several places in England.

Clay, Claye (*Eng.*) Dweller at the clayey place.

Clayton (*Eng.*) One who came from Clayton (village on clayey soil), the name of several towns in England.

Cleary, Clery (*Ir.*) Grandson of Cleireach (cleric or clerk).

Cleaves, Cleve, Cleave (*Eng.*) Dweller at the cliff or rock or steep descent, or at the bank of a river.

Clemenceau (*Fr.*) Descendant of little Clement (merciful).

Clemens, Clemons, Clemmons (*Scot., Ger.*) Descendant of Clemens (merciful).

Clemenson, Clemensen, Clemmensen (*Dan.*) The son of Clementius (merciful).

Clemente, Clementi Clemento (*It.*) Descendant of Clemente (merciful).

Clements, Clement (*Scot., Fr.*) Descendant of Clement (merciful).

Clendenning, Clendenin (*Scot.*) One who came from Glendinning (glen of the fair hill), in Scotland.

Cleveland, Cleaveland (*Eng.*) One who came from Cleveland (hilly district), in Yorkshire.

Clew, Clewes, (*Eng.*) Dweller at a hollow or ravine.

Cliff, Clive, Cliffe (*Eng.*) Dweller near a steep descent or slope, or a steep rock.

Clifford (*Eng.*) One who came from Clifford (ford at a cliff), the name of several places in England; dweller at the shallow river crossing with the steep bank.

Clifton (*Eng.*) One who came from Clifton (homestead on hill slope or bank of river), the name of various places in England.

Cline (*Ger.*) An Anglicization of the German, Klein, q.v.

Clinton (*Eng.*) Dweller at the hill enclosure.

Clithero (*Eng.*) One who came from Clitheroe (song-thrush hill), in Lancashire.

Close (*Eng.*) Dweller at an enclosure or fenced yard.

Cloud (*Eng., Scot.*) Dweller near the rock or mass of stone; the son of Leod (ugly).

Clough (*Eng.*) Dweller at a hollow or ravine.

Clougherty, Cloherty (*Ir.*) Dweller at, or near, a stone.

Cloutier (*Fr.*) One who made and sold nails.

Clow (*Eng.*) Dweller at a hollow or ravine.

Clyne, Clynes (*Scot.*) One who came from Clyne (a slope), the name of two places in Scotland.

Coady (*Eng.*) Dweller at, or near, a wood.

Coakley, Cokeley, Cokely (*Eng.*) Dweller in, or near, a wood frequented by wild birds.

Coan, Coen (*Ir.*) Grandson of Comhghan (twin).

Coates, Coats, Cote, Coate (*Eng.*) Descendant of one who occupied a cottage and tilled ten acres or less.

Cobb, Cobbe (*Eng.*) Dweller near the roundish mass or lump; descendant of Cobb, a pet form of Jacob (the supplanter).

Coburn (*Eng.*) One who came from Colburn (cool stream), in Yorkshire; dweller at a stream frequented by game birds.

Cochran, Cochrane (*Ir.*) Grandson of little Cogar (confident).

Codman (*Eng.*) One who carried, and sold goods from, a bag or pouch.

Cody (*Ir.*) The helper or assistant; the son of Odo or Otho (wealthy); grandson of Cuidightheach (helper).

Coe (*Eng.*) Dweller at the sign of the jackdaw.

Coffer, Cofer, Cofferer (*Eng.*) One who made coffers, boxes and chests; one who kept the treasure box, a treasurer; one who made and sold coifs, a kind of close-fitting cap for both sexes.

Coffey, Coffee (*Ir.*) Grandson of Cobhthach (victorious).

Coffin (*Eng., Fr.*) The bald man; one who sold baskets.

Coffman (*Ger.*) The merchant or tradesman, an Anglicization of Kaufmann.

Cogan, Coggan, Cogen (*Eng.*) One who came from Cogan (bowl), in South Wales; dweller in a bowl-shaped valley.

Coglianese (*It.*) One who came from Cogliano, in Italy; dweller on the Coglians, a peak on the Austrian-Italian border.

Cogswell (*Eng.*) Dweller at a spring frequented by game birds; one who came from Cogshall (Cogg's hill), in Cheshire.

Cohen, Cohn, Cohan (*Heb.*) The priest. This name indicates a family claiming descent from Aaron, the high priest.

Cokinos (*Gr.*) The ruddy-complexioned or red-haired man.

Colbert (*Eng.*) Descendant of Colbert (cool, bright).

Colburn, Colborne (*Eng.*) One who came from Colburn (cool stream), in Yorkshire; dweller near a cold stream.

Colby (*Eng.*) One who came from Colby (Koli's homestead), the name of places in Norfolk and Westmorland.

Cole, Coles (*Eng.*) Descendant of Cole, a pet form of Nicholas (people, victory).

Colegate, Colgate (*Eng.*) Dweller at a cool gap in a chain of hills.

Coleman, Colman (*Eng., Ir.*) Servant of Cole, pet form of Nicholas (people, victory); descendant of Coleman or Colman (little dove); an Anglicized form of Kuhlman, q.v.

Colfax (*Eng.*) Dweller at the sign of the black fox; a crafty person.

Collett, Collette, Collet (*Eng., Fr.*) Descendant of little Cole, a pet form of Nicholas (people, victory).

Colletti (*It.*) Dweller on, or near, a hill; descendant of little Cola, a pet form of Nicola (people, victory).

Colley, Collie (*Wel.*) Descendant of little Coll, a pet form of Nicholas (people, victory).

Collier, Colier (*Eng.*) One who worked, or dealt, in coal, a coal miner; one who made wood charcoal; one who worked in, or came from, the village of Caulieres in France.

Collins, Collings, Colin (*Eng.*) Son of little Cole, a pet form of Nicholas (people, victory).

Colomb, Colombe (*Fr.*) One who raised doves; descendant of Colomb (dove).

Colombo, Colombani, Colombini (*It.*) Same as Colomb, q.v.

Colonna (*It.*) Descendant of little Cola, a pet form of Nicola (people, victory).

Colquhoun (*Scot.*) One who formerly resided on the lands of Colquhoun (narrow corner or wood), in Dumbartonshire.

Colson, Coleson (*Eng.*) The son of Cole, a pet form of Nicholas (people, victory).

Colton (*Eng.*) One who came from Colton (Cola's homestead, or homestead on the Cole River), the name of several places in England.

Colvin (*Eng., Ir., Scot.*) Descendant of Calvin (bald); son of Anluan (great hero); one who came from Colleville (Col's farm), in Normandy; descendant of Ceolwine (ship, friend).

Combs, Combe, Combes, Comb (*Eng.*) Dweller at the deep hollow or valley.

Comerford (*Eng.*) One who came from Comberford (Combra's ford), in Staffordshire.

Comiskey (*Ir.*) The son of Cumascach (confuser).

Como (*It.*) Descendant of Como, a pet form of Giacomo (the supplanter).

Compton (*Eng.*) One who came from Compton (hollow estate), the name of many places in England.

Comstock (*Eng.*) Dweller in a deep valley; one who came from Comstock (monastery in a narrow valley), in England.

Conant (*Ir.*) Grandson of Conan (little hound).

Conboy (*Ir.*) Grandson of Cubuidhe (yellow hound).

Concannon (*Ir.*) Grandson of Cucheanainn (fair-headed hound).

Condit (*Fr.*) Merchant of pickled foods.

Condon (*Ir.*) Grandson of Cudubhan; one who came from Canton, in Glamorganshire.

Conforti (*It.*) One who enjoyed comfort.

Congdon (*Eng.*) One who came from Congdon (king's hill) in Cornwall.

Conklin, Conkling (*Du.*) Descendant of the petty king or chieftain.

Conley, Conly (*Ir.*) Grandson of Conghalach (valorous).

Conlon, Conlin (*Ir.*) Grandson of little Conall (high or mighty).

Conn (*Ir.*) Descendant of Conn, pet form of Constantine (constant).

Connaghty, Conaty (*Ir.*) One who came from the province of Connacht, in Ireland.

Connell, Connal (*Ir.*) Grandson of Conall (high or powerful).

Connelly, Connolly, Connally (*Ir.*) Grandson of Conghal or Conghalach (valorous), the names of seven Irish saints.

Connery, Conrey (*Ir.*) Grandson of Conaire (dog keeper).

Connors, Connor, Conners, Conner (*Ir.*) Grandson of Concobair (meddlesome), or of Conchor (high will or desire).

Conrad, Conrath (*Ger.*) Descendant of Conrad (bold, counsel).

Conroy, Conry (*Ir.*) The son of Curaoi (hound of the plain).

Considine, Costin (*Eng.*) Descendant of Constantine (constant).

Constable (*Eng.*) Originally count of the stable, later a military or civil officer; governor of a royal fortress.

Constantine (*Eng.*) Descendant of Constantine (constant).

Conti, Conte (*It.*) A nobleman, the count; one in the service of a count.

Converse, Conyers (*Eng., Fr.*) One who has been converted (to the Christian religion); one who came from Coignieres in France.

Conway (*Ir., Scot.*) Grandson of Connmhach; dweller at the sign of the yellow hunting dog; one who came from Conway (noisy or stormy), in Scotland.

Coogan, Cogan (*Ir.*) Son of Cogain (contention or strife).

Cook, Coke, Cooke (*Eng.*) One who prepared food.

Cooksey, Cooksie (*Eng.*) One who came from Cooksey (Cucu's island), in Worcestershire.

Cooley (*Ir., Eng.*) The son of the servant of St. Mochuille; descendant of little Cole, a pet form of Nicholas (people, victory).

Coolidge, Cooledge (*Eng.*) Dweller near a pool of cold water; one who came from Cowlinge (Cul's or Cula's people), in Suffolk.

Coombs, Coombes (*Eng.*) One who came from Coombes (valleys), in Sussex.

Coon, Coons (*Ger.*) An Anglicization of the German Kuhn, q.v.

Cooney (*Eng.*) Dweller at the sign of the rabbit; one thought to possess the characteristics of a rabbit.

Cooper, Couper, Cowper (*Eng.*) One who made and sold casks, buckets and tubs.

Cooperman (*Eng.*) The servant or helper of one who made casks, buckets and tubs.

Coopersmith (*Eng.*) The smith who made tubs and casks; variant of Coppersmith, q.v.

Copeland, Copland (*Eng.*) One who came from Copeland (bought land), in Cumberland.

Copley (*Eng.*) Dweller at the meadow on top of the hill.

Copp, Coppe (*Eng.*) Dweller at the top or summit of a hill.

Coppersmith (*Eng., Ger.*) One who worked in copper and brass.

Coppinger (*Eng.*) Dweller at the hilltop meadow.

Copple (*Eng.*) One who came from Coppull (peaked hill), in Lancashire.

Corbett, Corbet (*Eng., Fr., Ir.*) Dweller at the sign of the raven; the son of Corbet (raven).

Corbin, Corbyn, Corban (*Eng., Fr., Ir.*) Dweller at the sign of the raven; descendant of Coirbin (little chariot).

Corcoran, Corcrane, Cochrane, Corkran (*Ir.*) Grandson of Corcran (dim. of Corcair, purple).

Cordell (*Fr.*) One who made and sold light rope.

Cordes (*Fr.*) One who came from Cordes (ropes), in France; one who made rope.

Corey, Cory, Corry (*Ir.*) Dweller in, or by, a hollow; grandson of Corradh or Corra (spear).

Corkery (*Ir.*) Grandson of Corcair (purple).

Corley (*Eng.*) One who came from Corley (cranes' forest) or Coreley (slope frequented by cranes), in Shropshire and Warwickshire respectively.

Corliss, Corlis (*Eng.*) The cheerful or merry person.

Cormac, Cormack (*Ir.*) Grandson of Cormac (son of Corb, or son of a chariot, charioteer).

Corman, Cormann (*Ger.*) One who raises, or deals in, grain.

Cormier (*Fr.*) Dweller at, or near, a sorb tree.

Cornelius (*Eng.*) Descendant of Cornelius (hornlike).

Cornell, Cornel (*Eng.*) Descendant of Cornelius (hornlike); dweller at the dogwood-tree hill.

Corner (*Eng.*) Dweller at a nook or angle of land; a coroner or crown officer charged with the care of the private property of the king.

Cornish (*Eng.*) One who came from Cornwall (the Welsh in Cornavia), a county in England.

Cornwall, Cornwallis (*Eng.*) One who came from the county of Cornwall (the Welsh in Cornavia).

Cornwell (*Eng.*) One who came from Cornwell (crane's stream), in Oxfordshire; a variant of Cornwall, q.v.

Corona (*It.*) One who played the part of a king in the pageants and festivals; dweller at the sign of the crown.

Corrado (*It.*) Descendant of Corrado (able, counsel).

Corrigan (*Ir.*) Grandson of Corragan, a dim. of Corra (spear).

Corso (*It.*) Descendant of Corso, a pet form of Bonaccorso.

Corson (*Eng., Fr.*) One who came from Coursan or Courson, the names of several places in France; one who made and sold tight-fitting vestments.

Corwin (*Eng.*) Dweller near the white enclosure or castle.

Cosentino, Cosenza (*It.*) One who came from Cosenza, or the northern section of Calabria, in Italy.

Cosgrave, Cosgrove (*Ir.*) Grandson of Coscrach (victorious).

Costa (*It.*) Dweller on a hillside.

Costain (*Eng.*) Descendant of Constantine (constant).

Costanzo, Costanza (*It.*) Descendant of Costanzo (constant or firm of purpose).

Costello, Costelloe (*Ir.*) The son of Oisdealbh; one who is like a fawn or deer.

Coster (*Du.*) The sexton. *See* Koster.

Cote, Cott (*Eng.*) Dweller at a cottage, a manor inhabitant who worked only ten acres or less.

Coton (*Fr.*) Descendant of little Cot, a pet form of Nicolas (people's victory).

Cotter, Cottle (*Eng.*) A cottager who tilled only five or ten acres in a manor.

Cotton, Coton (*Eng.*) One who came from Coton or Cotton, the names of various places in England; dweller at the cottages.

Cottrell, Cottrill (*Eng.*) Dweller in a small cottage.

Couch (*Eng.*) One who couches and carpets, an upholsterer; one who had red hair.

Coughlin, Coughlan, Coghlan, Caughlin (*Ir.*) Grandson of Cochlan (dim. of cochal, a hooded cloak).

Coulon, Colon (*Fr.*) A variant of Colomb, q.v.

Coulter (*Eng.*) One who tended colts, a colt herd.

Courtney, Courtenay (*Ir., Fr.*) Descendant of Cuirnin (little horn or drinking cup); one who came from Courtenay, the name of two places in France.

Cousins, Cousin (*Fr.*) The cousin or kinsman.

Coutts, Coote (*Eng.*) Dweller at the sign of the coot; a nickname applied to a stupid person.

Covell, Covel (*Eng.*) Dweller in a small chamber or cave; one who came from Colville (Col's farm), in Normandy.

Coveney (*Eng.*) One who came from Coveney (bay island), in Cambridgeshire.

Covier (*Fr.*) One who made barrels, a cooper.

Covington (*Eng.*) One who came from Covington (homestead of Cufa's people), in Huntingdonshire.

Cowan, Cowen (*Ir., Scot.*) Dweller at a hollow; worker in metal, a smith; a corruption of Colquhoun, q.v.; grandson of Comhghan (a twin).

Coward, Cowherd, Cowart (*Eng.*) One who tended cows.

Cowie (*Eng., Scot.*) Dweller at the cow island or river pasture; one who came from Cowie (wood), the name of several places in Scotland.

Cowley (*Eng.*) One who came from Cowley (Cufa's meadow, cow meadow, or clearing where charcoal was burned), the name of several places in England.

Cox, Cocks (*Eng.*) Dweller at the sign of the cock, a common signboard; dweller near a small hill or clump of trees; variants of Cook, q.v.

Coyle (*Ir.*) The son of Dubhghall (the black stranger).

Coyne (*Ir.*) Grandson of Conn (reason; a freeman).

Cozzi, Cozza, Cozzo (*It.*) Descendant of Cozzi, a pet form of names ending in -cozzo, as Francescozzo (little Francesco) and Domenicozzo (little Domenico); one with an unusual head.

Crabtree (*Eng.*) Dweller at, or near, a crab-apple tree.

Craft (*Eng.*) Dweller in the small, enclosed field.

Craig, Cragg, Craige (*Scot., Eng.*) Dweller at, or near, a rock or crag.

Craigie (*Scot.*) One who came from Craigie (at the rock), the name of several places in Scotland.

Crain, Craine (*Eng.*) Variants of Crane, q.v.

Cram, Cramb (*Eng., Scot.*) One who came from Crambe (the bends), in Yorkshire; one who came from Crombie (crooked place), in Banffshire.

Cramer, Creamer (*Ger.*) The shopkeeper or tradesman; one who traveled through the country buying butter, hens and eggs which he carried to the market in a cram, or pack, on his back.

Crandall, Crandell, Crandle (*Eng.*) One who came from Crondall (a hollow), in Hampshire; dweller in a valley frequented by cranes.

Crandon, Cranden (*Eng.*) One who came from Crandon (cranes' hill), in Somerset.

Crane, Cran (*Eng.*) Dweller at the sign of the crane; one who lived near the Crane river in England.

Cranshaw (*Scot.*) One who came from Cranshaws (wood frequented by cranes), in Scotland.

Craven, Cravens, Cravener (*Eng.*) One who came from Craven (garlic), in Yorkshire.

Crawford (*Scot., Eng.*) One from Crawford (crow's pass), in Lanarkshire; dweller near a river crossing where crows were seen.

Crawley (*Eng.*) One who came from Crawley (crows' wood or hill), the name of several places in England.

Creedon, Creeden, Creaton (*Eng., Ir.*) One who came from Creeton (Craeta's homestead), in Lincolnshire; grandson of Criochan; one who came from Creaton (rocky homestead), in Northamptonshire.

Creighton, Cregan, Creighan (*Eng., Ir.*) One who came from Creaton (rocky homestead), in Northamptonshire, or from Creighton (rocky homestead), in Staffordshire; grandson of Criochan (little blind one, or small person).

Crenshaw (*Eng.*) One who lived near the grove frequented by cranes. *See also* Cranshaw.

Crimmons, Crimmings (*Ir.*) Grandson of Cruimin (little bent one).

Crist, Criss (*Eng.*) Descendant of Crist, a pet form of Christian (follower of Christ) and Christopher (Christbearer).

Criswell, Creswell (*Eng.*) One who came from Cresswell (stream where water cress grew), in Derbyshire. There were parishes named Cresswell in Northumberland and Staffordshire also.

Crittenden, Crittendon (*Eng.*) One who came from Criddon, formerly Critendone (Cridela's hill), in Shropshire.

Crocker (*Eng.*) One who made earthen pots, a potter.

Crockett, Crocket (*Eng.*) The little crooked or deformed person.

Croft, Crofts (*Eng.*) One who came from Croft (enclosure), the name of several places in England; dweller at the small, enclosed field.

Crofton (*Eng.*) One who came from Crofton (homestead with an enclosure, or homestead by a hill), the name of several places in England.

Croke, Croak, Croake (*Eng.*) Dweller at a nook or bend in a river; variants of Crook, q.v.

Crompton (*Eng.*) One who came from Crompton (homestead in the bend of a river), in Lancashire.

Cromwell (*Eng.*) One who came from Cromwell (winding stream), in Nottinghamshire.

Cronin, Cronen (*Ir.*) Descendant of the little brown-complexioned or swarthy man.

Cronkhite (*Ger., Du.*) One who was ill, an invalid.

Crook, Crooks, Crooke (*Eng., Scot.*) One who came from Crook (hill, or bend of a river), the name of several places in England and Scotland; same as Croke, q.v.

Crooker (*Eng.*) Dweller at a nook or bend; variant of Crocker, q.v.

Crosby, Crosbie, Crossby (*Eng., Scot.*) One who came from Crosby (village at the cross), the name of several villages in England and Scotland.

Cross, Crosse, Crouse, Cruce (*Eng.*) One who lived near a cross at a roadside dedicated to some saint, it often serving as a marker or guidepost.

Crossley, Crosley (*Eng.*) One who lived at the glade, or meadow, by the cross.

Crotty (*Ir.*) Grandson of Crotach (hunchbacked).

Crouch, Croucher (*Eng.*) Dweller near a cross; one who came from Crouch (cross), now Crouch End, in Middlesex.

Crowder, Crowther (*Eng.*) One who played a crowd, an ancient Celtic stringed instrument.

Crowe, Crow (*Eng.*) Dweller at the sign of the crow; one thought to possess the characteristics of a crow.

Crowell, Crowel (*Eng.*) One who came from Crowell (crows' stream), in Oxfordshire.

Crowles (*Wel.*) Descendant of one who came from Crowle (winding), villages in Worcestershire and Lincolnshire.

Crowley, Crolley (*Ir.*) The son of Roghallach; grandson of Gruadhlaoch (tough hero).

Crowninshield (*Eng.*) Dweller at the sign of the crown and shield.

Crozier (*Eng.*) One who bears a cross, or has something to do with a cross; the bearer of a bishop's crook or pastoral staff.

Cruickshank, Cruckshank, Cruikshank (*Scot.*) Dweller at, or near, the crooked projecting point of a hill; a person with bow legs.

Crum, Crume (*Eng.*) The crooked, or deformed, person.

Crummie, Crummy (*Scot.*) Dweller on the lands of Crummy which belonged to the Abbey of Culross.

Crump, Crumb (*Eng.*) The crooked, maimed or deformed person.

Cruse, Crews (*Eng.*) Dweller near a cattle pen; the nimble or lively person; dweller at, or near, a cross.

Crutchfield (*Eng.*) Dweller at, or in, the field on the hill; one who came from Cruchfield (hill field), in Berkshire.

Cruz (*Sp., Port.*) Dweller at, or near, a cross.

Cryer (*Eng.*) One appointed to make public announcements in the village.

Cuddy, Cuddie (*Eng.*) Descendant of Cuddy, a pet form of Cuthbert (famous, bright).

Culbertson (*Eng.*) The son of Culbert or Colbert (cool, bright).

Cullen, Cullens, Cullins (*Ir., Eng., Scot.*) Grandson of Cuileann (holly); a cub or puppy, an affectionate term; the handsome person; dweller in, or near, a small wood; dweller near a holly tree; one who came from Cullen (little nook), in Scotland.

Cullinan, Cullinane (*Ir.*) Grandson of little Cuileann (holly).

Culver (*Eng.*) Dweller at the sign of the culver or dove.

Cummings, Cummins, Cumming, Cumine (*Scot.*) One who came from Comines, in Flanders.

Cuneo (*It.*) One who came from Cuneo, a province in Italy.

Cunniff, Cunniffe, Conniff (*Ir.*) The son of Cudubh (black hound).

Cunningham (*Scot.*) One who came from Cunningham (rabbit farm), in Ayrshire; one who came from a royal manor.

Curcio, Curcione (*It.*) One of low stature; one who tended goats; dweller at the sign of the goat.

Curley, Curly, Curle (*Scot.*) Dweller near Curley (bend or turn in the road), in Scotland; one who came from Curley, in France; one who had curly hair.

Curran, Corran (*Ir.*) Grandson of Corran (dim. of Corradh, spear).

Currier (*Eng.*) One who dressed leather.

Curry, Currie (*Ir., Eng.*) Grandson of Corra (spear); one who came from Curry, the name of several places in England.

Curtin (*Ir.*) Grandson of Cartan; the son of the hunchbacked man.

Curtis, Curtiss (*Eng.*) One with courtlike, or elegant, manners, well bred.

Cusack, Cusick, Cusac (*Ir., Eng., Ukr.* One who came from Cussac (Cotius place), in France; one who was a member of a cavalry troop on the Russian steppes, a Cossack.

Cushing (*Eng.*) Descendant of little Cuss, a pet form of Custance or Constance (firm of purpose).

Cushman (*Eng.*) One who made cuish or thigh armor.

Custer (*Eng.*) One who made feather beds and cushions.

Cuthbertson (*Eng., Scot.*) The son of Cuthbert (famous, bright).

Cutler (*Eng.*) One who made, repaired or sold knives and other cutting instruments.

Cutter (*Eng.*) One who cut cloth.

Cutting (*Eng.*) The son, or family, of Cutha (famous); a corrupt form of the French *Cotin* or *Cottin* which are the diminutives of the terminal syllable of Jacquot or Nicot.

Cuyler (*Du.*) An archer or crossbowman.

Cwik (*Pol.*) A cunning fellow.

Cygan (*Pol.*) One of a wandering Caucasian race, a gypsy.

Cyr (*Fr.*) Descendant of Cyr (teacher); one who came from St. Cyr, in France.

Czaja (*Pol.*) Dweller at the sign of the large lapwing; one with some of the characteristics of a large lapwing.

Czajka (*Pol., Ukr., Rus.*) One with some of the characteristics of a small lapwing or gull; one who operated a small boat.

Czajkowski (*Pol., Ukr.*) One who came from Czajkow(o), (the gulls' settlement), the name of many places in Poland and Ukraine.

Czarnecki (*Pol.*) One who came from Czarne (black), the name of several places in Poland; the dark-complexioned man.

Czarnik (*Pol.*) One who came from Czarnik (black), in Poland; the little swarthy or dark-complexioned man.

Czech (*Ger.*) One who came from Bohemia (home of the Boii).

Czerniak (*Pol.*) One who came from Czernia (black), a village in Poland; dweller near the Czernia River; the dark-complexioned man.

Czernocky (*Cz.-Sl.*) The black-eyed man.

Czerwinski (*Pol.*) One who came from Czerwien (red dye), in Ukraine.

Dabbs (*Eng.*) The son of Dabb, a pet form of Robert (fame, bright).

Dabrowski (*Pol.*) Dweller in, or near, the oak grove; one who came from Dabrova (oak grove).

Dacey, Dacy (*Eng., Fr.*) One who came from the south; one who came from Acy, in France.

Dacosta (*Port.*) Dweller along the coast or shore.

Daggett (*Eng.*) Descendant of little Dagr (day), or Daegga (day).

D'Agostino, Dagostino (*It.*) Descendant of Agostino (August).

Dahl, Dahle (*Nor., Ger.*) Dweller in the valley.

Dahlberg (*Sw.*) Valley mountain.

Dahlgren (*Sw.*) Valley branch.

Dahlin (*Sw.*) One who came from the valley or dale.

Dahlman, Dallman (*Sw.*) Valley man.

Dahlquist (*Sw.*) Valley twig.

Dahlstrom (*Sw.*) Valley stream.

Daigle (*Ger.*) Descendant of Dago, a pet form of names beginning with Tag (the day), as Dagobald, Dagwart and Dagomar.

Dailey, Daily (*Ir.*) Grandson of Dalach (frequenting assemblies).

Dailide (*Lith.*) One who worked with wood, a carpenter.

Dale, Dales (*Eng.*) Dweller in the valley.

D'Alessandro, Dalessandro (*It.*) The son of Alesandro (helper of mankind).

Dallas (*Scot.*) One who came from the old barony of Dallas (place on the plain), in Moray.

Dalrymple (*Scot.*) One who came from the lands of Dalrymple (field on the curving stream), in Ayrshire.

Dal Santo (*It.*) Descendant of Santo (the saint).

Dalton (*Eng.*) One who came from Dalton (village in the valley), the name of several places in England.

Daly, Daley (*Ir.*) Grandson of Dalach (frequenting assemblies).

Damato, D'Amato (*It.*) Descendant of Amato (beloved).

Damico, D'Amico (*It.*) The son of Amico (friend).

Damm, Dammann (*Eng., Ger.*) Dweller, or worker, at the dam or dike.

D'Amore, Damore (*It.*) Descendant of Amore (love, or, sometimes, child of love).

Danahy, Danehy, Dannahy (*Ir.*) Grandson of Duineachaidh (humane).

D'Ancona (*It.*) One who came from the province, or city, of Ancona (elbow), in Italy.

D'Andrea (*It.*) The son of Andrea (manly).

Dane, Dain (*Eng.*) One who came from Denmark (forest of the Danes); dweller near the Dane River, in Cheshire.

Danek (*Ger.*) One who came from Denmark (forest of the Danes).

Danforth, Danford (*Eng.*) One who came from Denford (ford in a valley), in Berkshire.

D'Angelo, Dangelo (*It.*) The son of Angelo (an angel).

Daniels, Danielson, Daniel (*Wel., Eng.*) The son of Daniel (judged of God); the son of the Welsh Deiniol (attractive).

Danilevicius (*Lith.*) The son of Danil (judged of God).

Danner (*Ger.*) Dweller at, or near, a fir tree.

Dante (*It.*) Descendant of Durand (lasting).

Danziger, Danzig (*Ger.*) One who came from Danzig (the Danes' town, or town of the Goths), in Poland.

Darby (*Eng., Ir.*) One who came from Darby or Derby (both names meaning place frequented by wild animals), the names of several places in England; grandson of Diarmaid (free man).

Darcy (*Fr.*) One who came from Arcy (stronghold), in France.

Dare, Dares (*Eng.*) Descendant of Deor (brave, or bold).

Darling (*Eng.*) Descendant of Deorling (beloved).

Darlington (*Eng.*) One who came from Darlington (village of Deornoth's people), in Durham.

Darnell, Darnall (*Eng.*) One who came from Darnall (hidden nook), in Yorkshire.

Darrell, Darrett (*Eng.*) Descendant of little Deor (brave, or bold).

Darrow, Darrough, Darrah, Darragh (*Ir.*) The son of Dubhdarach (black man of the oak).

Darwin (*Eng.*) Dweller near the Derwent (clear water), a river in Lancashire; descendant of Deorwine (dear, friend).

Dasilva (*Port.*) Dweller in the wood or thicket.

Dauber, Daube (*Eng.*) One who plastered buildings or whitewashed walls.

Daugherty (*Ir.*) Grandson of Dochartach (unfortunate).

Daum, Daume (*Ger.*) One with a large or unusual thumb; also possibly shortened from Daumler, i.e., one who squeezed the thumb during an inquisition, a torturer.

Davenport (*Eng.*) One who came from Davenport (town on the Dane River), in Cheshire.

Davey, Davie, Davy (*Scot.*) Descendant of little David (beloved).

Davidson, Davids, David (*Scot., Wel.*) The son of David (beloved).

Davis, Davies (*Eng., Wel.*) The son of Davie, a pet form of David (beloved).

Davison (*Eng.*) The son of Davy or Davie, pet forms of David (beloved).

Davy, Davie (*Scot., Eng.*) Descendant of Davie or Davy, pet forms of David (beloved).

Dawes, Dawe, Daw (*Wel.*) Descendant of Daw, a pet form of David (beloved); dweller at the sign of the jackdaw; one lacking in wits, a simpleton.

Dawson (*Eng.*) The son of Daw, a pet form of David (beloved).

Day, Dey, Daye (*Eng., Wel.*) The dairy worker; kneader of bread; female servant, but the term was used later of men; descendant of Dai, a pet form of Dafydd (beloved).

Days (*Wel.*) Descendant of Dai, a pet form of Dafydd (beloved).

Deacon, Dekan (*Eng.*) One who assisted priest or minister.

Deakins (*Wel.*) The son of little Deak, a pet form of David (beloved).

Deal, Deale, Deals (*Eng.*) One who came from Deal (valley), in Kent; dweller on the allotted land.

Dean, Deane (*Eng.*) Dweller at the valley or woodland pasture; one who was the head of a body of canons of a cathedral church; a member of a dean's entourage.

Dearborn (*Eng.*) Dweller near a stream frequented by wild animals.

Deasy, Deacy, Deasey (*Ir.*) One who came from the Decies (people), of Waterford.

De Bartolo (*It.*) The son of Bartolo (son of Talmai, furrow).

De Boer (*Du.*) One who tilled the soil, a farmer; one who rose from the peasant class.

De Carlo (*It.*) The son of Carlo (man).

Decker, Dekker, Deckert (*Ger., Du.*) One who covers roofs with tile, straw or slate; one who came from Deck or Decker, the names of places in Germany.

De Courcey (*Fr.*) One who came from, or who owned, the fief of Courcey (passageway).

Dee, Dea (*Ir.*) Grandson of Deaghadh (good luck).

Deegan, Degan, Deagan, Deagon (*Ir.*) Grandson of Dubhceann (black head).

Deer, Deere (*Scot.*) One who came from Deer (forest), in Aberdeenshire.

Deering, Dearing (*Eng.*) Descendant of Deoring (beloved).

Degen, Degener, Degner (*Ger.*) One who made rapiers; descendant of Thegan, a pet form of names commencing with Degen (young warrior), as Deganhart and Theganbert; the young warrior or follower; descendant of Degenher (young warrior, army).

De George, De Giorgio (*It.*) The son of George (farmer).

Degnan, Degmon, Degman (*Eng., Ir.*) The servant who worked in a dairy; variant of Dignan, q.v.

De Graff, de Graaf, De Graaff, De Graf (*Ger., Du.*) The count, or, in England, an earl.

de Groot, de Groote (*Du.*) The big, or tall, man; one who came from Groot (large place), in Holland.

de Haan (*Du.*) Dweller at the sign of the cock.

Dehn, Dehne, Dehnel (*Ger.*) Descendant of Dehn, a pet form of names beginning with Degen (young warrior), as Deganhart, Theganbald and Degenher; descendant of Dano, a pet form of names beginning with Dane (the Dane), as Danaold and Danafrid.

De Jong, De Jonge, De Jonghe (*Du.*) One who was younger than another with whom he was associated; the younger son.

Delacroix (*Fr.*) Dweller near the cross. *See* Cross.

Delage (*Fr.*) One who had charge of the hedges or fences.

Delaney, Delany (*Ir.*) Descendant of the challenger; grandson of Dubslaine or Dubhslainge (black of the Slaney).

Delano (*Fr.*) One who came from Delanoe (of the wet land), in France; dweller in, or near, a marsh.

Delatre, Delattre (*Fr.*) Dweller in a house containing a tiled hearth.

Delavigne (*Fr.*) Dweller in, or near, the vineyard.

De Leo (*It.*) The son of Leo (lion).

De Leonardis (*It.*) The son of Leonardo (lion, hard).

Dell (*Eng.*) Dweller at the deep hollow or vale.

Delmar (*Sp.*) Dweller near the sea.

De Long, De Longe (*Fr.*) One who came from Long (large place), the name of several places in France.

Delorey (*Fr.*) Dweller at, or near, a granary.

Delorme (*Fr.*) One who came from Lorme (elm tree), the name of several places in France.

Del Rio (*Sp.*) Dweller near the river.

De Luca (*It.*) The son of Luca (light).

De Marco (*It.*) The son of Marco (belonging to Mars, the god of war).

Demaree (*Fr.*) Dweller near the sea.

Demers (*Eng.*) One who built dams.

Deming (*Eng.*) One who came from Migny or Migne, in France.

Demopoulos, Demopulos (*Gr.*) The son of Demos, a pet form of Demosthenes (strong with people), or of Demetrius (of Demeter, the goddess of fertility and harvests).

Demos (*Gr.*) Descendant of Demos, a pet form of Demosthenes (strong with people), or of Demetrius (of Demeter, the goddess of fertility and harvests).

Dempsey (*Ir.*) Descendant of Dymasa or Diomasach (proud).

Demski (*Pol.*) Dweller at, or near, an oak tree.

Denham, Denman (*Eng.*) One who came from Denham (homestead in a valley, or the hill of Dunn's people), the name of several places in England; dweller in a valley.

Denis, Deny (*Fr.*) Descendant of Denis (belonging to Dionysus, the Grecian god of wine).

Dennehy, Denehy (*Ir.*) Grandson of Duineachaidh (humane).

Dennen (*Ir.*) Grandson of Doineannach (stormy or tempestuous).

Denning (*Eng.*) The son of Dene (the Dane).

Dennis, Denis (*Eng., Ir.*) Descendant of Denis (belonging to Dionysius, Grecian god of wine); descendant of the brown fighter or warrior.

Dennison, Denison, Denson (*Eng., Ir.*) Son of Denis (belonging to Dionysius, Grecian god of wine); son of the brown fighter or warrior.

Denny, Denney, Dennie (*Scot., Eng.*) One who came from Denny (wet land), a town and parish in Stirlingshire, or from Denny (Danes' island), in Cambridgeshire; pet form of Dennis, q.v.

Dent (*Eng.*) One who came from Dent (hill), in Yorkshire.

Denton, Denten (*Eng.*) One who came from Denton (homestead in a valley), the name of many places in England.

D'Entremont (*Fr., Swis.*) Dweller between the mountains; one who came from Entremont, in Switzerland.

Depew, Depue, Dupuy (*Fr.*) Dweller on, or near, a hill.

Derby (*Eng.*) One who came from Derby (homestead frequented by wild animals), in Derbyshire.

De Rosa, De Rose (*It.*) The son of Rosa or Rose (rose).

Derrick, Derricks, Derrickson (*Eng.*) Descendant of Derrick, a pet form of Theodoric (people, rule).

De Salvo (*It.*) The son of Salvo (salvation).

Descartes (*Fr.*) Dweller in the outskirts of a town, a suburbanite.

De Simone (*It.*) The son of Simone (gracious hearing).

De Smet, De Smedt, De Smidt (*Du.*) The worker in metal, the smith.

Desmond (*Ir.*) One who came from south Munster.

Desmoulins (*Fr.*) Dweller near the mill.

Despagne (*Fr.*) One who came from Spain.

De Stefano, De Stefani (*It.*) The son of Stefano (crown or garland).

Detweiler, Detwiler (*Swis., Ger.*) One who came from Datweil, in Canton Zurich.

Deutsch, Deutscher, Deutch, Deutschmann, Deutschman, Deutsche (*Ger.,*

Du.) One who came from Germany, a German.

Devaney, Devanie (*Ir.*) Descendant of the cormorant or diving sea bird; descendant of Dubheannaigh (black of Eanach, a place name).

Deveaux, Deveau (*Fr.*) Dweller in a valley.

Dever (*Ir.*) Descendant of the successful one; grandson of Dubhodhar (black Odhar).

Devereaux, Devereux (*Fr.*) One who came from Evreux, in France.

Devine (*Ir., Fr.*) Descendant of the little poet; one who came from Vins, in France.

De Vito (*It.*) The son of Vito (life).

Devitt (*Ir.*) The son of little David (beloved).

Devlin (*Ir.*) Descendant of the plasterer or dauber; one who came from Dublin (black pool).

de Vries (*Du.*) The Frisian, i.e., one who came from the province of Friesland (curled hair, or free).

Dewar (*Scot.*) One who came from Dewar (dark, plowed land), in Midlothian; an official who had custody of the relic of a saint.

Dewberry (*Eng., Fr.*) One who came from Dewsbury (David's fort), in Yorkshire; one who lived at the edge of town, a variant of the French, Dubarry.

Dewey (*Wel.*) Descendant of little Dew, a pet form of David (beloved).

De Witt, De Wit, De Witte (*Du.*) The light-complexioned or white-haired man.

Dexter (*Eng.*) One who dyed cloth.

De Young (*Du.*) Partial Anglicization of De Jong, q.v.

Diamond (*Eng.*) Descendant of Daymond (day, protection); dealer in diamonds.

Diaz (*Sp.*) The son of Diago, corrupted form of Diego (supplanter).

Di Benedetto (*It.*) The son of Benedetto (blessed).

Dick, Dicke, Dicks, Dickes (*Ger., Eng.*) The large or fat man; descendant of Dick, a pet form of Richard (rule, hard).

Dickens, Dicken, Dickins (*Eng.*) The son of little Dick, pet form of Richard (rule, hard).

Dickerson (*Eng.*) The son of the dike, or ditch, maker.

Dickey, Dickie (*Eng.*) Descendant of little Dick, a pet form of Richard (rule, hard).

Dickinson (*Eng.*) The son of little Dick, a pet form of Richard (rule, hard).

Dickman, Dickmann, Dickerman (*Ger.*) The big or fat man.

Di Domenico (*It.*) The son of Domenico (the Lord's day).

Dieckmann, Dieckman (*Ger.*) Dweller at, or near, a dike or embankment.

Diehl (*Ger.*) Descendant of Diehl from Dudo, a pet form of names beginning with Diet (people), as Theudoricus, Teuduin and Theudulf.

Diemer (*Ger.*) One who came from Diehmen, in Germany.

Diener, Dienner (*Ger.*) One who was a servant.

Dietrich, Diedrich, Diederich, Dietrick, Dieterich (*Ger.*) Descendant of Theodoricus (people, ruler).

Dietz, Dietsch, Dietze, Dietzel, Dietzen (*Ger.*) Descendant of Teuzo, a pet form of names beginning with Diet (people), as Theudoald, Theotwig, and Theudulf.

Diggins (*Eng.*) The son of little Digg, or Dick, pet forms of Richard (rule, hard).

Diggs (*Eng.*) Descendant of Digg, a pet form of Richard (rule, hard).

Di Giovanni (*It.*) The son of Giovanni (gracious gift of Jehovah).

Dignan, Dignum, Digman (*Ir.*) Grandson of little Dubhceann (black head).

Dill, Dille (*Eng.*) Descendant of Dill or Dila (spoiler).

Dillard, Dillards (*Eng.*) Descendant of little Dill (spoiler).

Dillingham (*Eng.*) One who came from Dullingham (the village of Dulla's people), in Cambridgeshire.

Dillon (*Ir.*) Descendant of little Dill or Dillo (spoiler).

Dilworth, Dillworth (*Eng.*) One who came from Dilworth (homestead where dill was grown), in Lancashire.

Di Maggio (*It.*) Descendant of Maggio (name given to one born in the month of May).

Dineen, Dinneen (*Ir.*) Grandson of little Donn (brown).

Dingle (*Eng.*) Dweller in the deep dell or narrow valley; one who came from Dingle, in Lancashire.

Dingwall, Dingwell (*Scot.*) One who formerly lived on the lands of Dingwall (meeting of the local council), in Ross.

Dinsmore, Densmore (*Eng.*) One who came from Dinmore (great hill), in Herefordshire.

Dinwiddie, Dinwoodie (*Scot.*) One who came from the lands of Dinwoodie (hill with the shrubs), in Dumfriesshire.

Dion, Dionne (*Fr.*) Descendant of Dion (Grecian god of wine); one who came from Dionne, in Burgundy.

Diorio, DiOrio (*It.*) The son of Iorio or Orio, pet forms of Onorio (honor).

Dirksen (*Dan.*) The son of Dirk, a pet form of Diederik (people, rule).

Disney (*Eng.*) One who came from Isigny, in Normandy.

Dittmann, Dittman (*Ger.*) Descendant of Teutman (people, man).

DiVito (*It.*) The son of Vito (life).

Dix (*Eng.*) Descendant of Dick, a pet form of Richard (rule, hard).

Dixie, Dixey (*Eng.*) Descendant of little Dick, a pet form of Richard (rule, hard).

Dixon, Dickson (*Eng.*) The son of Dick, a pet form of Richard (rule, hard).

Doane, Doan, Done (*Eng., Ir.*) Dweller at, or near, the slope of a hill; grandson of Dubhan (black).

Dobbins, Dobbin, Dobyne, Dobynes, Dobbyn (*Eng.*) Descendant of little Dob, a pet form of Robert (fame, bright).

Dobbs, Dobb (*Eng.*) The son of Dobb or Dob, pet forms of Robert (fame, bright).

Doble, Double (*Eng.*) Descendant of little Dob, a pet form of Robert (fame, bright).

Dobler (*Ger.*) One who lived in the wooded valley or ravine.

Dobry (*Pol.*) The good man.

Dobson (*Eng.*) The son of Dob, a pet form of Robert (fame, bright).

Dockery (*Eng.*) One who came from Dockray (hollow), in Cumberland.

Doctor (*Scot., Ger.*) One who practiced medicine; one who was highly educated, generally a teacher.

Dodd, Dodds, Dod, Dods (*Eng.*) Descendant of Dod (rounded summit).

Dodge (*Eng.*) Descendant of Dodge, a pet form of Roger (fame, spear).

Dodson (*Eng.*) The son of Dod (rounded summit).

Doe (*Eng.*) Dweller at the sign of the doe or female deer.

Doering (*Ger.*) One who came from Thuringia, in Germany.

Doerr, Dorr (*Ger.*) Descendant of Isidorus (gift of Isis); descendant of Dioro, a pet form of names beginning with Teuer (dear), as Diurard and Deorovald.

Doherty, Dougherty (*Ir.*) Grandson of Dochartach (hurtful or unfortunate).

Dolan (*Ir.*) One with a dark complexion or black hair; a variant of Doolin, q.v.

Dole (*Eng.*) Dweller at the division of land or boundary mark.

Doll, Dolle (*Eng., Ger.*) Dweller at a division of land or boundary mark; descendant of Doll, a pet form of names beginning with Dult (patience), as Dultwic and Duldfrid.

Dollar (*Scot.*) The man from Dollar (dale of plowed land), in Clackmannanshire.

Dollarhide (*Eng.*) One who owned and tilled a hide of land (about 120 acres).

Dombrowski (*Pol.*) A variant of Dabrowski, q.v.

Dominick, Domenico, Domenick, Dominic (*It.*) Descendant of Dominick (the Lord's day), a name sometimes given to one born on Sunday.

Domino (*It.*) Descendant of the little, good man.

Domke, Dompke (*Ger.*) Descendant of little Dom (judgment); dweller in a small house.

Donahue, Donohue, Donaghue, Donoghue, Donohoe (*Ir.*) Descendant of Donough (brown battler).

Donaldson, Donald, Donalds (*Scot., Eng.*) The son of Donald (dark or brown-haired stranger).

Donato, Donat (*It.*) Descendant of Donato (given).

Donegan, Dongan (*Ir.*) Descendant of the little, brown man; grandson of little Donn (brown).

Donlan, Donlon, Donlin (*Ir.*) Grandson of little Domhnall (world mighty).

Donnellan, Donelan, Donelon, Donelin (*Ir.*) Grandson of little Domhnall (world mighty).

Donnelly, Donnelley, Donley (*Ir.*) Grandson of Donnghal (brown valor); descendant of the dark-complexioned, valiant man.

Donner (*Ger.*) Descendant of Donner (Thunar, the god of thunder).

Donofrio, D'Onofrio (*It.*) The son of Onofrio (supporter of peace).

Donovan (*Ir.*) Grandson of Donndubhan (brown Dubhan); grandson of Donndamhan (little, brown poet).

Doody (*Ir.*) One with dark complexion or black hair; grandson of Dubhda (black).

Dooley (*Ir.*) Grandson of Dubhlaoch (black hero); descendant of the dark warrior.

Doolin, Doolan, Dooling, Doolen (*Ir.*) Grandson of Dubhfhlann (black Flann); the defiant man.

Doolittle (*Eng.*) From the French *de l'hôtel,* referring to one who lived in the mansion house or palace; a loafer or idle person.

Doonan (*Ir.*) Grandson of little Donn (brown).

Doppelt (*Ger.*) One who was a double or twin.

Doran, Dorran (*Ir.*) The alien or foreigner.

Dore, Dorat (*Fr.*) One who gilds, a gilder.

Dorfman, Dorfmann (*Ger.*) One who formerly lived in the village.

Dorgan (*Ir.*) Grandson of little Dorchaidhe (dark man).

Dorman, Dohrmann, Dohrman, Dormand (*Eng., Ger.*) The beloved, or dear, man; one who had charge of the door or gate.

Dorn, Dorner, Dorne (*Eng.*) One who came from Dorn (stronghold), in Worcestershire.

Dorsch (*Ger.*) One who lived at the sign of the small codfish; one who grew and sold parsnips or cabbages.

Dorsett, Dorset (*Eng.*) One who came from Dorset, a county in England.

Dorsey (*Ir., Fr.*) Grandson of Dorchaidhe (dark man); one who came from Arcy (stronghold), in France.

Doss, Dose (*Ger.*) Descendant of Doss or Dose, forms of Teuzo, pet forms of names beginning with Diet (people), as Theudoricus and Theudoald.

Dotson (*Eng.*) The son of Dudd (fat, clumsy person), or of Dot (lazy, listless person).

Doty, Doughty (*Eng.*) The brave, strong man.

Doubek (*Cz.-Sl.*) Dweller near a small oak tree.

Doucette, Doucet, Doucett (*Fr.*) The sweet person, a name given an amiable person, sometimes ironically, however.

Douglas, Douglass (*Scot.*) Dweller at the black water or stream.

Dover (*Eng.*) One who came from Dover (the waters), a village in Kent.

Dow (*Ir.*) One with a dark complexion or black hair.

Dowd, Doud, Dowds (*Ir.*) One with a swarthy complexion, black; grandson of Dubhda (black).

Dowdell, Dowdall (*Eng.*) One who came from Dowdale (valley frequented by doves or does).

Dowell, Dowel (*Ir.*) Grandson of Dubhghall (black foreigner); descendant of the dark foreigner.

Dowling (*Ir.*) Grandson of Dunlang, an ancient Irish name; grandson of Dubhfhlann (black Flann).

Downey, Downie (*Scot., Ir.*) One who came from Downie, the name of several places in Scotland; dweller at the little hill; the brown-haired man; grandson of Dunadhach (belonging to a fort).

Downing, Downings (*Eng.*) Descendant of Dunn (dark brown); dweller at the hill or hill pasture.

Downs, Downes, Down (*Eng.*) Dweller on, or near, the hill or hill pasture.

Doyle (*Ir., Eng.*) Grandson of Dubhghall (black foreigner); the swarthy stranger or foreigner; one who came from Oilly, in France.

Dozier (*Fr.*) Dweller in, or near, a water willow grove.

Drain, Draine (*Ir., Eng.*) Grandson of Drean (wren); dweller at, or near, the drain.

Drake, Drakes (*Eng.*) Dweller at the sign of the dragon; one so nicknamed because of a dragon in his coat of arms; one with the qualities of a male duck; one who played the part of a dragon in the mysteries and miracle plays.

Draper (*Eng.*) One who made, or sold, woolen cloth.

Draye, Dray, Drey (*Eng.*) Descendant of Drew, Dru or Drogo (carrier).

Drayton (*Eng.*) One who came from Drayton (homestead near a portage, or on a narrow strip of land), the name of many places in England.

Drell (*Rus.*) Dweller at the sign of the arrow.

Drennan, Drennen (*Ir.*) Grandson of Draighnean (blackthorn).

Dressler, Dresser, Dressel (*Eng.*) One who finishes textile fabrics to give them a nap or smooth surface.

Drew, Drews, Drewes (*Eng.*) Descendant of Drew, Dru or Drogo (carrier), or of Drew, a pet form of Andrew (manly).

Drexel, Drexler (*Ger.*) One who turned a lathe, a turner.

Dreyer, Dryer, Dreier, Dreher (*Ger.*) One who fashioned objects on a lathe, a turner.

Dreyfus, Dreyfuss, Dreifuss, Dreifus (*Ger.*) One who made trivets; three feet; one who came from Treves or Trier (place of the tribe of the Treviri), in Germany.

Drinkwater (*Eng.*) One known as a teetotaler, i.e., one who drank water.

Driscoll (*Ir.*) Grandson of Eidirsceol (interpreter).

Driver (*Eng.*) One who drove a herd of cattle, especially to distant markets; same as Carter, q.v.

Droege (*Ger.*) Dweller on dry land; a droll person.

Drone, Dron, Drown (*Scot.*) One who came from Dron (hill ridge), in Perthshire; dweller at the rump or hill ridge.

Drooker (*Ger.*) A printer.

Drozd (*Pol., Ukr.*) One with some characteristic of a thrush; dweller at the sign of the thrush.

Drucker (*Ger., Du.*) A printer; one who pressed cloth.

Drummey, Drummy (*Ir.*) Grandson of Druim (black); descendant of the black person.

Drummond (*Scot.*) One who came from the barony of Drummond or Drymen (a ridge), in Scotland.

Drury (*Eng.*) A sweetheart or lover.

Dryden (*Scot.*) One who came from Dryden (dry valley), in Edinburgh.

Drysdale (*Scot.*) One who came from Dryfesdale (valley of the Dryfe River), in Scotland.

Duane (*Ir.*) Descendant of the fisherman; grandson of Dubhan (little black person).

Duarte (*Port., Sp.*) Descendant of Duarte (rich, guardian).

Dube, Dub, Duba (*Fr.*) One who raised and sold feather-legged pigeons; dweller at the sign of the feather-legged pigeon.

Dubiel (*Cz.-Sl., Pol., Ukr.*) One who was strong as an oak.

Dubin (*Rus.*) Dweller near an oak tree.

Du Bois, Dubosc, Duboscq (*Fr.*) Dweller in, or near, a small wood.

Dubow, Du Bow (*Rus., Ukr., Cz.-Sl.*) The son of Dub (oak).

Dubuisson (*Fr.*) Dweller near a bush; one who lived at the sign of the bush.

Ducey (*Ir.*) Grandson of Dubhghur (black choice).

Duckert (*Ger.*) Descendant of Tuchard (worth, brave).

Duckett (*Eng.*) Descendant of little Duke, a pet form of Marmaduke (sea leader).

Duckworth (*Eng.*) One who came from Duckworth (Ducca's homestead), in Lancashire.

Duda (*Pol., Ukr.*) One who played a bagpipe.

Duddy (*Ir.*) Grandson of Dubhda (black).

Dudek (*Cz.-Sl.*) One who played a bagpipe.

Dudley (*Eng.*) One who came from Dudley (Dudda's meadow), in Worcestershire.

Dudzik (*Pol.*) One who came from Dudki or Dudy (settlement of the Dudki family), in Poland; one who played the bagpipe.

Duff (*Ir.*) Grandson of Dubh (black); one with a swarthy complexion, black.

Duffin (*Ir.*) The little person with a dark complexion; descendant of Dolphin or Dolfin (Delphian); grandson of Dubhfionn (black Fionn).

Duffy (*Ir.*) Grandson of Dubhthach (black).

Dufour (*Fr.*) The official who operated the public oven, a baker.

Duggan, Dugan, Duigan (*Ir., Wel.*) Grandson of Dubhagan (little black one); descendant of little Dug, a Welsh pet form of Richard (rule, hard).

Dugo (*It.*) The son of Ugo (spirit).

Duke, Dukes (*Eng.*) Descendant of Duke, a pet form of Marmaduke (sea leader).

Dull (*Scot.*) The man who came from Dull (a plain), a village and parish in Perthshire.

Dulles (*Eng.*) One who came from the village of Dulas (dark river), in Herefordshire; dweller near the Dulas River, in England.

Dumas (*Fr.*) Dweller on the little farm.

Dumelle, Du Melle (*Fr.*) One who came from Melle (ring), in France.

Dumont, Du Mont (*Fr.*) One who lived on, or near, a hill.

Dunbar (*Scot.*) One who lived on the lands of Dunbar (fort on the height), in Scotland.

Duncan, Duncanson (*Ir., Scot.*) Descendant of Donnchad (brown warrior).

Dunham (*Eng.*) One who came from Dunham (the homestead on the hill), the name of several places in England.

Dunlap, Dunlop (*Scot.*) One who came from the lands of Dunlop (hill at the bend), in Ayrshire.

Dunmore (*Scot.*) One who came from Dunmore (big hill), the name of several places in Scotland.

Dunn, Dunne (*Ir.*) The dark-brown complexioned one; grandson of Donn (brown).

Dunning (*Scot., Ir.*) One who came from Dunning (little hill or fort), in Perthshire; the little brown-haired man; grandson of little Donn (brown).

Dunphy, Dunfey (*Ir.*) Grandson of Donnchadh (brown warrior).

Dunton (*Eng.*) One who came from Dunton (village on a hill), the name of several places in England.

Dupont (*Fr.*) One who lived near a bridge.

Dupree, Du Pree, Dupre (*Fr.*) Dweller in a meadow.

Dupuis, Dupuy (*Fr.*) One who lived near, or who owned, a well or spring; one from Le Puy, in France.

Durand, Duran (*Fr.*) Descendant of Durand (lasting).

Durante, Durant (*It.*) Descendant of Durand (lasting).

Durbin (*Eng.*) One who came from Durban, in France.

Durham (*Eng.*) One who came from Durham (island with a hill), in Durham.

Durkee (*Rus., Ukr.*) The stupid or dull man.

Durkin, Durkan (*Ir.*) The son of Duarcan (the gloomy one).

Durward, Dorward (*Scot.*) One who held the office of doorkeeper of the Abbey.

Dusek (*Pol.*) Descendant of Dusek (little ghost or spirit).

Dust (*Eng.*) Descendant of Dust, a pet form of Thurstan (Thor's stone); one with a dust-colored complexion.

Dustin (*Eng.*) One who came from Duston (dusty homestead), in Northamptonshire.

Duszynski (*Pol.*) One who came from Durzyn or Duzyn, the name of villages in Poland.

Dutton (*Eng.*) One who came from Dutton (Dudda's homestead), in Cheshire.

Duval, Deval, Duvall (*Fr.*) Dweller in the valley.

Dvorak (*Cz.-Sl.*) One who belonged to the lord's estate, a vassal; a courtier or attendant at the court of a prince.

Dwight (*Eng.*) Descendant of Dwight or Diot, possibly pet forms of Dionysus (Greek god of wine); the light-complexioned person.

Dwinell (*Fr.*) Descendant of little Douin, a pet form of Hardouin (hard, friend).

Dwyer, Dwyar (*Ir.*) Descendant of the dark, tawny man; grandson of Dubhodhar (black Odhar).

Dybas (*Pol., Ukr.*) One who fights by lurking or lying in ambush; a foundling.

Dye (*Eng.*) Descendant of Dye, a pet form of Dionysus (Greek god of wine).

Dyer, Deyer, Dier, Dyers (*Eng.*) One who dyed cloth.

Dyke, Dykes (*Eng.*) Dweller on, or near, a dike or embankment.

Dykstra (*Du.*) Dweller on, or near, a dike or embankment.

Dyson (*Eng.*) The son of Dy or Dye, pet forms of Dionysus (Grecian god of wine).

Dziedzic, Dziedzik (*Pol.*) One who rented land to another, a landlord.

Eagle, Eagles (*Eng.*) Descendant of Aegel (noble); dweller at the sign of the eagle; one who came from Eagle (oak wood), in Lincolnshire.

Eames (*Eng.*) The son of the uncle.

Earl, Earle, Earles, Earls (*Eng.*) Descendant of an earl; one connected in some way with an earl's household; one who came from Earle (hill with an enclosure), in Northumberland.

Early, Earley (*Eng.*) One who came from Earley (eagle wood), in Berkshire; dweller by the earl's meadow.

East (*Eng.*) One who came from an easterly place; dweller at the east end of the village.

Easterling (*Eng.*) A merchant who came from the shores of the Baltic having a reputation for honest dealings, giving rise to the word "sterling."

Eastman (*Eng.*) One who came from the east; descendant of Eastmund or Estmunt (east, protection); one who came from the Baltic countries.

Easton (*Eng.*) One who came from Easton (the eastern homestead), the name of several places in England.

Eaton (*Eng.*) One who came from Eaton (homestead on a river, or island), the name of various places in England.

Ebel, Eble, Ebell (*Ger., Fr.*) Descendant of Ebilo or Eble (boar).

Eberhardt, Eberhart, Eberhard (*Ger.*) Descendant of Eberhard (boar, strong).

Eberle, Eberlein, Eberling (*Fr., Ger.*) Descendant of little Ebilo (boar), or of little Eber, a shortened form of Eberhard (boar, strong).

Ebert (*Ger.*) Descendant of Ebert, a pet form of Eberhard (boar, strong).

Ebner (*Ger.*) Dweller in the lowlands.

Eby, Ebey (*Eng., Swis.*) Descendant of Eby, a pet form of Ebbe or Ebba (boar).

Eccles (*Eng., Scot.*) One who formerly lived in the village of Eccles (church), there being two of that name in Scotland and three in England; dweller near a church.

Echols, Echoles (*Eng., Scot.*) Dweller near the church; one who came from Eccles (church), the name of several places in England and Scotland.

Eck, Ecke (*Ger.*) One who lived at the corner; dweller at a steep slope.

Ecker, Eckmann, Eckerman (*Ger.*) Dweller on a farm located on a steep slope.

Eckert, Eckardt, Eckart, Eckhart, Eckard (*Ger.*) Descendant of Agihard (sword edge, brave).

Ecklund (*Sw.*) Oak grove.

Economos (*Gr.*) One who managed a large household, a steward.

Eddy, Eadie, Eady, Eddie (*Eng.*) Descendant of little Ead or Ede (rich), pet forms of names beginning with Ead, such as Edward, Edmund and Edgar.

Edelman, Edelmann (*Ger., Du.*) The nobleman; a noble or good man; the husband of Edel or Adele (noble).

Edelson (*Eng.*) The son of Edel or Adel (noble).

Edelstein, Edelstone (*Ger.*) Precious stone.

Eden, Edens (*Eng.*) Descendant of little Ede or Ead (prosperity).

Eder, Ederer (*Ger.*) One who lived near the Eder River, in West Germany.

Edgar (*Eng.*) Descendant of Edgar (rich, spear).

Edge (*Eng.*) One who came from Edge (edge or hillside), the name of places in Cheshire and Shropshire.

Edgerly, Edgerley (*Eng.*) One who came from Edgerley (Ecgheard's meadow), in Shropshire.

Edgett (*Eng.*) Descendant of little Ecga (sword).

Edison, Edson (*Eng.*) The son of Edie or Eadie, pet forms of Edmund (rich, protector), Edward (rich, guardian), Edwin (rich, friend), etc.

Edlund (*Sw.*) Heath grove.

Edmonds, Edmunds (*Wel.*) The son of Edmond or Edmund (rich, protector).

Edwards (*Wel.*) The son of Edward (rich, guardian).

Egan, Eagan (*Ir.*) The son of little Aodh (fire).

Eggert, Eggers, Egger (*Ger.*) Descendant of Agihard (sword edge, brave).

Eggleston, Egleston, Egelston (*Eng.*) One who came from Eggleston, in Durham, or Egglestone, in Yorkshire, both meaning Ecgel's homestead.

Ehlert, Ehlers (*Ger.*) Descendant of Adalhard (noble, brave), or of Adalhari (noble, army).

Ehrensperger, Ehrenberg (*Ger.*) One who came from Ehrensperg (hill of honor), the name of three places in Germany.

Ehrhardt, Ehrhard, Ehret, Ehrhart (*Ger.*) Descendant of Erhart (honor, brave).

Ehrlich (*Ger.*) The honest man.

Eich, Eichler, Eichmann (*Ger.*) Dweller near an oak tree.

Eichhorn (*Ger.*) Dweller at the sign of the squirrel.

Eichstaedt, Eichstadt (*Ger.*) One who came from Eichstaedt (place where oaks grew), in Germany.

Eifel, Eifler (*Ger.*) One who came from, or who dwelt in, a mountainous district.

Einhorn (*Ger.*) Dweller at the sign of the unicorn; one thought to possess the characteristics of a one-horned animal.

Einstein (*Ger.*) One who lines, or encloses, with stone, a mason; dweller in a stone enclosure.

Eiseman, Eisman, Eismann, Eisemann, Eisenmann, Eissman (*Ger.*) One who works with, or deals with, iron; descendant of Isanman (iron, man); an alteration from Isaac (he who laughs).

Eisen (*Ger.*) One who worked with iron.

Eisenberg, Eisenberger (*Ger.*) One who came from Eisenberg (iron mountain), in Thuringia.

Eisenhower, Eisenhauer (*Ger.*) The iron cutter, or iron miner; maker of eisenhauers, a saber or sword blade capable of shearing an iron nail.

Eisenstadt, Eisenstaedt (*Ger.*) One who came from Eisenstaedt (iron place), the name of a village in Austria.

Eisenstein (*Ger.*) One who came from Eisenstein (iron stone), in Germany.

Eisner (*Ger.*) One who deals in ironware.

Eklund (*Sw.*) Oak grove.

Ekstrom (*Sw.*) Oak stream.

Eland, Elander (*Eng.*) Dweller on an island.

Elder (*Eng.*) One who is older than another with whom he is associated; dweller at, or near, an elder tree.

Eldridge, Eldredge (*Eng.*) One who came from Elbridge (plank bridge), in Kent.

Elias (*Eng.*) Descendant of Elias (Jehovah is my God).

Elish (*Eng.*) Descendant of Elisha (God is salvation).

Elkin, Elkins (*Eng.*) Descendant of little Elie, a pet form of Elias (Jehovah is my God).

Ellard (*Eng.*) Descendant of Alward or Elward (elf guardian), or of Eliard (little Elias).

Ellaway (*Wel.*) Descendant of Elwy (gain).

Ellen (*Eng., Ger.*) Dweller at, or near, the Ellen, a river in Cumberland; dweller near an elder tree; one who came from Ellen (elbow), the name of three places in Germany.

Eller (*Ger.*) Dweller at, or near, an alder tree; one who came from Ellen (elbow), the name of three places in Germany, or from Eller, the name of five places in Germany.

Ellingswood (*Eng.*) Dweller near the wood of Ella's people, possibly a lost place name.

Ellington (*Eng.*) One who came from Ellington (the homestead of Ella's people), in Huntingdonshire.

Elliott, Elliot, Eliot (*Eng.*) Descendant of little Elijah or Elias (Jehovah is my God).

Ellis, Ellison (*Eng.*) Descendant of Ellis (God is salvation).

Ellman, Ellmann (*Ger.*) Descendant of Hellmann, a German Jewish synonym for Samuel (God hath heard); one who came from Germany, a German.

Ellsworth (*Eng.*) One who came from Elsworth (Elli's homestead), in Cambridgeshire.

Elmer (*Eng.*) Descendant of Aylmer (noble, famous).

Elmore (*Eng.*) One who came from Elmore (shore where elms grew), in Gloucestershire.

Elsdon (*Eng.*) One who came from Elsdon (Ellis' valley), in Northumberland.

Else, Elsen, Elser, Elsner (*Ger., Du.*) Dweller at, or near, the alder tree; one who came from Elsen (alder), in Germany.

Elson, Elsen (*Eng., Dan.*) The son of Ell, a pet form of Ellis (God is salvation), and Elias (Jehovah is my God); one who came from Elson (Elli's homestead or hill), in Shropshire.

Elston (*Eng.*) One who came from Elston (the homestead of Ethelsige or

Aelfwig or Elias), the name of three manors in England.

Elvidge (*Eng.*) Descendants of Alfwig (elf, war).

Elwell (*Eng.*) One who came from Elwell (the wishing well), in Dorset.

Ely (*Eng.*) One who came from Ely (eel district), in Cambridgeshire.

Emanuel (*Eng.*) Descendant of Emanuel (God is with us).

Emerson, Emmerson (*Eng.*) The son of Emery (industrious).

Emery, Emory (*Eng.*) Descendant of Emery (industrious).

Emmett, Emmet, Emmons (*Eng.*) Descendant of little Emery (industrious).

Emslie, Emsley (*Eng.*) Dweller at the elm grove; one who came from Helmsley (Helm's wood or island), in Yorkshire.

Enders, Endres (*Nor.*) Descendant of Ander (manly).

Endicott (*Eng.*) Dweller at the end cottage.

Eng, Enge (*Nor., Du., Chin.*) Dweller in, or near, the meadow; dweller at the lane or narrow street; one who came from Eng, a district in China.

Engberg (*Sw.*) Meadow mountain.

Engel, Engle, Engels, Engles (*Ger., Du.*) The man from England; one who lived in the meadow or grassland.

Engelhardt, Engelhard, Engelhart, Englehart, Englehardt (*Ger.*) Descendant of Engelhard (angel, hard).

Engelman, Engelmann, Engelsman (*Ger.*) One who came from England, an Englishman; dweller at the sign of the angel.

England, Englund (*Eng.*) Dweller at the ing-land or meadow land.

English (*Eng.*) An Englishman. Possibly the name was acquired while outside of England and brought back.

Engstrom (*Sw.*) Meadow stream.

Ennis, Ennes (*Eng., Ir.*) Dweller at the island or secluded place; grandson of Aonghus (one choice).

Enos (*Eng., Fr.*) Descendant of Enos (mortal man).

Enright, Enwright (*Ir.*) The son of Innreachtach or Ionnrachtach (unlawful).

Enriquez, Enriquiz (*Sp.*) The son of Enrique (home ruler).

Epps, Epp (*Ger.*) Descendant of Epp, a pet form of names beginning with Eber (boar), as Eburhard and Eburwin.

Epstein, Eppstein (*Ger.*) One who came from Eppstein (Eppo's stone), in Germany; one who came from Ebstein, a place no longer in existence, in Styria.

Erb, Erbe (*Ger.*) Descendant of Arpus, a pet form of names beginning with Erbe (inheritance), as Erbhart and Arbrich.

Erdmann, Erdman (*Ger.*) The land worker or farmer.

Erhardt, Erhard, Erhart (*Ger.*) Descendant of Erhart (honor, brave).

Erickson, Ericsson, Ericksen, Ericson (*Nor., Sw.*) The son of Eric (ever king).

Erikson, Eriksen (*Dan., Nor., Sw.*) The son of Erik (ever king).

Erlandson (*Sw.*) Son of Erland (foreigner).

Ernst, Ernest (*Ger.*) Descendant of Ernst (earnestness).

Erskine (*Scot.*) One who came from Erskine (green ascent), in Renfrewshire.

Ervin, Erwin (*Eng., Ger.*) Descendant of Erwinne or Eorwine (sea, friend).

Eskridge (*Eng.*) One who came from Askrigg (narrow corner of land), in Yorkshire.

Esposito (*It.*) Descendant of Esposito (exposed), a name sometimes given to a foundling.

Esser (*Ger.*) One who came from Essen, in Germany.

Estabrook, Estabrooke, Estabrooks, Esterbrook (*Eng.*) Dweller at the easterly stream.

Estes (*Eng.*) The son of East (easterly), or Est (gracious).

Estey, Esty (Eng.) Dweller at the east island, or the east enclosure.

Ettinger, Etting (*Ger.*) One who came from Oettingen, in Bavaria.

Eubanks, Ewbank (*Eng.*) Dweller on the ridge where yew trees grew.

Eustice, Eustace, Eustis (*Eng.*) Descendant of Eustace (steadfast).

Evanoff, Evanow (*Rus.*) The son of Evan (gracious gift of Jehovah).

Evans (*Wel.*) The son of Evan (young warrior).

Evensen, Evenson (*Sw.*) The son of Even (gracious gift of Jehovah).

Everett, Everette, Everitt, Everard (*Eng.*) Descendant of Everard (boar, strong).

Evers, Everson (*Eng.*) The son of Ever, a pet form of Everard (boar, strong).

Ewald, Ewaldt, Ewalt (*Ger.*) Descendant of Ewald (eternity, power); one who advised as to the law.

Ewers, Ewer (*Eng.*) The servant or household officer who supplied guests at the table with water to wash their hands, etc; a water-bearer.

Ewert, Ewart (*Eng.*) One who came from Ewart (homestead on a stream), in Northumberland; one who tended ewes.

Ewing, Ewen, Ewins (*Eng.*) Descendant of Ewen (warrior).

Exman (*Eng., Ger.*) One who made and sold axes; dweller in a nook or corner.

Faber, Fabri, Fabre, Fevre (*Fr.*) The worker in metals, a smith.

Fabian, Fabyan (*Eng.*) Descendant of Fabian (bean-grower).

Factor, Facktor, Facter (*Ger.*) One who managed a business or estate for another.

Fagan (*Ir.*) Descendant of Pagan (the rustic).

Fahey, Fahy (*Ir.*) Descendant of the reasonable man; grandson of Fathadh (foundation).

Fair, Fayer, Faires (*Eng.*) The light-complexioned or handsome man; one who lived or worked at the fair or market.

Fairbanks, Fairbank (*Eng.*) Dweller on, or near, the ridge where bulls or sheep were confined.

Fairchild (*Eng.*) The handsome youth; the son-in-law.

Fairfax (*Eng.*) One who had blond hair.

Fairfield (*Eng.*) One who came from Fairfield (beautiful field or hog field), the name of places in Derbyshire and Worcestershire.

Fairless (*Eng.*) Dweller near the bull meadow; one who traveled alone, i.e., without a companion or equal.

Fairley, Fairleigh, Fairlie (*Eng.*) One who came from Fairlee (beautiful glade), in Wight, or from Fairley (fern clearing), in Shropshire.

Fairweather, Fayerweather (*Eng.*) One who worked only in good weather; one with a happy disposition.

Falbo (*It.*) Descendant of Flavio (blond).

Falco, Falcone (*It.*) Dweller at the sign of the hawk or falcon; a bold, keen-eyed or nimble person; dweller near, or on, the Falco Mountain, in Italy; one who came from Falcone (falcon), in Sicily.

Falconer (*Eng.*) One who kept and trained falcons or hawks to hunt game.

Falk, Falke (*Ger., Nor.*) One who took care of the falcons or hawks; one who hunted with falcons; dweller at the sign of the falcon.

Falkenberg (*Sw.*) One who came from Falkenberg (falcon mountain), a city in Sweden.

Fall (*Eng.*) Dweller at, or near, the Fal, a river in Cornwall; dweller near the waterfall.

Fallon, Falloon, Fallin, Fallen (*Ir.*) Grandson of Fallamhan (ruler).

Falls (*Eng.*) Dweller at the fallow lands.

Falvey (*Ir.*) Grandson of Failbhe (lively).

Fanning, Fannon, Fannin (*Ir.*) Descendant of the little, blond man; grandson of little Fionn (fair).

Fantasia (*It.*) Imagination, a name to describe an eccentric or insane person.

Farber (*Ger.*) One who dyed cloth.

Farina, Farino (*It.*) One who ground grain, a miller.

Farinella (*It.*) One who conveyed flour from the mill to the home.

Farkas, Farkash (*Hun.*) One who lived at the sign of the wolf; one with wolflike qualities.

Farley, Farleigh (*Eng., Ir.*) The man who came from Farley or Farleigh (fern-covered clearing), the names of several places in England; grandson of Faircheallach (super war).

Farmer (*Scot.*) One who farmed the revenue, a tax collector.

Farnham, Farnum (*Eng.*) One who came from Farnham (homestead where ferns or thorns grew), the name of various places in England.

Farnsworth, Farnworth (*Eng.*) One who came from Farnworth (homestead where ferns grew), in Lancashire.

Farquhar, Farquharson (*Scot.*) The son of Farquhar (friendly).

Farr (*Eng., Scot*) Dweller at the sign of the bull or boar; one who came from Farr (passage), in Sutherland.

Farragut (*Scot.*) A nickname, the good traveler.

Farrand, Ferrand (*Eng., Fr.*) Descendant of Ferrand, a contraction of Ferdinand (journey, venture); one who had iron-gray, or graying, hair.

Farrar (*Scot.*) A corruption of Farquhar (friendly).

Farrell, Farrall (*Ir.*) Grandson of Fearghal (super valor).

Farren, Farrin (*Ir.*) Grandson of Arachan.

Farrington (*Eng.*) One who came from Farrington (manor where ferns grew), in Somerset.

Farris, Faris (*Ir.*) Grandson of Fearghur (better choice).

Farrow (*Eng.*) Dweller at the sign of the boar or pig.

Farwell (*Eng.*) One who came from Farewell (beautiful stream), in Staffordshire.

Fasano (*It.*) The pheasant, a nickname given to a dullard.

Faubus (*Ger.*) From Phoebus (bright), a name taken by Jews as equivalent to Me'ir and Uriboth with the same meaning.

Faulkenham, Faulkingham (*Eng.*) One who came from Falkenham (Falta's homestead), in Suffolk.

Faulkner, Falkner, Falknor (*Eng.*) The falconer, i.e., one who keeps and trains falcons or hawks to hunt game.

Faure, Faur (*Fr.*) One who worked in metal, a smith.

Faust (*Ger.*) Descendant of Faustus (fortunate).

Fawcett, Faucett (*Eng.*) One who came from Fawcett (multicolored hillside), in Westmorland.

Fay, Faye (*Eng., Ir.*) One who came from Fay or Faye (beech tree), in France; descendant of the reasonable man; grandson of Fathadh (foundation).

Fazio, Fazzi, Fazzio (*It.*) One who acted as a watchman or sentinel; dweller by a beech tree.

Fears, Feare, Fear (*Eng.*) One who was a companion or friend to another.

Featherstone, Featherston (*Eng.*) One who came from Featherstone (a tetralith, i.e., three upright stones and a headstone), the name of places in Northumberland and Yorkshire.

Feder, Fedder (*Ger.*) Dweller at the sign of the feather.

Fee (*Ir.*) Grandson of Fiach (raven).

Feeley, Feely (*Ir.*) Grandson of Fitcheallach (chess player).

Feeney, Feeny (*Ir.*) Descendant of the soldier.

Feigenbaum (*Ger.*) Dweller near a fig tree.

Feikema (*Du.*) The man, or servant, to Feike, Frisian form of Frederick (peace, rule).

Feil, Feiler (*Ger.*) One who was mercenary; one who came from Feil, in Pfalz.

Fein (*Ger.*) Refined.

Feinberg (*Ger.*) Dweller near the Feinberg (fair mountain), in Austria.

Feingold (*Ger.*) Fine gold.

Feinstein (*Ger.*) Fine stone.

Fekete (*Hun.*) One with a swarthy complexion, black.

Feld, Felde (*Eng., Ger.*) Dweller at land free from wood, a field.

Feldman, Feldmann, Feltman, Feltmann (*Ger.*) The worker in the field or open country.

Feldstein (*Ger.*) Field stone.

Felix (*Eng.*) Descendant of Felix (happy).

Fell, Fells, Fels (*Eng., Ger.*) Dweller on, or near, the rocky mountain; one who dealt in hides or furs.

Feller, Fellner, Felman, Fellerman (Ger.) One who dealt in furs.

Fellows, Fellowes (*Eng.*) One who was a partner or associate of another; dweller near the newly cultivated land.

Felsenthal (*Ger.*) Dweller in a rocky valley.

Felt, Feldt (*Ger.*) Dweller in the field.

Felton, Felten (*Eng.*) One who came from Felton (homestead in open country), the name of several places in England.

Feltz, Felz (*Ger.*) The large, or tall, man.

Fenn, Fenner, Fenne (*Eng.*) Dweller at the marsh, or fen.

Fennell (*Eng.*) Dweller at, or near, the corner of the marsh.

Fennelly (*Ir.*) Grandson of Fionnghalach (fair or valorous).

Fennessey, Fennessy (*Ir.*) Grandson of Fionnghus (fair choice).

Fenstermacher, Fenstermaker (*Ger.*) One who made windows.

Fenton (*Eng.*) One who came from Fenton (homestead in a marsh), the name of several places in England.

Fenwick (*Eng., Scot.*) One who came from Fenwick (farm by a marsh), the name of places in Northumberland and Yorkshire, also a village in Scotland.

Ferber (*Ger.*) A painter or stainer.

Ferdinand (*Eng.*) Descendant of Ferdinand (journey, venture).

Ferguson, Fergus (*Scot.*) The son of Fergus (manly strength, or super choice).

Fern, Fearn (*Scot.*) One who came from Fearn (alder tree), in Scotland; dweller by an alder tree.

Fernald (*Fr.*) The worker in iron, or one who dealt in iron, a dim. form.

Fernandez, Fernandes (*Sp.*) Son of Fernando (journey, venture).

Ferrara, Ferrera (*It.*) One who came from Ferrara, (Forum Allieni), a province in Italy.

Ferraro, Ferrari, Ferrero, Ferreri, Ferrario (*It.*) A worker in metals, a smith.

Ferreira (*Port.*) One who came from Ferreira (iron mine or workshop), the name of numerous places in Portugal.

Ferrell, Ferrall, Ferrill (*Ir.*) Grandson of Fearghal (super valor).

Ferrick (*Ir., Fr.*) The son of little Pier (rock); one who had large anklebones.

Ferris, Ferrise (*Ir., Fr.*) Variant of Farris, q.v.; one who shoes horses or works with iron.

Ferro, Ferrone, Ferroni (*It.*) Dweller near where iron was mined.

Ferry (*Eng., Fr.*) Dweller at, or near, a ferry; one who operated a ferry; descendant of Ferry, a pet form of Frederic (peace, ruler).

Feuer (*Eng., Ger.*) One who worked in metals, a smith.

Feuillet, Feuillette (*Fr.*) Dweller at the sign of a leaf, used generally to represent a wine merchant.

Fewkes (*Eng.*) The son of Fulk (people's guard).

Ficht, Fichter, Fichtner (*Ger.*) Dweller at, or near, a fir tree.

Fick, Ficke, Fickes (*Eng.*) Descendant of Fech, or Feche, (fated to die).

Fickett (*Eng.*) Descendant of little Fech (fated to die).

Fidler, Fiedler, Fiddler (*Eng., Ger.*) One who played a fiddle or stringed instrument.

Fielding (*Eng.*) Dweller near the fields or the meadow of the open country.

Fields, Field, Feld (*Eng.*) Dweller in the open country, or land free of trees.

Fifer, Fife (*Scot.*) One who came from Fife. *See* Fyfe.

Fifield (*Eng.*) One who came from Fifield (an estate of five hides, i.e., as much land as could be tilled by five plows), the name of several places in England.

Figura (*Sp., It.*) One with an unusual face or appearance.

Files (*Eng.*) Dweller on the level field or plain; one who came from The Fylde (level field), in Lancashire.

Filip (*Eng.*) Dweller at a hayfield or plot of newly cultivated land.

Filipiak (*Pol.*) The son of Filip (lover of horses).

Fillmore, Filmore (*Eng.*) Descendant of Filimar or Filomor (very famous).

Finch, (*Eng.*) Dweller at the sign of the finch; the simple-minded person.

Fincher (*Eng.*) One who trained and sold finches.

Finder (*Ger.*) One who discovered things or invented new processes.

Fine (*Eng., Ger.*) The fine or elegant person; a clever man.

Finger, Fingar (*Ger.*) One with a peculiar or unusual finger; one who came from a place using this word in some transferred sense.

Fink, Finke, Finck, Fincke (*Ger.*) Dweller at the sign of the finch.

Finkel, Finkle (*Ger.*) Dweller at the sign of the little bird; descendant of Finkel (little bird), a popular woman's name in the Middle Ages.

Finkelstein, Finklestein (*Ger.*) Pyrites; descendant of Finkel (little bird), with the addition of "stein" to give the name a German look and sound. *See* Finkel.

Finkler (*Ger.*) The birdcatcher.

Finley, Finlay, Findlay, Findley (*Scot.*) Descendant of Fionnla (fair hero); one who came from Findlay (clear calf), in Scotland.

Finn, Finne, Fynn (*Ir.*) Descendant of little Fionn (fair).

Finnegan, Finnigan, Finegan, Finigan (*Ir.*) Descendant of little Fionn (fair).

Finney (*Ir.*) Descendant of the soldier.

Fiore, Fiori (*It.*) Dweller at, or near, a place where flowers are grown.

Fischer (*Ger.*) One who caught or sold fish.

Fischl, Fischel (*Ger.*) Dweller at the sign of the little fish; the little dealer in fish.

Fish, Fisch (*Eng., Ger.*) A fisherman or dealer in fish; dweller at the sign of the fish.

Fisher (*Eng.*) One who caught or sold fish.

Fishman (*Eng.*) A fisherman or seller of fish.

Fisk, Fiske (*Sw.*) A fisherman, often a Swedish soldier name.

Fitch (*Eng.*) One who came from Fitz (Fita's spur of land), in Shropshire; dweller at the sign of the fitch, the European polecat; one with the characteristics of a polecat.

Fithian (*Eng.*) Descendant of Fithian, a variant of Vivian (alive).

Fitzgerald, Fitz Gerald (*Eng., Fr., Ir.*) The son of Gerald (firm, spear).

Fitzgibbons, Fitzgibbon (*Eng., Ir.*) The son of Gibbon or little Gib, a pet form of Gilbert (pledge, bright).

Fitzhenry (*Eng.*) The son of Henry (home ruler).

Fitzmaurice, Fitzmorris (*Eng., Ir.*) The son of Maurice or Morris (moorish or dark-skinned).

Fitzpatrick (*Ir., Eng.*) The son of Patrick (noble or patrician).

Fitzsimmons, Fitzsimons (*Ir., Eng.*) The son of Simon (gracious hearing).

Flack, Flach (*Ger.*) Dweller at the plain or level field.

Flagg, Flagge (*Eng.*) One who came from Flagg (sod, turf), in Derbyshire.

Flaherty (*Ir.*) Grandson of Flaithbheartach (bright ruler).

Flanagan, Flanigan, Flannigan, Flannagan (*Ir.*) The little ruddy man; grandson of little Flann (red).

Flanders (*Eng.*) One who came from Flanders (plain), a medieval county extending along the coast of the Low Countries.

Flannery, Flanery (*Ir.*) Grandson of Flannabhra (red eyebrows).

Flasch, Flesch (*Ger.*) Dweller at the sign of the flask or bottle, generally designating a tavern.

Flauter (*Eng.*) One who played a flute.

Flavin (*Ir.*) Grandson of little Flaitheamh (lord).

Flaxman, Flexman (*Eng.*) One who dressed or sold flax.

Fleche (*Fr.*) The archer.

Fleck (*Eng., Ger.*) One with a disfiguring spot or mark.

Fleischer, Fleisher (*Ger.*) One who cut and sold meats, a butcher.

Fleischhauer (*Ger.*) The hewer or cutter of meat, a butcher.

Fleischman, Fleischmann, Fleishman (*Eng., Ger.*) One who sold meat, a butcher.

Fleming, Flemming (*Eng.*) One who came from Flanders (plain), a medieval county extending along the coast of the Low Countries.

Fletcher, Flecher (*Eng.*) One who made or sold arrows, and sometimes bows as well.

Flick (*Eng.*) A variant of Fleck, q.v.

Flight (*Eng.*) One who fought with the longbow; the contentious man, one engaged in strife.

Flink, Flinker (*Du., Ger.*) The sturdy, stalwart man; the quick, active man.

Flint (*Eng.*) Descendant of Flint (rock or flint); one who came from Flint, a town and county in Wales.

Flood (*Eng.*) Dweller at, or near, the place where a stream often overflows; descendant of Floyd (gray).

Florek (*Pol.*) Descendant of little Flor, a pet form of Florian (flowering).

Florence (*Eng.*) Descendant of Florence (flourishing), a name for both men and women in the Middle Ages; one who came from Florence (flourishing), in Italy.

Flores (*Sp.*) Dweller near where flowers grew.

Florian (*Eng.*) Descendant of Florian (flowery or blooming).

Flory, Fleury (*Fr.*) One who came from Fleury (place where flowers grew), the name of several places in France; descendant of Flory, a pet form of Florence, Flora and Florian (blooming).

Flowers, Flower (*Eng.*) One who made arrows; descendant of Flower or Flour (flower).

Floyd (*Wel.*) Descendant of Lloyd (gray).

Flynn, Flinn (*Ir.*) The red-haired or ruddy-complexioned man.

Foerster, Foerstner (*Ger.*) A forest warden or gamekeeper.

Fogarty, Fogerty (*Ir.*) Descendant of the exiled man.

Fogel, Fogle (*Ger., Du.*) Dweller at the sign of the bird; one with birdlike characteristics.

Fogg (*Eng.*) Descendant of Fogg, a pet form of Fulcher (people, army).

Folan (*Ir.*) The son of little Faol (wolf).

Foley, Foly (*Ir.*) Grandson of Foghlaidh (plunderer).

Folger, Folgers (*Ger.*) A follower or vassal; descendant of Folcger (folk, spear).

Folk, Folkes (*Eng.*) Descendant of Fulk (people).

Follansbee (*Eng.*) One who came from Follingsby (origin obscure), in Durham.

Follett, Follette (*Fr.*) The little foolish person.

Folsom (*Eng.*) One who came from Foulsham (Foghel's homestead), in Norfolk.

Fontana, Fontano, Fontanetta (*It*). Dweller at, or near, a spring.

Foote, Foot (*Eng.*) Dweller at the lower part of the hill.

Foran (*Ir.*) Descendant of the little, cold man.

Forbes, Forbis (*Scot.*) One from Forbes (field place), in Aberdeenshire.

Ford, Forde (*Eng.*) Dweller, or worker, at a stream crossing.

Foreman, Forman (*Eng.*) One who tended pigs; an overseer.

Forget, Forgett (*Fr.*) Descendant of Fargeau (of iron), a variant of Ferreolus, bishop of Limoges in the sixth century; dweller, or worker, at the little forge.

Forney (*Ice.*) Descendant of Forni (ancient one).

Forrest, Forest (*Eng.*) Dweller at, or in, a large wood or forest.

Forristall, Forrestall (*Ir.*) Custodian of the forest, a gamekeeper.

Forsberg (*Sw.*) Waterfall mountain.

Forst, Forste (*Ger.*) Dweller in, or near, a forest.

Forster, Forrester, Forester (*Eng.*) A forest warden, or gamekeeper, a manor official.

Forsyth, Forsythe (*Scot.*) One who came from Forsyth, in Scotland; descendant of Fearsithe (man of peace).

Fort, Forte (*Eng., It., Fr.*) Descendant of Fort (strong); the strong man.

Fortier (*Fr.*) One employed at a fortress; one who made and sold gimlets.

Fortin (*Eng., Fr.*) One who came from Forton (homestead by a ford), the name of several places in England; dweller near the little fort; descendant of little Fort (strong).

Fortuna (*It.*) Descendant of Fortuna (good fortune), a name sometimes given to foundlings.

Fortunato (*It.*) The fortunate person.

Fortune (*Eng., Scot.*) The fortunate or lucky person; one who came from the lands of Fortune, in East Lothian.

Fosco (*It.*) One with a dark complexion.

Foss, Fosse (*Ger., Eng.*) Dweller at the sign of the fox; one with the qualities of a fox; dweller near a waterfall; dweller near a ditch or trench.

Foster (*Eng.*) A forest warden, or gamekeeper, a manor official.

Foulkes, Ffoulkes, Foulke, Foulk (*Wel., Eng.*) Descendant of Foulk or Fulk (people). An early form of a capital *F* was *ff*.

Fountain, Fountaine, Fontaine (*Fr.*) Dweller at, or near, a spouting spring.

Fournier (*Fr.*) One who baked bread, a baker.

Fowle (*Eng.*) Dweller at the sign of the bird, especially a game bird.

Fowler (*Eng.*) The birdcatcher or gamekeeper.

Fox, Foxx (*Eng.*) Dweller at the sign of the fox; one with some of the qualities of a fox.

Foy, Foye (*Eng., Ir.*) One who came from Foy (the church of St. Mwy), in Herefordshire; the reasonable man.

Francis, Francois (*Wel., Eng., Fr.*) Descendant of Francis or Francois (the free).

Frank, Franks, Franke, Franck, Francke, Franken (*Ger.*) One who came from Franconia, in central Germany; the free man; descendant of Frank (free or courageous).

Frankel (*Ger., Fr.*) Descendant of little Frank (free); one who came from France; one who came from Franken, an old duchy in south central Germany.

Frankenberger (*Ger.*) One who came from Frankenberg (the hill of the Franks), in Saxony.

Frankfort, Frankfurt, Frankfurter (*Ger.*) One who came from Frankfort or Frankfurt (ford of the Franks), in Germany.

Franklin, Franklyn (*Eng.*) A freeholder who held substantial land for which he paid only a small rent and who rendered little or no service to the lord.

Franz, Frantz, France, Franze (*Ger.*) Descendant of Franz (the free); descendant of Franz, a pet form of Franciscus (free).

Franzen (*Sw.*) The son of Franz (the free).

Frawley (*Ir.*) Grandson of Fergal or Farrell (super valor).

Frazier, Fraser, Frazer, Frasier (*Scot. Ir.*) One who came from Friesland, the Frisian.

Frech, Freake (*Ger.*) The bold man.

Frederick, Fredrick, Fredericks, Fredricks (*Ger., Eng.*) Descendant of Frederick (peace, ruler).

Fredrickson, Fredricksen, Fredriksen, Fredrikson (*Sw., Nor., Dan.*) The son of Fredrik (peace, ruler).

Freeburn, Freeborn (*Eng.*) Descendant of Freeburn (free, sword).

Freed, Frid (*Sw.*) Peace (of mind or soul), a Swedish soldier name.

Freedman (*Ger.*) Variant of Friedman, q.v.

Freeland (*Eng.*) Dweller, or worker, on land held without obligation of rent or service.

Freeman (*Eng.*) The free man, one whose status was just above that of a serf, one who owned land but was not of noble birth.

Freese (*Eng.*) One who came from Friesland, in Holland.

Freitag, Freytag (*Ger.*) Descendant of Freitag, the name sometimes given to one born on Friday.

Fremling (*Sw.*) The stranger or recent arrival.

French, Ffrench (*Eng., Scot.*) One who came from France, a Frenchman. An early form of a capital *F* was *ff*.

Freund, Freundt (*Ger.*) The friend.

Frey (*Nor.*) One who worshiped Frey, the Norse god of love, marriage and fruitfulness.

Freyer, Friar (*Eng.*) A member of a religious order, a friar or brother; a nickname for a guildsman.

Frick, Fricke (*Eng.*) The bold or brave man.

Fried, Friede (*Ger.*) Descendant of Fried, a pet form of Friedrich (peace, ruler).

Friedlander, Friedland (*Ger.*) One who came from Friedland (peaceful country), the name of towns in Brandenburg and Mecklenburg, Germany.

Friedman, Friedmann (*Ger.*) Descendant of Friduman (peace or security, man); a Germanized form of the name Solomon (peaceful).

Friedrich, Friedrichs (*Ger.*) Descendant of Friedrich (peace, ruler).

Friel (*Ger.*) Descendant of Friel, a variant of Fride (peace).

Friend (*Ger., Eng.*) An esteemed person, a friend.

Fries, Friese, Friesen, Friess (*Ger.*) One who came from Frisia, in northern Germany.

Frigo (*It.*) One who came from Friesland.

Frisbie, Frisby, Frisbee, Frisbey (*Eng.*) One who came from Frisby (the Frisians' village), the name of two places in Leicestershire.

Fritsch, Fritsche, Fritscher (*Ger.*) Descendant of Fritz, a pet form of Friedrich (peace, ruler).

Fritz, Fritze (*Ger.*) Descendant of Fritz, a pet form of Friedrich (peace, ruler).

Frizzell, Frissell, Frizell (*Scot.*) Early forms of Frazier, q.v.

Froehlich, Froelich, Frohlich, Fralick (Ger.) The merry or cheerful person; the wise person.

Fromm, From, Frome (*Ger.*) The quiet, pious or devout man.

Frost (*Eng., Wel.*) Descendant of Frost (one born at the time of frost); a contraction of Forrest, q.v.; one cold in behavior or temperament.

Fry, Frye (*Eng.*) The free man, i.e., free of obligations to the lord of the manor.

Fryer (*Eng.*) A member of a religious order, a friar or brother.

Fu (*Chin.*) Teacher.

Fuchs (*Ger.*) One who lived at the sign of the fox; one with foxlike characteristics.

Fujii (*Jap.*) Dweller at a well around which wistaria grew.

Fujikawa (*Jap.*) Dweller near a river where wistaria grew.

Fujimoto (*Jap.*) Dweller where wistaria grew.

Fulbright (*Eng.*) Descendant of Fulbeorht (people, bright).

Fulk, Fawke, Fawkes (*Eng.*) Descendant of Fulk (people).

Fulkerson, Fulcher (*Eng.*) The son of Fulker (people, guard), or Fulk (people).

Fuller (*Eng.*) One who cleaned and thickened cloth.

Fullerton (*Eng.*) One who came from Fullerton (the village of the birdcatchers), in Hampshire.

Fulton (*Scot.*) One who came from Fulton (fowl enclosure), in Roxburghshire.

Funk, Funke, Funck (*Ger.*) The sparkling or animated person.

Furlong (*Eng.*) Dweller at, or near, the furlong, a designation of an area rectangular in shape, and as long as the distance the plow went without turning.

Furman, Fuhrman, Fuhrmann (*Ger.*) One who conveyed passengers by boat across a stream, a ferryman.

Furness, Furniss (*Eng.*) One who came from Furness (podex headland), in Lancashire.

Furst, Fuerst, First (*Ger.*) One who acted the part of a prince in play or pageant; member of a prince's entourage.

Fyfe, Fyffe (*Scot*) One who came from Fife or Fifeshire (named after Fib, one of the sons of Cruithne, legendary father of the Picts).

Gabel, Gable, Gabl, Gaebel (*Ger.*, Eng.). One who made and sold agricultural implements, such as pitchforks; dweller by a fork in the road; one who came from Gabel (fork), in Germany; descendant of little Gabe, a pet form of Gabriel (God is my strength).

Gabor (*Hun.*) Descendant of Gabor, Hungarian form of Gabriel (God is my strength).

Gabriel (*Eng., Fr.*) Descendant of Gabriel (God is my strength).

Gabrielsen, Gabrielson (*Dan., Nor.*) The son of Gabriel (God is my strength).

Gaffey (*Ir.*) The son of Eochaidh (rich in cattle).

Gaffney, Gafeney (*Ir.*) Descendant of Gawain (calf).

Gage (*Eng.*) One who acted as pledge for another in the courts.

Gagliano (*It.*) Variant of Gallo, q.v

Gagnon (*Fr.*) One who cultivated a plot of land, a peasant farmer.

Gaines, Gaynes (*Eng.*) Descendant of Gegn (straight).

Gainsboro, Gainsborough (*Eng.*) One who came from Gainsborough (Gegn's fort), in Lincolnshire.

Gajda (*Rus., Cz.-Sl.*) One in the habit of using *gajda,* meaning, "hi," or "hey," in exclamations; dweller in, or near, a wood.

Gajewski (*Pol.*) Dweller in, or near, a wood.

Galbraith, Galbreath, Galbreth (*Scot.*) A stranger or foreigner, especially the foreign Briton.

Gale (*Wel., Eng.*) Dweller near a jail; a gay or lively person.

Galer, Gayler, Gaylor (*Eng.*) A jail keeper or turnkey.

Gales (*Eng.*) One who came from Wales, a Welshman.

Gall, Galle, Gahl (*Scot.*) The stranger or foreigner.

Gallagher, Gallaher, Galliger, Galligher (*Ir.*) The foreign helper or assistant; grandson of Gallchobhar (foreign help).

Gallant, Galante (*Eng., Fr.*) The gay, polite, brave person; one in gay or fine attire.

Gallas (*Fr.*) A variant of Gallant, q.v.

Gallery (*Scot.,* Ir.) One who came from Gallery (stranger Gael), in Angus; descendant of the gray youth.

Galligan (*Ir.*) Descendant of the little white one.

Gallivan (*Ir.*) Grandson of Gealbhan (bright, white).

Gallo (*It.*) Nickname given because of some resemblance to a rooster, possibly strutting like one; dweller at the sign of the rooster.

Galloway, Gallaway (*Scot.*) One who came from Galloway (white hill-face), a district in Scotland.

Gallup, Galup, Galut, Gallop (*Fr.*) A flat-bottomed boat used to load and unload ships, the surname being applied to the crew members.

Galvin, Galvan (*Ir.*) Grandson of Gealbhan (bright, white).

Gamble, Gambell, Gambill (*Eng.*) Descendant of Gamel (old).

Gannet (*Eng.*) One who came from Gannat, a town in central France.

Gannon (*Ir.*) Descendant of the fair-haired man.

Gans, Ganz, Gantz, Gansz (*Ger.*) One who lived at the sign of the goose; one with the qualities of a goose.

Gant (*Fr.*) One who made and sold gloves.

Garber, Garbrecht, Garbers (*Ger.*) Descendant of Garber, a variant of Garibert (spear, bright).

Garcia (*Sp.*) Descendant of Garcia, Spanish form of Gerald (spear, firm).

Gardner, Gardiner (*Eng., Fr.*) One who tended a garden, cultivating flowers and vegetables.

Garfield (*Eng.*) Dweller on the grassy land or pasture.

Garfinkel, Garfinkle (*Ger.*) Carbuncle, a red precious stone or the garnet-cut cabochon, probably one who dealt in these stones.

Garland (*Eng.*) Descendant of Gaerland (spear, land); dweller at the triangular field; dweller at the sign of the garland.

Garner, Garnier (*Eng.*) Descendant of Garner or Warner (protection, warrior).

Garnett, Garnet (*Eng.*) Descendant of little Guarin, or Garnet (protection, friend).

Garofalo, Garofolo, Garofala, Garafolo (*It.*) Dweller near where soapwort (Bouncing Bet) was grown; dweller near a clove tree.

Garrett, Garatt (*Eng.*) Descendant of little Gerard (spear, firm).

Garrick (*Eng.*) One who came from Garrick (Gara's dwelling), in Lincolnshire.

Garrison (*Wel., Eng.*) The son of Garry, a pet form of Garrath (spear, firm).

Garrity, Garity (*Ir.*) The son of Aireachtach (member of a court or assembly).

Garroway, Garraway (*Eng.*) A spear warrior; one who came from Garway (Guoruoe's church), in Herefordshire.

Garth, Garthe (*Eng.*) Dweller in an enclosed yard or on a farm.

Gartner, Gaertner (*Ger.*) One who tended a garden, cultivating flowers and vegetables.

Garvey, Garvie (*Ir.*) Descendant of Gairbhit (rough peace).

Garvin, Garven, Garvan (*Ir.*) Grandson of little Garbh (rough).

Gary, Garry (*Ir.*) Grandson of Gadhra (hound or hunting dog).

Gaskill, Gaskell (*Eng.*) One who came from Gaisgill (wild-goose valley), the name of places in Westmorland and Yorkshire.

Gasper, Gaspar (*Eng.*) Descendant of Gasper or Jasper (master of the treasure). *See* Kaspar.

Gasser, Gasse, Gass (*Ger.*) One who lived on an alley.

Gast (*Fr., Ger., Du.*) Dweller near an uncultivated field; one who came from a distance, a stranger.

Gaston (*Eng.*) One who came from Gascony, in France.

Gately (*Eng.*) One who came from Gately (clearing where goats were kept), in Norfolk.

Gates (*Eng.*) One who lived in, or near, the gate or gap in a chain of hills.

Gatewood, Gatwood (*Eng.*) Dweller in, or by, the wood frequented by goats; dweller at the entrance to the wood.

Gatto, Gattone, Gatti (*It.*) Dweller at the sign of the cat; one thought to possess some of the qualities of a cat.

Gatton (*Eng.*) One who came from Gatton (enclosure where goats were kept), in Surrey.

Gatz, Gatsch (*Ger.*) Descendant of Gato, a pet form of Gadafrid (comrade, peace).

Gaudet, Gaudette (*Fr.*) Descendant of little Gaud (ruler).

Gaughan, Gaughen (*Ir.*) Descendant of little Gaibhteach (plaintive).

Gault, Gaul (*Scot.*) The stranger or foreigner.

Gauss, Gaus, Gause (*Ger.*) Dweller at the sign of the goose; one with some characteristic of a goose.

Gauthier (*Fr.*) Descendant of Gautier (ruler, army).

Gavin (*Scot., Ir.*) Descendant of Gavin (hawk of battle); grandson of Gabhadhan (dim. of Gabhadh, want or danger).

Gawlik (*Pol.*) One who came from Gawlik, in Poland; descendant of little Gawel (God is my strength).

Gay, Gaye (*Eng.*) The merry or blithe person; one in the habit of wearing colorful apparel.

Gaylord, Gaillard (*Eng.*) The gay or blithe person; descendant of Gaillard (gay).

Gaynor, Gainer (*Ir.*) Son of the light-complexioned or white-haired man.

Geary (*Ir.*) Grandson of Gadhra (hound or hunting dog).

Gebhardt, Gebhart, Gebhard, Gebert (*Ger.*) Descendant of Gebahard (gift, brave); the generous person, one who gladly and freely gave.

Gee (*Eng.*) The crooked or deformed person; one who came from Gee, in Cheshire.

Gehrke, Gehrkens (*Ger.*) Descendant of little Gero, a pet form of Gereman (spear, man).

Geier (*Ger.*) Dweller at the sign of the vulture; one with the characteristics of a vulture.

Geiger (*Ger.*) One who played a violin.

Geis, Geiser, Geiss, Geisser, Geise (*Swis.*) One who came from Geiss (place where goats graze), in Switzerland; descendant of Geiss, a variant of Giso, a pet form of names beginning with Gis (spear).

Geisler, Geissler, Gessler (*Ger.*) Descendant of Gisalhar (spear, army); one who was a vassal or feudal tenant; one who beat another; one who butchered goats and small animals; one who came from Geislar or Geisler, the names of places in Germany.

Geist (*Ger.*) Descendant of Geist (spirit); one who came from Geistingen (Geist's settlement), in Germany.

Gelb (*Ger.*) The yellow-haired or blond man; descendant of Gelb, a pet form of Gilbert (pledge, bright).

Gelderman, Geldermann, Gellerman (*Du.*) One who came from Gelders, a province in Holland.

Gelfand, Gelfond (*Pol., Ger.*) One who loaned money on the security of personal property pledged in his keeping, a pawnbroker; variant of Helfand, q.v.

Gellatly, Galletly, Gillatly (*Scot., Eng.*) Variants of Golightly, q.v.

Geller (*Ger.*) Descendant of Gelther (sacrifice, army); one who is known for shrieking; one who came from Geldern, in Prussia.

Gelman, Gellman (*Ger.*) The money man, perhaps a money changer.

Gemmell, Gemmill (*Nor.*) One born at the same time as another, a twin.

Genovese (*It.*) One who came from Genova (head of the water), a province in Italy.

Gentile, Gentle (*It., Eng.*) One with polished, well-bred manners, or of a gentle or benign character; originally, one not a Christian.

Gentry (*Eng.*) A courteous person; one of noble birth.

Geoghegan, Gegan (*Ir.*) The son of little Eochaidh (racing horse).

Georgacas, Georgakas (*Gr.*) Descendant of big or fat Georgios (farmer).

Georgacopoulos, Georgopulos (*Gr.*) The son of Georgios (farmer).

George (*Wel., Fr.*) Descendant of George (farmer); dweller at the sign of St. George.

Georges, Georget (*Fr.*) Descendant of George (farmer).

Georgescu (*Rom.*) Descendant, or follower of, George (farmer).

Geraci, Gerace (*It.*) One who came from Gerace, in Italy.

Geraghty, Geraty, Gerraughty (*Ir.*) The son of the assemblyman.

Gerard, Gerald, Geralds (*Eng.*) Descendant of Gerard or Gerald (spear, firm).

Gerber (*Ger.*) One who prepared leather, a tanner or currier.

Gerhardt, Gerhard, Gerhart (*Ger.*) Descendant of Gerhard (spear, hard).

Gerlach (*Ger.*) Descendant of Gerlach or Gerolah (spear, tournament).

Germain (*Fr.*) Descendant of Germain (spear, people).

German, Germain, Germaine, Germann (*Eng., Ger.*) The man from Germany; descendant of German (a German).

Gerrish, Gerish (*Wel., Eng.*) The showy or resplendent person.

Gershon, Gerson (*Heb.*) Descendant of Gershon or Gershom (violent expulsion).

Gerstein, Gersten (*Ger.*) Dweller at, or in, the barley field; one who came from Gersten (barley field), in Germany.

Gerstenberg, Gerstenberger (*Ger.*) One who came from Gerstenberg (barley mountain).

Gerstung (*Ger.*) One who came from Gerstungen (barley-field village), in Thuringia.

Gertz, Goertz, Gertsch, Gerz (*Ger.*) Descendant of Goertz, a pet form of Gerhard (spear, brave), also of other names commencing with Ger, as Geremar, Geribald and Germund.

Gesell (*Ger.*) One bound by an agreement to serve another in learning an art or trade, an apprentice.

Getchell, Gatchell (*Eng.*) One who came from Gatesgill (shelter for goats), in Cumberland.

Geyer, Gey (*Ger.*) Dweller at the sign of the vulture; one who came from Gey, in Germany; one with the characteristics of a vulture.

Gfroerer, Gfrorer (*Ger.*) One to whom soldiers came for superstitious protection in battle.

Giacomini (*It.*) Descendant of little Giacomo (the supplanter).

Giannini (*It.*) Descendant of little Giani, a pet form of Giovanni (gracious gift of Jehovah).

Gianopoulos, Gianopolis, Gianopolus (*Gr.*) The son of Joannes (gracious gift of Jehovah).

Gibbons, Gibbon, Gibons, Gibbins (*Eng.*) Descendant of little Gib, a pet form of Gilbert (pledge, bright).

Gibbs, Gibb (*Eng.*) Descendant of Gib, a pet form of Gilbert (pledge, bright).

Giblin (*Eng.*) Descendant of little Gib, a pet form of Gilbert (pledge, bright).

Gibson (*Eng.*) The son of Gib, a pet form of Gilbert (pledge, bright).

Giddings (*Eng.*) One who came from Gidding (Gydda's people), in Huntingdonshire, or Gedding (Gydda's people), in Suffolk.

Giese, Gies, Giess (*Ger.*) Descendant of Giso, pet form of names beginning with Gis (spear), as Gisbert, Gisber and Gissold.

Giffin, Giffen (*Eng., Scot.*) Descendant of little Giff, a pet form of Geoffrey (pledge, peace); one who came from Giffen (ridge), in Ayrshire.

Gifford (*Eng., Scot.*) Descendant of Giffard (give, bold); one with fat cheeks.

Giglio, Gigli (*It.*) Dweller where lilies grew; dweller on the peak.

Gilbert, Gilbertson, Gilberts (*Eng.*) Descendant of Gilbert (pledge, bright).

Gilchrist, Gilchriest, Gilcrest (*Scot.*) The servant of Christ.

Gildea (*Ir.*) The servant or disciple of God.

Giles, Gile (*Eng.*) Descendant of Giles (shield-bearer).

Gilfoyle, Gilfoy (*Ir.*) The son of the servant or devotee of St. Paul.

Gill (*Ir.*) The son of the foreigner.

Gillard, Gillarde (*Eng.*) The gay or blithe person; descendant of Gaillard (gay).

Gillen, Gillan, Gillon (*Ir.*) Descendant of the little servant or youth.

Gillespie (*Scot., Ir.*) The servant of the bishop.

Gillette, Gillett, Gillet (*Fr.*) Descendant of little Giles, Gilles or Gille, a variant of the Latin, Aegidius (shield or protection).

Gilliam, Gilliams, Guilliams, Guillam (*Eng.*) Descendant of Guilliam (resolution, helmet), the name of William as influenced by the French Guillaume.

Gilligan (*Ir.*) Descendant of the little servant or youth.

Gillis (*Scot., Ir.*) The servant or disciple of Jesus.

Gillogly (*Ir.*) The son of the gluttonous lad.

Gilman, Gillman (*Eng.*) The servant of Gill, a pet form of Gilbert (pledge, bright) and of Gillian (downy-bearded or youthful).

Gilmartin (*Ir.*) The son of the servant of St. Martin.

Gilmore, Gilmour, Gilmer (*Ir.*) The son of the servant or devotee of Mary.

Gilroy (*Ir.*) The son of the red youth.

Gilson (*Eng.*) The son of Gill, a pet form of Julian (downy-bearded or youthful) and several other names; one who came from Gilson (Gydel's hill), in Warwickshire.

Gimbel, Gimble, Gimpel (*Ger.*) Dweller at the sign of the red finch; a blockhead or dunce.

Ginn, Genn (*Eng., Ir.*) Descendant of Ginn or Genn, pet forms of Guinevere (fair lady) or of Eugene (wellborn); one with a fair complexion.

Ginsberg, Ginsburg, Gunzburg (*Ger.*) One who came from Gunzburg, in Bavaria.

Giordano (*It.*) Descendant of Giordano (flowing down), a name given to one baptized in the River Jordan.

Gipson, Gipp, Gips (*Eng.*) The son of Gip, a pet form of Gilbert (pledge, bright).

Girard, Giraud, Geraud, Gerault (*Fr.*) Descendant of Girard (spear, firm).

Giroux (*Fr.*) Descendant of Giroux (old man), or Girulf (spear, wolf).

Gittins, Gittings (*Wel.*) The rough or unkempt man.

Givens, Given (*Scot., Eng.*) Descendant of little Gib, a pet form of Gilbert (pledge, bright).

Glab, Glabe (*Pol.*) Dweller in, or near, the deep hole or ravine.

Gladney, Gladny (*Eng., Pol.*) Dweller at the narrow enclosure; the gaunt or hungry man.

Gladstone (*Scot.*) One who came from Gledstanes (kite's rock), in Lanarkshire.

Gladwin (*Eng.*) Descendant of Gladwin (kind friend).

Glancy, Glancey (*Ir.*) The son of Flannchadh (ruddy warrior).

Glasgow (*Scot.*) One who came from Glasgow (greyhound, or green hollows), in Lanarkshire.

Glass, Glasser, Glaser (*Eng.*) One who made or sold glassware.

Glassman, Glassmann (*Ger., Eng.*) One who dealt in glass.

Glatz (*Ger.*) The bald man.

Glavin (*Ir.*) Grandson of Glaimhim (glutton).

Glazer, Glazier (*Eng.*) One who made and sold glass.

Gleason, Gleeson (*Ir.*) The descendant of the little, green man, possibly referring to the color of his clothes.

Glendenning, Glendinning (*Scot.*) One who came from Glendinning (glen of the fair hill), in Dumfriesshire.

Glenn, Glen (*Wel.*) Dweller in the glen or valley.

Glennon (*Ir., Eng.*) The son of Lennan (small coat); one who came from Glendon (clean hill), in Northamptonshire.

Glick, Glickman, Glicker, Glickerman (*Ger.*) The lucky or fortunate man.

Glidden (*Eng.*) A variant of Gladwin, q.v.

Glover (*Eng.*) One who made or sold gloves.

Glowacki (*Pol.*) One with a large or peculiar head.

Gluck (*Ger.*) The lucky person.

Gluckstein (*Ger.*) Lucky stone.

Glynn (*Wel.*) Dweller in the narrow valley.

Goddard (*Eng.*) Descendant of Goddard (God, hard).

Godfrey (*Eng.*) Descendant of Godfrey (God's peace).

Godwin (*Eng.*) Descendant of Godwin (God's friend).

Goebel, Goble, Gobel (*Ger.*) Descendand of Godbeald (God, brave).

Goethe (*Ger.*) An abbreviation of one of the old German names beginning with Gott (God), as Gottfried (Godfrey), or Gotthardt (Goddard).

Goetz, Getz, Gotz, Goettsche, Gosch (*Ger.*) Descendant of Goetz, a pet form of Godizo (God); the beautiful person.

Goff (*Ir.*) The worker in metals; the ruddy or red-haired man; son of Eochaidh (rich in cattle).

Goggin, Goggins, Gogins, Goggans (*Ir.*) One who came from Cogan, a parish in Glamorganshire.

Goins, Goines, Goinges, Goin (*Fr.*) Descendant of Gudin (God's friend).

Gold, Golde (*Eng.*) The son of Gold or Golda, Old English personal names derived from the metal.

Goldberg, Goldberger (*Ger.*) One who came from Goldberg (gold mountain), the name of five places in Germany.

Goldblatt (*Ger.*) Gold leaf.

Golden, Golding, Goulding (*Eng.*) Descendant of Goldwin (gold, friend).

Goldenberg (*Ger.*) One who came from Goldenberg (gold mountain), in Germany.

Goldfarb (*Ger.*) Gold color.

Goldfine, Goldfein (*Ger.*) Gold fine.

Goldman (*Eng.*) The servant of Gold or Golda (gold).

Goldsberry, Goldsbury, Goldsborough (*Eng.*) One who came from Goldsborough (Godhelm's or Golda's fort), the name of several places in England.

Goldsmith, Goldschmidt, Gildsmith, Gouldsmith (*Eng., Ger.*) One who made or sold gold articles, a jeweler, later a banker.

Goldstein (*Ger.*) Gold stone; one who used a goldstein, a touchstone used by a goldsmith to test gold; dweller at the sign of the gollstein, a topaz emblematic of the goldsmith's shop.

Goldsworthy (*Eng.*) One who came from, or worked on, Gold's farm; one who came from Galsworthy (slope where bog myrtle grew), in Devonshire.

Goldthwait, Goldthwaite (*Eng.*) One who came from Gold's clearing.

Golenpaul (*Rus.*) Dweller in, or near, an open field.

Golightly (*Eng.*) A messenger or runner who was fleet of foot.

Golub (*Rus.*) Dweller at the sign of the pigeon or dove; one with some of the qualities of a pigeon.

Golz, Goltz (*Ger.*) One without a beard, a boyish man.

Gomberg (*Rus., Ger.*) One who came from Homburg (high fortified place) or Homberg (high mountain), the names of several places in Germany.

Gomes (*Port.*) The son of Gomo, a pet form of Gumesindo or Gumersindo (man, path).

Gomez (*Sp.*) The son of Gomo, a pet form of Gomesano (man, path).

Gonzalez, Gonzales (*Sp.*) The worker in metals, a smith; the son of Gundisalv (battle, elf).

Gooch (*Wel., Ir.*) The red-haired or ruddy man; son of Eochaidh (rich in cattle).

Good, Goode (*Eng.*) Descendant of Goda or Gode (good), which is also the first element in many names such as Godmund, Godric and Godwine. In these names it often refers to God; occasionally it refers to the good man.

Goodale (*Eng.*) A nickname meaning "good ale," given to a brewer who makes good ale; variant of Goodall, q.v.

Goodall, Goodell (*Eng.*) One who came from Gowdall (corner overgrown with marigold), in Yorkshire.

Goodenough, Goodnough, Goodnow, Goodenow (*Eng.*) Said to be a nickname for one who was sufficient or satisfactory in some sense.

Goodfellow (*Eng., Scot.*) One who was a pleasant companion, a jolly person.

Goodfriend (*Eng.*) The amiable or pleasant companion.

Goodhue (*Eng.*) One who was an able and competent servant.

Gooding (*Eng.*) Descendant of Goding, or sometimes of Godwin (God's friend).

Goodman (*Eng., Scot.*) Descendant of Godmann (good man), or of Gudmund (war, protection); a landowner who held as a sub-tenant.

Goodrich, Goodrick (*Eng.*) One who came from Goodrich (Godric's castle), in Herefordshire; descendant of Godric (God's rule).

Goodridge (*Eng.*) Descendant of Godric (God's rule); one who came from Goodrich (Godric's castle), in Herefordshire.

Goodsmith (*Eng.*) An able and competent worker in metals.

Goodspeed (*Eng.*) A wish of success, possibly a nickname for one who frequently voiced it.

Goodwin, Goodwine, Goodwyn (*Eng.*) Descendant of Godwin (God's friend).

Gora (*Pol.*) Dweller on, or near, a mountain.

Goranson (*Sw.*) The son of Goran (farmer).

Gordon, Gorden, Gordan (*Scot., Eng.*) The man from Gordon (spacious hill), in Scotland; one who lived on, or near, a three-cornered hill or wedge-shaped piece of land.

Gore (*Eng.*) One who lived near, or on, the triangular piece of land; one who tilled such a piece; one who came from Gore (triangular land), in Kent.

Gorecki, Goralski, Goral (*Pol.*) One who lived on, or near, the mountain.

Gorham (*Eng.*) One who lived on the triangular homestead.

Gorman (*Ir.*) The descendant of the little, blue man, possibly referring to the color of his clothes.

Gormley (*Ir.*) Grandson of Goirmghialla (blue hostage), Goirmghiolla (blue servant), or Goirmrhleaghach (blue spearman).

Gorny, Gorney (*Fr.*) One who came from Gournay (Gornus' estate), in France.

Gorski, Gorska, Gorske (*Pol.*) Dweller on, or near, a mountain.

Gorton (*Eng.*) One who came from Gorton (dirty homestead), in Lancashire.

Goss, Gosse (*Eng., Ger., Fr., Hun.*) Dweller in, or near, a moor or wood; a Goth; a shortened form of names beginning with the element god; dweller near a hedge of thorns; dweller at the sign of the goose; one who came from the former town of Goss, in Austria.

Gosselin, Goslin (*Eng.*) Descendant of Goselin or Jocelin (just).

Gosswiller (*Ger.*) One who came from Gersweiler, the name of two places in Germany.

Gott (*Ger.*) A shortened form of a longer name containing the word "God."

Gottlieb (*Ger.*) Descendant of Gottlieb (God, love).

Gottschalk, Gottschall (*Ger.*) Descendand of Gotesscalc (God's servant).

Goudy, Goudie, Gowdy (*Scot.*) Descendant of little Gold or Golda (gold).

Gough (*Eng., Ir.*) The ruddy or red-haired man; son of Eochaidh (rich in cattle).

Gould (*Eng.*) Descendant of Gold or Golda, Old English personal names derived from the metal.

Gow, Gowan, Govan, Gove (*Scot., Ir.*) The worker in metals, a smith; one who came from Govan, in Lanarkshire.

Graber, Grabner (*Ger.*) One who dug in the ground, a digger.

Grabowski (*Pol.*) One who came from Grabow(o) (birch tree), in Poland.

Grace (*Eng.*) The large or fat person. *See also* Gras.

Graczyk (*Pol.*) The little man who played a musical instrument, a musician.

Grady, Gradie (*Ir.*) Grandson of Grada (noble, illustrious).

Graff, Graf, Groff (*Ger.*) The earl or count; overseer in a lord's establishment.

Grafton (*Eng.*) One who came from Grafton (homestead by a grove), the name of several places in England.

Graham, Grahame (*Eng., Scot.*) Dweller at the gray homestead.

Gran (*Nor.*) Dweller near the spruce tree.

Grandclement (*Fr.*) Descendant of tall Clement (merciful).

Grande, Grand (*Fr.*) The large or fat man.

Granger, Grange, Grainger (*Eng., Scot.*) One who was in charge of a farmhouse with outbuildings; one who came from Grange (farm), the name of many places in Scotland.

Granquist (*Sw.*) Spruce, twig.

Grant, Grand (*Eng., Fr., Scot.*) The large or fat man.

Gras, Grass (*Fr., Eng.*) One who came from Grasse or Gras, in France; the large or fat person; dweller at the grass or green.

Grauer, Grau (*Ger.*) The gray man, probably referring to an old, gray-haired man.

Graver (*Eng.*) One who engraved or carved wood, stone, metal or the like; one who digs in the ground.

Graves, Greaves (*Eng.*) Descendant of the grave, a minor official appointed by the lord of the manor to supervise his tenants' work; dweller in, or near, a grove.

Gray, Graye (*Eng.*) The gray-haired man; one who came from Gray, in France.

Grayson (*Eng.*) The son of Greve (earl), or of the Grave. *See* Graves.

Graziano, Graziani, Grazian (*It.*) The polite, gracious man.

Greco, Grego (*It.*) One who came from Greece.

Green, Greene (*Eng.*) Dweller at, or near, the village green, or grassy ground.

Greenberg, Greenburg (*Ger.*) One who came from Grunberg (green mountain), in Hesse, Germany.

Greenblatt (*Ger.*) Green leaf.

Greenfield (*Eng.*) Dweller at the verdant field or pasture.

Greenlaw (*Scot.*) One who came from Greenlaw (verdant hill), the name of several places in Scotland.

Greenleaf (*Eng.*) One dressed in green leaves, representing a wild man in public pageants.

Greenlee (*Eng.*) Dweller in the verdant wood or glade.

Greenman (*Eng.*) Dweller at the sign of the green man; a forest warden (who dressed in green); one who enacted that part in plays and pageants.

Greenough (*Eng.*) One who came from Greenhaugh (green enclosure), in Northumberland.

Greenspan, Greenspon, Greenspahn (*Ger.*) One who made and used or sold verdigris, a substance much used in early chemical arts.

Greenstein, Greenstone (*Ger.*) Green stone.

Greenwald (*Ger.*) Dweller in the green forest.

Greenwood (*Eng.*) Dweller in the verdant wood or forest.

Greer (*Scot.*) A contraction of MacGregor, q.v.

Greet, Grete (*Eng.*) The great or large person; dweller near the Greet River (gravelly stream), in Nottinghamshire; one who came from Greet, the name of several villages in England.

Gregg, Greg, Greggs (*Eng.*) Descendant of Greg, a pet form of Gregory (watchman).

Gregoire, Gregori (*Fr.*) Descendant of Gregoire (watchman).

Gregory, Gregor, Gregorson (*Eng., Scot.*) Descendant of Gregor (watchman).

Greig (*Eng.*) Descendant of Greg, a pet form of Gregory (watchman).

Grenier (*Fr.*) One who operated a granary.

Gresham, Grisham (*Eng.*) One who came from Gresham (grazing farm), in Norfolk.

Grey (*Eng.*) Same as Gray, q.v.

Gridley (*Eng.*) Dweller in, or near, Grida's wood.

Grieco (*It.*) One who came from Greece.

Griffin, Griffen (*Eng.*) Dweller at the sign of the griffin, a fabulous monster, half lion and half eagle; one with a ruddy complexion; descendant of Griffin or Griffith (fierce lord).

Griffith, Griffiths (*Wel.*) Descendant of Griffith (fierce lord).

Griggs, Grigg (*Eng.*) Descendant of Greg, a pet form of Gregory (watchman).

Grigsby (*Eng.*) Dweller at the homestead belonging to Grig, a pet form of Gregory (watchman).

Grill, Grille (*Ger.*) One who came from Grill, the name of several places in Germany and Austria; dweller at the sign of the cricket.

Grimes (*Eng.*) Descendant of Grim (mask). *See* Grimm.

Grimm, Grim, Grimme (*Eng., Ger.*) Descendant of Grim (mask), the first element of names like Grimbald, Grimkell and Grimulf; the fierce, savage person.

Grinnell, Grindle, Grindel (*Eng.*) One who came from Grindle (green hill), in Shropshire.

Griswold (*Eng.*) Dweller at a wood frequented by pigs.

Groff (*Du.*) The coarse or boorish man.

Grogan (*Ir.*) Grandson of little Gruag (hair of the head) or of little Grug (fierceness).

Groh, Grohe, Grohman, Grohmann (*Ger.*) The gray-haired man.

Gromek (*Pol.*) A nickname meaning little thunderbolt.

Gromyko (*Rus.*) Thunder, an adopted name.

Groner, Groener, Gruner, Gruener (*Ger.*) One who came from Grone (green), in West Germany; descendant of Gronhari (green, army).

Groot, Groote (*Du.*) The big, or tall, man; one who came from Groot (large place), in Holland.

Grootstadt (*Du.*) One who came from the big city.

Gros (*Fr.*) The fat man.

Gross (*Ger.*) The large or fat person.

Grosser (*Eng.*) The merchant in gross, or wholesaler.

Grosskopf (*Ger.*) One with a large head.

Grossman, Grossmann (*Ger.*) The large or fat man.

Grossschmidt (*Ger.*) One who made heavy iron articles; the large smith.

Grosvenor (*Eng.*) The chief or royal huntsman.

Groth, Grothe (*Ger.*) The large or fat man.

Grove, Groves (*Eng.*) One who lived in, or by, the small wood.

Grover (*Eng.*) Dweller in, or near, a grove.

Gruber, Grube (*Ger.*) One who lived near a ditch or quarry.

Grund, Grundman, Grundmann (*Ger.*) One who dwelt in the valley or bottom land.

Grunewald, Gruenewald, Gruenwald (*Ger.*) Descendant of Gronwald (green, forest); dweller in, or near, the green forest.

Gudaitis (*Lith.*) The son of the White Russian.

Gudde (*Ger.*) Dweller near a bush, or at the sign of the bush.

Guenther, Guenthner (*Ger.*) Descendant of Guntard (war, bold).

Guerrero, Guerrieri (*It., Sp.*) One who engaged in combat, a warrior.

Guest (*Eng.*) The accepted stranger, a newcomer.

Guido, Guidi (*It.*) The son of Guy (wood).

Guild (*Scot.*) A variant of Gold, q.v.

Guilford (*Eng.*) One who came from Guilford (ford where marigolds grew), in Surrey.

Guilfoyle, Gilfoyle, Gilfoil (*Ir.*) The son of the servant or devotee of St. Paul.

Guillotin, Guillemet, Guillet, Guilotte (*Fr.*) Descendant of little William (resolution, helmet).

Guiney (*Ir.*) Descendant of the prisoner.

Gulbrandsen, Gulbransen (*Nor.*) The son of Gulbrand (war, sword).

Gump (*Eng.*) Dweller on, or near, the flat place.

Gunderson, Gundersen (*Nor.*) The son of Gunder (war).

Gunn (*Scot.*) Descendant of Gunn (war); also an abridged form of many longer names, like Gunnarr, Gunulf, Gunnhildr, etc.

Gunnar, Gunnarson (*Nor., Sw., Ice.*) Descendant of Gunnarr (war, battle).

Gunnell (*Eng.*) Descendant of Gundwulf (war, wolf).

Gunning (*Nor., Eng.*) Descendant of Gunning or Gunnic (war or strife); the son of Gunn.

Gunther, Gunter (*Ger., Eng.*) Descendant of Gunter (war, bold).

Guptill (*Scot.*) Dweller at the sign of the fox; one with foxlike characteristics.

Gurney, Gurnee, Gurnea (*Fr.*) One who came from Gournay (Gornus' estate), in France.

Gurry (*Fr.*) Descendant of Gurie or Guris (rich, powerful).

Gustafson, Gustavson (*Sw.*) The son of Gustav (Goth's staff).

Guth (*Ger.*) The good, stout-hearted or agreeable man; descendant of Godo, a pet form of names beginning with Gott (God), as Goteleib, Godulf and Godelmar.

Guthrie (*Scot.*) One who came from the barony of Guthrie (windy place), in Angus.

Gutierrez (*Sp.*) The son of the small man.

Gutknecht (*Ger.*) The good or able servant.

Guttman, Gutman, Gutmann, Guttmann (*Ger.*) Descendant of Gudmund (war, protection); the able or efficient servant.

Guy (*Eng.*) Descendant of Guy (wood).

Guzik (*Pol.*) The little button, a nickname.

Guzzo, Guzzi (*It.*) Descendant of Guzzo or Guzzi, pet forms of Francesguzzi, Domenicuzzi and the like.

Gwynn, Gwinn, Gwin, Gwynne (*Wel.*) The light-complexioned person.

Haack, Haak, Haake (*Du.*) Dweller at the bend or hook in the river.

Haag (*Du.*) Dweller in, or near, the hedged enclosure; keeper of the hedges or fences; one who came from The Hague (the hedge).

Haan (*Du.*) Dweller at the sign of the cock.

Haas, Haase, Hase (*Du., Ger.*) Dweller at the sign of the hare; one thought to possess some of the characteristics of a hare.

Haber, Hafer, Haberkorn (*Ger.*) One who grew oats; dweller near where oats grew.

Hack (*Eng.*) Dweller at the gate, or entrance, to a forest; descendant of Hake, a pet form of Hakon (high kin).

Hacker (*Eng.*) One who cultivates the soil with a hoe or hack; a maker of hacks.

Hackett (*Eng.*) Descendant of little Hack or Hache (hook).

Haddad, Hadad (*Syr.*) One who worked in metal, a smith.

Hadley (*Eng.*) One who came from Hadleigh (heather-covered clearing), the name of several places in England.

Hafner, Haffner (*Ger.*) One who fashioned pottery, a potter.

Hagedorn (*Du.*) Dweller near a hawthorn tree.

Hagen, Hagan (*Ir., Ger.*) Dweller at, or near, the thorn fence; descendant of Hagano (forest man); dweller in a grove.

Hager, Hagar (*Eng.*) The tall, slender man; the wild, untamed man; descendant of Hagar (flight, or a stranger).

Haggerty, Hagerty, Hagarty, Haggarty (*Ir.*) Grandson of Eigceartach (unjust).

Hagstrom, Haggstrom (*Sw.*) Pasture, or willow, stream.

Hahn, Hahne (*Ger.*) One who lived or worked at the sign of the cock.

Haight, Haigh (*Eng.*) One who came from Haigh (enclosure), the name of places in Lancashire and Yorkshire.

Haines (*Eng.*) One who came from Haynes (enclosures), in Bedfordshire; dweller near the hedged enclosures.

Hajduk (*Ukr.*) A footman in Hussar or Cossack uniform; a messenger.

Hajek (*Cz.-Sl.*) Dweller in, or near, a small wood or grove.

Haldemann, Haldeman, Halde (*Ger.*) Dweller on the mountainside; one who came from Halden, a common place name in Switzerland.

Hale, Hales, Hele (*Wel., Eng.*) Dweller at the corner, nook, small hollow, or secret place; one who came from Hale or Hales, the names of several places in England.

Haley (*Eng.*) Dweller at the way, or passage, leading to the hall.

Halfacre (*Eng.*) Dweller on a homestead consisting of half an acre; one who tilled only half an acre.

Halfknight (*Eng., Scot.*) One who held his land of the lord of the manor at half a knight's fee.

Halford (*Eng.*) One who came from Halford (ford in a narrow valley, or hawkers' ford), the name of places in Devonshire and Shropshire.

Halfpenny, Halpenny (*Ir.*) Grandson of Ailpin (little, stout person).

Halfyard (*Eng.*) Dweller at half a yardland, or homestead consisting of half a yardland (about fifteen acres); one who tilled half a yardland.

Haliburton, Halliburton (*Scot.*) One who came from Halyburton (village by the holy enclosure), in Berwickshire.

Hall (*Eng.*) Dweller in, or near, the manor house; servant in the principal room of the manor house; dweller at the rock or stone, generally a boundary marker.

Hallam, Hallum (*Eng.*) One who came from Hallam or Halam (corner or remote valley), the names of several places in England.

Hallberg (*Sw.*) Boulder mountain.

Haller, Halle (*Ger., Eng.*) One who came from Halle (saltworks), in Germany; same as Hall, q.v.

Hallett (*Eng.*) Descendant of little Hal, a pet form of Harry or Henry (home ruler).

Halliday, Holliday (*Eng.*) Descendant of Halliday, a name sometimes given to a child born on a Sunday or other holy day.

Halligan, Hallihan, Hallaghan (*Ir.*) Grandson of little Aille (handsome or beautiful); descendant of the little handsome man.

Hallisey, Hallissey, Hallisy (*Eng.*) One who came from Hollesley (hollow meadow), in Suffolk.

Hallman, Hallmann (*Eng., Ger.*) The servant in the hall or manor house.

Halloran, Halleran (*Ir.*) Grandson of Allmhuran (stranger from beyond the sea).

Hallowell, Halliwell (*Eng.*) One who came from Haliwell, in Middlesex, or Halliwell, in Lancashire, both meaning holy spring.

Halper (*Heb., Ger.*) Variant of Halperin, q.v.

Halperin, Halpern, Halprin (*Heb., Ger.*) A money changer; one who came from Heilbronn (holy well), in Wurttemberg.

Halpin (*Ir., Fr.*) Grandson of Ailpin (little stout person); a money changer.

Halstead, Halsted (*Eng.*) One who came from Halstead (place of shelter for cattle), the name of several places in England.

Halvorsen, Halverson (*Nor.*) The son of Halvor (firm, prudence).

Ham (*Eng.*) One who came from Ham (meadow on a stream), the name of many places in England. *See also* Hamm.

Hamann, Hamman (*Ger.*) Descendant of Hamann, a variant of Johannes (gracious gift of Jehovah); one who came from Hamm, in Germany.

Hamburg, Hamburger (*Ger.*) One who came from Hamburg, in Germany.

Hamill, Hamel, Hamil (*Eng.*) One who came from Hammill (Hamela's wood), in Kent; descendant of little Hamo or Hamon (home).

Hamilton (*Eng., Scot.*) One who came from Hambleton (bare or treeless hill), the name of several villages in England; one who lived at Hamela's farm or enclosure.

Hamlin, Hamlet, Hamling, Hamlett, Hamlyn (*Eng.*) Descendant of little Hamo or Hamon (home).

Hamm (*Eng., Ger.*) One who lived on, or near, the enclosed plot of land; descendant of Hamo (home); dweller at the low, wet meadow; one who came from Hamm, in Germany.

Hammarskjold (*Sw.*) Hammer, shield.

Hammer, Hamer, Hammar (*Eng., Ger.*) Dweller at the pasture ground; one who came from Hamm, in Germany; dweller at the low, wet meadow.

Hammersmith, Hammerschmidt (*Eng., Ger.*) One from Hammersmith (blacksmith's shop), now a part of London; the smith who worked with a hammer.

Hammond, Hammons, Hammonds, Hammon (*Eng.*) Descendant of Hamo or Hamon (home); descendant of Heahmund (chief, protector).

Hampton (*Eng.*) One who came from Hampton (enclosure in a village, or high village), the name of several places in England.

Hancock, Handcock, Hancox, Handcox (*Eng.*) Descendant of little Hane, a pet form of John (gracious gift of Jehovah).

Hand (*Eng.*) Dweller at the sign of the hand.

Handel, Handell (*Ger.*) Descendant of little Hand or Hanto, pet forms of names beginning with Hand (hand), as Hantbert and Hantwin; a peddler or tradesman.

Handelman, Handleman (*Ger.*) The merchant or shopkeeper.

Handler, Haendler (*Ger.*) One who bought and sold goods, a dealer or trader.

Handy (*Eng.*) The polite, courteous man; one who came from Hanby (Handi's stream or Hundi's village), the name of two places in Lincolnshire; descendant of Handi.

Haney, Hanney, Hannay (*Eng., Ir.*) One who came from Hanney (island frequented by wild cocks), in Berkshire; grandson of Eanna (bird).

Hanke, Hank, Hankes, Hanks (*Ger.*) Descendant of Hanke, a pet form of Heinrich (home ruler).

Hankins, Hankinson, Hankin (*Eng.*) The son of little Hane, a pet form of John (gracious gift of Jehovah).

Hanley, Handley, Hanly (*Eng., Ir.*) One who came from Hanley (high meadow), in Staffordshire, or from Handley, with the same meaning, the name of several places in England; grandson of Ainte (beauty, also a hero or warrior).

Hanlon (*Ir.*) Grandson of Anluan (great hero or warrior).

Hanna, Hannah, Hannay (*Scot., Eng.*) Descendant of Senach (old, wise), or of Annan (grace); one who came from Hannah (Hanna's island), a parish in Lincolnshire.

Hannaford (*Eng.*) One who came from Handforth or Hanford (cock's ford), the names of several places in England.

Hannigan, Hanigan, Hanihan (*Ir.*) Grandson of little Annadh (delay); descendant of the little, slow man.

Hannon, Hannan (*Ir.*) Grandson of little Annadh (delay).

Hanrahan (*Ir.*) Grandson of little Anradh (warrior or champion).

Hans (*Ger.*) Descendant of Hans, a pet form of Johannes (gracious gift of Jehovah).

Hanscom, Hanscomb (*Eng.*) One who came from Hascomb (witches' valley), in Surrey.

Hansen, Hanson (*Dan., Nor., Sw.*) The son of Hans, a diminutive of the Teutonic Johannes (gracious gift of Jehovah).

Harcourt (*Eng.*) One who came from Harcourt (hawker's cottage), in Shropshire, or from Harcourt, in France.

Harder, Harders (*Eng., Ger.*) Dweller at, or near, the hard or firm embankment; one who took care of animals, a herder.

Hardiman (*Eng.*) The servant of Hardy (bold).

Harding, Hardin (*Eng.*) Descendant of Hardwin or Harding (firm, friend); the son of Hard (firm).

Hardt (*Ger.*) One who came from Haardt (woods); dweller at, or near, a wood.

Hardwick, Hardwicke (*Eng.*) One who came from Hardwick (sheep pasture), the name of several places in England.

Hardy, Hardie (*Fr., Scot., Eng.*) Descendant of Hardi, a short form of Hardouin (bold, friend); one who came from Hardy (Hard's island), in Lancashire.

Hare (*Eng.*) Dweller ot the sign of the hare; one thought to possess some of the characteristics of a hare.

Hargrave, Hargraves, Hargreaves (*Eng.*) One who came from Hargrave (hares' grove), the name of several places in England.

Hargrett, Hargett, Harget, Hargitt (*Ger.*) Variants of Hergott, q.v.

Hargrove, Hardgrove (*Eng.*) Variants of Hargrave, q.v.

Harker (*Eng.*) One who keeps and trains hawks to hunt game; one who sells wares from place to place, a peddler.

Harkins, Harkin (*Ir., Eng.*) Descendant of Ercan (red, speckled); or of little Har, a pet form of Harry or Henry (home ruler).

Harkness (*Eng., Scot.*) Dweller near the (heathen) temple, or on, or near, the cape or headland.

Harlan, Harland (*Eng.*) Dweller at the land infested with hares.

Harley (*Eng.*) One who came from Harley (hares' wood), the name of places in Shropshire and Yorkshire.

Harlow (*Eng.*) One who came from Harlow (meeting place), the name of places in Essex and Northumberland.

Harmon, Harman, Harmen (*Eng.*) Descendant of Herman (army, man).

Harms (*Ger., Du.*) Descendant of Hariman or Herman (army, man); one who came from Harms, in Germany.

Harnack (*Ger.*) The hard-necked or obstinate person.

Harnden (*Eng.*) One who came from Horndon (hill where thorns grew, or hornlike hill), the name of several places in England.

Harney, Hartney (*Ir.*) Grandson of Athairne (fatherly).

Harold, Harrold, Harroldson (*Eng.*) Descendant of Harold (powerful warrior); one who came from Harrold (gray wood), in Bedfordshire; occasionally from the office of herald, i.e., one who bore messages from rulers or commanders or acted as heralds in tourneys.

Harper (*Eng., Scot.*) One who played the harp at fair and festival, or for an important lord, often an hereditary official.

Harrell, Harrel (*Eng.*) One who came from Harel, in Normandy; descendant of little Harry, an English form of Henry (home ruler).

Harrigan (*Ir.*) Grandson of little Anradh (champion).

Harriman (*Eng.*) The servant to Harry (home ruler).

Harrington (*Eng., Ir.*) One who came from Harrington (the heath-dwellers' enclosure), in Northamptonshire; grandson of the tall or powerful man.

Harris, Harrison, Harries (*Wel., Eng.*) The son of Harry, the English version of Henry (home ruler).

Harry (*Wel.*) Descendant of Harry, a form of Henry (home ruler).

Hart, Harte (*Eng.*) Dweller at the sign of the hart or stag, the adult male of the red deer; one who came from Hart (stag island), in Durham.

Hartfield, Hartsfield (*Eng.*) One who came from Hartfield (open land frequented by stags), in Sussex.

Hartford (*Eng.*) One who came from Hartford (stag ford) or Hereford (army ford), the names of several places in England.

Hartig (*Du.*) The strong, robust man.

Hartigan (*Ir.*) Grandson of little Art (stone or bear).

Hartley (*Eng.*) One who came from Hartley (stag clearing), the name of several places in England.

Hartman, Hartmann (*Ger.*) Descendant of Hartmann (strong, man).

Hartnett, Harnett (*Ir.*) Grandson of Artneada (battle bear).

Hartshorn, Hartshorne (*Eng.*) One who came from Hartshorne (stags' headland), in Derbyshire.

Hartstone, Hartstein (*Ger.*) Dweller near a hard stone.

Hartung, Hardung, Harting (*Ger.*) The son of Hart (strong); descendant of Harto, a pet form of names beginning with Hart, as Hardher, Hardmod or Hartnagel.

Hartwell (*Eng.*) One who came from Hartwell (stags' spring or stream), the name of three places in England.

Hartwig, Hartwich, Hartweg, Hartewig (*Ger.*) Descendant of Harduwich (hard, battle).

Harty (*Eng.*) One who came from the Isle of Harty (stag island), in Kent.

Harvard (*Eng.*) Descendant of Hereward (army, protection).

Harvey, Hervey (*Eng.*) Descendant of Harvey (bitter, or carnage-worthy).

Harwich (*Eng.*) One who came from Harwich (camp), in Essex.

Harwood, Harewood (*Eng.*) One who came from Harwood or Harewood (gray wood or hares' wood), the names of several places in England.

Haskell (*Ger.*) Descendant of Ezekiel (God is powerful), from a Yiddish form.

Haskins, Haskin (*Eng.*) Descendant of little Aesc (ash, spear or ship).

Hass, Hasse (*Ger.*) Descendant of Hazzo (combat); variant of Haas, q.v.

Hassel, Hassell, Hasselman, Hasselmann (*Ger., Eng.*) One who came from Hassel (place where hazel trees grew), the name of many places in Germany; one who came from Hassall (witches' corner), in Cheshire; dweller near a hazel tree.

Hassett, Hassey (*Ir.*) Grandson of Aisidh (strife).

Hastie, Hastey, Hasty (*Scot., Ir.*) The impatient, violent person; the son of Hodge, a pet form of Roger (fame, spear).

Hastings (*Eng.*) One who came from Hastings (Haesta's people or violence), in Sussex; descendant of Hasting or Haesten (violence).

Hatch (*Eng.*) Dweller by the gate or entrance to a forest; one who came from Hatch (gate), the name of several places in England.

Hatcher (*Eng.*) Dweller near the gate, or entrance, to a forest.

Hatfield (*Eng.*) One who came from Hatfield (heather field), the name of various places in England.

Hathaway, Hatheway (*Eng.*) Dweller at the heath road.

Hathorne, Hathorn (*Eng.*) Variants of Hawthorne, q.v.

Hatt (*Eng.*) One who made head coverings; dweller near a clump of trees; dweller at the sign of the hat.

Hatter (*Eng.*) One who made or sold hats.

Hauck, Hauk, Hauke (*Ger.*) Descendant of Hauck, a pet form of Hugo (spirit).

Haug, Haugen, Hauge (*Nor.*) Dweller on, or near, a pasture; dweller near a small hill or burial mound.

Haupt (*Ger.*) One with a large or unusual head; dweller at the top of the hill or mountain; dweller at the sign of the head.

Hauser (*Ger.*) Dweller in a house for which a money rent is paid; descendant of Hauser, a pet form of Balthasar (Bel has formed a king); one who came from Hausen, in Germany.

Havel, Havill (*Ger.*) Dweller near the Havel, a river in Germany.

Haver (*Eng.*) Dweller at the sign of the buck or male goat.

Haviland, Haverland (*Fr., Ger.*) Dweller on, or near, an oat field; one who came from Havelland (oat land), in Germany.

Havlik, Havlick, Havlicek (*Cz.-Sl., Ukr.*) Descendant of Havlik, a pet form of Gabriel (God is my strength).

Havoc (*Eng.*) Dweller at the sign of the hawk; one with the characteristics of a hawk.

Hawes, Haws, Haw (*Eng.*) Dweller at the hedged enclosure; descendant of Haw or Hal, pet forms of Harry or Henry (home ruler).

Hawk, Hawke, Hawkes (*Eng.*) Descendant of Haw or Hal, pet forms of Harry or Henry (home ruler); dweller at the sign of the hawk; one with the characteristics of a hawk.

Hawkins, Hawkinson, Hawkings (*Eng.*) The son of little Haw or Hal, pet forms of Harry or Henry (home ruler).

Hawley (*Eng.*) One who came from Hawley (hall in the wood or clearing), in Hampshire, or Hawley (holy glade), in Kent.

Haworth (*Eng.*) One who came from Haworth (hawthorn enclosure), in Yorkshire; a variant of Hayward, q.v.

Hawthorne, Hawthorn (*Eng.*) One who came from Hawthorn (hawthorn tree), a village in Durham; dweller near a hawthorn tree.

Hayden, Haydin, Haydon (*Ir., Eng.*) Descendant of the armored man; one who came from Heydon (hay valley or hill), the name of places in Cambridgeshire and Norfolk).

Hayes, Hays, Hay (*Eng.*) Dweller at the hedge or hedged enclosure; keeper of the hedges or fences; one who came from Hayes (enclosure), a common name of minor places in England.

Hayman, Haymon, Haymond (*Eng.*) One who made, repaired or trimmed hedges.

Hayne, Hayn, Hain (*Eng.*) One who came from Hayne (hedges), the name of minor places in England; keeper of the hedges or fences.

Haynes (*Eng.*) One who came from Haynes (enclosures), in Bedfordshire; dweller near the hedged enclosures.

Haynie, Hainey (*Eng., Ir.*) One who came from Hanney (island frequented by wild cocks), in Berkshire; grandson of Eanna, an old Irish saint.

Hayward (*Eng.*) The manorial official who had charge of the hedges and was guardian of the cultivated land to protect it from straying cattle.

Haywood (*Eng.*) One who came from Haywood (enclosed wood), the name of several places in England.

Hazard, Hazzard (*Fr.*) One who played games of chance, a gambler.

Hazel, Hazell, Hasel (*Eng.*) Dweller at, or near, the hazel bushes.

Hazeltine, Hazeldean (*Eng.*) Dweller in the valley where hazel trees grew.

Hazelton (*Eng.*) One who came from Hazleton (homestead with hazel bushes), in Gloucestershire.

Hazelwood, Hazlewood (*Eng.*) One who came from Hazlewood (wood where hazel bushes grew), the name of several places in England.

Hazen, Hazan (*Eng., Sp.*) One who came from Hazon (enclosed sandy meadow), in Northumberland; one who served as cantor in the synagogue.

Hazlett, Hazlitt, Hezlitt (*Eng.*) Dweller at the hazel copse or wood.

Head (*Eng.*) Dweller at the upper end of some natural feature such as wood, land, valley and the like; one with a large or peculiar head; one who came from Hythe (landing place), in Kent.

Headland (*Eng.*) Dweller at, or near, the headland, the area reserved at the end of the field for the turning of the plows and for access by the villagers to the different ridges or plots.

Headley (*Eng.*) One who came from Headley (clearing overgrown with heather), the name of several places in England.

Heald (*Eng.*) Dweller on a slope or bend.

Healy, Healey, Hely (*Eng., Ir.*) One who came from Healaugh (high clearing or wood), the name of several places in England; grandson of the skillful or learned man.

Heaney, Heany (*Ir.*) Grandson of Eanna, an early Irish saint.

Heap, Heaps (*Eng.*) Dweller at, or near, a heap, i.e., hill.

Heard, Herd, Herde (*Eng.*) One who tended domestic animals, a herdsman.

Hearn, Herne, Hearne (*Ir.*) Descendant of the little fearful or distrustful one; grandson of Eachthigheirn (horse lord).

Hearst (*Eng.*) Dweller on, or near, a copse or wooded eminence.

Heath, Heth (*Eng.*) One who came from Heath (wasteland with low shrubs), the name of several places in England.

Heaton (*Eng.*) One who came from Heaton (homestead on high land), the name of several places in England.

Hebbard, Hebard, Hebberd (*Eng.*) Descendant of Hibbert (high, bright).

Hebel, Hebele (*Nor., Ger.*) Descendant of Hebald (high, strong).

Hebert (*Ger.*) Descendant of Hebert (combat, bright).

Hecht, Hechter (*Ger.*) Dweller at the sign of the pike (fish); one who fished for, or sold, pike.

Heck, Hecker, Hecke (*Eng.*) Dweller near the gate, or entrance, to a forest.

Heckmann, Heckman, Hecktman (*Ger.*) One who took care of the hedges or fences.

Hedberg (*Sw.*) Heath mountain.

Hedge, Hedges, Hedger (*Eng.*) Dweller by a hedge.

Hedlund (*Sw.*) Heath grove.

Hedrick, Hedrich (*Ger.*) Descendant of Haidrich (heath, rule).

Hedstrom (*Sw.*) Heath stream.

Heffernan, Hefferren, Heffern (*Ir.*) Grandson of Ifearnan.

Heffner, Hefner (*Ger.*) One who fashioned pottery, a potter.

Heffron (*Ir.*) Grandson of little Eimhear; grandson of little Amhra (prosperous or eminent).

Hegarty (*Ir.*) Variant of Haggerty, q.v.

Hegg, Hegge (*Eng.*) One who lived near the hedged or fenced enclosure.

Hegy (*Hun.*) One who lived on, or near, a hill.

Heidemann, Heideman, Heide, Heid (*Ger.*) Dweller on, or near, the unimproved or wild land.

Heiden, Heider, Heidinger (*Ger., Du.*) Dweller on, or near, uncultivated land covered by coarse grass and low bushes; the rustic or countryman.

Heil, Heile, Heyl (*Ger.*) Descendant of Heilo, a pet form of names beginning with Heil (salvation or holy), as Heilker and Hailwich.

Heilman, Heilmann (*Ger.*) The sound or healthy man; descendant of Hellmann, a German Jewish synonym for Samuel (God hath heard); descendant of Heilman (salvation, man).

Heim (*Ger.*) Descendant of Heimo (home), a pet form of names beginning with Heim, as Heimard, Heimrich and Heimoald.

Heiman, Heimann (*Ger.*) Descendant of Hagiman (enclosed place, man); one who came from Hagen (enclosed place), in Germany; descendant of Hyam (life).

Hein, Heine, Heinen (*Ger.*) Descendant of Heino, a pet form of names beginning with Hein (home or protection), such as Heinfrid, Heinrich and Heinhard, or beginning with Hag (hedged place), as Haganrich and Haginold.

Heinemann, Heineman (*Ger.*) The servant to Hagano (forest, man), a pet form of names beginning with Hag (hedged place), as Haganrich and Haginold; caretaker of a wood or forest.

Heinrich, Heinrichs (*Ger.*) Descendant of Heinrich (home ruler).

Heintzleman, Heinzelman (*Ger.*) Variants of Heinemann, q.v.

Heinz, Heintz, Heinze, Heins (*Ger.*) Descendant of Heinz, a contraction of Heinrich (home ruler).

Heiser (*Ger.*) Dweller on, or near, uncultivated land covered by coarse grass and low bushes.

Heisler, Heissler (*Ger.*) One who worked by the day, a day laborer.

Heitz (*Ger.*) Descendant of Heizo, a pet form of Heinrich (home ruler), also a pet form of names beginning with Heid (heath), as Haidrich and Haidulf.

Held, Heldt, Helt (*Ger., Du., Eng.*) The hero or champion; one who lived on the slope or declivity.

Helfand (*Ger.*) One who came from Helfand, in Saarburg; dweller at the sign of the elephant.

Hellberg (*Sw.*) Boulder mountain.

Heller, Helle (*Ger.*) One who came from Halle, in Germany; one nicknamed after the old heller, an obsolete copper coin worth about a fourth of a cent.

Helliwell (*Eng.*) One who came from Haliwell (holy spring), in Middlesex; dweller at the holy well or spring.

Hellman, Hellmann (*Eng., Ger.*) Dweller in a deep, wide valley; one who settled on communal land; descendant of Hellmann, a German Jewish synonym for Samuel (God hath heard).

Hellyer (*Eng.*) One who covered roofs with thatch, slate or tile, a roofer.

Helm, Helme (*Eng., Du., Ger., Sw.*) Dweller near the roofed shelter for cattle; dweller at the elm tree; descendant of Helmo, a pet form of names beginning with Helm, as Helmhart, Helmold and Helmarich; descendant of Helm (helmet); helmet.

Helms (*Eng*). Dweller at the elm trees.

Helwig, Hellwig, Hellweg, Helwich (*Ger.*) Descendant of Haluig (man, fight); dweller at, or near, a military road; one who came from Hellweg (army road), in Germany; descendant of Hiltiwic (fight, fight); descendant of Hailwich (holy, fight).

Hemenway, Hemingway (*Eng.*) Dweller at the road to Heming's estate, or to Hemma's people.

Hemmer, Hemm, Hemme (*Eng.*) Dweller near the border; one who came from The Hem (the border), in Shropshire.

Hempel, Hemphill, Hemple (*Eng., Ger.*) One who came from Hempshill (Hemede's hill), in Nottinghamshire; descendant of Haginbald (hedged place, bold).

Hench, Henche (*Ger.*) Descendant of Hink, a pet form of names beginning with Hagin (hedged place), as Haginbald, Haginher and Haganrich.

Henderson, Henryson (*Eng., Scot.*) The son of Henry (home ruler).

Hendricks, Hendrick, Hendrich, Hendrix (*Ger.*) Descendant of Heinrich (home ruler).

Hendrickson, Hendricksen (*Sw., Dan.*) The son of Hendrick (home ruler).

Hendriks, Hendrikse (*Du.*) The son of Hendrik (home ruler).

Hendry, Hendrie, Hendries (*Eng.*) Descendant of Henry (home ruler).

Heneghan, Henehan, Henaghan (*Ir.*) Grandson of Eidhneachan (origin obscure, but by some authorities thought to mean bird).

Henke, Henkel, Henk, Hencke, Henkes (*Ger.*) Descendant of Hagano or Heino (hedged place), a pet form of names so beginning, such as Haginold, Haginwarth and Haganrich.

Henley (*Eng.*) One who came from Henley (high wood or clearing, or one frequented by wild birds), the name of several places in England.

Henneberry (*Eng.*) One who came from Henbury (high fort), in Gloucestershire.

Hennessy, Hennessey, Hensy (*Ir.*) Grandson of Aonghus (one choice).

Henning, Hennings, Hennig (*Eng., Ger.*) Dweller at the meadow frequented by wild birds such as moorhens or partridges; descendant of Hann, a pet form of Johannes (gracious gift of Jehovah).

Henrici (*It., Ger.*) Descendant of little Henry (home ruler).

Henriksen, Henrikson (*Dan., Sw., Nor.*) The son of Henrik (home ruler).

Henry, Henri (*Eng., Fr.*) Descendant of Henry (home ruler).

Hensel, Henschel, Hentschel, Hensle, Henzel (*Ger.*) Descendant of little Hans, a pet form of Johannes (gracious gift of Jehovah).

Henshaw (*Eng.*) Dweller in, or near, the grove frequented by wild birds, as moorhens, partridges, etc.

Hensley (*Eng.*) Dweller in the wood frequented by wild birds.

Henson, Hensen (*Nor.*) The son of Hens, a pet form of Johannes (gracious gift of Jehovah).

Hepburn (*Eng., Scot.*) One who came from Hebburn or Hepburn (high tumulus), in Northumberland; one who lived by the dog-rose tree at the brook.

Herald (*Eng.*) One who held the office of herald and delivered formal messages or proclamations from a sovereign or general, later charged with duties concerning armorial bearings and questions of precedence; a variant of Harold, q.v.

Herbert, Herberts (*Wel., Eng.*) Descendant of Herbert (army, bright).

Herbst, Herbster (*Ger.*) One who harvests crops.

Herdman (*Eng.*) One employed to herd cattle, sheep or other animals.

Hergott, Herigodt, Herget, Hergert (*Ger.*) Descendant of Heregod (army, Goth), or of Hariger (army, spear).

Herlihy, Herlihey (*Ir.*) Descendant of the underlord.

Herman, Hermann (*Eng., Ger., Du.*) Descendant of Herman (army, man).

Hermanson, Hermansen (*Eng., Sw., Dan., Nor.*) The son of Herman (army, man).

Hernandez (*Sp.*) Son of Hernando (journey, venture).

Herndon (*Eng.*) Dweller in a nook, or corner, by a hill.

Hernon (*Ir.*) Grandson of Iarnan, a name of obscure origin.

Herold, Herrold (*Eng.*) Variants of Herald and Harold, q.v.

Herr, Herre (*Ger.*) One who was lord of the manor.

Herrera, Herrero (*Sp.*) The worker in iron, a smith.

Herrick (*Eng.*) Descendant of Hereric (army, rule).

Herring, Hering (*Ger., Eng., Scot.*) Descendant of Hering (son of Here, army); one who fished for, and sold, herring, an important article of food in medieval England; dweller at the sign of the herring.

Herriot, Herriott (*Fr.*) Descendant of little Henry (home ruler).

Herrmann, Herrman, Heerman, Heermann (*Ger.*) One who served in the army; descendant of Hariman (army, man).

Herron, Heron (*Eng.*) Dweller at the sign of the heron.

Hersey (*Eng.*) One who came from Herse (railed place), the name of several hamlets in France.

Hersh, Hershey, Hersch, Herrscher (*Ger.*) Dweller at the sign of the red deer; one with some characteristic of a deer.

Hertel, Hertle (*Fr., Ger.*) Desecendant of little Hart (strong), or of little Hert, a pet form of Hertrich (strong, powerful).

Herter (*Du.*) One who took care of a flock, a herdsman.

Hertz, Herz (*Ger.*) Dweller at the sign of the heart; a courageous man.

Herzberg (*Ger.*) One who came from Herzberg (red-deer mountain), the name of two towns in West Germany.

Herzog (*Ger.*) One who led an army; a duke.

Hess, Hesse (*Ger.*) One who came from Hesse (the hooded people), in Germany.

Hesslich (*Du.*) The ugly person.

Hester (*Ger.*) Dweller at, or near, a young tree, especially a beech tree.

Hetherington (*Eng.*) One who came from Hetherington (village of the dweller on a heath), in Northumberland.

Heuer (*Ger.*) One who tilled a piece of land on which he paid rent; one who mowed hay.

Hewes, Hewson (*Eng.*) The son of Hew, a variant of Hugh (spirit); one who was servant to another.

Hewitt, Hewett, Hewlett (*Eng.*) Descendant of little Hew, a variant of Hugh (spirit).

Heyden (*Eng.*) One who came from Heydon (hay valley), in Cambridgeshire.

Heyman, Heymann (*Ger.*) Descendant of Hagimar (hedged place, famous); variants of Heiman, q.v.

Heyn, Heyne (*Ger.*) Descendant of Heino or Hagano, pet forms of names beginning with Hag (hedged place), as Heinpreht and Haginold.

Heywood (*Eng.*) One who came from Heywood (high or enclosed wood), the name of places in Lancashire and Wiltshire; dweller in, or near, an enclosed wood.

Hibbard, Hibbert, Hibberd (*Eng.*) Descendant of Herbert (army, bright).

Hickenlooper (*Du.*) The battle runner or messenger.

Hickey, Hicklin, Hickok, Hickox (*Eng.*) Descendant of little Hick, a pet form of Richard (rule, hard).

Hickman (*Eng.*) The servant of Hick, a pet form of Richard (rule, hard).

Hicks, Hickson (*Eng.*) The son of Hick, a pet form of Richard (rule, hard); the son of Hicca (courage).

Higbee, Higby, Higbie, Higbe (*Eng.*) One who came from Hyge's settlement.

Higginbotham, Higginbothan, Higginbottom, Higginbothom (*Eng.*) Dweller in, or near, the valley owned by Higgin, q.v.

Higgins, Higgin, Higginson, Higgens, Higgs (*Eng.*) The son of little Higg or Hick, pet forms of Richard (rule, hard).

High (*Eng.*) Dweller on the high place, such as an eminence or hill.

Highsmith, Hysmith (*Eng.*) The tall worker in metals; the smith on the higher place.

Hightower (*Eng.*) Dweller in, or near, the tall tower.

Hildebrand, Hildebrandt, Hildebrant, Hildenbrand, Hilderbrand (*Eng., Ger.*) Descendant of Hildebrand (battle, sword).

Hildreth (*Eng.*) Descendant of Hildefrith (war, peace).

Hill, Hills (*Eng.*) Dweller on, or near, a hill, or on rising ground; one who came from Hill (hill), the name of various places in England.

Hillebrand, Hillenbrand (*Ger.*) Descendant of Hildebrand (battle, sword).

Hiller (*Eng.*) Dweller on, or near, a hill; one who constructed slate roofs.

Hilliard (*Eng.*) Dweller at the hill enclosure; descendant of Hildyard (war, enclosure).

Hillman (*Eng.*) Dweller on, or near, a hill.

Hillson (*Eng.*) The son of Hild (war).

Hillstrom, Hellstrom (*Sw.*) Boulder stream.

Hilton (*Eng.*) One who came from Hilton (hill village), the name of several villages in England.

Himmel, Himmler, Himel (*Ger.*) Heaven or sky.

Himmelblau, Himelblau (*Ger.*) Heaven blue.

Hinchcliffe, Hinchcliff, Hinchliffe, Hinchliff, Hinchsliff (*Eng.*) Dweller near an overhanging cliff.

Hinckley, Hinkley (*Eng.*) One who came from Hinckley (Hynca's homestead), in Leicestershire.

Hindmarch, Hindmarsh (*Eng.*) Dweller on, or near, the low, wet land where deer were found.

Hines, Hinds, Hine, Hindes (*Eng.*) One who was a domestic servant.

Hinkle, Hinkel, Hinkler (*Ger.*) Dweller at the sign of the little chicken; an affectionate name for a friend; descendant of Hinkel, a pet form of Heinrich (home ruler).

Hinton (*Eng.*) One who came from Hinton (homestead on high land, or the monk's homestead), the name of many places in England.

Hintz, Hintze, Hinsch, Hinz, Hinze (*Ger.*) Descendant of Heino (hedged place), a pet form of names beginning with Hag, as Haginold, Heinarad and Haginher.

Hirsch, Hirsh (*Ger.*) Dweller at the sign of the hart; one thought to possess some characteristic of a hart.

Hirschberg (*Ger.*) One who came from Hirschberg (red-deer mountain), the name of two towns in Germany and one in Lower Silesia.

Hirtle (*Ger.*) Descendant of Herto, a pet form of names commencing with Hart (strong), as Hardolt, Hardulf and Hardwin.

Hiscock, Hiscox (*Eng.*) Descendant of little Hick, a pet form of Richard (rule, hard).

Hislop (*Eng.*) Dweller at a high or enclosed land in a marsh where hazel trees grew.

Hitchcock, Hitchcox (*Eng.*) Descendant of little Hitch, a pet form of Richard (rule, hard).

Hitchings, Hitchins, Hitchens, Hitchen (*Eng.*) One who came from Hitchin (the Hicce tribe), in Hertfordshire; the son of little Hitch or Hick, pet forms of Richard (rule, hard).

Hitchman (*Eng.*) The servant of Hitch or Hick, pet forms of Richard (rule, hard).

Hitler, Hittler (*Ger.*) One who supervised saltworks.

Hixson, Hixon (*Eng.*) The son of Hick, a pet form of Richard (rule, hard); one who came from Hixon (Hyht's hill), in Staffordshire.

Hjelm (*Sw.*) Helmet.

Hoadley (*Eng.*) One who came from Hoathly (heather-covered clearing), in Sussex.

Hoar, Hoare (*Eng.*) The gray-haired man.

Hoard (*Eng.*) Keeper of the hoard or treasure; contraction of Howard, q.v.

Hoban, Hobin (*Ir.*) Grandson of Uban, a name of uncertain meaning.

Hobart, Hobert (*Eng.*) Corruption of Hubert (mind, bright).

Hobson, Hobbs (*Eng.*) The son of Hob, a pet form of Robert (fame, bright).

Hoch, Hoche (*Ger.*) The high, or tall, man; descendant of Hoch, a pet form of names beginning with Hoch (high), as Hochbert and Hochmuot.

Hodgdon (*Eng.*) One who came from Hoddesdon (Hod's hill), in Hertfordshire.

Hodges, Hodge, Hodgson (*Wel., Eng.*) Descendant of Hodge, a pet form of Roger (fame, spear).

Hodgkins, Hodgkinson, Hodgkin, Hodgin, Hodgins (*Eng.*) The son of little Hodge, a pet form of Roger (fame, spear).

Hoegh, Hoeh (*Dan.*) Dweller on a spur of land.

Hoekstra (*Du.*) Dweller at the corner place, or on a hook of land.

Hoel, Hoell, Hoelle (*Eng.*) Descendant of Hoel (eminent).

Hoey (*Ir.*) Grandson of Eochaidh (horseman).

Hofbauer (*Ger.*) One who worked a farm.

Hofer, Hoefer, Hoefner (*Ger.*) One who owned or worked a farm; one who came from Hof (farm), in Germany.

Hoff, Hof (*Ger.*) Dweller in a courtyard or fenced-in place; one who came from Hof (farm), in Germany.

Hoffman, Hoffmann, Hofmann, Hofman (*Ger.*) One who worked a large farm either as owner or manager; the farm, or manor, servant.

Hofmeister, Hoffmeister (*Ger.*) The steward or head servant.

Hofstetter, Hostetter (*Ger., Swis.*) One who came from Hofstetter, the name of several villages in Germany and Switzerland.

Hogan (*Ir.*) Grandson of little Og (young).

Hoger (*Du.*) Dweller at the higher place.

Hogg, Hogge, Hoggs (*Eng.*) Dweller at the sign of the hog or young sheep; descendant of Hoga (careful or prudent); a nickname applied to a coarse, self-indulgent, gluttonous or filthy person; descendant of Hodge, a pet form of Roger (fame, spear).

Hoglund (*Sw.*) High grove.

Hojnacki (*Pol.*) Dweller near a pine tree.

Hoke, Hoker (*Eng.*) Dweller near the spur, bend or corner, referring to some natural feature.

Holbrook, Holbrooks (*Eng.*) One who came from Holbrook (stream in a deep ravine), the name of several places in England.

Holcomb, Holcombe, Holcum (*Eng.*) One who came from Holcombe (deep ravine), the name of several places in England.

Holden, Holdener (*Eng.*) One who came from Holden (deep valley), in Yorkshire.

Hole, Holl (*Eng.*) Dweller at the hollow, or low land.

Holic, Holich (*Cz.-Sl.*) One who cut hair, a barber.

Holland, Hollander (*Eng.*) One who came from the Netherlands; dweller on the low land; one who came from Holland (land on, or by, a projecting ridge of land), the name of several places in England.

Holleb, Hollub, Holub (*Ger., Pol.*) Dweller at the sign of the dove; one with dovelike characteristics.

Holliday, Holiday (*Eng.*) Descendant of Halliday or Haliday (name given to one born on Sunday or other holy day).

Hollingsworth (*Eng.*) One from Hollingworth (holly enclosure), the name of places in Cheshire and Lancashire.

Hollins, Hollin (*Eng.*) Dweller near the holly trees.

Hollis (*Eng.*) Dweller at, or near, the holly tree.

Holloway (*Eng.*) One who came from Holloway (hollow or sunken road), in Middlesex.

Holly, Holley, Hollie (*Eng.*) Dweller at, or near, a holly tree.

Holm, Holme (*Dan., Eng., Nor.*) Dweller at, or near, the holly tree; dweller on, or near, the hill; one who came from Holme (island), the name of many places in England; dweller on the small island, or on the spot of dry land in a fen.

Holman, Holmen (*Nor.*) Dweller on the island.

Holmberg (*Sw., Nor.*) River island mountain; dweller near, or on, a hill on the island, or dry land in a fen.

Holmes (*Eng.*) Dweller at, or near, the holly tree, or on a river island, or on, or near, a hill; dweller on a piece of dry land in a fen.

Holmgren (*Sw.*) River island branch.

Holmquist (*Sw.*) River island twig.

Holst, Holste (*Ger.*) Dweller in a forest.

Holt, Holte, Holts (*Eng.*) Dweller by the wood or copse; one who came from Holt (wood), the name of various places in England.

Holton (*Eng.*) One who came from Holton (homestead on a spur of land, or in a remote valley, or by a hollow or belonging to Hola), the name of various places in England, with these different meanings.

Holtz, Holz (*Ger.*) Dweller in, or near, a grove; one who came from Holz or Holzen (grove), in Germany.

Holtzman, Holzman, Holzmann (*Ger.*) One who cut wood in the forest; dweller in the forest.

Holyoke (*Eng.*) Dweller at a sacred oak.

Homan, Homann, Hohmann, Hohman (*Ger.*) The high or tall man; descendant of Homan (high, man).

Homer (*Eng.*) Dweller at the small island or land partially surrounded by streams; dweller on a spot of dry land in a marsh.

Honeywell (*Eng.*) Dweller at, or near, a spring or well where honey was found.

Hong (*Chin.*) From the dynasty of that name.

Hood, Hodder (*Eng.*) One who made head coverings or hoods; one who came from Hood (shelter), the name of places in Devonshire and Yorkshire; descendant of Hood or Hud, a pet form of Richard (rule, hard).

Hoogland, Hooglant (*Du.*) Dweller on the high land.

Hooker, Hooks, Hook (*Eng.*) One who lived near the spur, river bend or corner, referring to some natural feature; one who came from Hook (hook, corner, headland or hills), the name of various places in England.

Hooper, Hoopes, Hoops, Hoper (*Eng.*) One who made hoops, a cooper; one who lived on the hop, a piece of enclosed land in a marsh.

Hooton (*Eng.*) One who came from Hooton (homestead on the spur of a hill), the name of several places in England.

Hoover (*Ger.*) Feudal tenant of a German hide of land (about 120 acres).

Hope (*Eng.*) Dweller on the raised or enclosed land in the midst of a marsh or wasteland; dweller in a small, enclosed valley, especially a smaller one branching out from the main valley; dweller in a hollow among the hills.

Hopkins, Hopkinson, Hopkin (*Wel., Eng.*) The son of little Hob, a variant of Rob, pet forms of Robert (fame, bright).

Hoppe, Hopp (*Eng.*) Descendant of Hop or Hob, pet forms of Robert (fame, bright).

Hopper, Hoppers (*Eng.*) One who danced at fair and festival; one who lived on the raised or enclosed land in the midst of a marsh.

Hopson (*Eng.*) The son of Hop or Hob, pet forms of Robert (fame, bright.)

Horan (*Ir.*) Descendant of the belligerent or warlike one; grandson of little Anradh (warrior or champion); grandson of Odhar (dark gray).

Horder (*Eng.*) One who kept the hoard, a treasurer.

Horn, Horne (*Eng., Ger.*) One who lived near the hornlike projection, probably a projecting hill or spur of land; dweller at a nook or corner.

Hornblower (*Eng.*) One who blows a horn, a trumpeter.

Hornburg, Hornberg, Hornberger (*Ger.*) One who came from Hornburg (mountain fortress), the name of twelve places in Germany.

Horner (*Eng., Ger.*) One who made horn spoons, combs, etc; one who blows a horn, a trumpeter; descendant of Hornher (horn, army).

Hornung, Horning (*Ger.*) Descendant of Horno, a pet form of names beginning with Horn (horn).

Horsley (*Eng.*) One who came from Horsley (pasture for horses), the name of several places in England.

Horton (*Eng.*) One who came from Horton (village on muddy land), the name of various places in England.

Horwath, Horvath (*Hun.*) One who came from Croatia.

Horwich, Horwitch (*Eng.*) One who came from Horwich (gray wych-elms), in Lancashire.

Horwitz, Horowitz, Horvitz (*Cz.-Sl., Rus.*) One who came from Horice or Horitz (mountainous place), in Bohemia; the son of the mountaineer.

Hoskins, Hoskin, Hoskinson, Hoskings, Hosking (*Eng., Wel.*) Descendant of little Os or Hos, pet forms of Osbert, Osgood, Osmund and similar names; sometimes a corruption of Hodgkin, q.v.

Host, Hostler, Hoste, Hoster (*Eng.*) One who kept a public place of lodging, the landlord of an inn.

Hotchkiss, Hotchkins, Hotchkin (*Eng.*) The son of little Hodge, a pet form of Rodger or Roger (fame, spear).

Hotchner (*Scot., Eng.*) One who drove cattle.

Hough (*Eng.*) One who came from Hough (spur of hill), in Cheshire.

Houghton (*Eng.*) One who came from Houghton (homestead on the spur of a hill), the name of various places in England.

Houlihan, Houlahan (*Ir.*) Grandson of little Uallach (proud).

House (*Eng.*) Dweller near, or in, an unusual house, perhaps a religious house or convent; servant in such a house.

Houser, Hooser (*Eng.*) One who made, or dealt in hose, i.e., stockings or socks.

Houston (*Scot.*) One who came from Houston (Hugh's town), in Scotland.

Hovland, Hoveland (*Nor.*) One who came from Hovland (hay land), in Norway.

Howalt (*Ger.*) Descendant of Hugold (spirit, rule).

Howard (*Eng.*) Descendant of Howard (keeper of the swords); a corruption of Hayward, q.v.

Howe, Howes, How (*Eng.*) Descendant of How, a variant of Hugh (spirit); dwellers on, or near, a projecting ridge of land, a promontory; one who came from Howe (hill), the name of places in Norfolk and Yorkshire.

Howell, Howells, Howel (*Eng., Wel.*) Descendant of Howell (eminent); descendant of little How, a variant of Hugh (spirit).

Howie, Howey (*Scot.*) Descendant of little How, a variant of Hugh (spirit).

Howland (*Eng.*) Dweller at, or near, a hillock.

Howley (*Eng.*) One who came from Howle (hill), in Shropshire.

Howorth, Howarth (*Eng.*) One who came from Howarth (hawthorne enclosure), a parish in Lancashire, or from Haworth, in Yorkshire; descendant of Howard (keeper of the swords).

Hoy, Hoye (*Eng., Ir., Chin.*) Dweller at a bluff or hill; grandson of Eochaidh (horseman); sea.

Hoyer, Hoier (*Ger.*) One who makes hay; one who came from Hannover, a city and province in Germany; descendant of Hucger (spirit, spear).

Hoyle (*Eng.*) Dweller in, or near, a hollow, or low land.

Hoyne (*Ir.*) Grandson of Eoghan (wellborn).

Hoyt, Hoyte (*Du., Ir.*) Descendant of Hoyte; grandson of Ud.

Hrdlicka (*Cz.-Sl.*) Dweller at the sign of the dove; an affectionate name for a friend.

Hrncir (*Cz.-Sl.*) One who made earthen utensils, a potter.

Hruby, Hrubec (*Cz.-Sl.*) One with a gruff or low voice.

Hruska (*Cz.-Sl.*) Dweller near a pear tree.

Hubbard, Hubbart (*Eng.*) Descendant of Hubert (spirit, bright).

Hubbell, Hubble (*Eng.*) Descendant of Hubbold or Hubald (mind, bold).

Huber (*Ger.*) Feudal tenant of a German hide of land (about 120 acres).

Hubert, Hubbert, Hubberts (*Eng.*) Descendant of Hubert (mind, bright).

Hubsch (*Ger.*) The handsome man.

Huck (*Fr.*) Descendant of Huc, a pet form of Hugo (spirit).

Huddleston, Huddlestun (*Eng.*) One who came from Huddleston (Huda's homestead), in Yorkshire.

Hudson, Hutson (*Eng.*) The son of Hudde, a pet form of Richard (rule, hard).

Huebner, Hubner (*Ger.*) One who worked a hube, a plot of land of about 120 acres.

Huey (*Eng., Ir.*) Descendant of little Hugh (spirit); variant of Hoey, q.v.

Huff, Huf, Huffer (*Ger., Eng.*) Dweller or worker on a hube, a farm of about 120 acres; dweller on, or by, a bluff or hill or hollow; one who came from Huffen, in Germany.

Huffman (*Ger.*) Worker on a hube, a farm of about 120 acres.

Hufschmidt (*Ger.*) The smith who made shoes.

Huggins (*Eng.*) Descendant of little Hug, a pet form of Hugh (spirit).

Hughes, Hugh (*Wel., Eng.*) The son of Hugh (spirit).

Huguelet (*Fr.*) Descendant of very little Hugues (spirit).

Hull (*Eng.*) An early spelling of Hill, q.v.; one who lived near the Hull (muddy river), a river in Yorkshire; one who came from Hull (hollow), in Cheshire.

Hult (*Sw.*) Copse.

Hultgren (*Sw.*) Copse branch.

Hume, Humes, Hum (*Eng.*) Dweller on a river island or plot of land enclosed by a bend in a stream; dweller near a holly tree.

Hummel, Hummell (*Ger.*) A nickname for an excited person; one who came from Hummel (bumblebee), in Germany; descendant of Hummo or Humbold (Hun, brave).

Humphrey, Humphreys, Humphries, Humphryes, Humphury (*Wel., Eng.*) Descendant of Humphrey (supporter of peace).

Hungerford (*Eng.*) One who came from Hungerford (ford where people starved), in Berkshire.

Hunnewell (*Eng.*) Dweller near a spring or well where honey was found.

Hunt, Hunter, Hunte (*Eng.*) One who hunted game, a huntsman.

Huntington (*Eng.*) One who came from Huntington (hill or place where men hunted), the name of several places in England.

Huntley (*Eng.*) One who came from Huntley (wood of the huntsmen), in Gloucestershire.

Hurd, Hird (*Eng.*) One who tended domestic animals.

Hurlburt, Hurlbert, Hurlbut, Hurlbutt (*Eng.*) Descendant of Hurlbert (army, bright); one proficient with a hurlebatte in the medieval game of hurling; one who used a hurlbat in combat.

Hurley (*Eng.*) One who came from Hurley (homestead in a corner), the name of places in Berkshire and Warwickshire.

Hurst (*Eng.*) One who lived by, or in, the wood or copse, or on the knoll or hillock.

Hurt (*Eng.*) Dweller at the sign of the hart or stag, the adult male of the red deer; one thought to have some characteristic of the hart or stag.

Hurwitz, Hurwich, Hurvitz (*Cz.-Sl.*) One who came from Horovice, Horice or Horitz (mountainous place), in Bohemia; the son of the mountaineer.

Husak (*Cz.-Sl.*) One who lived at the sign of the gander; one with the characteristics of a gander.

Husband, Husbands (*Eng.*) One who owned and cultivated a husbandland (about 26 acres), a middle class of English villagers who lived in a house instead of a cote; one who tilled the soil, a farmer.

Huss, Hus, Husch, Huscher (*Ger.*) Dweller at the sign of the goose; one with the qualities of a goose; descendant of Huss, a pet form of Hugo (spirit).

Hussey (*Eng., Scot.*) One who wore hose; one who came from Houssay (holly grove), in Normandy, or from Housay, in Scotland.

Huston (*Scot.*) A variant of Houston, q.v.

Hutchins, Hutchings, Hutchens (*Eng.*) Descendant of little Hutch, a pet form of Hugh (spirit).

Hutchinson, Hutchison, Hutcherson, Hutcheson (*Eng., Scot.*) The son of little Hutch, a pet form of Hugh (spirit).

Huth (*Eng.*) Dweller at the landing place or harbor.

Hutter, Huttner, Hutten, Huttel (*Ger.*) One who came from Hutten (small house), in Germany; dweller in a cottage.

Hutton (*Eng.*) One who came from Hutton (village on the spur of a hill), the name of many places in England.

Hyatt, Hiatt (*Eng.*) Dweller at the high gate.

Hyde (*Eng.*) One who lived on a homestead consisting of one hide, i.e., as much land as could be tilled with one plow.

Hyder (*Eng.*) One who prepared hides for tanning.

Hyland, Hylander (*Eng.*) Dweller at the high land or field.

Hyman, Hymen (*Heb.*) Descendant of Hyam (life).

Hynes, Hyne, Hynds (*Eng.*) One who worked as a domestic servant.

I (*Chin.*) The first Chinese syllable of a Manchu's name, which serves as the family name.

Ianson (*Scot.*) The son of Ian, Gaelic form of John (gracious gift of Jehovah).

Ickes, Icke (*Eng.*) Descendant of Hick, a pet form of Richard (rule, hard).

Idris (*Wel.*) Descendant of Idris (ardent lord).

Illingsworth, Illingworth (*Eng.*) One who came from Illingworth (homestead of Illa's people), in Yorkshire.

Illsley, Ilsley (*Eng.*) One who came from Ilsley (Hild's meadow), in Berkshire.

Imhof (*Ger.*) Dweller in the court.

Ing, Inge (*Eng.*) Dweller at, or near, a swampy meadow.

Ingalls (*Eng.*) Descendant of Ingeld (Ing's tribute); one who came from Ingol (Inga's valley), in Lancashire.

Ingersoll, Ingersol (*Eng.*) One who came from Inkersall (the monks' field), in Derbyshire.

Ingham (*Eng.*) One who came from Ingham (Inga's estate), the name of several places in England.

Inglis, Ingles, Ingle (*Scot.*) One who came from England, an Englishman.

Ingram, Ingraham (*Eng.*) Descendant of Ingram (Ing's raven—Ing was a mythical Scandinavian hero); one who came from Ingram (grassland enclosure), in Northumberland.

Inlander (*Eng.*) One who dwelt by, or worked on, the land belonging to the lord of the manor; one who came from the interior to dwell by the sea.

Inman, Inmon (*Eng.*) One who kept a lodginghouse or inn.

Innes, Innis, Inniss (*Scot.*) One who came from the barony of Innes (island), in the parish of Urquhart, Moray.

Ippolito (*It.*) Descendant of Ippolito (he who sets horses free).

Iredell, Iredale (*Eng.*) One who came from Airedale (valley of the Aire River), in Yorkshire.

Ireland (*Eng.*) One who came to England from Ireland.

Irish (*Eng.*) One who came from Ireland.

Irons (*Eng., Scot.*) One who came from Airaines (brass), in France.

Irvine, Irving, Irvin (*Scot.*) One who came from Irvine or Irving (green river), the names of several villages in Scotland.

Irwin (*Eng., Scot.*) Descendant of Erewine (sea friend); one who came from Irvine (green river), in Ayrshire.

Isaacson, Isaac, Isaacs, Isacson, Isakson (*Eng.*) The son of Isaac (he who laughs).

Isbell, Isabell, Isabel (*Eng.*) Descendant of Isabel (oath to Baal); an English variant of Elizabeth (oath of God).

Isenberg (*Ger.*) One who came from Eisenberg (iron mountain), the name of two towns in Germany.

Isham (*Eng.*) One who came from Isham (village on the Ise River), in Northamptonshire.

Israel, Israelson (*Heb.*) Descendant of Israel (champion of God).

Ivanov, Ivan (*Rus., Bulg.*) The son of Ivan (gracious gift of Jehovah).

Ivers (*Eng.*) Descendant of Iver (archer).

Iversen, Iverson, Ivarson (*Dan., Sw., Nor.*) The son of Iver (archer).

Ivert (*Eng.*) One who came from Iver (edge or steep slope), in Buckinghamshire.

Ivory, Ivery, Ivry (*Eng.*) One who came from Ivry or Ivory, in Normandy; descendant of Ivor or Ivory (archer).

Ivy, Ivie, Ives, Ivey (*Eng.*) Descendant of Ivo (yew); one who came from St. Ives, the name of several places in England.

Izzo, Izzi (*It.*) A nickname given to one thought to possess some of the characteristics of a snail; dweller near a holm oak.

Jablonski (*Pol.*) One who lived near an apple tree.

Jachim (*Eng., Ger.*) Descendant of Jachim or Joachim (may Jehovah exalt).

Jack (*Scot.*) Descendant of Jack, a pet form of John (gracious gift of Jehovah).

Jackman (*Eng.*) The servant of Jack.

Jackson, Jaxon (*Eng.*) The son of Jack, a pet form of John (gracious gift of Jehovah).

Jacob (*Ger.*) Descendant of Jacobus (the supplanter).

Jacobi, Jacoby (*Fr., Ger.*) Descendant of Jacob (the supplanter).

Jacobson, Jacobs, Jacobsen, Jacob (*Eng., Wel., Dan., Sw.*) The son of Jacob (the supplanter).

Jacques, Jaques (*Fr.*) Descendant of Jacques (the supplanter).

Jaeger, Jager (*Ger.*) One who hunted for game, a huntsman.

Jaffe, Jaffee, Jaffey (*Heb.*) Descendant of Jaffe, a pet form of Japheth (increase); variants of Joffe, q.v.

Jahn (*Sw.*) Descendant of Jahn (gracious gift of Jehovah).

Jahnke, Janicke (*Ger.*) Descendant of little Jahn, a pet form of Johannes (gracious gift of Jehovah).

Jakob (*Ger.*) Descendant of Jakob (the supplanter).

Jakobi, Jakoby (*Ger.*) Descendant of Jakob (the supplanter). Scholars sometimes added the Latin ending *-i*.

Jakobsen (*Dan.*) The son of Jakob (the supplanter).

Jakubowski (*Pol.*) The son of Jakob (the supplanter).

James (*Wel., Eng.*) Descendant of James, Old French form of Jacob (the supplanter).

Jamison, Jameson, Jamieson, Jamie, Jemison (*Scot.*) The son of Jamie, Scotch pet form of James (the supplanter).

Jana, Janas (*Cz.-Sl.*) Descendant of John (gracious gift of Jehovah).

Janda (*Cz.-Sl.*) Descendant of Yan (gracious gift of Jehovah).

Janes, Jaynes (*Eng.*) Descendant of Jan, a form of John (gracious gift of Jehovah).

Janicki, Janicke (*Pol.*) Descendant of Jan (gracious gift of Jehovah).

Janik (*Pol.*) Descendant of little Jan (gracious gift of Jehovah).

Janis (*Lith.*) Descendant of Jan (gracious gift of Jehovah).

Janisch, Janish, Janitch, Janush, Janusch (*Ger., Cz.-Sl.*) Descendant of little Jan, a pet form of Johannes (gracious gift of Jehovah).

Janiszewski (*Pol.*) One who came from Janiszew(o) (Jan's place), in Poland.

Janke, Janicke, Jankel (*Ger.*) Descendant of little Jan, a pet form of Johannes (gracious gift of Jehovah).

Jankowski, Janowski (*Pol.*) The son of Jan (gracious gift of Jehovah).

Janosfi (*Hun.*) The son of John (gracious gift of Jehovah).

Janowicz, Janowiez, Janczyk (*Pol.*) The son of John (gracious gift of Jehovah).

Jansen, Janson, Jansson, Janssen, Jans, Janse (*Du., Dan., Nor., Sw.*) The son of Jan, Dutch and Scandinavian form of John (gracious gift of Jehovah).

Jantzen, Janzen (*Du.*) The son of Jan (gracious gift of Jehovah).

Janus, Janusz (*Pol.*) A follower of Janus (the ancient Roman deity with two opposite faces).

Jardine, Jarden, Jardin (*Scot., Fr.*) Dweller at, or near, a garden.

Jarecki (*Pol.*) The lord of the village of Jarek, in Poland; one who came from Jarek.

Jaros, Jarosz (*Pol., Ukr.*) Descendant of Jaros (young).

Jarrell, Jarrells (*Eng.*) Descendant of Jarrold, a variant of Gerald (spear, firm).

Jarrett, Jarratt (*Eng.*) Descendant of Gerard (spear, firm).

Jarvi, Jarvinen (*Finn.*) Dweller at, or near, a lake.

Jarvis (*Eng.*) Descendant of Gervais or Gervase (spear, servant).

Jasinski (*Pol.*) Descendant of little Jas, a pet form of Jan (gracious gift of Jehovah).

Jason, Jasin (*Eng.*) Descendant of Jason (healer).

Jasper, Jasperson (*Eng.*) Descendant of Jasper (master of the treasure). *See* Kaspar.

Jaworski (*Pol.*) One who came from Jaworow (maple tree), in Poland.

Jay, Jaye (*Eng.*) One who talked incessantly, or was gaily dressed, after the jay; dweller at the sign of the jay.

Jefferson, Jeffers (*Eng.*) The son of Geoffrey or Jeffrey (God's peace).

Jeffries, Jeffrey, Jeffery, Jefferies (*Eng.*) Descendant of Geoffrey or Jeffrey (God's peace).

Jenkins, Jenkinson, Jenks (*Wel., Scot., Eng.*) The son of little Jen or Jenk, pet variants of John (gracious gift of Jehovah).

Jenner (*Scot.*) One who operated an engine of war (an aphetic form of "engineer").

Jennings (*Eng.*) Descendant of Jen, a pet variant of John (gracious gift of Jehovah).

Jennison, Jenison (*Eng.*) The son of Jenny, a pet form of the French Jean (gracious gift of Jehovah).

Jensen, Jenssen, Jenson, Jenzen (*Dan., Nor.*) The son of Jens, a variant of John (gracious gift of Jehovah).

Jepsen, Jeppesen, Jepson (*Dan., Nor.*) The son of Jep, a pet form of Jacob (the supplanter).

Jeremiah (*Wel.*) Descendant of Jeremiah (exalted of Jehovah).

Jerman, Jarman (*Eng.*) One who came from Germany; descendant of German (a German); descendant of Gereman (spear, man).

Jerome (*Eng.*) Descendant of Jerome (holy name).

Jeske, Jeschke, Jeschek (*Ger., Cz.-Sl.*) Descendant of little Jesch, a pet form of Johannes (gracious gift of Jehovah); one with the characteristics of a hedgehog.

Jesse, Jess, Jessee, Jessie (*Eng.*) Descendant of Jesse (Jehovah is).

Jessen (*Dan.*) The son of Jesse, a pet form of Johan (gracious gift of Jehovah).

Jessup, Jessop, Jessopp (*Eng.*) Descendant of Joseph (He shall add).

Jewell (*Eng.*) Descendant of Jewell or Joel (Jehovah is God).

Jewett (*Eng.*) Descendant of little Jew, a pet form of Julian (downy-bearded or youthful).

Jimenez (*Sp.*) Descendant of the house or family of Simon (gracious hearing).

Jindra (*Cz.-Sl.*) Descendant of Jindrich (ruler of the home).

Jirik (*Cz.-Sl.*) Descendant of little Jiri (farmer).

Job, Jobe (*Eng.*) Descendant of Job (persecuted).

Joffe, Joffee (*Heb.*) The handsome or beautiful person; variants of Jaffe, q.v.

Joffre, Joffrey, Jofre (*Fr.*) Descendant of Geoffray or Godefroi (God's peace).

Johannes, Johann (*Ger.*) Descendant of Johannes or Johann (gracious gift of Jehovah).

Johanson, Johansen, Johannsen, Johansson (*Sw., Dan.*) The son of Johan (gracious gift of Jehovah).

Johns, John (*Wel., Eng.*) Descendant of John (gracious gift of Jehovah).

Johnson, Johnsen, Johnsson (*Eng., Dan,. Nor., Sw.*) The son of John (gracious gift of Jehovah).

Johnston, Johnstone (*Scot.*) The man from Johnston (John's manor), in Dumfriesshire; also confused with Johnson, q.v.

Joiner (*Eng.*) One who worked with wood, a carpenter.

Joki (*Finn.*) Dweller near a river.

Jolly, Jolley, Jolie, Joly, Jollie (*Fr.*) One who was agreeable or pleasant.

Jones, Jonas (*Wel., Eng.*) The son of Jone, the Welsh pronunciation of John (gracious gift of Jehovah).

Jonikas, Jonynas (*Lith.*) Descendant of little Jon (gracious gift of Jehovah).

Jonsson (*Sw.*) The son of Jon (gracious gift of Jehovah).

Joost, Joos (*Du.*) Descendant of Joost or Just (the just).

Jordan, Jorden, Jourdain, Jordon (*Eng., Fr.*) Descendant of Jordan or Jourdain (flowing down), a personal name sometimes given to one who was baptized with holy water from the River Jordan.

Jorgensen, Jorgenson (*Dan., Nor.*) The son of Jorgen (farmer).

Joseph, Josephson, Josephs (*Eng.*) Descendant or son of Joseph (He shall add).

Joslyn, Joslin, Jocelyn, Joslun, Josslin, Josselyn (*Eng.*) Descendant of Jocelyn or Joscelin (the just).

Jost (*Ger.*) Descendant of Jodocus (fighter), or of Justinus (the just).

Joy, Joye (*Eng., Ir.*) Descendant of Joy (joyful); one given to exhibitions of happiness.

Joyce (*Eng., Ir.*) Descendant of Joyce (joyful), a masculine name in medieval times.

Joyner (*Eng.*) One who worked with wood, a carpenter.

Jozwiak (*Pol.*) The son of Jozwa (He shall add).

Judd, Jude, Jud (*Eng.*) Descendant of Jude or Judah (confession); descendant of Jud, a pet form of Jordan (flowing down).

Judge (*Eng., Ir.*) One who occupied the office of judge; a translation of the Irish Brehon, with the same meaning.

Judkins (*Eng.*) The son of little Jud, a pet form of Jordan (flowing down), or of Jud or Jude (confession).

Judson (*Eng.*) The son of Jud. *See* Judd.

Julian, Julien, Julius (*Eng.*) Descendant of Julian (downy-bearded or youthful).

Jung, Junge (*Ger.*) One who is younger than another with whom he is associated.

Jungblut, Jungbluth, Jungblud (*Ger.*) The young man or youth.

Jungmann, Jungman (*Ger.*) The young servant.

Jurek (*Pol.*) Dweller at, or on, a hill.

Jurgens, Jurgen (*Du.*) Descendant of Jurgen (farmer).

Jurgensen, Jurgenson (*Dan.*) The son of Jurgen (farmer).

Just (*Eng.*) The fair-dealing or righteous person; descendant of Just, a pet form of Justus and Justin (the just).

Justice, Justus, Justis (*Eng.*) Descendant of Justus (the just); one who performed the functions of a judicial officer, a judge.

Justin, Justen, Justyn (*Eng.*) Descendant of Justin (the just).

Kabat (*Pol.*) One who made and sold overcoats; one who wore an unusual overcoat.

Kaczmarek (*Pol.*) The son of a bartender.

Kadlec (*Cz.-Sl.*) Descendant of Karlec, a pet form of Karl (man); a worker or day laborer.

Kadow (*Pol., Ukr., Rus.*) One who made and sold barrels, a cooper.

Kaebisch, Kabisch (*Ger.*) The feeble, languid man.

Kafka (*Cz.-Sl.*) One who lived at the sign of a bird.

Kagan, Kagen (*Pol., Rus.*) The rabbi or teacher.

Kaganovich, Kaganoff (*Rus.*) The son of the rabbi or priest.

Kahn, Kahne, Kahan, Kahane (*Ger.*) Descendant of Cagano, a pet form of names commencing with Gegen (against), as Gaganhard and Geginheri; German variants of Cohen, q.v.; dweller at the sign of the boat; one who owned or operated a boat.

Kaiser, Kayser, Keyser, Kyser (*Ger.*) Descendent of Caesar, i.e., emperor; one who took that part in the Purim plays.

Kalas, Kallas (*Gr., Pol.*) One who coated the inside of pots and pans; one who came from Kalisz, a city in Poland.

Kalata, Kaleta, Kalita (*Pol., Rus., Ukr.*) Dweller in a corner or pocket.

Kalina (*Rus., Pol., Ukr.*) Dweller at, or near, a guelder-rose or snowball tree.

Kalinowski (*Pol.*) One who came from Kalinow(o) (guelder-rose or snowball), in Poland.

Kalish (*Pol.*) One who came from Kalisz, in Poland.

Kallen (*Ger.*) Dweller at the sign of the cock.

Kallio (*Finn.*) Dweller near a rock or cliff.

Kalvaitis (*Lith.*) The son of the smith, or worker in metals.

Kamen (*Pol., Rus., Ukr.*) Dweller at, or near, a stone, a boundary mark.

Kamin (*Ukr., Rus.*) One who lived in a hut with a fireplace; dweller at, or near, a stone, a boundary mark.

Kaminski, Kaminsky (*Pol., Rus.*) Dweller near a stone or boundary mark.

Kamm (*Ger.*) Dweller on the ridge or crest of a mountain.

Kammerer, Kamerer (*Ger.*) A superintendent or overseer.

Kamp, Kampf, Kampe, Kamps (*Eng., Ger.*) The warrior or soldier; also an athlete or wrestler.

Kane, Kahane (*Ir.*) Descendant of the warrior; grandson of Cathan (warrior).

Kangas (*Finn.*) Dweller in, or near, a heath or moor.

Kania (*Pol., Ukr.*) Dweller at the sign of the hawk; one with the qualities of a hawk.

Kann, Kanne (*Ger.*) Dweller at the sign of the jug, sometimes carved on doors of homes of Levites since it is the duty of the Levites to pour water over the hands of the priests before they bless the congregation.

Kanter, Kantor (*Ger.*) The soloist who sang liturgical music in the synagogue.

Kaplan, Kaplin, Kaplon (*Ger., Pol.*) Descendant of the chaplain or high priest.

Kapp, Kappe (*Ger.*) Descendant of Kapp, a pet form of Kaspar (treasure); one who made hooded cloaks or mantles; dweller at the sign of the cap.

Kappel, Kapell, Kappeler (*Ger., Hun.*) One who came from Kapelle (chapel), in Germany; dweller near a chapel.

Kapustka (*Pol.*) The cabbage head, a term of contempt for a stupid person.

Karas, Karras (*Gr.*) One with a swarthy complexion.

Karczewski (*Pol.*) Dweller at, or near, an unusual stump.

Karel, Karels (*Du.*) Descendant of Karel (man).

Karl, Karle (*Eng., Ger.*) The husbandman or rustic; descendant of Karl (man); one who came from Karl (man), in Germany.

Karlin, Karlinsky (*Rus.*) Descendant of little Karl (man).

Karlson, Karlsen, Karlsson (*Sw.*) The son of Karl (man).

Karner (*Ger.*) One who drove a cart, a carter; dweller near a charnel house.

Karp (*Du.*) Dweller at the sign of the carp.

Karpenstein (*Swis.*) One who carves or chisels inscriptions on stone.

Karr, Karre (*Ir.*) Grandson of Carra (spear).

Karson (*Sw.*) The son of Karl (man).

Kasper, Kaspar (*Ger.*) Descendant of Kaspar or Casper (master of the treasure), the traditional name of one of the Wise Men who went to Bethlehem to worship the infant Jesus.

Kasprzyk (*Pol.*) The son of Kasper (treasure).

Kass, Kase, Kasch, Kaese (*Ger.*) Descendant of Kass, a pet form of Cazo; one with the characteristics of a blackbird.

Kassel (*Ger.*) One who came from Kassel, in Prussia.

Kastner, Kaster, Kasten, Kassner (*Ger., Du.*) The manager of a granary; one who made cabinets.

Katz (*Heb.*) An abbreviation of *kohen tzedek,* priest of righteousness, therefore, a priest.

Katzenberg, Katzenberger (*Ger.*) One who came from Katzenberg (cats' mountain).

Katzman, Katzmann (*Ger.*) Descendant of Cazo; the priest. *See* Katz.

Kaufman, Kaufmann, Kauffman, Kauffmann (*Ger.*) The merchant or tradesman.

Kavanaugh, Kavanagh (*Ir.*) Grandson of little Caomh (comely) or Caomhan, the names of fifteen Irish saints.

Kawa (*Pol., Ukr.*) One who dealt in coffee.

Kay, Kaye (*Eng., Scot.*) Descendant of Gaius (rejoice); dweller near the wharf or boat landing place.

Kazmierczak (*Pol.*) The son of Kazimierz (show forth peace).

Keane, Kean (*Ir., Eng.*) Descendant of the warrior; variant of Keen, q.v.

Kearney (*Ir.*) Grandson of Carney (victorious in battle).

Kearns, Kerns, Kernes (*Ir.*) Descendant of the little black one.

Keating, Keatinge (*Ir.*) Descendant of the reasonable or urbane person; grandson of Ceatfhaidh (sense).

Keaton (*Eng.*) One who came from Ketton (estate of the Kesteven people), in Rutland.

Keats, Keets, Keate (*Eng.*) Descendant of Keat (lively); or of Ket, an abbreviation of one of the names beginning with Ketil (cauldron); descendant of Kit, a pet form of Christopher (Christbearer).

Keck, Kecker (*Ger.*) One who is full of life, brave.

Keddy, Keddie, Keady (*Scot.*) The son of Adie, a pet form of Adam (red earth).

Keefe, Keeffe (*Ir.*) Grandson of Caomh (beautiful, gentle).

Keegan (*Ir.*) The son of little Aodh (fire).

Keeler (*Eng.*) One who worked on a keel or longboat, a seaman or bargeman.

Keeley, Keely, Kealy, Kealey (*Ir.*) Descendant of the slender man; grandson of Caollaidhe, an ancient Irish name of uncertain meaning.

Keen, Keene (*Eng., Ir.*) The quick, sharp person; grandson of Cathan, a pet form of some name commencing with Cath, as Cathair or Cathal.

Keenan (*Ir.*) Grandson of little Cian (ancient).

Keeney (*Ir.*) Grandson of Cianach (ancient).

Kefauver (*Ger.*) One who made and sold vats.

Kehoe, Keho (*Ir.*) The horseman or jockey.

Keil (*Ger.*) One who is supercilious or wanton; dweller on, or near, a wedge-shaped piece of land.

Keith (*Scot.*) One who lived on the lands of Keith (wood), in East Lothian.

Kelleher, Kelliher, Keleher, Kellegher (*Ir.*) Grandson of Ceiteachar (spouse-loving).

Keller, Kellner (*Fr., Eng., Ger.*) One employed in a storeroom, particularly a food storage place; one who made or sold cauls or kells, a cap or hairnet for women.

Kellogg, Kellock (*Eng.*) One who slaughtered hogs.

Kelly, Kelley (*Ir.*) Grandson of Ceallach (contention).

Kelsey, Kelsie (*Eng.*) One who came from Kelsey (Cenel's island or high land in a marsh), in Lincolnshire.

Kelso (*Scot.*) One who came from Kelso (chalk height), in Roxburghshire.

Kemble (*Eng.*) One who came from Kemble (from Camulos, the name of a Celtic god), in Gloucestershire.

Kemnitz, Kemnitzer (*Ger.*) One who came from Kemnitz (stone), the name of various places in Germany.

Kemp, Kempf, Kempfer, Kemph (*Eng., Ger.*) The warrior or soldier; an athlete or wrestler; dweller in an enclosure belonging to one person.

Kemper (*Eng.*) A soldier or warrior; one who combed wool or flax.

Kempton (*Eng.*) One who came from Kempton (Cempa's homestead), in Shropshire.

Kendall (*Eng.*) One who came from Kendal (valley of the Kent River), in Westmorland.

Kendrick, Kendricks (*Eng.*) Descendant of Kenrick (royal, rule).

Kendzior, Kendziora, Kendzierski (*Pol.*) One who had curly hair.

Kennard (*Eng.*) Descendant of Cenhard (bold, strong), or of Cynehard (royal, strong).

Kennedy (*Scot.*) One with an ugly or misshapen head; descendant of Kennedy (head armor).

Kennelly, Kenneally, Kenealy (*Ir.*) Grandson of Ceannfhaoladh (wolf head, or learned man).

Kenney, Kenny (*Ir.*) Grandson of Cionaodh (fire sprung).

Kenniston, Kennison (*Eng.*) One who came from Kensington (homestead of Cynesige's people), in Middlesex; the son of Kenny (ardent love).

Kenrick (*Eng.*) Descendant of Cenric or Kenric (bold, ruler), or of Cynric (royal, ruler).

Kent (*Eng.*) One who came from the county of Kent (open country), in the southeast corner of England.

Kenyon, Kennon (*Eng., Ir.*) One who came from Kenyon (Enion's mound), in Lancashire; the son of Coinin (rabbit), or of Finghin (fair offspring).

Keough, Keogh (*Ir.*) The son of Eochaidh (horseman).

Kerber (*Ger.*) One who came from Korb (basket), in Germany.

Kerman (*Eng.*) Dweller at, or near, a pond or bog.

Kern, Kerns (*Ger., Ir.*) Descendant of Kern, a pet form of Gernwin (desire, friend); one who came from Kern (kernel), in Germany; grandson of Ceirin (little, black one).

Kernan, Kiernan (*Ir.*) Son of the lord or owner of the village.

Kerner (*Ger.*) One who drives a cart, a carter; one who grinds grain, a miller; one who came from Kern (kernel), in Germany.

Kerr (*Eng., Ir.*) Dweller at, or near, a marsh, especially one grown up with low bushes; dweller near a fort.

Kerrigan (*Ir.*) Grandson of little Ciar (black).

Kersey (*Eng.*) One who came from Kersey (cress island), in Suffolk.

Kershaw (*Eng.*) Dweller at, or near, the copse on the marsh, i.e., a boggy wood.

Kersten, Kerstein, Kersting (*Ger.*) Descendant of Christianus (follower of Christ).

Kerwin, Kirwan (*Ir.*) One with a dark complexion.

Kessel, Kessell, Kesselman (*Ger., Eng.*) One who made and sold kettles; dweller in, or near, a fort or castle; one who came from Kessel (castle), the name of many places in Germany.

Kessler, Kestler, Kesseler (*Ger.*) One who made kettles; one who came from Kessel (castle), the name of many places in Germany.

Ketchum, Ketcham (*Eng.*) One who came from Caecca's homestead.

Kettering (*Eng.*) One who came from Kettering (estate of Cytringas), in Northamptonshire.

Kettle, Kettles, Ketill (*Ice.*) Descendant of Ketill (cauldron).

Kettunen (*Finn.*) One who lived at the sign of the fox; one with foxlike qualities.

Keyes, Keys, Key (*Scot.*) Dweller near the wharf or boat landing place.

Khokhlov (*Rus.*) The man from Ukraine, a slightly contemptuous term.

Khrushchev (*Rus.*) The son of the cockchafer, a large beetle; one with some characteristic of a large beetle.

Kibbee, Kibbe, Kibby (*Eng.*) One who came from Keadby (Keti's homestead), in Lincolnshire, or from Kearby (Kaeri's homestead), in Yorkshire.

Kidd, Kidde (*Eng., Scot.*) Dweller at the sign of the young goat; descendant of Kid, a pet form of Christopher (Christ-bearer).

Kidder (*Eng.*) One who tends or trains hawks for hunting.

Kiefer, Keefer, Kieffer (*Ger.*) One who made and sold casks, a cooper; one who had charge of the wine cellar.

Kiely (*Ir.*) Grandson of Cadhla (beautiful or graceful).

Kieran, Kearon (*Ir.*) Grandson of Kieran (little, black one), the name of fifteen Irish saints.

Kilborn, Kilbourn, Kilbourne, Kilburn, Kilborne (*Eng.*) One who came from Kilbourne or Kilburn (stream by a kiln), the names of several places in England.

Kilbride, Kirkbride (*Scot., Ir.*) One who came from Kilbride (church of St. Brigit), in Lanarkshire; the son of the servant or devotee of St. Bridgid.

Kilby (*Eng.*) One who came from Kilby (Cilda's homestead), in Leicestershire.

Kilcoyne (*Ir.*) The son of the gentle youth.

Kilduff (*Ir.*) The son of the black youth.

Kiley (*Ir.*) Grandson of Cadhla (beautiful or graceful).

Kilgallen, Kilgallon (*Ir.*) The son of the servant of St. Caillin.

Kilgore, Kilgour, Killgore (*Ir.*) Dweller in the wood where goats are kept; one who tended goats.

Kilham, Killam, Killham (*Eng.*) One who came from Kilham (kiln for drying brick), the name of places in Northumberland and Yorkshire.

Killeen, Killen (*Ir.*) Grandson of Cillin, a pet form of Ceallach (war).

Killelea, Killilea (*Ir.*) The son of the gray youth.

Killian, Kilian, Killion (*Ir.*) Grandson of Cillin or Cillean, pet forms of Ceallach (war).

Killkelly (*Ir.*) The son of the devotee of St. Ceallach (war or strife), the name of three Irish saints.

Kilpatrick (*Ir.*) Son of the servant of St. Patrick.

Kilroy (*Ir.*) Son of the red-haired man.

Kimball, Kimble, Kimbel, Kimbell (*Eng.*) One who came from Kimble (royal hill), in Buckinghamshire.

Kimbrough (*Eng.*) Descendant of Cyneburh (royal stronghold).

Kimmel, Kimmich, Kimmell (*Ger.*) One who produced and sold caraway seeds.

Kimmerle (*Ger.*) Descendant of little Khunemar (race, famous); descendant of little Gundemar (war, famous).

Kincaid, Kinkaid, Kinkade, Kinkead, Kincaide (*Scot.*) One who came from Kincaid (head of the pass), in Stirlingshire.

King (*Eng.*) One who played the part of the king in a play or pageant; one connected in some way with the king's household.

Kingsbury, Kingsberry, Kingsbery (*Eng.*) One who came from Kingsbury (the king's fort), the name of several places in England.

Kingsley, Kinsley (*Eng.*) One who came from Kingsley (the king's wood), the name of several places in England.

Kingston (*Eng.*) One who came from Kingston (the king's manor), the name of many places in England.

Kinney, Kinnie (*Ir.*) Grandson of Cionaodh (fire sprung).

Kinsella (*Ir.*) Descendant of the Cinnsealaigh (head stained), a clan in Wexford, Ireland.

Kinsey (*Eng.*) Descendant of Cynesige (royal victory); one who came from Kilnsey (Cynel's island), in Yorkshire, or from Kingsley (the king's wood), the name of several places in England.

Kinsley (*Eng.*) One who came from Kinsley (Cyne's meadow), in Yorkshire.

Kinzie (*Eng.*) Variant of Kinsey, q.v.

Kipke (*Ger.*) Descendant of little Kippo, a pet form of names beginning with Geben (gift), as Gebahard, Giperich and Gebald.

Kipp, Kippes (*Ger.*) Dweller at the peak of the hill or mountain; descendant of Kippo, a pet form of names beginning with Geben (gift), as Gebahard, Giperich and Gebald.

Kirby, Kirkby (*Eng.*) One who came from Kirby or Kirkby (village with a church), the names of various places in England.

Kirchhoff, Kirchoff (*Ger.*) Dweller at, or near, a churchyard; one who came from Kirchhofen (churchyard), in Germany.

Kirchner, Kircher (*Ger.*) A minor official of a church who had charge of the sacristy and its contents.

Kirk, Kirke (*Scot.*) Dweller near a church.

Kirkland (*Scot.*) Dweller on, or near, the land of the church.

Kirkpatrick (*Scot.*) One who came from Kirkpatrick (church of St. Patrick), the name of several places in Scotland.

Kirkwood (*Scot.*) Dweller in, or near, the wood belonging to the church.

Kirsch, Kirsh (*Ger.*) One who grew and sold cherries; dweller at the sign of the cherry; one who came from Kirsch (cherry place), in Germany.

Kirschbaum, Kirschenbaum, Kirshenbaum, Kirshbaum (*Ger.*) Dweller at, or near, a cherry tree.

Kirschner, Kirshner (*Ger.*) One who prepared skins, a furrier.

Kiss (*Hun.*) The small man.

Kissane (*Ir.*) Grandson of Casan (little, curly one).

Kissel (*Ger.*) Descendant of little Giso, a pet form of names beginning with Geisel (staff), as Gisher, Gisemar and Gisulf.

Kisser (*Eng.*) One who made and sold leg armor.

Kistler, Kistner (*Ger.*) One who made boxes.

Kitchen, Kitching, Kitchener (*Eng.*) One employed in a kitchen, especially one in charge of the kitchen in a monastery.

Kite (*Eng.*) Dweller at the sign of the kite or hawk.

Kitterman (*Ger.*) One who came from Gitter (railing), in Germany; one who cemented things.

Kittner, Kittnar (*Ger.*) One who came from Kutten, in Saxony.

Kitto, Kittoe (*Ir., Ger.*) The left-handed man; descendant of Kitto, a pet form of Christianus (follower of Christ).

Kittridge, Kittredge (*Scot.*) The son of Sitreac or Sitrig (true victory).

Kivi (*Finn.*) From residence near a stone.

Kizenberger (*Ger.*) One who came from Kitzeberg or Kinzenberg, in Germany.

Klass, Klaas (*Du.*) Descendant of Nicolaas (people's victory).

Klaus (*Ger.*) Descendant of Klaus, pet form of Nicolaus (people's victory).

Klausner, Klauser (*Ger.*) One who came from Klaus, in Germany; dweller near a sluice or floodgate; one who acted as rabbi of a conventicle.

Klecka (*Pol., Rus.*) One who came from Kleck (house), in Byelorussia, or from Klecko (house), in Poland; dweller near the Kleca River in Byelorussia.

Kleiman, Kleimann (*Ger.*) Dweller on clay ground; one who came from Klei (clay), the name of various places in Germany.

Klein, Kline, Kleine (*Ger.*) The small man; the neat or nice mean.

Kleinschmidt, Kleinsmith (*Ger.*) One who made small metal objects, such as locks and nails; the small worker in metals.

Klemm, Klemme, Klemmer (*Ger.*) Descendant of Klem, a pet form of Clemens (merciful); dweller at, or near, a narrow passage or steep slope.

Klima (*Pol., Ukr., Cz.-Sl.*) Descendant of Klim, a pet form of Klemens (merciful).

Klimas (*Lith.*) Descendant of little Kliment (merciful).

Klimek (*Pol.*) Descendant of little Klim, a pet form of Klemens (merciful).

Kling, Klinge, Klingen (*Ger.*) Dweller at, or near, a mountain stream; one who came from Kling, Klinge or Klingen (rushing stream), the names of many places in Germany.

Klingelschmidt (*Ger.*) One who made bells.

Klinger, Klingler, Klingner (*Ger.*) One who made and sold blades or swords.

Klink, Klinke, Klinck (*Du., Ger.*) Dweller near a rushing stream or ravine; dweller near a field gate; dweller near a corner; dweller on, or near, a low hill.

Klopp (*Du., Ger.*) Descendant of Klopp, a pet form of names beginning with Lut (loud or distinct), as Chlodbald and Chlodobert; shortened form of Kloppman, q.v.

Kloppman, Klopper (*Du.*) The official who attached seals or marks of approval to pieces of cloth, by stamping them.

Kloss (*Ger.*) Descendant of Nicholas (people's victory).

Klotz (*Ger.*) One with no manners.

Klug, Kluge (*Ger.*) The wise or learned man.

Kmiec (*Pol.*) One who tills the soil, a farmer.

Kmiecik (*Pol.*) The little farmer.

Knapp (*Eng.*) Dweller at the top of the hill; one who came from Knapp (hilltop), in Hampshire.

Knecht (*Ger.*) One who was a servant.

Knickerbocker (*Du.*) An American surname, not found in Holland, possibly a nickname for a military man, meaning "clay marble baker."

Knifesmith, Knysmith (*Eng.*) One who made small swords and knives.

Knight (*Eng., Wel.*) A military servant of the king; one who held land in exchange for military service to be rendered to king or lord; descendant of Cniht (youth or servant).

Knoll (*Eng.*) Dweller at the top of the hill.

Knorr, Knor (*Ger.*) Dweller near a knot or protuberance, or small hump or hill.

Knott (*Eng.*) Dweller at a rocky hilltop; descendant of Knut (hill, or white-haired).

Knowland (*Eng.*) Dweller at the knoll, or hilltop land.

Knowles (*Eng., Scot.*) Dweller near a small, round hill.

Knowlton (*Eng.*) One who came from Knowlton (homestead by a knoll), the name of places in Dorset and Kent.

Knox, Knows (*Scot.*) One who lived on the lands of Knock (hill), in Renfrewshire and in various other places in Scotland; one who lived on, or near, a hill or prominence.

Knudsen, Knudson (*Dan., Nor.*) The son of Knud or Canute (hill, or white-haired).

Knudtson, Knudtzon, Knudtsen (*Dan.*) The son of Canute or Knut (hill, or white-haired).

Knuth (*Dan., Sw., Nor., Pol.*) Descendant of Knut or Canute (hill, or white-haired); dweller at, or on, a hill; one with an aggressive nature.

Knutson, Knutsen (*Sw., Nor.*) The son of Knut or Canute (hill, or white-haired).

Kobus, Kobusch (*Du.*) Descendant of Kobus, a pet form of Jacobus (the supplanter).

Koch (*Ger.*) One who prepared food, a cook.

Kochan (*Pol., Ukr.*) Descendant of Kochan (beloved); dweller near the Kochan, a small river in Ukraine.

Kocourek (*Cz.-Sl.*) One with the characteristics of a small tomcat.

Koehler, Koeller, Koller, Kohler (*Ger.*) The charcoal-burner or coal worker.

Koenig, Konig (*Ger.*) One who played the part of the king in plays; a servant of the king.

Koepke (*Ger.*) Descendant of little Kob, a pet form of Jacobus (the supplanter).

Koepp, Koeppe (*Ger.*) Descendant of Kob, a pet form of Jacobus (the supplanter).

Koerner (*Ger.*) Dweller near a mill; one who dealt in grain.

Koestner, Koester (*Ger.*) One who was an underofficer of a church and had charge of the sacristy and its contents; one who came from Koesten, in Germany.

Kogan (*Pol., Rus., Ukr.*) One who performed sacerdotal functions, a priest.

Kohl, Kohlman, Kohlmann (*Ger.*) One who grew and sold cabbage.

Kohler (*Ger.*) One who burned charcoal; one who came from Koehlen or Koehler, in Germany.

Kohn, Kohnen (*Ger.*) Descendant of Kuno, a pet form of names beginning with Kun (brave), as Chunrad and Kunimund; variants of Cohen, q.v.

Kohout (*Cz.-Sl., Ukr.*) Dweller at the sign of the rooster.

Kolar (*Cz.-Sl.*) The wheelmaker or wheelwright.

Kolb, Kolbe (*Ger.*) Descendant of Kolb, a pet form of names beginning with Kol (helmet), as Kolbert and Kohlhardt; one who had hair cut short.

Koller (*Ger.*) One who made leather harness; a variant of Kohler, q.v.

Kolodziej (*Pol.*) One who made wheels and wheeled vehicles.

Konieczny (*Pol.*) Dweller at the end, or outskirts, of the village.

Konikowski (*Pol.*) One who took care of ponies.

Konrad, Konrath (*Ger.*) Descendant of Conrad (bold, counsel).

Konstanty (*Pol.*) Descendant of Konstanty (constant).

Koopman, Koopmann (*Du.*) The merchant or tradesman, a peddler.

Kopec (*Ukr.*) Dweller near a boundary hill.

Kopecky, Kopeck (*Cz.-Sl.*) Dweller on, or near, a hill.

Kopf (*Ger.*) Generally a shortened form of a name with this element meaning head; one whose head was unusual or distinctive in some manner.

Kopp, Koppe (*Ger.*) Descendant of Kob, a pet form of Jacobus (the supplanter); dweller at the head or uppermost part of some topographical feature; descendant of Kopp, from Gobbo, a pet form of Godabald (God, bold) and Godaberht (God, bright).

Koranda (*Cz.-Sl.*) One who operated a raft or flatboat; one who cleaned bark from trees.

Korb (*Ger.*) One who made and sold baskets; one who came from Korb (basket), in Germany.

Korelev (*Rus.*) One connected in some way with a king's household.

Korman, Kormann (*Ger.*) One who grew, or dealt in, grain.

Korn, Korner (*Ger.*) One who grew and sold corn or grain.

Kornfeld, Kornfield (*Ger.*) Dweller at, or near, a grain field.

Kos (*Cz.-Sl.*) One who lived at the sign of the blackbird; shortened form of various other names of which this is the root.

Kosciuszko (*Pol.*) Descendant of Koscia, a pet form of Konstanty (constant).

Kosiek (*Pol.*) Descendant of little Kos (blackbird); dweller at the sign of the little horse.

Kosinski (*Pol.*) One who came from Kosin(o) (scythe), in Poland.

Koski (*Finn.*) Dweller near the rapids or waterfall.

Kosowski (*Pol.*) One who came from Kosow (scythe), in Poland.

Koss, Kosse (*Ger.*) Descendant of Koss, a pet form of Godizo (God).

Kostecki (*Pol., Ukr.*) One who came from Kostki (bone), the name of many places in Poland; dweller near the Kostka, a little river in Ukraine.

Kostelny (*Ukr.*) One employed to take care of a church, a sexton.

Koster, Kostner, Kuster (*Ger.*) An underofficer of a church who had charge of the sacristy and its contents.

Kosygin (*Rus.*) The reaper.

Kott, Kot, Kotte (*Ger.*) Descendant of Godo, a pet form of names commencing with Gott (God), as Gotahard, Godowin and Godeman; dweller in the little house or cottage.

Kotz (*Ger.*) Descendant of Gutz, a pet form of Godizo (God); one who came from Kotz, in Germany.

Kouba, Kuba (*Cz.-Sl.*) Descendant of Kuba, a pet form of Jakub (the supplanter).

Kovacs, Kovac, Kovatch, Kovach, Kovats (*Hun.*) The worker in metals, a smith.

Kovalik (*Pol.*) The little worker in metals.

Kovar (*Cz.-Sl.*) The worker in metals, a smith.

Kovarik (*Cz.-Sl.*) The little smith, or worker in metals.

Kowalczyk (*Pol.*) The son of the smith.

Kowalski, Kowalewski, Kowal, Koval (*Pol.*) The worker in metals, a smith.

Kowalsky (*Rus.*) The worker in metals, a smith.

Koza, Kozak, Koziol (*Cz.-Sl., Pol.*) One who takes care of goats; one who is like a goat in some respect.

Kozlowski, Kozlowsky (*Pol., Rus.*) One who took care of the goats.

Kracke, Krack (*Ger.*) Dweller at the sign of the raven or crow; one thought to possess the characteristics of a crow.

Kraemer, Kraehmer (*Ger.*) Same as Kramer, q.v.

Kraft, Krafft (*Ger.*) The strong or powerful man.

Krahe, Kray, Krah (*Ger.*) Dweller at the sign of the crow; one thought to possess the characteristics of a crow.

Krajewski (*Pol.*) Dweller at the outskirts of the town.

Krakow, Krakowski, Krakover (*Pol.*) One who came from Krakow (the town of Duke Krak), in southern Poland.

Kral, Krall (*Cz.-Sl.*) One connected in some way with a king's household; one who played the part of a king in pageants.

Kramer, Krammer (*Du., Ger.*) The shopkeeper or tradesman; one who traveled through the country buying butter, hens and eggs which he carried to the market in a cram or pack on his back.

Kramp, Kram (*Ger.*) One who came from Kramp (edge); dweller at the brim or edge.

Kranz, Krantz, Krantzler (*Ger.*) One who came from Kranz or Krantz (wreath), in Germany; one with a prominent nose.

Krasnoshtanov (*Rus.*) One known for wearing red pants.

Krause, Kraus, Krauss (*Ger.*) Descendant of the curly-headed man.

Kravitz, Kravetz, Kravets, Krawetz, Krawitz, Kravits (*Cz.-Sl., Pol., Ukr.*) One who made outer garments, a tailor.

Krawczyk (*Pol.*) The son of the tailor.

Krebs (*Ger.*) Dweller at the sign of the crab; one who came from Krebes, in Germany.

Kreisler (*Ger.*) One who operated a lathe, a turner.

Krejci (*Cz.-Sl.*) One who made outer garments, a tailor.

Kremer (*Ger.*) Same as Kramer, q.v.

Krenz, Krentz (*Ger.*) A variant of Kranz, q.v.

Kress, Kresse (*Ger.*) Descendant of Kress, a pet form of Erasmus (amiable).

Kretschmer, Kretchmer, Kretchmar, Kretzschmar (*Ger.*) One who sold ale and wine, a tavernkeeper.

Krieger (*Ger., Du.*) The warrior or champion; descendant of Gregorius (watchman).

Kriz, Kritz (*Ger.*) Dweller at, or near, a cross; one who proclaimed the orders or messages of a court.

Kroeger, Kroger (*Du.*) A publican or innkeeper.

Krohn (*Ger.*) Descendant of Grun (green), a pet form of names beginning with Grun, as Gruonrik and Gronwald; dweller at the sign of the crane.

Kroll, Krol (*Pol.*) One connected in some way with a king's household; one who played the part of a king in pageants.

Krom (*Du.*) The cripple.

Krone, Kron, Kroner (*Ger.*) Dweller at the sign of the Kron (crest); descendant of Krone, a pet form of Cruanhart and Gronhari (green, army).

Kronenberg, Kronenberger (*Ger.*) One who came from Kronenberg or Cronenberg (crown mountain), in West Germany.

Kropp, Kropf, Kropfel, Kropfl (*Ger.*) Descendant of Kropp, a pet form of names beginning with the element *hrod* (fame), as Hrodobert, Hrodgaer, Rotbrand, etc.; one who came from Kropp, in Germany; one who had a prominent goiter.

Kross (*Scot., Ger.*) One who came from Cross (a cross), formerly spelled Kross, in the Orkney Islands; the curly-headed man.

Krowa (*Pol.*) One who took care of cows.

Krueger, Kruger (*Ger.*) A publican or innkeeper.

Krug, Krugman (*Ger.*) A publican or innkeeper.

Krull (*Ger.*) The curly-headed man.

Krupa (*Pol., Ukr.*) One with some real or fancied resemblance to a grain of barley.

Krupp (*Ger.*) Descendant of Krupp or Ruppo, pet forms of names beginning with Hrod (fame); variant of Kropp, q.v.

Kruse (*Ger.*) The curly-haired man.

Krushchev (*Rus.*) The son of a cockchafer, a large bettle; one with some characteristic of a large beetle.

Kubiak (*Pol.*) The son of Kuba, a pet form of Jakob (the supplanter).

Kubicki (*Pol.*) Descendant of Kuba, a pet form of Jakob (the supplanter).

Kubik (*Pol., Rus., Ukr.*) Descendant of Kubik, a pet form of Jakob (the supplanter).

Kubilius (*Lith.*) One who made tubs.

Kubilunas (*Lith.*) The son of the tubmaker.

Kucera (*Cz.-Sl.*) One with curly hair.

Kucharski (*Pol.*) One who prepared food, a cook.

Kuchenbecker (*Ger.*) One who baked cakes.

Kuehl (*Ger.*) One with a cold personality.

Kuester (*Ger.*) An underofficer of a church who had charge of the sacristy and its contents.

Kuhl (*Ger.*) One who lived near a pool.

Kuhlman, Kuhlmann (*Ger.*) The man who lived at, or near, the pool.

Kuhn, Kuhne, Kuehn, Kuehne, Kuhns, Koons (*Ger.*) One who was bold or keen.

Kujawa (*Pol.*) One who came from Kujawy, a province in Poland.

Kukla (*Ukr., Rus.*) One who had some real or fancied resemblance to a puppet; one who operated a puppet show.

Kula (*Pol., Ukr.*) Dweller at the sign of the ball, or at some natural feature shaped like a ball.

Kulik (*Rus.*) Dweller at the sign of the snipe or stilt bird; one with some quality of a snipe.

Kulikowski (*Pol.*) One who came from Kulikow(o) (Kulik's settlement), the name of many places in Poland.

Kummer (*Ger.*) Descendant of Khunemar (race, famous), or of Gundemar (war, famous); one who came from Kummer, the name of several places in Germany.

Kunkel (*Ger.*) Dweller at, or near, deep water; one from the distaff side, perhaps an effeminate man; descendant of Kuno, a pet form of names beginning with Kuhn (bold), as Kuniald and Chunrad.

Kuntz, Kunz, Kunze, Kunst, Koontz, Koonce (*Ger.*) Descendant of Conrad (bold, counsel).

Kurath (*Ger.*) Descendant of Chuonrad (bold, counsel).

Kurek (*Pol., Cz.-Sl.*) Dweller at the sign of the cock; one thought to possess some characteristic of a cock.

Kurland, Kurlander (*Ger.*) One who came from Kurland or Courland (country of the Cours), in Latvia.

Kurowski (*Pol.*) One who came from Kurowo (cock), the name of many places in Poland.

Kurth (*Ger.*) Descendant of Kurth, a pet form of Kunrath (bold, counsel).

Kurtz, Kurz (*Ger.*) The short man.

Kus (*Ger., Pol.*) The small person.

Kusch, Kush (*Ger.*) Descendant of Godizo (God).

Kusek (*Pol.*) Descendant of little Kus or Kusy, a nickname meaning "short tail," probably referring to a dog.

Kushner, Kushnir, Kushmar (*Pol., Cz.-Sl., Ukr.*) One who made fur coats, a furrier.

Kuss, Kusse (*Ger.*) Descendant of Kus, a pet form of Marcus (belonging to Mars, the god of war), and of Dominicus (the Lord's day).

Kuta (*Pol., Ukr.*) One who came from Kuta (corner), in Poland; dweller in a corner or angle of land.

Kutz (*Ger.*) Descendant of Gutz, a pet form of Godizo (God).

Kuyper, Kuiper (*Du.*) The cask maker, a cooper.

Kuznetsov (*Rus.*) The worker in metals, a smith.

Kuzniar (*Cz.-Sl.*) One who prepared skins or furs, a furrier.

Kwiatkowski (*Pol.*) One who came from Kwiatkow(o) (flower place), in Poland.

Kyle (*Eng.*) Dweller near the Kyle (narrow), a river in Yorkshire.

LaBarbera (*It.*) Descendant of Barbera (the stranger).

LaBelle (*Fr.*) The handsome man.

Labno (*Pol.*) The light-complexioned or white person.

LaBuda (*It.*) One who came from Buda (Buda's town), in Hungary.

Lacey, Lacy (*Eng.*) One who came from Lassy or Lessay (Latius' estate), in Normandy.

Lach (*Ger.*) Dweller at, or in, the bushes or small wood; dweller near a small pool.

Lachman, Lachmann (*Ger.*) Dweller at, or near, a pool or lake; a nickname given to one who is continually laughing; dweller near a small wood or underbrush.

Lackey, Lackie (*Eng., Ir.*) One who attended another, a footman; dweller at a stony or rocky place.

Lackland (*Scot.*) One who owned no land; one who came from Lochlann, i.e., Norway.

Lacour, Lacourt (*Fr.*) The short or small man.

LaCroix (*Fr.*) Dweller at, or near, a cross; one who carried the cross in a procession. *See* Cross.

LaCrosse (*Fr.*) A partially Englished form of La Croix, q.v.

Ladd (*Eng.*) A serving man or attendant.

Lafayette (*Fr.*) Dweller at, or near, a small beech grove.

Laffite, Laffitte (*Fr.*) Dweller at a boundary stone or marker.

LaGuardia (*It., Sp.*) Dweller near an outpost; a guard; one who came from LaGuardia (outpost), in Italy.

Lahey (*Ir.*) Grandson of Flaitheamh (lord, ruler).

Lahr (*Ger.*) One who came from Lahr (empty, deserted), in Germany; descendant of Lahr, a pet form of Hilarius (cheerful).

Lahti (*Finn.*) Dweller near the bay.

Lain, Laine, Layne (*Eng.*) Dweller by certain tracts of arable land at the foot of the Sussex Downs.

Laing (*Scot.*) The tall man.

Laird (*Scot.*) An owner of land or houses, a landlord.

Lake (*Eng.*) Dweller at a stream or brook; dweller in a dried-up watercourse in the moors.

Lakin (*Rus.*) Descendant of Lakeh (the weary one), a woman's name.

Lally (*Fr.*) One who came from Ally, in central France.

LaMantia (*It.*) One who came from Amantea, in Italy.

Lamb, Lambe (*Eng.*) Dweller at the sign of the lamb; one with some characteristic of a lamb.

Lambert, Lambart, Lamberty, Lamberts, Lambertson (*Eng., Du.*) Descendant of Lambert (land, bright).

Lambrecht, Lamprecht, Lambrechts, Lambright (*Ger.*) Descendant of Lambrecht (land, bright).

Lamkin, Lampkin, Lampkins (*Eng.*) Descendant of little Lamb, a pet form of Lambert (land, bright).

Lamont, Lamond, Lemond, Limont (*Scot.*) The lawman or lawyer.

Lampert (*Eng.*) One who came from Lamport (long marketplace), the name of several places in England; a variant of Lambert, q.v.

Lamson, Lampson (*Eng.*) The son of Lam, a pet form of Lambert (land, bright).

Lancaster (*Eng.*) One who came from Lancaster (Roman camp on the Lune River), the county town of Lancashire.

Lance (*Eng.*) Descendant of Lance (land), also a pet form of Lancelot (very little Lance).

Land, Landis, Landise, Landes, Lande (*Eng.*) Dweller in, or near, the cultivated field.

Landau, Landauer (*Ger.*) One who came from Landau (meadowland), the name of three towns in Germany.

Landers, Lander, Landor (*Eng.*) One who washed and bleached flax, wool, cloth, etc.

Landon (*Eng., Fr.*) One who came from Langdon (long hill), the name of several places in England; descendant of Lando (land).

Landreth (*Eng., Scot.*) One who came from Lanreath (court of justice), in Cornwall.

Landry, Landrey, Landro (*Fr.*) Descendant of Landry (country, powerful).

Landsman (*Scot.*) One who tended the open wood.

Lane, Layne (*Eng.*) One who lived near the rural road, or narrow way between fences or hedges.

Lang, Lange (*Ger., Eng., Scot.*) The tall man.

Langan (*Ir.*) Grandson of little Long (long or tall).

Langbauer (*Ger.*) The tall tiller of the soil, or farmer.

Langdon (*Eng.*) One who came from Langdon (long hill), the name of several places in England.

Langer (*Ger.*) The tall man; one who tilled the soil, a farmer.

Langford (*Eng.*) One who came from Langford (long ford), the name of several places in England.

Langille, Langill (*Scot., Eng.*) One who came from Langwell (long field), the name of places in Caithness and in Ross and Cromarty, or from Langhale (long, flat land), in Norfolk.

Langley, Langlie (*Eng.*) One who came from Langley (long wood or clearing), the name of many places in England.

Langlois, Langlais (*Fr.*) The Englishman or man from England.

Langner (*Ger.*) One who came from Langen (long place), in Germany.

Langston (*Eng.*) One who came from Langstone (long stone), villages in Devonshire and Hampshire.

Langton (*Eng.*) One who came from Langton (long homestead, or hill), the name of several places in England.

Lanier (*Fr.*) One who dressed, wove or sold wool.

Lannon, Lannan, Lannen (*Ir.*) Grandson of little Leann (cloak or mantle).

Lansford (*Eng.*) One who came from Landford (lane ford), in Wiltshire, or from Langford (Landa's ford), in Nottinghamshire.

Lansing (*Eng.*) One who came from Lancing (people of Wlenca), in Sussex.

Lantz, Lanz (*Ger.*) Descendant of Lanzo or Lando (land).

Lanza, Lanzi, Lanzo (*It.*) A mercenary German soldier; one who fought with a lance; descendant of Lanza, a pet form of Lancillotto (manservant).

Lapham (*Eng.*) One who came from Lopham (Loppa's homestead), in Norfolk.

Lapin (*Rus.*) One who had big feet.

Lapinski (*Pol.*) One who came from Lapy (claws), a city in Poland.

LaPorte (*Fr.*) Dweller near a city gate or other large gate.

Lapp, Lappe (*Ger.*) A foolish person.

Larcom, Larcome, Larcombe (*Eng.*) Dweller in Lar's valley.

Lardner, Lardiner, Larder (*Eng.*) The keeper of the larder, the place where provisions were stored.

Lark, Larke (*Eng.*) One with some characteristic of a lark; dweller at the sign of the lark; descendant of little Lar, a pet form of Laurence (laurel, symbol of victory).

Larkin, Larkins (*Eng.*) Descendant of little Lar, a pet form of Laurence (laurel, symbol of victory).

LaRocco, LaRocca (*It.*) Dweller near, or worker at, a fortress; dweller near a cliff.

Larousse (*Fr.*) The red-haired or ruddy man.

Larrabee (*Fr.*) Dweller at the riverbank.

Larson, Larsen, Larsson (*Sw., Dan., Nor., Eng.*) The son of Lars or Lawrence (laurel, symbol of victory).

LaRue (*Fr.*) Dweller on an important street.

Lash, Lasch (*Ger.*) Descendant of Lash, a pet form of Lazarus (help of God).

Laskowski, Lasko (*Pol.*) Dweller in, or near, a forest; one who came from Laskow(o), in Poland.

Lasky, Laskey, Laski, Laske (*Ger., Pol.*) One who came from Lask, in Poland; dweller on cleared land.

Lassen (*Ger.*) Descendant of Las, a pet form of Nikolaus (people's victory), or of Lars, a pet form of Laurentius (laurel, symbol of victory); the lazy or indolent man.

Lasser, Lassers, Laser, Lassar (*Ger.*) One who bled people; descendant of Lazarus (help of God).

Lassiter (*Eng.*) A variant of Lester, q.v.

Latchford (*Eng.*) One who came from Latchford (ford over a stream), the name of villages in Cheshire and Oxford.

Latham (*Eng.*) One who came from Latham or Laytham, both in Yorkshire, or Lathom in Lancashire, all three meaning barn enclosure.

Lathrop, Lathrope (*Eng.*) One who came from Lowthorpe (Logi's farm), in Yorkshire.

Latimer, Latimore, Lattimore, Latturner, Lattner (*Eng.*) The Latiner or translator of Latin, an interpreter.

Lau, Laue (*Ger.*) Dweller at the sign of the lion; one who came from Laue or Lauen (lion), in Germany.

Lauder, Lawder, Lawther (*Scot.*) One who came from Lauder (Lowther, famous warrior), in Berwickshire.

Lauer (*Ger.*) One who tans skins; one who fights by ambushing another; one who came from Lau or Laue (lion), in Germany.

Laughlin (*Ir.*) Variant of Loughlin, q.v.

Laughton (*Eng.*) One who came from Laughton (homestead where leeks were grown, or enclosed homestead), the name of several places in England.

Laurence (*Wel.*) Descendant of Laurence (laurel, symbol of victory).

Laurent (*Fr.*) Descendant of Laurent (laurel, symbol of victory); one who came from Lorraine, a medieval kingdom and duchy in Europe.

Laurie (*Scot.*) Descendant of little Laurence (laurel, symbol of victory).

Lausche, Lausch, Lauch (*Ger.*) Dweller near quicksand.

Lauterbach, Lauterback (*Ger.*) Dweller near the clear or pure brook; one who came from Lauterbach (clear brook), the name of many places in Germany.

LaValle, Laval (*Fr.*) Dweller in the valley.

LaVelle (*Fr.*) Dweller in, or one from, the town.

Lavender (*Eng.*) One who washed or bleached flax, wool, cloth, etc.

Lavery (*Ir.*) Descendant of the speaker or spokesman.

LaVigne, Lavigne (*Fr.*) Dweller at, or near, the vineyard.

Lavin, Lavine, LaVine (*Ir.*) Grandson of Flaitheamhan (little ruler), or of Lamh (hand).

Law, Lawe (*Eng.*) Dweller at a burial mound or hillock.

Lawler, Lawlor (*Ir.*) One who mumbled or was unable to speak plainly.

Lawless (*Eng.*) One deprived of the protection of the law, an outlaw.

Lawrence (*Eng.*) Descendant of Lawrence (laurel, symbol of victory).

Lawson, Laws (*Eng.*) The son of Law, a pet form of Lawrence (laurel, symbol of victory).

Lawton (*Eng.*) One who came from Lawton (enclosure on a hill), the name of villages in Cheshire and Herefordshire.

Lawyer, Lawman (*Eng.*) One who followed the legal profession, a lawyer.

Lay (*Eng.*) Dweller at a meadow or open place in a wood.

Layman (*Eng.*) An official declarer of the law; a lawyer.

Layton (*Eng.*) One who came from Layton (village on a stream, or homestead where leeks are grown), the name of several villages in England.

Lazar, Lazarus, Lazare (*Heb.*) Descendant of Lazarus (help of God).

Lazzara, Lazzaro, Lazzari (*It.*) A beggar.

Le (*Chin.*) Dweller near a pear tree.

Lea (*Eng.*) One who came from Lea (wood or clearing), the name of several places in England; dweller at, or near, the Lea (light), an English river.

Leach, Leech (*Eng.*) Dweller at, or near, the Leach (stream), a river in Gloucestershire; a bloodletter or physician.

Leader (*Eng.*) One who drove a vehicle, a carter.

Leaf, Leef, Leafe (*Eng.*) The beloved person.

Leahy, Leahey (*Ir.*) Grandson of Laochdha (heroic).

Leake, Leak, Leek (*Eng.*) One who came from Leake (stream), the name of several places, all on streams, in England; dweller near a stream or pool.

Leander (*Eng., Fr.*) Descendant of Leander (lion man).

Learned, Learnard (*Eng.*) Descendant of Leonard (lion, bold).

Leary (*Ir.*) Grandson of the keeper of calves.

Leavitt (*Eng.*) Variant of Levitt, q.v.

LeBeau (*Fr.*) The handsome man.

LeBlanc (*Fr.*) The white-haired or light-complexioned man.

Lebovitz (*Cz.-Sl., Yu.-Sl.*) The son of Leyba (life).

Lech (*Cz.-Sl.*) One of high birth or exalted rank, a noble.

Lederer (*Eng., Ger.*) One who drove a vehicle, a carter; one who tanned leather, a tanner.

Lederman, Ledermann (*Ger.*) One who tanned leather, a tanner.

Lee, Ley (*Eng.*) Dweller at the meadow, or open place in a wood; one who came from Lee, the name of various places in England.

Leeds (*Eng.*) One who came from Leeds (district on the river), in Yorkshire.

Leeper, Leaper (*Eng.*) One who made or sold baskets.

LeFevre, LeFebvre, LeFebre, LeFebure, LeFeber (*Fr.*) The worker in metals, a smith. Also found with the *F* not capitalized.

Leff (*Pol., Rus., Ukr.*) Descendant of Leff, a pet form of Leon (lion).

Lefferts, Leffert (*Du.*) The son of Leffert (dear, hard).

Legg, Legge (*Eng., Nor.*) Dweller in, or near, the meadow; one who had unusual legs; descendant of Leggr (leg).

Leggett, Leggitt (*Eng.*) One who represented a state as ambassador or legate. *See also* Liggett.

Legrand (*Fr.*) The tall man.

Lehmann, Lehman (*Ger.*) One who held land on feudal tenure, a vassal or villein.

Lehner, Lehn (*Ger.*) One who worked for a lord on a feudal estate.

Lehr (*Ger.*) Descendant of Lehr, a pet form of Hilarius (cheerful).

Leib (*Ger.*) Dweller at the sign of the lion; descendant of Leib, a variant of Laybo (life).

Leigh (*Eng.*) A variant of Lee, q.v.

Leighly (*Ger.*) Dweller at, or near, a small clump of low trees or bushes; dweller on ground recently cleared.

Leighton (*Eng.*) One who came from Leighton (homestead where leeks were grown), the name of several places in England.

Leith (*Scot.*) One who formerly resided in the town or territory of Leith (overflow), in Midlothian.

Lejeune (*Fr.*) One who was younger than another with whom he was associated.

Leland (*Eng.*) One who came from Leyland (fallow land), in Lancashire; dweller at, or near, the fallow or untilled field.

Lemaitre (*Fr.*) The master or overseer.

Lemke (*Ger.*) Descendant of little Lem, a pet form of Lambico (land); descendant of little Lampo, a pet form of names beginning with Land (land), as Landbald and Landebert; one who came from Lemke, in Germany.

Lemon, Lemmon, Lemons (*Eng.*) Dweller at, or near, the Lemon (elm), a river in Devonshire; the lover or sweetheart.

Lenard, Lennard (*Eng.*) Descendant of Leonard (lion, bold).

Lenihan, Lenehan, Lenahan (*Ir.*) Grandson of little Leannach (cloaked).

Lenk, Lenke (*Ger.*) Descendant of Lenk, a shortening of Lendeke, i.e. little Lando (land); the tall man.

Lennon (*Ir.*) Grandson of Lennane (small coat).

Lennox, Lenox (*Scot.*) One who came from the district of Lennox (place of elms), in Dumbarton.

Lenormand (*Fr.*) The Norman or man from Normandy.

Lentsch (*Ger.*) Descendant of little Lanzo, a pet form of Lando (land).

Lenz, Lentz (*Ger.*) Descendant of little Lanzo, a pet form of Lando (land).

Leo (*Eng.*) Descendant of Leo (lion).

Leon, Leone (*Gr., Sp.*) Dweller at the sign of the lion; nickname for a brave person; one who came from Leon (lion), an ancient kingdom and region in Spain.

Leonard (*Eng., Ger.*) Descendant of Leonard (lion, bold).

Leonardi, Leonardo (*It.*) Descendant of Leonardo (lion, bold).

Leonhardt, Leonhard (*Ger.*) Descendant of Leonhard (lion, bold).

Leopold, Liepold (*Ger.*) Descendant of Leudbald or Leopold (people, bold).

Leppert (*Ger.*) Descendant of Liebrecht (people, pride); dweller at the sign of the leopard.

Lerch, Lerche (*Ger.*) One with some characteristic of a lark; dweller at the sign of the lark; one who came from Lerche, in Germany.

Lerman (*Ger.*) One who came from Leer in Germany; one who taught others, a teacher.

Lerner (*Ger.*) One who came from Lern (to learn), in Germany.

Leroy (*Fr.*) One connected in some way with the king's household; one who played the part of a king in tournaments.

Leslie, Lesley, Lesslie (*Scot.*) One from Leslie (garden of hollies), in Aberdeenshire; descendant of Leslie (from the gray fort).

Lesniak (*Pol.*) Dweller in, or near, a forest.

Lesniewski (*Pol.*) One who came from Lesniew(o) (forest), the name of places in Poland and Ukraine.

Lesser (*Heb.*) Descendant of Eliezer (my God has helped), or of Elazar, a form of Lazarus (help of God).

Lester (*Eng.*) One who came from Leicester (dwellers on Legra River), a town and county in England.

Lesueur (*Fr.*) One who made shoes, a shoemaker.

Leszczynski (*Pol.*) Dweller near hazel bushes.

Lettenberger (*Ger.*) Dweller on, or near, a clay hill.

Lev (*Pol.*) Dweller at the sign of the lion; one with lion-like qualities; a shortened form of Levi, q.v., under Levy.

Leverenz, Leverence, Leverentz (*Ger.*) Descendant of Leverenz, a variant of Laurentius (laurel, symbol of victory).

Leverick (*Eng.*) Descendant of Leofric (dear, rule).

Levin, Levine (*Heb.*) Descendant of little Levi (united).

Levinson, Levenson, Lewin (*Eng., Ger.*) The son of Leofwin (dear, friend), but sometimes the son of little Levi (united).

Leviton, Levitan (*Heb.*) The large or heavy man; dweller at the sign of the leviathan.

Levitt, Levit (*Eng.*) One who came from Livet (wolf cub), in Normandy; descendant of little Levi (united).

Levy, Levi, Levey (*Heb.*) Descendant of Levi (united).

Lewandowski, Lewan (*Pol.*) One who came from Lewandow (Lewand's settlement), in Poland near Warsaw.

Lewis (*Wel., Eng.*) Descendant of Lewis (hear, fight).

Leyden, Leydon (*Eng., Du., Ger.*) Dweller at the meadow valley; a variant of Lydon, q.v.; one who came from Leiden (people), in Holland; descendant of Liuto (people).

L'Hommedieu (*Fr.*) The man God, probably referring to a servant of God.

Li (*Chin.*) One who lived near a plum tree.

Libby, Libbey, Libbe (*Scot., Ger.*) Descendant of Ibb, a pet form of Isobel (oath to Baal); a form of Elizabeth (oath of God); the beloved person.

Lichtenstein (*Ger.*) One who came from Lichtenstein (light stone), in Germany.

Lichter, Licht, Lichten, Lichte (*Ger., Du.*) The light-complexioned, or blond, man.

Lichterman (*Du., Ger.*) One who lit lamps, a lamplighter.

Liddell, Liddle (*Eng.*) One who came from Liddel (loud river valley), or dweller at the Liddel River, both in Cumberland.

Lieb (*Ger.*) The dear, beloved person; descendant of Lieb, a pet form of Liubwin (dear, friend).

Lieber (*Ger.*) Descendant of Lieber, a variant of Liubheri (dear, army); one who came from Liebau, in Germany.

Lieberman, Liebermann (*Ger.*) The beloved servant; the servant of Lieber.

Liebman, Liebmann (*Ger.*) Variants of Lieberman, q.v.

Lietz (*Ger.*) Descendant of Liuzo, a pet form of Liuto (people).

Liggett (*Eng.*) One who came from Lidgate (swing-gate), in Suffolk; dweller at a swinging gate; a variant of Leggett, q.v.

Liggins (*Eng.*) Descendant of little Lig, a pet form of Ligulf (spear shaft, wolf).

Light, Licht (*Eng., Ger.*) One who lived at the light place or clearing in the forest.

Lightbody (*Eng.*) A light, active person.

Lightbourne, Lightbown, Lightburn (*Eng.*) Dweller at the clear stream.

Lightfoot (*Eng.*) One who was fleet of foot.

Liland (*Nor.*) Dweller at the field where flax was grown.

Lilienfeld (*Ger.*) Lily field.

Lilienthal (*Ger.*) Lily valley.

Lilly, Lillie, Lilley (*Eng.*) One who came from Lilley (meadow where flax was grown), in Hertfordshire; dweller where lilies grew.

Lincoln (*Eng.*) One who came from Lincoln (lake colony), in Lincolnshire.

Lind, Linde (*Eng., Sw.*) Dweller by the lime tree; linden tree.

Lindahl (*Sw.*) Linden-tree valley.

Lindberg, Lindbergh (*Sw.*) Linden-tree mountain.

Lindell (*Eng.*) One who came from Lindal (lime-tree valley), in Lancashire.

Lindemann, Lindeman (*Ger.*) Dweller at, or near, the linden tree; dweller at, or near, the open court or assembly place.

Linden (*Sw.*) Dweller near the linden tree.

Lindenberg (*Sw.*) Linden-tree mountain.

Linder (*Eng.*) Dweller at, or near, a lime tree.

Lindgren (*Sw.*) Linden-tree branch.

Lindh (*Sw.*) Linden tree.

Lindholm (*Sw.*) Linden-tree island.

Lindley (*Eng.*) One who came from Lindley (glade where flax was grown), the name of several places in England.

Lindner (*Sw.*) Dweller near the linden tree.

Lindquist, Linquist (*Sw.*) Linden-tree twig.

Lindsay, Lindsey (*Scot., Ir.*) The man from Limesay or Lindesey (lime tree or linden isle), in Normandy; grandson of the sailor.

Lindstrom (*Sw.*) Linden-tree river.

Linehan, Linnehan (*Ir.*) Grandson of little Leannach (cloaked).

Lingley, Linley (*Eng.*) One who came from Linley (meadow where flax was grown), in Shropshire.

Link, Linke (*Eng., Du.*) Dweller at a ridge or bank separating strips of arable land on rising ground; one who was left-handed.

Linn, Linne (*Eng.*) Dweller at, or near, a pool or lake; dweller near a linden tree.

Linnell (*Eng.*) Descendant of Lionel (little Leon or lion).

Linscott (*Eng.*) Dweller in the cottage by the linden trees.

Linton (*Eng.*) One who came from Linton (homestead of flax or lime trees), the name of various places in England.

Lipinski (*Pol.*) Dweller near a linden tree.

Lipman, Lippman, Lippmann (*Ger.*) The servant of Lipp, a pet form of Phillip (lover of horses).

Lipp, Lippe (*Ger.*) Descendant of Lipp, a pet form of Philippus (lover of horses); one who came from Lipp or Lippe (bank of a river), the names of places in Germany.

Lippert (*Ger.*) Descendant of Liutperaht (people, pride); dweller in a clay and straw hut.

Lippincott (*Eng.*) Dweller in the cottage at the edge, or bank, or shore; one who lived in Lippa's cottage.

Lipscher (*Cz.-Sl.*) One who came from Libous (named after Queen Libousa), in Czechoslovakia.

Lipschultz, Lipshultz (*Ger.*) One who came from Lippschutz, in Germany.

Lipscomb, Lipscombe (*Eng.*) One who came from Letcombe (ledge in the valley), in Berkshire, or from Liscombe (enclosed hollow), in Buckinghamshire; dweller in Lipp's valley.

Lipsey (*Eng.*) Descendant of Lepsi, a variant of Leofsige (dear, victory).

Lipsky, Lipski, Lipske (*Rus., Pol.*) One who came from Lipsk, in Poland; dweller near a linden tree.

Lipson (*Ger.*) The son of Lip, a pet form of Philippus (lover of horses); Americanized version of Lipschultz, q.v.

Lipton (*Eng.*) One who came from Lepton (homestead in an abyss), in Yorkshire.

Liska, Lisak (*Cz.-Sl.*) One who dwelt at the sign of the fox; one with some of the qualities of a fox.

Lisowski (*Pol.*) One who came from Lisow(o) (fox), in Poland.

Liss, Lis, Lisse (*Pol.*) One who lived at the sign of the fox; one with some foxlike characteristic.

List (*Ger.*) Descendant of List, a pet form of Listhard (clever, strong).

Lister (*Eng., Ger.*) One who dyed cloth; one who came from Liste, in Germany.

Liston (*Eng.*) One who came from Liston (Leofsige's homestead), in Essex.

Litchfield (*Eng.*) One who came from Litchfield (hill slope), in Hampshire.

Lithgow (*Scot.*) One who came from Linlithgow (dear broad lake), former name of West Lothian, also capital city of West Lothian, in Scotland.

Litt (*Eng.*) The small or short man.

Little, Littell (*Eng.*) The small or short man.

Littlefield (*Eng.*) Dweller in, or near, the small field or open place in a wood.

Littlejohn (*Eng.*) The small man named John (gracious gift of Jehovah), to distinguish him from other Johns.

Littleton (*Eng.*) One who came from Littleton (small homestead), the name of various places in England.

Littlewood (*Eng.*) Dweller in, or near, a small wood or grove; one who came from Littleworth (small homestead), in Berkshire.

Litwin, Litvin (*Pol.*) One who came from Lithuania.

Livermore (*Eng.*) One who came from Livermere (lake where rush or iris grew), in Suffolk.

Livingston, Livingstone (*Scot.*) One who came from the lands, now parish, of Livingston (abode of Leofwine, dear friend), in West Lothian.

Llewellyn, Llewellin (*Wel.*) Descendant of Llewellyn (lion-like).

Lloyd, Loyd, Lloyds (*Wel.*) From *llwyd,* meaning both brown and gray, referring to the complexion or hair.

Lobdell (*Eng.*) Dweller in the deep hollow infested by spiders.

LoBello (*It.*) One with an attractive physique.

LoBianco, Lobianco (*It.*) The light-complexioned or white-haired man.

LoCascio, Locascio (*It.*) Descendant of Cassius (vain).

Loch (*Scot.*) Dweller by a lake.

Locke, Lock (*Eng.*) One who lived by an enclosure of some kind.

Lockett (*Eng.*) Dweller by, or in, a small enclosure.

Lockhart (*Scot.*) Descendant of Locard (enclosure, small).

Lockwood (*Eng.*) One who came from Lockwood (enclosed wood), in Yorkshire.

Lockyer, Locksmith (*Eng.*) One who made locks.

Lodge (*Eng.*) Dweller in the cottage or hut.

Loeb (*Ger.*) One who came from Löbau (dear meadow), in Germany.

Loeffler (*Ger.*) One who made spoons.

Loeschhorn (*Ger.*) One who cleaned lamps; one who made and sold leather horns, used as drinking utensils.

Loewe, Loew (*Ger.*) Variants of Lowe, q.v.

Loewy, Loevy (*Ger.*) Dweller at the sign of the lion; one with lion-like characteristics; descendant of Levi (united).

Lofton (*Eng.*) One who came from Lufton (Luca's homestead), in Somerset.

Loftus, Lofthouse (*Eng.*) One who came from Lofthouse or Loftus (house with an upper floor), both places in Yorkshire; one who lived in a house with an upper story.

Logan, Lagen, Login (*Scot., Ir.*) One who came from Logan (little hollow), in Ayrshire; grandson of the little weak person.

Loggins, Loggin, Login (*Scot.*) One who came from Logan (little hollow), in Scotland; dweller near a small ravine.

Logsdon (*Eng.*) One who came from Longsdon (long ridge), in Staffordshire.

Loizzo, Loizzi (*It.*) One with the characteristics of a snail.

Lomax (*Eng.*) One who came from Lomax (flat alluvial land by a pool), in Lancashire.

Lombard (*Eng.*) One who came from Lombardy (long-bearded men), in Italy.

Lombardo, Lombardi (*It.*) One who came from Lombardia (country of the Longobardi), a province in Italy; a shopkeeper, from the fact that many from Lombardia set up shop in Sicily.

London (*Eng.*) One who came from London (place of Londinos, or from a tribal name), in England.

Lonergan (*Ir.*) The little, strong, fierce man.

Long (*Eng.*) The tall man.

Longenecker (*Ger., Swis.*) One who formerly resided in Longenegg, in Switzerland.

Longfellow (*Eng., Fr.*) The tall partner or companion; one who came from Longueville (great town), in France.

Longfield (*Eng.*) One who came from Longfield (long field), in Kent; one who lived at, or in, the long, narrow field.

Longley (*Eng.*) Dweller in, or near, the extensive meadow or open place in a wood; variant of Langley, q.v.

Longo, Longi (*It.*) The tall man.

Longstreet (*Eng.*) Dweller on a long paved road, especially an ancient Roman road.

Longwood (*Eng.*) Dweller in, or near, the big wood or forest.

Longworth (*Eng.*) One who came from Longworth (large homestead), the name of places in Berkshire and Lancashire.

Loomis, Lomas, Lummas (*Eng.*) One who came from Lomax (flat alluvial land by a pool), in Lancashire.

Looney (*Ir.*) A warrior or soldier; descendant of Luinneach (merry or jovial).

Loos, Loose, Loosen, Looser (*Ger., Fr., Du.*) One who came from Loose, Loosen, Loos, or Lohsa, in Germany; descendant of Laus, a pet form of Nicolaus (people's victory); one who came from Loos, in France; the crafty or cunning person.

Lopata, Lopat (*Pol.*) One who worked with a shovel.

Lopez, Lopaz (*Sp.*) The son of Lope or Lupe (wolf).

Lord (*Eng.*) One who was master or head of the household; the lord's servant; nickname given to one assuming superior rank.

Lordan, Lorden (*Eng.*) The lazy person or vagabond.

Lorel (*Eng.*) A worthless person, a rogue.

Lorenz, Lorentz (*Ger.*) Descendant of Lorenz (laurel, symbol of victory).

Lorenzen, Lorentzen (*Ger.*) One who came from Lorenzen, in Schleswig; descendant of Lorenzen, a variant of Laurentius (laurel, symbol of victory).

Lorimer (*Eng.*) One who made bridle bits and spurs.

Loring (*Eng.*) One who came from Lorraine (dominion of King Lothar II), in France; dweller near a laurel tree; descendant of Loren, a pet form of Laurence (laurel).

Lothrop, Lowthorp (*Eng.*) One who came from Lowthorpe (Logi's farm), in Yorkshire.

Lott, Lotts (*Eng.*) Dweller on the apportioned share of land, i.e., the allotted land.

Lotz (*Ger.*) Descendant of Lotze, a pet form of Hludizo (clear, plain).

Loud (*Eng.*) Dweller near the Loud (the loud one), a river in Lancashire.

Louderback (*Ger.*) Dweller near the clear or pure brook; one who came from Lauterbach (clear brook), the name of many places in Germany.

Loughlin (*Ir.*) Grandson of Lochlainn (lake land); dweller near a lake or sea inlet; grandson of Lachtna (gray); grandson of the servant of St. Secundinus.

Louis (*Fr.*) Descendant of Louis (hear, fight).

Lounsbury, Lounsbery (*Eng.*) One who came from Londesborough (Lothen's fort), in Yorkshire.

Love (*Eng.*) Descendant of Love or Lufa, an Early English given name.

Loveday (*Eng.*) Descendant of Loveday (a name given to a child born on a loveday, i.e., a day appointed for reconciliations).

Lovejoy (*Eng.*) One who craved pleasure.

Lovelace, Loveless (*Eng.*) Descendant of Lovelace (love token); nickname for an unfriendly person.

Loveland (*Eng.*) One who came from Leaveland (Leofa's land), in Kent.

Lovell (*Eng.*) Descendant of little Love (wolf or love).

Lovely (*Eng.*) Dweller at, or near, Lufa's clearing or wood.

Lo Verde, Loverde (*It.*) Dweller at the green place.

Lovering (*Fr.*) One who came from Louvergny or Auvergni, places in France.

Lovett, Lovitt (*Eng.*) Descendant of little Love (wolf).

Loving, Lovinger (*Eng.*) One who came from Louvain, in Belgium.

Lowden, Louden, Loudon (*Scot.*) One who came from Loudoun (flame hill), in Ayrshire.

Lowe (*Ger., Eng.*) One with lion-like characteristics, bold; dweller at the sign of the lion; dweller at the mound, or burial mound, or heap of stones.

Lowell (*Eng.*) Dweller at the sign of the little wolf.

Lowenstein (*Ger.*) One who came from Lowenstein (lions' stone), in Germany.

Lowenthal (*Ger.*) Lions' valley.

Lowes, Lowis (*Scot.*) One who came from Lowes (lake), in Selkirkshire.

Lowry, Lowrey, Lowrie, Lowery, Lourie (*Scot.*) Descendant of Laurie, pet form of Lawrence (the laurel, symbol of victory).

Lubin, Lubinski, Lubinsky (*Pol., Rus.*) Dweller where lupine (herbs of the pea family) was grown for fertilizer.

Luby, Looby (*Pol., Rus., Ukr.*) The dear or beloved man.

Lucas, Lukas (*Eng., Pol.*) Descendant of Lucas or Luke (light).

Lucchesi, Lucchese (*It.*) One who came from Lucca, in Italy.

Luce, Lucet, Lucette (*Fr.*) Descendant of Louis (hear, fight), or of Luke (light).

Luck, Lucke (*Eng.*) Descendant of Luck or Luke (light).

Luckett (*Eng.*) Descendant of little Luck, an English variant of Luke (light).

Luckey, Lucky, Lukey (*Eng.*) Descendant of little Luck or Luke (light).

Luczak (*Pol.*) One who fought with a bow and arrow, a bowman.

Ludlow (*Eng.*) One who came from Ludlow (hill by the rapid), in Shropshire.

Ludwig (*Ger.*) Descendant of Ludwig (fame, warrior).

Luebke (*Ger.*) Descendant of little Luppo (people), a pet form of names beginning with Leute (people), as Liudberct and Liutbrand.

Lueck, Luecke (*Ger.*) Descendant of Liudiko (little people), a pet form of names beginning with Leute (people), as Liudman, Liuderich and Liutwin.

Luedtke, Ludtke (*Ger.*) Descendant of Liudiko (little people), a pet form of Liuto (people).

Luff (*Wel.*) Descendant of Luff, a variant of Love or Lufa (love or wolf).

Lufkin (*Eng.*) Descendant of little Luf, a pet form of Love or Lufa (love or wolf).

Lukasik, Lukasek (*Pol.*) Descendant of little Lukasz (light).

Lukaszewski, Lukasiewicz (*Pol.*) The son of Lukasz (light).

Lukes, Luke (*Eng.*) Descendant of Luke (light).

Lumpkin, Lumpkins (*Eng.*) Descendant of little Lam or Lump, pet forms of Lambert (land, bright).

Lumpp, Lump, Lumpe, Lum, Lumb (*Eng.*) Dweller at, or near, a deep pool or wooded valley; descendant of Lump, a pet form of Lambert (land, bright).

Lund, Lunde (*Sw.*) Grove.

Lundberg, Lundborg, Lundeberg (*Sw.*) Grove mountain.

Lundell (*Sw.*) Grove valley.

Lundgren, Lundgreen, Lungren (*Sw.*) Grove branch.

Lundin, Lundeen, Lundine (*Sw.*) One who came from Lund (grove), the name of a city and several villages in Sweden.

Lundmark (*Sw.*) Grove field.

Lundquist (*Sw.*) Grove twig.

Lundstrom (*Sw.*) Grove river.

Lundy, Lundie (*Eng.*) One who came from Lundy (puffin), an island in Devonshire.

Lunt (*Eng.*) One who came from Lunt (grove), in Lancashire.

Lupino, Lupina, Luppino (*It.*) Dweller at the sign of the little wolf.

Lupo, Lupa, Lupi, Luppo (*It.*) A nickname, referring to the wolf, given to one who was voracious or fraudulent; dweller at the sign of the wolf.

Lurie, Luria (*It.*) One who came from Luria (sorrowful), in Italy.

Lurton (*Eng.*) One who came from Larton (village on clayey soil), in Cheshire.

Lusk (*Pol., Ukr.*) One who came from Luck, a city in medieval Volhynia, in Western Ukraine.

Lustgarten (*Ger.*) Pleasure garden.

Lustig (*Ger.*) The jolly, merry or gay man; one who came from Lustig, in Germany.

Luther (*Eng., Ger.*) Descendant of Lothair (famous, warrior).

Lutz, Lutze (*Ger.*) Descendant of Luizo, a pet form of names beginning with

Luete (people), as Liutbald, Liutgard and Liutwin; one who came from Lutz (small place), in Germany.

Lux (*Ger.*) Descendant of Luks, a pet form of Lucas (light).

Lycos (*Gr.*) Dweller at the sign of the wolf; one thought to possess the qualities of a wolf.

Lydon, Lyden, Lyddon (*Eng.*) One who came from Lydden (pasture with a shelter), in Kent.

Lyford (*Eng.*) One who came from Lyford (ford where flax grew), in Berkshire.

Lyles, Lyle, Lisle (*Fr.*) Dweller on the small island.

Lyman, Lynam, Lynan, Lymon (*Eng., Ir.*) One who came from Lyham (homestead by a wood), in Northumberland; grandson of Laidghnean (snow birth).

Lynch, Lynk (*Eng.*) Dweller at the ridge or bank which separated strips of arable land often on a slope or rising ground.

Lyng, Lynge (*Eng.*) One who came from Lyng (hill), the name of places in Norfolk and Somerset.

Lynn, Lynne (*Eng.*) Dweller at, or near, a pool or lake.

Lyons, Lyon (*Eng., Scot.*) Descendant of Leon (lion); dweller at the sign of the lion.

Lytle, Lyte, Lyttle, Lytell (*Eng.*) The small or short man.

Lytton (*Eng.*) One who came from Litton (village on a roaring stream), the name of several places in England.

Maas (*Du., Bel.*) Dweller at, or near, the Meuse River in western Europe; one who made chain mail used as defensive armor.

McAdams, McAdam, MacAdams, MacAdam (*Scot., Ir.*) The son of Adam (red earth).

McAdoo, McAddo (*Ir.*) The son of Cudabh (black hound).

McAfee, McAffee, MacAffee (*Ir.*) The son of Dubhshithe (black man of peace).

McAllister, MacAllister, MacAlister (*Scot.*) The son of Allister or Alistair, Scotch forms of Alexander (helper of mankind).

MacAlpine, MacAlpin (*Scot.*) Son of Ailpean (elf).

Macaluso (*It.*) One who came from Macala, in Italy.

McAndrew, McAndrews (*Ir., Scot.*) The son of Andrew (manly).

McArdle (*Ir.*) The son of Ardghal (high valor).

MacArthur, McArthur (*Ir., Scot.*) The son of Arthur (valorous).

McAuliffe (*Ir.*) The son of Olaf (ancestor's relic).

McAvoy (*Ir.*) Son of the yellow-haired lad.

MacBean (*Scot.*) The son of Bean (life).

MacBeth (*Scot.*) Descendant of Macbeatha (son of life, a religious person), a personal name.

McBride, MacBride (*Ir.*) The son of the servant of St. Brigid.

McCabe, MacCabe (*Ir.*) Son of the hooded one.

McCaffrey, MacCaffray, McCaffrie (*Ir.*) The son of Godfrey (God's peace); the son of Eachmharcach (horse rider).

McCahey (*Ir.*) The son of the horseman or cavalryman.

McCain (*Ir.*) The son of Eoin, Irish form of John (gracious gift of Jehovah).

McCall, MacCall, McColl (*Ir.*) The son of Cathal (battle mighty), or of Cathmhaol (battle chief).

McCallum, MacCallum, MacCollom (*Ir., Scot.*) The son of the tender one, i.e., one who was like a dove.

McCambridge, MacCambridge (*Scot.*) The son of Ambrois (immortal).

McCann (*Ir.*) The son of Annadh (a storm).

McCarron, McCarren (*Ir.*) The son of little Ciar (black).

McCarthy, MacCarthy, McCarty (*Ir.*) The son of Carthach (loving).

McCartney (*Ir.*) The son of little Art (stone or bear).

McCauley, Macaulay, McCawley, Maccauly, MacAulay, MacAuley, MacAllay (*Scot., Ir.*) The son of Amlaib, a Scotch form of Olaf (ancestor's relic); the son of Amhalghaidh, an ancient Irish personal name.

McClain (*Ir.*) The son of the servant of St. John.

MacClamroch (*Scot.*) Son of the ready-handed or dexterous man; also, possibly, son of the ruddy-handed, or bloody-handed, person.

MacClellan, McClellan, McClelland, Macclelland, Macleland (*Scot.*) The son of the servant of St. Faolan, Fillan or Felan (little wolf).

McClendon, McClenton (*Ir.*) The son of little Leannach (cloaked, or mantled).

McCloskey, McClosky (*Ir.*) The son of Bloscadh.

McCloud (*Scot.*) Variant of McLeod, q.v.

McClure, MacClure (*Scot.*) The son of the servant of Odhar.

McCluskey, McClusky (*Ir.*) The son of Bloscadh.

McColgan (*Ir.*) The son of Colga.

McCollum, McCollom, McCollam (*Ir., Scot.*) The son of the tender one, i.e., one who was like a dove.

McConnell, MacConnell (*Ir.*) The son of Domhnall (world mighty).

McCord (*Ir., Scot.*) The son of Muircheartach (navigator).

McCorkle, McCorkel, McCorkell (*Scot.*) The son of Thorcull or Thorketill (Thor's kettle).

McCormick, McCormack, MacCormack, MacCormick, McCormac (*Ir.*) The son of Cormac (charioteer or son of Corb), the name of eight saints.

McCoy, MacCoy (*Ir.*) The son of Aodh (fire).

McCracken, McCrackin (*Ir.*) The son of Neachtan (the pure one).

McCray, McCrea, MacCrea, McCree (*Ir., Scot.*) Descendant of MacRaith (a given name, meaning son of grace or prosperity).

McCue (*Ir.*) The son of Aodh (fire).

McCullough, McCulloch, McCullock, McCullagh (*Scot.*) The son of Cullach (boar).

McCune (*Ir.*) The son of Eoghan (well-born).

McCurdy, MacCurdy (*Ir.*) The son of the navigator.

McCutcheon, MacCutcheon, McCutchan, McCutchen (*Scot.*) The son of Hutcheon, diminutive pet form of Hugh (spirit).

McDaniel, McDaniels, MacDaniel, MacDaniels (*Ir.*) The son of Domhnall (world mighty).

McDermott, MacDermott, McDermut, MacDermid (*Ir.*) The son of Diarmaid (the freeman or common man); the son of Diarmuit or Dermot (free from envy).

McDonald, MacDonald, McDonell, MacDonell (*Scot., Ir.*) The son of Donald (dark or brown-haired stranger); the son of Domhnall (world mighty).

McDonough, MacDonough, McDonagh (*Ir.*) The son of Donnchadh (brown warrior or strong warrior).

MacDougall, McDougall, MacDougal, McDougal, McDougald (*Scot., Ir.*) The son of Dougal (black stranger).

McDowell, MacDowell, McDowall, MacDowall (*Ir.*) The son of the dark foreigner.

MacDuff (*Scot.*) The son of Dubh (dark).

Mace (*Fr.*) One who came from Macy, Macey, or Mace (Mathieu's farm), in France.

McElligott (*Ir.*) The son of little Ulick, a pet form of William (resolution, helmet).

McElroy, MacElroy (*Ir.*) The son of the red youth.

McEvoy (*Ir.*) The son of the yellow-haired lad.

McEwen, McEwan, MacEwan (*Scot., Ir.*) The son of Eoghan (wellborn).

McFadden, MacFadden, McFaden, McFayden, McFadyen (*Scot., Ir.*) The son of little Pad, a pet form of Patrick (noble or patrician).

MacFarland, MacFarlane, MacFarlan (*Scot.*) The son of Parlan or Partholon (sea waves).

MacFee, MacFie (*Scot.*) The son of Dubhshithe (the black man of peace).

McGann, McGan (*Ir.*) The son of Annadh (a storm).

McGarry, McGary (*Ir.*) The son of Fearadhach (manly).

MacGee, McGee, MacGhee, Magee (*Ir.*) The son of Aodh (fire).

McGill (*Ir.*) The son of the foreigner; a shortened form of some surname commencing with MacGiolla (son of the servant of . . .).

MacGillicuddy, MacGillycuddy (*Ir.*) The son of the servant, or devotee, of Mochuda, an early Irish saint of Lismore.

MacGillivray, McGillvray, MacGilvray MacGilvra, McGilvery (*Scot.*) The son of Gillebhrath (servant of judgment or doom).

McGinley (*Ir.*) The son of Fionnghal (fair valor).

McGinnis, MacGinnis (*Ir.*) The son of Aonghus (one choice).

McGinty (*Ir.*) The son of Fionnachta (fair snow).

McGoldrick, MacGoldrick (*Ir., Scot.*) The son of Ualgharg (proud and fierce, or hot-tempered).

McGonagle, McGonigle, McGonnigal (*Ir.*) The son of Congal (high valor).

McGovern, MacGovern (*Ir.*) The son of little Samhradh (summer).

McGowan, MacGowan, McGowen (*Ir., Scot.*) The son of the smith or worker in metals.

McGrath, MacGrath (*Ir.*) Descendant of MacRaith (son of grace or prosperity), the full form being a given name.

McGraw (*Ir.*) Variant of McGrath, q.v.

MacGregor, McGregor, McGregory (*Scot.*) The son of Gregory (watchman).

McGrew (*Scot.*) The son of the brewer.

McGuinness, McGuiness (*Ir.*) The son of Aonghus (one choice).

McGuire, MacGuire (*Ir.*) The son of the pale or light-complexioned man.

McHale, MacHale (*Wel., Ir.*) The son of Howel (eminent).

McHenry (*Ir.*) The son of Henry (home ruler).

McHugh, MacHugh (*Ir.*) The son of Aodh (fire).

Maciejewski (*Pol.*) Descendant of Maciej, a pet form of Mateusz (gift of Jehovah).

McInerney, McInerny (*Ir.*) The son of the steward of church lands.

MacInnis, McInnis, MacInnes, McInnes, Maginnis (*Scot.*) The son of Innes (islet), q.v.; the son of Angus (excellent strength).

McIntosh, MacIntosh, Mackintosh (*Scot.*) The son of the chief or leader.

McIntyre, MacIntyre, McIntire (*Scot.*) The son of the carpenter or worker in wood.

McIsaac, MacIsaac, MacIsaacs (*Scot.*) The son of Isaac (he who laughs).

MacIver, McIver, MacIvor (*Scot.*) The son of Ivar or Iver (archer).

Mack, Mac (*Scot., Ir.*) Descendant of Mack or Mac (son), an abbreviation of one or another of the numerous Gaelic Mac- names.

McKay, MacKay, MacKey (*Scot.*) The son of Aoidh or Aodh (fire).

McKenna, MacKenna, McKenney, McKenny (*Ir.*) The son of the man beloved by Aodh (fire), the fire god.

MacKenzie, McKenzie (*Scot.*) The son of Coinneach (fair, bright).

McKeon, McKeown, McKeone (*Ir.*) The son of Eoghan (wellborn), or of Eoin (gracious gift of Jehovah).

Mackey, Mackie (*Ir.*) The son of Macdha (manly, or virile).

MacKey, McKee (*Ir.*) The son of Aodh (fire).

McKinley, MacKinley, McKinlay (*Scot.*) The son of Finlay (fair hero).

McKinney, MacKinney, McKinnie, McKinny (*Ir.*) The son of Cionaodh (fire sprung).

MacKinnon, McKinnon (*Scot.*) The son of Findgaine (fair-born).

Macklin, Mackling (*Ir.*) The son of Flann (the red).

McKnight, MacKnight (*Ir.*) The son of the knight.

Mackowiak (*Pol.*) One who came from Mackow(o) (Maciek's farm), the name of several places in Poland.

McLachlan (*Scot.*) The son of Lachlan (warlike).

McLain, McLane (*Ir.*) The son of the servant of St. John.

McLaren, McLaurin (*Scot.*) The son of Laurin or Laurence (the laurel, symbol of victory).

McLaughlin, MacLaughlin, McLoughlin, MacLachlan, McLaughlan (*Ir.*) The son of Lochlainn or Lochlann (Norway); the son of one who came from Norway.

MacLean, McLean, McLain, McLane (*Scot.*) The son of the servant of St. John (gracious gift of God).

MacLeish, McLeish, MacLish (*Scot.*) The son of the servant of Jesus.

McLellan, MacLellan, McLelland (*Scot., Ir.*) The son of the servant of St. Faolan (little wolf).

MacLennan, McLennan (*Scot.,*) The son of the servant of St. Finnian.

MacLeod, McLeod, McLoud (*Scot.*) The son of Leod (ugly).

McMahon, McMahan, MacMahon, McMahin (*Ir.*) The son of Mathghamhain (bear).

McMann (*Ir.*) Variant of McMahon, q.v.

McManus, MacManus (*Ir.*) The son of Maghnus (great).

McMaster, McMasters (*Scot.*) The son of the Master, i.e., a cleric.

MacMillan, McMillan, McMillen, McMillin (*Scot.*) The son of the bald, or tonsured, one.

McMorrow, McMurrough (*Ir.*) The son of Murchadh (sea warrior).

McMullen, MacMullen, McMullan, McMullin (*Ir.*) The son of little Maolan (little bald man).

McMurray, McMurry (*Ir., Scot.*) The son of Muireadhach (belonging to the sea, or a lord).

McNabb, MacNabb, McNab (*Scot.*) The son of the Abbot.

McNair (*Scot., Ir.*) The son of dark-brown John (gracious gift of Jehovah); the son of the heir, or of the steward, or of the smith, or of the stranger.

McNally, MacNally (*Ir.*) The son of the poor man.

McNamara, MacNamara (*Ir.*) The son of the hound of the sea, a name applied to a daring seaman.

McNamee, MacNamee (*Ir.*) The son of Cumidhe (hound of Meath).

McNaughton, MacNaught (*Scot., Ir.*) The son of Neachdain or Neachtan (the pure one).

McNeil, MacNeill, McNeill, MacNeil, McNeal, MacNeal (*Scot.*) The son of Naill or Neil (champion).

McNicholas, McNichols, McNichol, MacNichol (*Ir.*) The son of Nicholas (people's victory).

McNiff (*Ir.*) The son of Cu-dubh (black hound).

McNulty, MacNulty (*Ir.*) The son of the Ulidian (native of East Ulster).

McNutt (*Ir., Scot.*) The son of Nuadha (an ancient sea divinity); the son of Neachtan (the pure one).

Macomber, McComb, McCombs (*Scot.*) The son of Tom, a pet form of Thomas (a twin).

Macon, Masson (*Fr.*) One who built with stone or brick; one who came from Macon in France; descendant of Masson, a pet form of Thomasson (a twin); descendant of Macon (force, hard).

MacPhail, McPhail (*Scot.*) The son of Paul (small).

McPhee, MacPhee (*Scot.*) The son of Dubhshithe (the black man of peace).

MacPherson, McPherson (*Scot.*) The son of the parson.

McQuade, McQuaid, McQuaide (*Ir.*) The son of Wat, a pet form of Walter (rule, army).

MacQuarrie, McQuarrie, McQuire (*Scot.*) The son of Guaire (proud, noble).

McQueen, MacQueen, McQueyn (*Scot., Ir.*) The son of Suibhne (good going); the son of the peaceful or quiet man.

McRae, McRay, MacRae (*Scot.*) Descendant of Macrath (son of grace), the full form being a given name.

McReynolds (*Ir.*) The son of Reginald (powerful, force).

McShane (*Ir.*) The son of Eoin, Seon or Sean, all forms of John (gracious gift of Jehovah).

McSorley (*Scot., Ir.*) The son of Somhairle (viking or sailor, or summer wanderer).

McSweeney, MacSweeney, McSwiney, McSweeny (*Ir.*) The son of Suibhne (good going).

MacTavish (*Scot.*) The son of Tammas (a twin).

McTigue (*Ir.*) The son of Tadhg (poet or philosopher).

McVey, McVeigh, McVay, McVeagh, McVea (*Ir.*) Descendant of Mac an Bheathadh (son of life), the full form being a given name.

McWilliams, MacWilliams, McWilliam, MacWilliam (*Scot., Ir.*) The son of William (resolution, helmet).

Macy, Macey (*Eng.*) One who came from Macy, Macey or Mace, all in France; descendant of Maci, a pet form of Mathiu (gift of Jehovah).

Maday (*Pol.*) Descendant of Madey, the name of a Polish legendary hero.

Madden, Maddin (*Eng., Ir.*) Descendant of little Matthew (gift of Jehovah); grandson of little Madadh (dog).

Maddox, Maddock, Maddocks (*Eng., Wel.*) Descendant of Madog or Madoc (fortunate).

Madej (*Pol.*) One who came from Madej (Madey's settlement), in Poland; dweller near the Madej River, in Poland.

Mader, Madar, Madder (*Eng., Ger.*) One who dyes with, or sells, red dye stuff; one who came from Maden, in Germany; one who mows or harvests grain; descendant of Matheri (court, army).

Madigan (*Ir.*) Grandson of little Madadh (dog).

Madison (*Eng.*) The son of Mad, a pet form of Matthew (gift of Jehovah).

Madoc, Madog (*Wel.*) Descendant of Madog or Madoc (fortunate).

Madsen (*Dan.*) The son of Mad, a pet form of Mathies (gift of Jehovah).

Madura (*Pol.*) The wise or learned man.

Magee (*Ir.*) Variant of MacKey, q.v.

Mager (*Du.*) The slender, gaunt person.

Magg, Mag, Maggs (*Ger., Eng.*) Descendant of Magg, a pet form of names beginning with Mag (blood relationship), as Magafrid and Magbald; descendant of Magg, a pet form of Margaret (pearl).

Maggio, Maggini (*It.*) Descendant of Maggio (one born in the month of May).

Maggiore (*It.*) Descendant of the eldest son.

Magill (*Ir.*) The son of the foreigner.

Magner (*Ir.*) Descendant of little Maghnus (great).

Magnuson, Magnus (*Sw.*) The son of Magnus (great).

Magoun, Magoon, Magowan (*Ir.*) The son of the smith or worker in metals.

Maguire (*Ir.*) The son of the pale or light-complexioned man.

Maher (*Ir.*) Grandson of Meachar (hospitable).

Mahler (*Ger.*) One who painted buildings and ships, a painter; one who came from Mahlau, in Germany.

Mahon, Mahan, Mahone (*Ir.*) Grandson of little Moch, a pet form of some early name commencing with Moch; the son of one with bearlike characteristics.

Mahoney, Mahony (*Ir.*) Grandson of Mathghamhain (bear).

Maier (*Ger., Du.*) An overseer or head servant; later, a farmer; one who cut and gathered grain, a reaper.

Main, Maine (*Eng., Fr.*) Descendant of Magino (strength); one who came from Maine, in France; the strong man.

Maitland (*Scot., Eng.*) Dweller at, or on, the meadow or pasture land.

Majewski (*Pol.*) One born in the month of May.

Majka (*Yu.-Sl., Bulg.*) The mother's son, probably referring to a widow's son.

Major (*Eng.*) The larger man.

Makepeace (*Eng.*) One who acted as a peacemaker or mediator.

Maki (*Finn.*) One who lived on, or near, a hill.

Makowski (*Pol.*) Dweller where poppies grew; one who came from Makow(o) (poppy), in Poland.

Malcolm, Malcom, Malcomb (*Scot.*) Descendant of Malcolm (devotee of St. Columba, dove).

Malecki, Malec (*Pol.*) The little man.

Malek, Malik (*Rus., Pol.*) The small man.

Malenkov (*Rus.*) The son of a little man.

Malin, Malina, Malinowski (*Pol.*) Dweller where raspberries grew; one who came from Malinowo, in Poland.

Malkin, Malkinson (*Eng.*) Descendant of Malkin, a pet form of Mary (bitterness), also of little Mal, a pet form of Matilda (might, battle).

Malkowski (*Pol.*) One who came from Malkowo (little), in Poland.

Mallard (*Eng.*) Dweller at the sign of the wild drake, or common wild duck.

Mallett, Mallette, Mallet, Malet (*Eng., Fr.*) Descendant of little Mal, a pet form of names like Malcolm, Malculf and Maldred; descendant of little Malo or Maclou, a saint of the seventh century.

Mallin, Mallen, Mallinson (*Eng.*) Descendant of little Mall, a pet form of Mary (bitterness), or of Matilda (might, battle).

Mallory, Malory, Mallery (*Eng.*) The unhappy or unfortunate man.

Malloy (*Ir.*) Grandson of Maolaodha (servant of St. Aedh).

Malmberg (*Sw.*) Ore mountain.

Malone (*Ir.*) Grandson of the servant or devotee of St. John.

Maloney (*Ir.*) Grandson of Maoldomhnaigh (devoted to Sunday, or to the church).

Malonson, Malanson (*Fr.*) The sick, or infirm, man.

Maloof, Malouf (*Arab.*) The well-known or famous man.

Malthus (*Eng.*) Dweller at a house in which malt is prepared and stored.

Maly, Maley, Mally, Malley (*Cz.-Sl.*) The small person.

Malyshev (*Rus.*) The small man, little boy.

Mancuso, Mancini, Mancinelli (*It.*) One who was left-handed.

Mandel, Mandell, Mandl (*Ger.*) Descendant of little Manto (pleasure or joy).

Manfred (*Eng.*) Descendant of Manfred (man, peace).

Mangan, Mangin (*Ir.*) Grandson of Mongan (little, hairy one).

Maniates, Maniatis (*Gr.*) One who came from Mane, an idefinite district in Greece.

Manley, Manly (*Eng.*) One who came from Manley (common wood), in Cheshire.

Mann, Man, Manns (*Ger., Eng.*) The vassal or servant; one who came from the Isle of Man, a Manxman.

Mannheimer, Mannheim (*Ger.*) One who came from Mannheim (servant's home), in Germany.

Manning (*Eng.*) The son of the servant; descendant of Manning (little person).

Mannion, Manion (*Ir.*) Grandson of Mainnin or Maincin (little monk).

Manolatos (*Gr.*) The son of Manolis (God is with us).

Manos (*Gr.*) Descendant of Manos, a pet form of Manolis (God is with us).

Mansfield (*Eng.*) One who came from Mansfield (open land by the hill named Mam), in Nottinghamshire.

Manson, Mansen (*Sw., Nor., Dan., Eng.*) The son of Man, a pet form of Magnus (great); the son of the servant.

Mantell, Mantel (*Eng.*) One who made and sold cloaks or mantles.

Manuel, Manual (*Eng., Scot.*) Descendant of Emmanuel (God with us); one who came from Manuel, in Stirlingshire.

Manz, Manze (*Ger.*) Descendant of Manz, a pet form of Manto (pleasure or joy).

Mapes (*Wel., Eng.*) The son of Map (son), or of Mab, a pet form of Mabel (amiable).

Maple, Maples, Mapel, Maypole (*Eng.*) Dweller at, or near, a maple tree, or at the sign of the maypole.

Mapp, Mapps (*Eng., Wel.*) Descendant of Map (son); descendant of Mabb, a pet form of Mabel or Amabel (amiable).

Marais (*Fr.*) One who lived near a marsh.

Marangopoulos (*Gr.*) The son of the carpenter.

Marble, Marple, Marbles (*Eng.*) One who came from Marple (hill by the boundary valley), in Cheshire.

March (*Eng.*) Dweller at the boundary mark; the same as Marsh, q.v.; one who came from March (boundary), in Cambridgeshire.

Marchand, Marchant, Marcand, Marquand (*Fr.*) The tradesman or merchant.

Marchese (*It.*) One with the title of marquis; one connected in some manner with a marquis' household.

Marchetti (*It.*) Descendant of little Marco (belonging to Mars).

Marciniak (*Pol.*) The son of Marcin (belonging to Mars).

Marckwardt, Markwardt, Markvart, Markwart (*Ger.*) The warden of the marches, or frontier watchman or guard; descendant of Marcward (border, guard).

Marco (*It.*) Descendant of Marco (belonging to Mars).

Marcus (*Eng.*) Descendant of Marcus, the Latin form of Mark (belonging to Mars, the god of war).

Marden (*Eng.*) One who came from Marden (pasture for mares, or boundary hill), the name of places in Kent and Sussex.

Marder (*Ger.*) Dweller at the sign of the marten; dweller in a place infested by martens.

Marek (*Pol.*) Descendant of Marek (belonging to Mars).

Mares (*Cz.-Sl.*) Dweller at, or near, a marsh.

Margolis, Margulis, Margulies (*Ukr., Rus.*) Descendant of Margaret (pearl).

Marinello, Marinelli, Marinella (*It.*) A nickname given to one thought to possess some quality of the ladybug; dweller at the sign of the ladybug.

Marino, Marini, Marina (*It.*) Descendant of Marino or Marinus (of the sea).

Marion, Marian (*Fr.*) Descendant of little Mary (bitterness).

Marison (*Eng.*) The son of Mary (bitterness).

Marker, Markers (*Eng.*) One who marks game, i.e., notes the spot to which it has retired, for the hunter; dweller at, or near, a landmark or boundary.

Markey (*Ir.*) The horseman or rider.

Markham (*Eng.*) One who came from Markham (village on the boundary), in Nottinghamshire.

Markiewicz (*Pol., Rus.*) The son of Marek (belonging to Mars).

Markley, Markle (*Eng., Scot.*) Dweller in, or near, the wood on the boundary; one who came from the lands of Markle (hill where there are horses), in East Lothian.

Markowitz, Markovitz (*Cz.-Sl., Yu.,-Sl.*) The son of Mark (belonging to Mars).

Markowski (*Pol.*) One who came from Markowo (Marek's place), in Poland.

Marks, Mark (*Eng.*) Dweller at the boundary or boundary mark; descendant of Mark (belonging to Mars, the god of war); one who came from Marck (frontier district), in France; one who came from Mark (boundary house), in Somerset.

Markus (*Ger.*) Descendant of Mark (belonging to Mars, the god of war).

Marland, Marlan (*Eng.*) One who came from Marland (land on a lake), in Devonshire; dweller on the land by the lake.

Marley (*Eng.*) One who came from Marley (boundary, or pleasant, wood), villages in Devonshire and Kent.

Marlowe, Marlow (*Eng.*) One who came from Marlow (lake remains), in Buckinghamshire; dweller at the hill by the lake.

Maroney, Marone (*Ir.*) Variants of Moroney, q.v.

Marquardt, Marquard, Marquart (*Ger.*) The warden of the marches, or frontier watchman or guard; one who came from Marquard (border guard), in Germany; descendant of Marcward (border guard).

Marquis, Marquiss (*Eng., Fr.*) Descendant of Marcus (belonging to Mars); one connected in some manner with a marquis' household.

Marriott (*Eng.*) Descendant of little Mary (bitterness).

Mars, Marrs, Marr (*Scot., Eng.*) One who came from the parish of Mar (a tribal name), in Aberdeenshire, or from Marr (marsh), in Yorkshire; dweller at, or near, a marsh.

Marsden (*Eng.*) One who came from Marsden (boundary valley), the names of villages in Lancashire and Yorkshire.

Marsh, Mersh (*Eng.*) One who lived on, or near, the swamp or tract of soft, wet land.

Marshall, Marschall, Marshell (*Eng., Ger.*) One who cared for horses, especially one who treated their diseases; a shoeing smith; later, an official in a king's or high noble's household having charge of military affairs.

Marsters (*Eng.*) Variant due to pronunciation of Masters, q.v.

Marston (*Eng.*) One who came from Marston (homestead by a marsh), the name of many places in England.

Marszalek (*Pol.*) The officer in the household of a medieval king, prince or noble having charge of military affairs.

Martell, Martel (*Eng., Fr.*) The worker who used a hammer in a smithy; a nickname for a warrior.

Martensen, Martinson, Martinsen (*Dan.*) The son of Marten (belonging to Mars, the god of war).

Marti, Marta, Marte (*Swis., It.*) Descendant of Marti (belonging to Mars); descendant of Marti (Tuesday), a name sometimes given to one born on Tuesday.

Martikke (*Ukr.*) Descendant of Martycki (belonging to Mars, the god of war).

Martin, Marten, Martens, Martyn (*Fr., Eng.*) Descendant of Martinus (belonging to Mars, the god of war).

Martinek (*Cz.-Sl.*) Descendant of little Martin (belonging to Mars, the god of war).

Martinet, Martineau (*Fr.*) Descendant of little Martin (belonging to Mars, the god of war).

Martinez (*Sp.*) The son of Martin (belonging to Mars, the god of war).

Martini, Martino (*It.*) Descendant of Martini (name sometimes given to one born on Tuesday).

Marvin (*Eng.*) Descendant of Marvin (sea Finn), or of Marwin (sea, friend).

Marx, Marxen, Marxsen (*Ger., Eng.*) The son of Mark or Marcus (hammer); dweller at a mark or boundary stone.

Marzano (*It.*) Descendant of Marzano or Marzia (belonging to Mars).

Marzec (*Pol.*) Descendant of one born in the month of March.

Marzullo, Marzulli (*It.*) Descendant of Marzullo (name sometimes given to one born in March).

Masaryk (*Cz.-Sl.*) The little man who cut and sold meat, the little butcher.

Masek (*Cz.-Sl.*) One who sold meat, a butcher; descendant of Masek, a pet form of Mathes (gift of Jehovah).

Maslanka (*Ukr.*) One who had some characteristics of buttermilk; one who sold buttermilk.

Maslankowski (*Pol.*) One who came from Maslankow(o) (buttermilk).

Mason (*Eng.*) The builder with stone or brick.

Mass (*Ger.*) Descendant of Mass, a pet form of Thomas (a twin).

Massa, Masso (*It.*) Dweller in the upland or lowland; descendant of Masso, a pet form of Tomasso (a twin).

Massey, Massie (*Eng., Fr.*) One who came from Massy or Macey (Mathieu's farm), in Normandy; descendant of Massey, a pet form of Thomas (a twin).

Masters (*Eng.*) Descendant of the teacher or schoolmaster.

Masterson (*Eng.*) The son of the leader or teacher.

Mather, Mathers (*Eng.*) One who cut grass, a mower; descendant of Mathhere (power, army).

Matheson, Mathisen, Mathison, Mathewson (*Scot., Dan.*) Son of Matthew (gift of Jehovah); descendant of Matgamna (bear).

Mathiesen, Matthiesen (*Dan.*) The son of Mathies (gift of Jehovah).

Mathieu (*Fr.*) Descendant of Mathieu (gift of Jehovah).

Matlock (*Eng.*) One who came from Matlock (oak where a meeting was held).

Matson, Mattson (*Eng.*) The son of Mat or Matt, pet forms of Matthew (gift of Jehovah).

Matsumoto (*Jap.*) One who came from Matsumoto (original pine), a town in Japan.

Matteson, Mattes, Matt (*Eng.*) The son of Matt, pet form of Matthew (gift of Jehovah).

Matthews, Mathews, Matthew, Mathew (*Wel., Eng.*) The son of Matthew (gift of Jehovah).

Matthies, Matthias (*Ger., Eng.*) Descendant of Matthies or Matthias (gift of Jehovah).

Matthis, Matthes (*Ger.*) Descendant of Matthes (gift of Jehovah).

Mattinen (*Finn.*) The son of Matti (gift of Jehovah).

Matus, Matous (*Cz.-Sl., Pol.*) Descendant of Matus (gift of Jehovah).

Matuszak, Matousek, Matushek (*Cz.-Sl., Pol.*) The son of Matus or Matous (gift of Jehovah).

Matz (*Ger.*) Descendant of Mazo, a pet form of Math (assembly place), or from Matz, a pet form of Matthaus (gift of Jehovah).

Mau (*Ger.*) One who came from Maua, in Germany.

Maul, Maule, Maull (*Ger., Eng.*) One with a large, or animal-like mouth; one who came from Maule (mouth), in France; descendant of Mall, a pet form of Matilda (might, battle).

Maurer (*Ger.*) One who builds with stone, a mason.

Max (*Ger.*) Descendant of Max, a pet form of Maximilian (the greatest).

Maxey (*Eng.*) One who came from Maxey (Maccu's island), in Northamptonshire.

Maxim, Maxime (*Eng., Fr.*) The greatest, a nickname; descendant of Maxime (greatest).

Maxwell (*Eng.*) Dweller by the big spring.

May, Mayes, Mays (*Eng., Fr.*) Descendant of May, a pet form of Matthew (gift of Jehovah).

Mayberry (*Eng.*) Dweller at, or near, the tribal hill.

Maybury (*Eng.*) One who came from Maesbury (Maerec's fort), in Somerset.

Mayer (*Ger.*) An overseer or head servant; later, a farmer.

Mayfield (*Eng.*) One who came from Mayfield (field where madder or mayweed grew), the name of places in Staffordshire and Sussex.

Mayhew (*Eng.*) Descendant of Mayheu or Matthew (gift of Jehovah).

Maynard (*Eng.*) Descendant of Maynard (strength, hardy).

Mayo (*Eng.*) Descendant of Mayo, a pet form of Matthew (gift of Jehovah).

Mazeika (*Lith.*) The small man.

Mazur, Mazurek (*Pol.*) One who came from Mazury or Masuria, a former East Prussian province, now a part of Poland.

Mazurkiewicz (*Pol., Ukr.*) The son of Mazur (one who came from the province of Mazowsze, in Poland).

Mazzone, Mazzoni (*It.*) Dweller at the sign of the fish; descendant of big Mazzo, a pet form of Giacomazzo (the supplanter); the slow-moving man; dweller at, or near, a field or meadow.

Mazzuca, Mazzucca (*It.*) Descendant of Mazzo, a pet form of Giacomazzo (the supplanter).

Mc. *See* Mac. All Mc names are listed as if spelled *Mac.*

Mead, Meade (*Eng., Ir.*) Dweller at the grassland or meadow; the man from Meath (middle).

Meadows, Medow, Meadow (*Eng.*) Dweller at, or near, the field where grass is grown for hay.

Meagher (*Ir.*) Grandson of Meachar (hospitable).

Means, Mean, Menes (*Eng.*) Dweller near the common or unenclosed land.

Meany, Meaney (*Scot.*) One who came from the lands of Mennie, in Aberdeenshire.

Mears, Meers, Mear, Meares (*Eng.*) Dweller at, or near, the lake or pond; dweller at the boundary line.

Medford (*Eng.*) One who came from Meaford (ford at the junction of streams), in Staffordshire.

Medina (*Sp.*) Dweller at, or near, the market; one who had returned from Medina (market), the holy city of Islam, in Arabia; one who came from Medina.

Meehan, Mehan (*Ir.*) Grandson of Miadhachan (dim. of miadhach, honorable).

Meeks, Meek (*Eng.*) The mild or humble person.

Meier (*Ger.*) An overseer, or head servant; later, a farmer.

Meissner, Meisner (*Ger.*) One who came from Meissen (place on the river Meissa), in Saxony.

Meister, Mester (*Ger.*) One who was master of a trade; a learned person or teacher; an artist.

Melanson, Melancon, Melonson (*Fr.*) The sick or infirm man.

Melas (*Gr.*) The swarthy man, black.

Melcher, Milker, Melker (*Ger., Eng.*) One who milked cows or goats; a seller of milk; descendant of Melchior (king of the light).

Mele (*Pol., Ukr., Rus.*) The pleasant or charming person.

Melin, Melind, Meline (*Fr.*) Descendant of Amelin (labor, bright).

Mellen, Melling, Mellon (*Eng.*) One who came from Melling (the people of Malla), the name of two places in Lancashire.

Melor, Meller (*Eng.*) One who came from Mellor (bare hill), in Derbyshire.

Melnick (*Cz.-Sl., Ukr.*) One who ground grain, a miller.

Melnikov (*Rus.*) One who ground grain, a miller.

Melone, Meloni, Mellone (*It.*) Descendant of Melone, a pet form of Giacomelli (the supplanter); one who grew and sold melons.

Melton (*Eng.*) One who came from Melton (mill homestead), the name of several places in England.

Meltzer, Melzer, Meltzner (*Ger.*) One who brews, a brewer; one who came from Meltz, in Germany.

Melville (*Scot.*) One who came from Melville in Scotland or Maleville (bad town), in Normandy.

Melvin (*Scot.*) A variant of Melville, q.v.

Menard (*Eng., Fr.*) Descendant of Maynard (strength, hardy).

Mencken, Menken (*Ger.*) One who lived in a monastery.

Mendel, Mendell (*Ger.*) Descendant of Mendel (knowledge or wisdom), a dim. of Menahem.

Mendelsohn, Mendelson, Mendelssohn (*Ger.*) Son of Mendel (knowledge or wisdom).

Mendez, Mendes (*Sp.*) Descendant of Mendel (knowledge or wisdom).

Mendoza (*Port., Sp.*) One who came from Mendoza (cold or high mountains).

Menzies, Menees (*Scot.*) One who came from Meyners, in Normandy.

Mercer, Mercier (*Eng., Fr.*) One who dealt in silks, velvets and other costly materials; a peddler or merchant of small wares.

Merchant (*Eng.*) The tradesman.

Mercurio (*Sp.*) Descendant of Mercurio (from the god, Mercury).

Meredith, Meridith (*Wel.*) Descendant of Maredudd (sea lord).

Merkel, Merkle, Merkell, Merkl (*Ger.*) Descendant of little Merk or Mark (belonging to Mars, the god of war).

Merker, Merk, Merke (*Ger.*) One who came from Merke (boundary), in Germany; descendant of Marchari (boundary, army).

Merriam (*Eng.*) The gay or merry man.

Merrick, Merick, Merricks (*Eng., Scot.*) Descendant of Merick or Almeric (work, rule); one who came from Merrick (pronged or branching place), in Kirkcudbright.

Merrifield, Merryfield (*Eng.*) One who came from Merevale (pleasant valley), in Warwickshire.

Merrill, Merrell (*Eng.*) Descendant of Muriel, Miriel or Merel (sea, bright).

Merriman, Merryman, Merrymon (*Eng.*) A gay or pleasant man; one who followed a knight or outlaw.

Merritt (*Fr.*) One who tills the soil for which he pays rent, a tenant farmer; the small leader of the village.

Merriweather, Merryweather, Merriwether (*Eng.*) A gay, blithe or agreeable person.

Mertes (*Ger.*) Descendant of Mertin or Martinus (from Mars, the god of war).

Mertz, Merz (*Ger.*) Descendant of Mertz, a pet form of Mertens (from Mars, the god of war), or of Maro, a pet form of names beginning with Mar (famous), as Maruin and Maroald; one who came from Mertz, in Germany; one who sold small articles.

Meserve, Meservey (*Fr.*) One who measured land, a surveyor.

Mesirow, Meserow (*Pol., Rus., Ukr.*) Dweller on a row or strip of land between ditches.

Messer (*Eng.*) One who had charge of the fields, especially one appointed to oversee the reapers or mowers.

Messina (*It.*) One who came from Messina, in Italy.

Messinger, Messenger (*Eng.*) One who carried communications.

Metcalf, Metcalfe (*Eng.*) Dweller at, or near, the meadow where calves are kept.

Metz (*Ger.*) One who came from Metz (in the middle), in Lorraine; descendant of Metz, a pet form of Matthias (gift of Jehovah), or of Mark (belonging to Mars), or of names beginning with Macht (might), as Mahtfrid and Mahtulf.

Metzger, Metzler (*Ger.*) One who sold or handled meat, a butcher.

Meyer, Meyers (*Ger., Heb.*) An overseer, or head servant; later, a farmer; derived from the Hebrew *me'ir* (light).

Meyner, Meiner (*Ger.*) Descendant of Maganhar (strength, army); one who came from Meyn, in Germany.

Micek (*Pol.*) One who made and sold caps.

Miceli, Micelli, Micele (*It.*) Descendant of Michele (who is like God).

Michaelis (*Ger.*) Descendant of Michael (who is like God).

Michaels, Michael (*Eng.*) Descendant of Michael (who is like God).

Michaelson, Michaelsen (*Eng., Dan.*) The son of Michael (who is like God).

Michal, Mical (*Pol., Cz.-Sl.*) Descendant of Michal or Mical (who is like God).

Michalak, Michalek, Michalik, Michalec (*Pol.*) The son of Michal (who is like God).

Michalowski, Michalski (*Pol.*) Descendant of Michal (who is like God).

Michels, Michel (*Eng., Fr.*) Descendant of Michel (who is like God).

Michelson, Michelsen (*Nor.*) The son of Michel (who is like God).

Middendorf (*Ger.*) One who came from Middendorf (middle village), in Germany.

Middleton (*Eng.*) One who came from Middleton (the middle homestead or village), the name of many villages in England.

Mielke (*Ger.*) Descendant of little Miel, a pet form of Aemilius (industrious); descendant of little Milan (beloved), a pet form of names beginning with Mil (beloved), as Miloslaw and Milobrat.

Mika (*Pol.*) Descendant of Mika, a pet form of Marika (bitterness).

Mikkelsen (*Dan., Nor.*) The son of Mikkel (who is like God).

Mikkonen (*Finn.*) The son of Mikko (who is like God).

Mikos (*Gr.*) Descendant of Michos, a pet form of Michael (who is like God).

Mikrut (*Pol.*) The little one; descendant of Mikolaj (people's victory).

Mikula (*Pol., Rus., Ukr.*) Descendant of Mikolaj (people's victory).

Milano, Milani, Milanesi (*It.*) One who came from Milano (middle of the plain), in Italy.

Milazzo (*It.*) One who came from Milazzo, in Italy.

Milburn, Milbourn, Milbourne (*Eng.*) One who came from Milburn, Milbourne or Milborne (millstream), the names of various places in England.

Miles (*Wel.*) Descendant of Miles (soldier).

Milewski (*Pol.*) One who came from Milew(o) (dear), in Poland.

Milford (*Eng.*) One who came from Milford (ford by a mill), the name of several places in England.

Milgram, Milgroom, Milgrim (*Eng.*) One who came from Malham (stony place), in Yorkshire; descendant of Milegrim (Grimr with the big mouth).

Millard (*Fr., Eng.*) Dweller at, or near, a field of millet; descendant of Milhard (dear, strong); the keeper of a mill, a miller.

Miller, Milner, Millar (*Eng.*) One who grinds grain.

Milligan, Milliken, Millikin, Millican, Millikan (*Ir.*) Grandson of Maolagan (little, bald one).

Million (*Fr.*) Dweller at, or near, a small field of millet; descendant of little Milo (soldier), or of little Emile (industrious).

Millman (*Eng.*) One who operates a mill, a miller.

Mills, Mill, Milne, Milles (*Eng.*) Dweller at, or near, a mill.

Milos (*Cz.-Sl., Yu.-Sl.*) Descendant of Milos (pleasant).

Milton (*Eng.*) One who came from Milton (middle homestead, or mill homestead), the name of many places in England.

Mims, Mimms (*Eng.*) One who came from Mimms (origin obscure), the name of places in Hertfordshire and Middlesex.

Minkus (*Lith.*) Descendant of Minkus, a pet form of Minkantas (remember, suffer).

Minnick, Minnich (*Ger.*) Descendant of Minnich, a contracted form of Dominicus (Sunday child).

Minor, Miner (*Eng.*) One who worked in a mine; a soldier who undermines a fortress.

Minot, Minott (*Fr.*) One who measured goods.

Minsky (*Rus.*) One who came from Minsk, in Byelorussia.

Minster (*Eng.*) One who came from Minster (monastery), the name of places in Kent and Oxfordshire; dweller near a monastery.

Minter (*Eng.*) One who coined money.

Minton (*Eng.*) One who came from Minton (village by a mountain), in Shropshire.

Mintz, Mintzer (*Ger.*) Descendant of Magino, a pet form of names beginning with Magan (strength), as Maginbald, Maginhard and Maganrad; one who came from Mainz (great water), in Germany.

Miranda, Mirando (*Port., Sp.*) One who came from Miranda (admired place), the name of places in Spain and Portugal.

Mitcham, Mitchum, Mitchem (*Eng.*) One who came from Mitcham (great homestead), in Surrey.

Mitchell, Mitchel (*Eng.*) Descendant of Michael (who is like God).

Mix (*Eng.*) The son of Mick, a pet form of Michael (who is like God); one who came from Mix, in France.

Mixon, Mixson (*Eng.*) The son of Mick, a pet form of Michael (who is like God); one who came from Mixon (dunghill), in Staffordshire.

Mlynar (*Cz.-Sl.*) One who ground grain, a miller.

Mlynek, Mlejnek (*Cz.-Sl.*) The little miller or grinder of grain.

Moberg, Moburg (*Sw.*) Heath mountain.

Mobley, Moberly (*Eng.*) One who came from Mobberley (glade with an assembly mound), in Cheshire.

Mock (*Ger.*) The plump or fat man; the clumsy or awkward man.

Mockler (*Ger., Ir.*) The plump or fat man; the bad clerk or clergyman.

Moe, Moen (*Nor.*) Dweller on the heath or low land.

Moeller, Moller (*Ger.*) One who ground grain, a miller.

Moffet, Moffett, Moffatt, Moffitt, Moffit (*Scot.*) One who came from Moffatt (long plain), in Dumfriesshire.

Mogge, Mogg (*Eng.*) Descendant of Mogg, a pet form of Margaret (pearl).

Moliere (*Fr.*) One who lived near the quarry from which millstones were obtained.

Moline (*Fr.*) One who came from Moline (mill), in France.

Moll (*Eng.*) One who paid a money rent to the lord of the manor in return for the land he held and worked for the lord only on special occasions; descendant of Moll (the foolish one), or of Mall, a pet form of Mary (bitterness).

Molnar, Molner, Molnor (*Hun.*) One who ground grain, a miller.

Moloney, Molony (*Ir.*) Grandson of Maoldomhnaigh (devoted to Sunday, or to the church).

Molotov (*Rus.*) Hammer, an adopted name.

Monahan, Manahan, Monaghan (*Ir.*) Descendant of the little monk, i.e., a tenant of ecclesiastical lands; grandson of Manachan (dim. of manach, a monk).

Monday (*Eng.*) One who occupied land in an English manor for which he worked for the lord one day a week, on Mondays; descendant of Monday (one born on Monday).

Money, Monnie (*Eng.*) One who came from Monnaie (mint), in France.

Monk (*Eng.*) One who was a male member of a religious order.

Monroe, Monro (*Scot.*) One who came from near the Roe River in Derry, Ireland; dweller near a red swamp.

Monson, Monsen (*Sw., Dan.*) The son of Mon, a pet form of Magnus (great).

Montague, Montagu (*Eng.*) One who came from Montacute or Mont Aigu (peaked hill), in Normandy.

Montefiore (*It.*) One who came from Montefiore (flower mountain), in Italy.

Moody, Moodie, Mudie (*Eng.*) The bold, impetuous, brave man.

Moon, Moone (*Eng.*) One who came from Mohon, in France; dweller at the sign of the moon.

Moore, Moor, More (*Eng.*) Dweller in, or near, the marsh or high wasteland.

Moorman (*Scot.*) The official in charge of the cattle on the marsh or waste ground.

Moran, Morane, Moraine (*Ir.*) Grandson of Moran (little great man); grandson of Mughron (slave seal).

Moravec, Moravek (*Cz.-Sl.*) One who came from Moravia (district of the marshy river), a former province in Czechoslovakia.

Mordecai (*Wel.*) Descendant of Mordecai (taught of God).

Moreau (*Fr.*) One who came from Moreau, the name of three places in France; the brown-skinned man, perhaps a Moor.

Morehead, Moorhead (*Scot.*) Variants of Muirhead, q.v.

Morehouse, Moorhouse (*Eng.*) Dweller in the house by the swamp or wasteland.

Moreland (*Eng.*) One who came from Morland (grove by a moor), in Westmorland; dweller near a swamp.

Morelli, Morello (*It.*) Descendant of little More, a pet form of Amore (love), or of Mauro (a Moor); the small, dark-complexioned man.

Moreno (*Sp.*) The dark-complexioned man.

Moretti, Moretta (*It.*) Same as Morelli, q.v.

Morey, Mora (*Ir.*) Grandson of Mordha (majestic).

Morgan (*Wel.*) Descendant of Morgan (great, bright).

Morgenthau (*Ger.*) Morning valley.

Moriarty (*Ir.*) Grandson of Muircheartach (expert navigator).

Morin (*Fr.*) One who had a dark complexion, a Moor.

Moritz, Morritz (*Ger.*) Descendant of Moritz, a variant of Mauritius (a Moor, dark).

Mork (*Nor.*) Dweller near the mork, or unenclosed land owned jointly by the surrounding landowners.

Morley (*Eng.*) One who came from Morley (wood by a marsh), the name of several places in England.

Moroney (*Ir.*) Grandson of Maolruanaidh (follower of Ruanaidh).

Morreale (*It.*) One who came from Morreale (royal mountain), in Italy.

Morrill, Morrell, Morrall, Morel, Morell (*Eng.*) The little, dark-complexioned man; descendant of Morel (dark-complexioned).

Morris, Morice (*Wel., Fr.*) Descendant of Maurice (Moorish, or dark-skinned).

Morrison, Morison (*Eng., Scot.*) The son of Morris (Moorish, or dark-skinned).

Morrissey, Morrisey (*Ir.*) Grandson of Muirgheas (sea prophet).

Morrow (*Eng.*) Dweller in the row of houses by the moor, i.e., marsh or wasteland.

Morse, Moors (*Eng.*) Dweller at, or near, a moor or marshy wasteland; the son of Moor (dark-complexioned man); one who came from North Africa.

Mortensen, Mortenson (*Dan., Nor., Sw.*) The son of Morten (from Mars, the god of war).

Mortimer, Mortimore (*Eng.*) One who came from Mortemer (stagnant water), in Normandy.

Morton (*Eng.*) One who came from Morton (homestead by a marsh), the name of many places in England.

Moser (*Fr.*) One who grew and sold vegetables.

Moses, Moseson (*Wel.*) Descendant of Moses (saved from the water).

Mosher, Moshier (*Ger.*) Dweller on, or near, the moor or swamp.

Moskal (*Pol., Ukr.*) A Russian soldier who came from Muscovy, a principality in west central Russia.

Moskovitz, Moskowitz (*Cz.-Sl., Yu.-Sl.*) The son of Mosko (saved from the water).

Moskovsky (*Rus.*) One who came from Moscow (mossy water).

Mosley, Moseley, Mosely (*Eng.*) One who came from Moseley (wood infested with mice, or Moll's wood), the name of places in Staffordshire and Worcestershire.

Moss, Mosse (*Eng.*) Descendant of Moss, a pet form of Moses (saved from the water); one who came from Moss (morass), in Yorkshire.

Mostyn, Moston (*Wel.*) One who came from Mostyn (field fortress), in Wales.

Motel (*Pol., Fr.*) Dweller at the sign of the butterfly; one thought to possess some characteristic of a butterfly; dweller near a small fortification.

Motley, Mottley (*Eng.*) One who made cloth of a mixed color.

Mott, Mote (*Eng.*) Dweller near a moat; dweller near a mound or embankment.

Moulin, Moulinier, Molinier, Moliner (*Fr.*) One who ground grain, a miller.

Moulton (*Eng.*) One who came from Moulton (Mula's homestead), the name of various places in England.

Moy (*Chin.*) Plum flower.

Moyer, Moyers (*Ir.*) The son of the steward.

Mozart (*Ger.*) Descendant of Muothart (spirit, strong).

Mraz (*Cz.-Sl.*) Descendant of Mraz (frost).

Mrazek (*Cz.-Sl.*) Descendant of little Mraz (frost).

Mroz, Mrozek (*Cz.-Sl.*) One with the qualities of a walrus, for example, fat, or mustached; one who lived at the sign of the walrus, or little walrus.

Mucha (*Pol., Ukr., Cz.-Sl., Rus.*) The fly, probably designating one with some characteristic of that insect; dweller at the sign of the fly.

Mudd (*Eng.*) Dweller at the muddy place.

Mudge (*Eng.*) Dweller in, or near, a swamp.

Mudgett (*Eng.*) Dweller in, or near, the little swamp.

Mueller, Muller (*Ger.*) One who ground grain, a miller.

Muench, Munch (*Ger.*) One who was a member of a religious order.

Muhr (*Ger.*) Dweller at the marsh land or moor; dweller near a wall.

Muir (*Scot.*) Dweller at, or near, a moor or heath.

Muirhead (*Scot.*) One who came from Muirhead (end of the moor), the name of several places in Scotland; dweller at the end of the marsh.

Mulcahy (*Ir.*) Grandson of Maolchatha (battle chief), or of Maolcathach (warlike chief), or of Maolchathaigh (follower of Cathach, warlike).

Mulder (*Du.*) One who ground grain, a miller.

Muldoon, Muldon (*Ir.*) Grandson of Maolduin (commander of the garrison).

Mulholland (*Ir.*) Grandson of Maolchallann (chief of the calends).

Mull (*Eng.*) One who lived, or worked, at the mill.

Mullaney, Mullane, Mullany (*Ir.*) Grandson of the follower or devotee of St. Senan (old, wise), the name of various Irish saints.

Mullen, Mullon, Mullan (*Ir.*) Grandson of Maolan (dim. of maol, bald); the son of the little, bald man.

Mulligan, Mulliken, Mullikin (*Ir.*) Grandson of Maolagan (little, bald one).

Mullins, Mullin (*Ir., Fr.*) Grandson of Maolan (dim. of maol, bald); one who came from Moulins or Moulines (mills), the names of several places in France; one who ground grain, a miller.

Mulroy (*Ir.*) Grandson of Maolruadh (red chief).

Mulvaney, Mulvany, Mulvanny, Mulvenny (*Ir.*) Grandson of one overly concerned with minor details, a fussy person; grandson of Maolmheana (follower of Meana).

Mulvey (*Ir.*) Grandson of Maolmiadhach (honorable chief).

Mulvihill (*Ir.*) Grandson of Maolmhichil (servant of St. Michael).

Mumford (*Eng.*) One who came from Mundford (Munda's river crossing), the name of several places in England.

Munch (*Nor.*) A male member of a religious order.

Mundt, Mund, Muntz, Munz (*Ger.*) Descendant of Mundo, a pet form of names beginning with Munt (protection), as Mundhart and Munderich.

Mundy, Munday (*Eng.*) Descendant of Monday, a name given to children in the Middle Ages born on a Monday; variants of Monday, q.v.

Munger (*Eng.*) One who sold things, a merchant.

Munk, Monk, Monek (*Eng.*) One who resided in a monastic establishment.

Munn, Munns (*Eng.*) One who resided in a monastic establishment, a monk.

Munoz, Muniz (*Sp.*) The son of Muno (hill), or of Nuno.

Munro, Munroe (*Scot.*) One who came from near the Roe River in Derry, Ireland; dweller near a red swamp.

Munson, Munsen (*Sw., Eng., Nor.*) The son of Mans, a pet form of Magnus (great); the son of Mun, a pet form of Edmund (rich, protector).

Murawski (*Pol.*) One who lived near an outstanding lawn.

Murchison, Murch, Murche (*Eng.*) The son of the dwarf.

Murdock, Murdoch (*Eng., Ir.*) Descendant of Murdoch (seaman).

Murgatroyd (*Eng.*) Dweller at Margaret's clearing.

Murillo (*Sp.*) One who came from Murillo de Rio de Leza, in Spain.

Murnane (*Ir.*) Grandson of Manannan (the name of an ancient Irish sea god).

Murphy, Murphey (*Ir.*) Descendant of Murchadh (sea warrior).

Murray, Murry, Murrie (*Scot.*) One who came from Moray (beside the sea), in Scotland.

Murrell (*Eng.*) A variant of Morrill, q.v.

Murtaugh, Murtagh (*Ir.*) Grandson of Muircheartach (expert navigator).

Muscarello, Muscarella (*It.*) One who grew the muscat or muscatel grape; one thought to possess the characteristics of a gnat.

Muse, Mews, Muhs (*Eng.*) Dweller near the hawk's cage; dweller at a mew, i.e., a range of stables, with coach houses, around an open space.

Musgrave, Musgrove (*Eng.*) One who came from Musgrave (grove overrun with mice), in Westmorland.

Musial (*Pol.*) Descendant of Musial (he was forced to).

Muskie (*Cz.-Sl.*) The strong or masculine person.

Mussolini (*It.*) A nickname, from some supposed resemblance to a gnat.

Mustanen (*Finn.*) Descendant of the swarthy or dark-complexioned man.

Muszynski (*Pol.*) One who came from Muszyn (fly), in Poland.

Muth (*Ger.*) Descendant of Muth, a pet form of Helmuth (helmet, courage); the brave or courageous man; descendant of Muth, a pet form of names beginning with Mut (spirit), as Muotfrid and Mothar.

Mutter (*Ger.*) The mother's son or mother's boy; dweller at, or near, a morass.

Mutziger (*Ger.*) One who came from Mutzig, in Germany.

Myers, Myer (*Ger.*) An overseer, or head servant; later, a farmer.

Myles (*Eng.*) Descendant of Miles (soldier).

Myrick (*Eng.*) Descendant of Merick, a pet form of Almeric (work, ruler).

Naber, Nabor, Nabors (*Eng.*) The nearby farmer.

Nachtigall (*Ger.*) One with the qualities of a nightingale; dweller at the sign of the nightingale.

Nadler (*Eng.*) One who made needles.

Nagel, Nagle, Nagler, Naegele, Nagele, Naegel (*Ger.*) One who made nails.

Nagy (*Hun.*) The big man.

Nance (*Eng.*) One who came from Nance (valley), in Cornwall; dweller in a valley.

Napier (*Eng.*) One who had charge of the napery, or table linen, in a large household.

Napoleon, Napoleone (*It.*) One who came from Neapolis (new city) in Italy; descendant of Napoleon (lion of forest).

Napoli, Napolitano (*It.*) One who came from Naples (the new city), in Italy.

Nardi, Nardo (*It.*) Descendant of Nardi, a pet form of Leonardo (lion-like), or Bernardo (bear, firm); dweller near a spindle tree; dweller near where lavender grew.

Nash (*Eng.*) Dweller "atten ashe," which by wrong division became "atte Nashe," i.e., at the ash tree; one who came from Nash (the ash trees), in Buckinghamshire.

Nason (*Fr.*) One who had a small nose.

Nathan, Nathanson (*Eng.*) Descendant of Nathan (gift of God).

Natterer (*Ger.*) One who caught and exhibited snakes; one who came from Natters, in Tirol.

Naughton, Naughten (*Ir.*) Grandson of Neachtan (the pure one).

Navarro, Navarra (*Sp.*) One who came from Navarro (plain among hills), an ancient kingdom in Spain.

Nawrocki (*Pol.*) One who came from Nawra or Nawry (converted), the names of places in Poland.

Naylor, Nayler (*Eng.*) One who made nails.

Neal, Neale, Neel (*Eng.*) Descendant of Nigel or Neil (champion).

Neary (*Ir.*) Grandson of Naradhach (happy, prosperous).

Neat, Neate (*Eng.*) One who cultivated a yardland (about 30 acres), or half a yardland, the middle class of English villagers.

Neave, Neef (*Ger., Eng., Bel.*) A nephew.

Nee (*Fr.*) One who came from Nee (swamp), in France; one who worked on a ship, a sailor.

Needham (*Eng.*) One who came from Needham (needy or poor homestead), the name of several places in England.

Neely, Neeley (*Ir.*) The son of Conghal (high valor).

Neff (*Ger.*) A nephew.

Neil, Neill (*Eng.*) Descendant of Neil (champion).

Neiman (*Ger.*) One who has but recently arrived in the locality, a stranger.

Nellis, Nelis (*Ir.*) The son of Niallghus (champion, choice).

Nelms (*Eng.*) Dweller at, or near, the elm trees.

Nelson, Neilson, Nelsen, Neilsen (*Sw., Nor., Dan.*) The son of Nel or Neil (champion).

Nemec (*Cz.-Sl.*) Word meaning dumb, applied to one who came from Germany, because he did not understand the Slavic tongue.

Nemecek (*Cz.-Sl.*) A dim. form of Nemec, q.v.

Nemeth (*Hun.*) One who came from Germany.

Nemitz, Nemetz (*Pol., Cz.-Sl., Rus.*) One who came from Germany, a German. Literally one who could not speak, i.e., a mute.

Neri, Nero (*It.*) Descendant of Neri, a pet form of names with this termination, as Raineri and Maineri; the dark-complexioned or black-haired man.

Nesbitt, Nesbit, Nesbet, Nisbet (*Scot.*) One who came from the old barony of Nesbit in the parish of Edrom, Berwickshire.

Nesmith, Naesmith, Naysmith, Nasmith (*Scot.*) The smith who made nails.

Ness, Nesse (*Eng., Scot.*) Dweller at a promontory or headland, or on low marshy ground.

Nestor, Nester (*Ir.*) The son of the short man of the halter.

Netzel (*Ger.*) Descendant of Nato, a pet form of names beginning with Nad (grace), as Nadhere and Nadold.

Neu (*Ger.*) Descendant of Neu (new), a pet form of names like Neubert, Neufred and Neuhardt; the young person.

Neubauer (*Ger.*) The recently settled villager or new farmer.

Neuberg, Neuberger (*Ger.*) One who came from Neuburg (new town), the name of two places in Germany.

Neuhaus, Neuhauser (*Ger.*) One who lived in the house recently built.

Neumann, Neuman (*Ger.*) The recent arrival or newcomer.

Neumark (*Ger.*) Dweller at the new boundary or boundary mark.

Neuwirth, Neuvirth, Neuwerth (*Ger.*) Descendant of Neubert (new, light.)

Neva (*Finn.*) Dweller at, or near, a swamp or marsh.

Neville, Nevill, Nevil (*Eng.*) One who came from Neville, (new town), in Normandy, or Neuville (new town), a common place name in France.

Nevins, Nevin, Nevens, Neven (*Ir.*) Grandson of Cnaimhin (little bone); the son of Naoimhin (little saint).

Newberg (*Eng., Ger.*) One who lived in, or dwelt near, the new castle.

Newberger, Newburger (*Ger.*) One who came from Neuburg (new town), the name of two places in Germany.

Newberry, Newbury (*Eng.*) One who came from Newbury (new fort or castle), in Berkshire.

Newby (*Eng.*) One who came from Newby (the new or recently founded settlement), the name of various places in England.

Newcomb, Newcombe, Newcom, Newcomer (*Eng.*) The newly settled stranger, a newcomer.

Newell (*Eng.*) A variant of Newhall, q.v.

Newhall (*Eng.*) Dweller, or worker in, the newly built hall or principal dwelling in the village.

Newhouse (*Eng.*) One who dwelt in the newly built house.

Newkirk (*Scot.*) Dweller near the recently built church.

Newland, Newlander, Newlands (*Eng.*) One who dwelt on, or near, the newly cleared or newly acquired land; one who came from Newland, the name of various places in England.

Newman, Newmann (*Eng.*) The recent arrival or newcomer.

Newmark (*Sw., Eng.*) New field; dweller at the new boundary or boundary mark.

Newsome, Newsom, Newson (*Eng.*) One who came from places now called Newsham, Newhouse, Newsam and Newsholme, all formerly spelled Neusum, or a similar spelling, and meaning "new houses," all in England.

Newton (*Eng., Scot.*) One who came from Newton (the recently founded homestead), probably the most common English place name, also the name of several places in Scotland.

Nicholas, Nichol, Nicol, Nicholl, Nicoll (*Wel., Eng.*) Descendant of Nicholas (people's victory).

Nichols, Nicholson, Nicholls (*Eng.*) The son of Nichol (people's victory).

Nickel, Nickells, Nickels, Nickerson, Nickell (*Eng.*) Descendant of Nickel (people's victory).

Nickelson, Nickelsen (*Sw., Nor.*) The son of Nickla (people's victory).

Niebuhr (*Ger.*) The newcomer or new peasant.

Nielsen (*Dan.*) The son of Niel (champion).

Niemann, Nieman (*Ger.*) One who has but recently arrived in the locality, a stranger.

Niemi (*Finn.*) Dweller on a cape or headland.

Niemiec (*Pol.*) Man who came from Germany. *See* Nemec.

Nierman, Niermann (*Ger.*) Dweller in the lower location, such as farther down the hill.

Nietzsche (*Ger.*) Descendant of little Neid, a pet form of Niedhardt (envy, strong).

Nightingale, Nightengale (*Eng.*) One who came from Nightingale, a village in Monmouthshire; dweller at the sign of the nightingale, a thrush.

Niles, Nilles (*Ger., Eng.*) Descendant of Nils, a pet form of Nicholas (people's victory); descendant of Nilles, a pet form of Cornelius (cornel tree); dweller "atten iles," i.e., at the islands.

Nilson, Nilsen, Nilsson (*Dan., Sw.*) The son of Nils (champion).

Nissen, Nisson (*Dan.*) The son of Nis, a pet form of Nils (champion), or Nicolaus (people's victory).

Nitti (*It.*) Descendant of Nitti, a pet form of Giovanitti (gracious gift of Jehovah).

Nitz, Nitsche, Nitsch (*Ger.*) Descendant of Nizo or Nitho, pet forms of names beginning with Neid (envy), as Nidolf and Nidmar; descendant of Nitz, a pet form of Nikolitsch (people's victory).

Nix (*Eng.*) The son of Nick, a pet form of Nicholas (people's victory).

Nixon, Nickson (*Eng.*) The son of Nick, a pet form of Nicholas (people's victory).

Niziolek (*Pol.*) One who was short in stature.

Noakes, Noak (*Eng.*) One who lived "atten oak," which by wrong division became "atte Noak," i.e., at the oak tree.

Noble, Nobile (*Eng.*) An illustrious or famous person, or one possessing dignity, or of high birth or exalted rank, a name sometimes given ironically.

Noel, Nowell, Noell, Noelle (*Fr., Eng.*) Descendant of Noel, a name given to a child born on Christmas Day.

Nolan, Nolen, Noland (*Ir.*) Grandson of little Nuall (noble, famous).

Noll (*Eng.*) Descendant of Noll, an old pet form of Oliver (elf host).

Noon, Noone (*Ir.*) Grandson of Nuadha (an ancient sea divinity).

Noonan (*Ir.*) Descendant of the little, beloved one.

Norbury (*Eng.*) One who came from Norbury (northern fort), the name of several places in England.

Norcott, Northcott, Northcutt (*Eng.*) Dweller at the northern cottage.

Norcross, Northcross (*Eng.*) One who lived near, or by, the north cross.

Nord (*Sw.*) North.

Nordberg, Norberg (*Sw.*) North mountain.

Nordby, Norby (*Nor.*) North village.

Nordstrom (*Sw.*) North river.

Norkus (*Lith.*) Descendant of Norkus, a pet form of Norkantas (wish, suffer).

Norman, Normand (*Eng.*) Descendant of Norman (the Northman); one who came from Normandy.

Noronha, Norona (*Port., Sp.*) One who came from Norona, in Spain.

Norris (*Eng.*) One who came from the north country, a northman; one who took care of another, a nurse.

North (*Eng.*) One who came from the north.

Northam (*Eng.*) One who lived on, or near, the enclosed piece of land to the north.

Northbrook (*Eng.*) One who lived at the stream to the north.

Northlake (*Eng.*) One who lived at the stream or brook to the north.

Northrop, Northrup, Northrip (*Eng.*) One who came from Northorpe (the northern farm), in Lincolnshire.

Northway (*Eng.*) One who lived by the path or road leading to the north or located north of another.

Norton (*Eng.*) One who came from Norton (the homestead or village north of another), the name of several villages in England.

Norwich, Norwick, Norwish (*Eng.*) One who came from Norwich (north town), in Cheshire.

Norwood (*Eng.*) One who came from Norwood (north of the wood), in Middlesex.

Noseworthy (*Eng.*) Dweller at a homestead on a neck of land.

Noto, Noti, Notto (*It.*) Descendant of Noto, a pet form of Giovannotti (gracious gift of Jehovah); one who came from Noto, a town in Sicily.

Nourse, Nurse (*Eng.*) One who attended, or took care of, sick people.

Novak, Novack, Novacek (*Cz.-Sl.*) The stranger or newcomer.

Novick (*Cz.-Sl., Pol.*) One who had but recently arrived in the vicinity, a newcomer.

Novotny, Novy (*Cz.-Sl.*) One who had but recently arrived in the vicinity, a newcomer.

Nowak (*Pol., Ukr.*) One who came from Nowaki (new), the name of places in Poland and Ukraine; dweller on new, or virgin, land.

Nowakowski (*Pol., Rus.*) One who came from Nowakowo (new), the name of places in Poland and Byelorussia.

Nowicki (*Pol., Ukr.*) One who had but recently arived in the vicinity, a newcomer.

Noyes, Noyce (*Eng.*) Dweller at, or near, a walnut tree.

Nuccio, Nucci (*It.*) Descendant of Nucci, a pet form of Giovannucci (gracious gift of Jehovah), and of other names terminating in -no, as Stefano and Marino.

Nudelman, Nudleman (*Ger.*) One who made and sold needles.

Nugent (*Ir.*) One who came from Nogent (fair, wet meadow), the name of several places in France.

Nunez (*Sp.*) The son of Nuno.

Nunn, Nunne (*Eng.*) Descendant of a nun; descendant of Nunna (monk); a nickname given to a demure man.

Nurnberg, Nurnberger (*Ger.*) One who came from Nurnberg (the fortress of the Noricii), in Germany.

Nusbaum, Nussbaum (*Ger.*) Dweller at, or near, the nut tree.

Nutt, Nute (*Eng.*) Descendant of Canute (kind, race).

Nutter (*Eng.*) One who collected and sold nuts.

Nuzzo (*It.*) Descendant of Nuzzo, a pet form of Gianuzzi (gracious gift of Jehovah).

Nyberg (*Sw.*) New mountain.

Nye (*Eng.*) Dweller at the island.

Nyholm (*Dan.*) Dweller at the new river island.

Nystrom (*Sw.*) New stream.

Oakes, Oaks (*Eng.*) Dweller at, or near, an oak tree.

Oakley (*Eng.*) One who came from Oakley or Oakleigh (oak wood), the name of several places in England.

Oates, Oatis, Oats (*Eng.*) Descendant of Odo (rich).

Oberdorf, Oberdorfer (*Ger., Swis.*) One who came from Oberdorf (upper village), the name of several villages in Switzerland.

Oberg (*Sw.*) Island, or brook, mountain.

Oberlander (*Swis.*) One who came from Oberland (high land), the name of several districts in Switzerland; dweller in the high lands or mountains.

Oberlin (*Ger.*) One who came from Oberlind (upper linden tree); in Germany; descendant of little Adubert (noble, bright).

Oberman, Obermann (*Ger.*) One who acted as a foreman or supervisor.

O'Boyle (*Ir.*) Grandson of Baoigheall (vain pledge).

O'Brien, O'Bryan, O'Brion (*Ir.*) Grandson of Bryan or Brian (hill).

O'Callaghan, O'Callahan (*Ir.*) Grandson of little Ceallach (war or strife).

Ochs (*Ger.*) Dweller at the sign of the ox; one with the qualities of an ox.

O'Connell (*Ir.*) Grandson of Conall (high powerful).

O'Connor, O'Conner, O'Conchor (*Ir.*) Grandson of Concobair (meddlesome), or of Conchor (high will or desire).

O'Day, O'Dea (*Ir.*) Grandson of Deaghadh (good luck).

Odom, Odem (*Eng.*) One who came from Odeham (Ode's homestead), in Devonshire; descendant of Adam, this being the Hebrew pronounciation of Adam; the son-in-law.

O'Donnell, O'Donill (*Ir.*) Grandson of Domhnall (world mighty).

O'Dwyer, O'Duire (*Ir.*) Descendant of Duibhidhir (black Odhar).

Offord (*Eng.*) One who came from Offord (upper ford), in Huntingdonshire.

Ogden, Ogdon (*Eng.*) Dweller in the oak valley.

Ogilvie, Ogilvy, Ogilby (*Scot.*) One who came from the barony of Ogilvie (high hill), in the parish of Glamis, in Angus.

Oglesby, Oglesbee (*Scot.*) Dweller at Odkell's or Egel's homestead; variants of Ogilvie, q.v.

O'Grady (*Ir.*) Grandson of Grada (noble, illustrious).

O'Halloran, O'Hallaren, O'Holleran, O'Halloren (*Ir.*) Grandson of Allmhuran (stranger from beyond the sea).

O'Hara (*Ir.*) Grandson of Eaghra (bitter, or sharp).

O'Hare (*Ir.*) Grandson of Ir (origin obscure); grandson of Aichear (bitter, angry).

O'Hart (*Ir.*) Grandson of Art (bear, stone, or noble).

Ohlson, Ohlsen (*Sw., Nor.*) The son of Olof or Olaf (ancestor's relic).

Ohm, Ohms (*Ger.*) The uncle.

O'Keefe, O'Keeffe (*Ir.*) Grandson of Caohm (beautiful, noble).

Olander (*Sw.*) Islander.

Oldenburg, Oldenburger (*Ger.*) One who came from Oldenburg (old fortification), the name of four places in Germany.

Oldfield (*Eng.*) Dweller near the old field, a designation given to a field after another has been cleared; one who came from Aldfield (old field), in Yorkshire.

Oldham, Oldam (*Eng.*) One who came from Oldham (old island), in Lancashire.

Olds, Oldis (*Eng.*) Dweller at the old house.

O'Leary (*Ir.*) Grandson of Laoghaire (calf keeper).

Olejniczak (*Pol.*) The son of one who made oil from sunflower seeds or linseeds for food purposes.

Oleksy (*Ukr.*) Descendant of Oleksiy (helper of mankind).

Oleson, Olesen (*Nor., Dan.*) The son of Ole, a pet form of Olaf (ancestor's relic).

Oliphant, Olivant (*Fr., Eng.*) One who dealt in ivory; one who played a horn, a trumpeter; dweller at the sign of the elephant; a corruption of Oliford or Holiford.

Oliva, Olive, Olivia, Olivo (*Sp., It.*) One who grew and sold olives; descendant of Olivo (olive); one with an olive complexion.

Oliver, Olivier (*Eng., Fr.*) Descendant of Oliver, or Olivier (elf, host, or an olive tree).

Olivier, Ollivier (*Fr.*) One who possessed an olive grove; descendant of Olivier (the olive).

Olmsted, Olmstead (*Du.*) Dweller at the homestead where elms grew.

Olney (*Eng.*) One who came from Olney (Olla's island or lonely glade), the name of places in Buckinghamshire and Northamptonshire.

Olson, Olsen, Olsson (*Nor., Sw.*) The son of Ole or Olaf (ancestor's relic).

Olszewski (*Pol.*) Dweller at, or near, the alder-wood tree.

O'Malley (*Ir.*) Grandson of Maille (noble or chief).

O'Mara, O'Meara (*Ir.*) Grandson of Meadhair (mirth).

Onderdonk (*Du.*) One who lived, or came from, below Donk, in Brabant.

Ondrus (*Cz.-Sl.*) Descendant of Andrew (manly).

O'Neill, O'Neil, O'Neal (*Ir.*) Grandson of Niall (champion or military hero).

Ooms (*Du.*) The son of the uncle.

Oosterhout (*Du.*) One who came from Oosterhout (east wood), in Holland.

Opdyck (*Du.*) One who lived on the dike.

Oppenheimer, Oppenheim (*Ger.*) One who came from Oppenheim (Oppo's place), in Germany.

Oran (*Eng.*) Dweller at the homestead on the river bank; one who came from Owram (ridge), in Yorkshire.

Orange (*Eng., Fr.*) One who came from Orange (town on the river Araise), in France.

Orchard, Orchart (*Eng., Scot.*) Dweller at a fruit garden; corruption of Urquhart, q.v., from its early pronunciation; one who came from Orchard, the name of several places in England and one in Scotland.

Orcutt (*Eng.*) Dweller in a hillside, or riverbank, cottage.

Ordway (*Eng.*) Descendant of Ordwig (spear, warrior).

O'Reilly, O'Reyly, O'Reely, O'Riley (*Ir.*) Grandson of Raghallach (the sportive one).

Orfevre (*Fr.*) One who made and sold gold articles.

Orlando, Orlandi (*It.*) Descendant of Orlando (fame, land).

Orloff, Orlov, Orlof (*Rus.*) One with eaglelike characteristics.

Orlowski (*Pol.*) Descendant of one with eaglelike characteristics.

Orman, Ormond, Ormand (*Wel.*) One who came from Ormond, in Ireland.

Ormsby, Ormsbee (*Eng.*) One who came from Ormesby (Orm's homestead), the name of several places in England.

Orne, Orn (*Sw.*) Eagle.

O'Rourke (*Ir.*) Grandson of Ruarc (Norse Hrothrekr); descendant of the restless man.

Orr (*Eng., Ir.*) One who lived near the border, bank, shore, hill or ridge; the pale person.

Orrick (*Scot.*) One who came from Orrock, in Fife.

Ortega (*Sp.*) Dweller at the sign of the grouse; one with the characteristics of a grouse.

Orth, Ort (*Ger.*) One who came from Orth (the place), in Germany; descendant of Ort, a pet form of names beginning with Ort (point), as Ortgis and Ordwig.

Ortiz (*Sp.*) The son of Ordono (the fortunate).

Ortmann, Ortman (*Ger.*) Descendant of Ortman (point, man); one who acted as an arbitrator or referee.

Orton (*Eng.*) One who came from Orton (homestead on a slope or upper homestead), the name of various places in England.

O'Ryan, O'Rian (*Ir.*) Descendant of the servant of the queen; grandson of Rian or Riaghan, or of a follower of Rian or Riaghan.

Orzechowski (*Pol.*) One who came from Orzechow(o); dweller near hazel bushes.

Osborne, Osborn, Osburn, Osbourne (*Eng.*) Descendant of Osborn (god, man); one who came from Osborne (Aust's stream), in Wight.

Oscarson (*Eng.*) The son of Oscar (god, spear).

Osgood (*Eng.*) Descendant of Osgood (divine goodness).

O'Shaughnessy (*Ir.*) Grandson of Seachnasach (elusive).

O'Shea, O'Shay (*Ir.*) Grandson of Seaghdha (majestic or learned).

Osman, Osmon, Osmond, Ozmun, Osmun, Osmund (*Eng.*) Descendant of Osmund (divine protector).

Osmanski (*Pol.*) One who came from Turkey.

Osowski (*Pol.*) Dweller near the aspen tree; one who came from Osow.

Oster (*Sw.*) East.

Osterberg, Osterberger (*Sw.*) East mountain.

Ostrand, Ostrander (*Sw.*) Island shore.

Ostrom (*Sw.*) Island stream.

Ostrowski (*Pol.*) Dweller on a river island; one who came from Ostrow (river island), in Poland.

O'Sullivan (*Ir.*) Grandson of Suileabhan (black-eyed).

Oswald, Oswaldt (*Eng.*) Descendant of Oswald (divine power).

Otis (*Eng.*) Descendant of Otis or Otes, forms of Odo (rich).

O'Toole (*Ir.*) Grandson of Tuatal (people mighty).

Ott, Otte (*Eng., Ger.*) Descendant of Otta or Otto (prosperity).

Otter (*Nor., Eng.*) Dweller at the sign of the otter; descendant of Otthar (terrible, army); dweller at the Otter (otter stream), a river in England.

Otto (*Ger.*) Descendant of Otto or Odo (rich).

Oudheusden (*Du.*) One who came from the village of Oud-Heusden (old Heusden or inn), in North Brabant.

Ouellette, Ouellet (*Fr.*) Dweller at the eye, or source, of the little stream or fountain.

Ousley, Owsley (*Eng.*) Dweller at, or in, the wood or meadow by the Ouse (water), the name of several streams in England.

Outerbridge (*Eng.*) One who came from Oughtibridge (Uhtred's bridge), in Yorkshire.

Ovcik (*Cz.-Sl.*) One who took care of a flock, a shepherd.

Overbey, Overby (*Eng.*) One who came from Overbury (upper earthwork or fort), in Worcestershire.

Overland (*Swis.*) One who came from Oberland (high land), the name of several districts in Switzerland; dweller in the high lands or mountains.

Overman (*Eng.*) Dweller on the bank of a river; one in charge in a coal mine.

Overstreet (*Eng.*) Dweller at a Roman road by a riverbank.

Overton (*Eng.*) One who came from Overton (homestead on a riverbank or ridge), the name of several places in England.

Owens, Owen (*Wel.*) The son of Owen (wellborn).

Oxford (*Eng.*) One who came from Oxford (ford for oxen), in Oxfordshire.

Oxnam (*Scot.*) One who came from Oxnam (oxen homestead), in Scotland.

Pabst, Papst (*Ger.*) One who performed sacerdotal functions; one whose function, behavior, spirit or appearance resembled that of a priest.

Pace (*Eng., It.*) Descendant of Pace or Pash, a name given to one born during the Passover festival or at Easter; descendant of Pace (peace), or of Pace, a pet form of Bonapace (good peace).

Pacelli (*It.*) Descendant of little Pace, a pet form of Bonapace (good peace).

Pacholski (*Pol.*) The boyish, or young, person.

Pacini (*It.*) Descendant of little Pace, a pet form of Bonapace (good peace).

Packard (*Fr.*) Descendant of Bacard (combat, strong).

Packer (*Eng.*) One who packed wool.

Pacovsky, Pacak, Paca (*Cz.-Sl.*) One who came from Pacov, in Bohemia.

Padden, Paden (*Ir.*) The son of Padin, a pet form of Patrick (noble or patrician).

Paddock (*Eng.*) One who came from Paddock (enclosure), now Paddock Wood, in Kent.

Paderewski (*Pol.*) The son of Patrick (noble or patrician).

Padgett, Padgitt, Pagett, Paget, Padget (*Eng., Fr.*) The young male servant; descendant of Padge, a variant of Madge, pet form of Margaret (pearl).

Padula (*It.*) Dweller at, or near, a swamp.

Page, Paige (*Eng.*) A male servant of the lowest grade, an attendant.

Pahl (*Ger.*) The bold, audacious man; descendant of Paulus (small); descendant of Baldo, a pet form of names beginning with Bald (bold), as Baldwig, Baldawin and Baldulf.

Paine, Pain (*Eng.*) The rustic or countryman, a pagan; descendant of Payen (villager, later heathen).

Painter, Paynter (*Eng.*) One who covers buildings and ships with paint; the official in charge of bread in a large household.

Paisley (*Scot.*) One who came from Paisley (pasture slope), in Renfrewshire.

Pajak (*Pol.*) One with spider-like characteristics; dweller at the sign of the spider.

Palermo (*It.*) One who came from Palermo (the spacious harbor), in Italy.

Polka (*Cz.-Sl.*) One who walked with a cane.

Palm (*Sw.*) Palm tree.

Palmer (*Eng.*) A palm-bearing pilgrim returned from the Holy Land.

Palmquist (*Sw.*) Palm-tree twig.

Paluch (*Pol.*) One with an unusual finger.

Palumbo (*It.*) Dweller at the sign of the dove.

Panek (*Pol.*) The little gentlemen; one who assumed the prerogatives of a gentleman.

Panico, Panici, Panicola (*It.*) Dweller in, or near, a field of millet; one who grew millet.

Panos (*Gr.*) Descendant of Panos, a pet form of Panayotis (pertaining to Our Lady).

Panozzo (*It.*) A variant of Panico, q.v.

Panter, Panther (*Eng., Scot.*) The official in charge of bread in a large household, a pantry-keeper.

Paoli (*It.*) Descendant of Paoli (small).

Papa (*It.*) One who performed sacerdotal functions, a priest; one whose function, behavior, spirit or appearance resembled that of a priest.

Papadopoulos, Papadopulos, Pappadopoulos (*Gr.*) The son of the priest.

Pape (*Eng.*) A variant of Pope, q.v.

Pappas, Papas (*Gr.*) The priest.

Paprocki (*Pol.*) Dweller where ferns grew.

Paquette, Paquet (*Fr.*) Descendant of Paschase (Easter devotions); the itinerant seller of fagots.

Paradis, Paradise (*Fr.*) One who played the part of Paradise in the ancient mystery plays.

Paradiso (*It.*) Dweller in, or near, a fruit grove or flower garden.

Pardo, Pardoe (*Sp., It.*) One who had gray hair; descendant of Pardo, a pet form of Leopardo (lion, hard).

Parent, Parente, Parenteau (*Fr.*) The father, probably a nickname; descendant of a priest, or other dignitary of the church.

Parenti (*It.*) One who had a child, a parent, or who stood in the place of a parent; one who came from Parenti, a place in Calabrese.

Parham (*Eng.*) One who came from Parham (homestead where pears grew), the name of places in Suffolk and Sussex.

Paris, Parris (*Eng.*) One who came from Paris (the marshy land of the Parisii), in France; one of the tribe of the Parisii.

Parisi, Pariso, Parisio (*It.*) One who came from Paros, in Greece.

Parker (*Eng., Wel.*) One in charge of a park for the lord of the manor; a gamekeeper.

Parkhurst (*Eng.*) Dweller in an enclosure on a wooded hill.

Parkinson, Parkin, Parkins, Parkison (*Eng.*) Descendant, or son of, Parkin, a pet form of Peter (rock).

Parkman (*Eng.*) One who had charge of a park for the lord of the manor; a gamekeeper.

Parks, Park, Parke, Parkes (*Eng.*) Dweller near the enclosed space stocked with game for use of the king or great nobles.

Parlee, Parlea (*Eng.*) One who came from Parley (glade where pears grew), the name of places in Dorset and Hampshire.

Parlin (*Eng.*) Descendant of little Par, a pet form of Peter (rock).

Parmelee, Parmele, Parmley (*Eng.*) Dweller at the meadow belonging to the palmer. *See* Palmer.

Parmenter, Parmentier (*Eng.*) One who made outer garments, a tailor.

Parnell (*Eng.*) Descendant of Parnel, a contraction of Petronella (little rock); descendant of Pernell, a pet form of Peter (rock).

Parr (*Eng.*) One who came from Parr (enclosure or district), in Lancashire.

Parrilli, Parrillo, Parrilla (*It.*) Descendant of little Parro, a pet form of Gasparro (treasure).

Parrish, Parish (*Eng.*) One who resided within the limits of the parish, a territorial division originally in the care of a single priest; one who had something to do with the organization or government of the parish.

Parry (*Wel.*) The son of Harry, a pet form of Henry (home ruler).

Parsons, Parson (*Wel., Eng.*) The son of the parson; the son of Par, a pet form of Peter (rock).

Partipilo (*It.*) One who came from Partipilo, in Italy.

Partlow (*Eng.*) One who came from Pathlow (path by a sepulchral mound), in Warwickshire.

Partridge (*Eng.*) Dweller at the sign of the partridge; one with some characteristic of a partridge.

Pascal, Paschal, Paschall (*Fr.*) Descendant of Pascal (Easter).

Paschke, Patschke (*Ger.*) Descendant of little Paulus (small).

Pass (*Eng.*) Descendant of Pash, a name given to one born during the Passover festival or at Easter.

Passman (*Eng.*) Dweller near the path or passageway.

Passmore (*Eng.*) Dweller near the path through the moor.

Pasternak (*Pol., Ukr., Rus.*) Dweller at the sign of the parsnip; one who grew and sold parsnips.

Pasteur (*Fr.*) The keeper of a flock, a shepherd.

Patch (*Eng.*) Descendant of Pache, a name given to one born during the Passover festival or at Easter.

Pate, Patt, Pait (*Scot., Eng.*) Descendant of Pate or Pait, pet forms of Patrick (noble or patrician).

Pathe (*Eng.*) Dweller near an important path or footway.

Patrick, Petrick, Patricks (*Eng.*) Descendant of Patrick (noble or patrician).

Patterson, Pattison, Paterson (*Scot., Eng.*) The son of Patrick (noble or patrician).

Patti (*It.*) Descendant of Patti, a pet form of Patrizio (noble or patrician).

Patton, Patten, Paton, Pattin (*Eng.*) Descendant of little Pat, a pet form of Patrick (noble or patrician).

Paul, Paull, Paule, Pawl (*Scot., Eng., Fr.*) Descendant of Paul (small); one who came from Paull (pole marking a ferry), in Yorkshire, or from Paul (church of St. Paulinus), in Cornwall.

Paulson, Paulsen, Poulson (*Sw., Nor., Dan., Eng.*) The son of Paul (small).

Paulus (*Ger.*) Descendant of Paulus (small).

Pauly, Pauli (*Eng., Ger.*) Descendant of little Paul (small).

Pavlik (*Ukr.*) Descendant of little Pavlo (small).

Pavlov, Pafko (*Cz.-Sl.*) The son of Paul (small).

Pawlak, Pawlik (*Pol.*) Descendant of little Pawel (small).

Pawlicki (*Pol.*) The son of Pawel (small).

Pawlowski (*Pol.*) One who came from Pawlow, in Poland.

Paxton (*Eng., Scot.*) One who came from Paxton, (Pack's homestead), the name of places in Huntingdonshire and in Berwickshire.

Payne, Paynes (*Eng.*) The rustic or countryman, a pagan; descendant of Payen (villager, later heathen).

Payton (*Eng.*) One who came from Peyton (Paega's homestead), in Suffolk; descendant of little Pate, a pet form of Patrick (noble or patrician).

Peabody, Peacock (*Eng.*) Dweller at the sign of the peacock; one with the qualities of a peacock.

Peak, Peake, Peaks (*Eng.*) One who lived at, or on, a pointed hill; one who came from Peak (hill), in Derbyshire.

Peale, Peel, Peal, Peele (*Eng.*) Dweller at a fortified residence or small castle; one who came from Peel (fortress), on the Isle of Man.

Pearce, Pearse (*Eng.*) Descendant of Piers (rock).

Pearl, Perl, Perle (*Ger., Eng.*) Descendant of Perle (pearl); one who came from Perl (pearl), in Germany.

Pearlman (*Ger.*) An Anglicized form of Perlman, q.v.

Pearsall (*Eng.*) One who came from Pearshall or Pershill (Per's hill), in Staffordshire.

Pearson (*Eng.*) The son of Pears, an early form of Peter (rock).

Peary, Peery (*Eng.*) Descendant of little Pear, a pet form of Peter (rock).

Pease, Peace (*Eng.*) Variants of Pace, q.v.

Peasley, Peaslee (*Eng.*) Dweller at the field where peas were grown.

Peavey (*Eng.*) One who came from Pavie, in France.

Pech, Peach (*Eng.*) One who came from Pech or Peche (peach), in Normandy; dweller at, or on, a peaked hill.

Peck, Pec (*Eng.*) Dweller at, or on, a pointed hill.

Peckham (*Eng.*) One who came from Peckham (homestead by a hill), the name of several places in England.

Pecora (*It.*) One who took care of sheep, a shepherd.

Peddle (*Eng.*) One who carries about goods for sale, a peddler.

Pedersen, Pederson, Peddersen, Pedderson (*Nor., Dan.*) The son of Peder (rock).

Peebles, Peeples (*Scot.*) One who came from Peebles (place of assembly), in Peeblesshire.

Peek (*Eng.*) Dweller at, or on, a pointed hill.

Peet, Peete (*Eng., Du., Scot.*) Descendant of Peet, a pet form of Pieter or Peter (rock); dweller near a hole or steep hollow; one who was delicate or a pampered pet.

Peirce (*Eng.*) A variant of Pierce, q.v.

Pelham (*Eng.*) One who came from Pelham (Peola's homestead), in Hertfordshire.

Pell (*Eng.*) Dweller at, or near, a pool.

Pellegrini, Pellegrino (*It.*) Descendant of Pellegrino (pilgrim).

Pelletier (*Fr.*) One who prepared skins, a skinner.

Pelton (*Eng.*) One who came from Pelton (Peola's homestead), in Durham.

Pelz (*Ger.*) One who made or sold fur coats.

Pemberton (*Eng.*) One who came from Pemberton (barley enclosure by the hill), in Lancashire.

Pembroke, Pembrook (*Wel., Eng.*) One who came from Pembroke (head or end of the land), a county in Wales.

Pence, Pentz, Penz (*Ger.*) Descendant of Benzo, a pet form of names beginning with Bar (bear) and Band (banner); one who came from Pentz, in Germany.

Pendergast, Pendergrass (*Eng., Ir.*) Descendant of Pendegast (head stranger); one who came from Prendergast, a parish in Pembrokeshire.

Pendleton, Pendelton (*Eng.*) One who came from Pendleton (hilltop village), in Lancashire.

Penn, Penna (*Eng.*) Dweller near a pen or sheepfold; one who came from Penn (enclosure, or hill), the name of places in Buckinghamshire and Staffordshire.

Pennell (*Eng., Fr.*) Descendant of little Pinn (peg), or of little Pain or Pagan (rustic or countryman); one who wore ragged, tattered clothing.

Penner, Pender (*Eng.*) Dweller at the pen enclosure.

Pennington (*Eng.*) One who came from Pennington (village that had to pay a penny tribute, or the village of Pinna's people), the name of several villages in England.

Penny, Penney (*Eng., Scot., Fr.*) Dweller at the sign of the feather; descendant of Penny.

Penrose (*Eng.*) One who lived at the head, or upper end, of the heath.

Pentecost (*Eng.*) Descendant of Pentecost (fiftieth), a name given to children born on that day.

Peoples (*Scot.*) One who came from Peebles (place of assembly), in Peeblesshire.

Pepper, Peppers (*Eng.*) One who dealt in pepper and other condiments.

Percival (*Eng.*) One who came from Percheval or Perceval (valley-piercer), in France; descendant of Percival (pierce valley).

Percy, Piercy, Piercey (*Eng.*) One who came from Perci or Percy (Persius' estate), in Normandy.

Perdue (*Fr., Eng.*) Descendant of Perdu (lost), a name given to a foundling; a nickname given to one addicted to use of the oath "By God," i.e., *par Dieu.*

Peregrine, Peregrin (*Eng.*) Descendant of Peregrine (wanderer); one who was a stranger in the community.

Perez (*Sp.*) The son of Pero, a pet form of Pedro (rock).

Perham (*Eng.*) One who came from Parham (homestead where pears grew), in Sussex.

Perkins, Perkinson (*Wel.*) The son of little Pier, a pet form of Peter (rock).

Perlman, Perelman (*Ger.*) Pearl man; one who buys and sells pearls or beads; the husband of Perl (pearl).

Perlmutter (*Ger.*) Dealer in mother of pearl; possibly a name taken by one whose mother was named Perl.

Perri (*It.*) Descendant of Piero (rock).

Perrin, Perron, Perret, Pierrot (*Fr.*) Descendant of little Pierre (rock).

Perry (*Wel., Eng.*) The son of Harry, English pet form of Henry (home ruler); dweller by the pear tree; descendant of little Pier, a pet form of Peter (rock); descendant of Perry, a pet form of Peregrine (wanderer).

Pershing, Pfoersching (*Ger.*) One who lived at, or near, a peach tree.

Person, Persson, Persons (*Sw., Nor., Fr.*) The son of Per (rock); descendant of little Pierre (rock); the parish priest.

Peter (*Ger., Eng.*) Descendant of Peter (rock).

Peters, Peterson, Petersen (*Wel., Eng., Dan., Sw.*) The son of Peter (rock).

Petersson (*Sw.*) The son of Peter (rock).

Petit, Pettit, Petiet (*Fr.*) The short or small man.

Petitperrin (*Fr.*) Descendant of short, little Pierre (rock).

Petkus (*Lith.*) Descendant of Petko, a form of Petr (rock).

Petofi (*Hun.*) The son of Peter (rock).

Petraitis (*Lith.*) The son of Petras (rock).

Petrakos, Petrakis (*Gr.*) Descendant of little Petros (rock).

Petrauskas, Petrauskis (*Lith.*) Descendant of little Petras (rock).

Petrescu (*Rom.*) Descendant, or follower of, Petre (rock).

Petri (*It.*) Descendant of Pietro (rock).

Petrie, Petry (*Scot.*) Descendant of little Peter (rock), or of little Patrick (noble or patrician).

Petrillo, Petrilli (*It.*) Descendant of little Pietro (rock).

Petrone, Petroni, Petronio (*It.*) Descendant of big Pietro (rock).

Petronis (*Lith.*) The son of Petras (rock).

Petroski (*Pol.*) Descendant of Peter (rock).

Petrov, Petroff (*Rus., Bulg.*) The son of Petr or Petur (rock).

Pettengill, Pettingell, Pettengell (*Eng.*) One who came from Portugal (the harbor).

Petterson, Pettersen (*Sw., Nor.*) The son of Petter (rock).

Pettiford (*Eng.*) The iron-footed person, a nickname.

Pettigrew (*Scot., Eng.*) Dweller at a grove frequented by cranes.

Pettis, Pettes, Pettas (*Eng.*) Dweller in the house by the pit.

Petty, Pettie, Pettee, Pettey (*Scot., Eng.*) One small in stature; one who came from Petty (piece), in Scotland.

Peyton (*Eng.*) One who came from Peyton (Paega's homestead), in Suffolk; descendant of little Pate, a pet form of Patrick (noble or patrician).

Pfaff (*Ger.*) One who performed sacerdotal functions, a priest; one whose behavior, spirit or appearance resembled that of a priest.

Pfau (*Ger.*) Dweller at the sign of the peacock; one thought to possess the characteristics of a peacock.

Pfeiffer, Pfeifer (*Ger.*) One who played a fife or a pipe, a piper.

Pfister (*Ger.*) One who made bread, a baker.

Pflueger, Pfleger (*Ger.*) One who plowed the fields.

Phelan, Phelon (*Ir.*) Grandson of little Faol (wolf).

Phelps, Philp (*Eng.*) Descendant of Philip (lover of horses).

Philbin (*Eng.*) Descendant of little Philip (lover of horses).

Philbrick (*Eng.*) One who came from Felbridge (bridge by a field), in Surrey, or from Felbrigg (plank bridge), in Norfolk.

Philhower (*Du.*) One who made files, a corruption of the original Villhouwer.

Phillips, Philipps, Phillip, Phillipp, Philipp, Philips (*Wel., Eng.*) The son of Philip (lover of horses).

Philpott, Philpot, Philipot (*Eng.*) Descendant of little Philip (lover of horses).

Phinney, Phinnie (*Ir.*) Descendant of the soldier.

Phipps (*Eng.*) Descendant of Phip, a pet form of Philip (lover of horses).

Phyfe (*Scot.*) A variant of Fyfe, q.v.

Piasecki (*Pol.*) Dweller on sandy soil.

Piazza, Piazzi (*It.*) Dweller on, or near, the square.

Picard, Pickard (*Fr.*) One who came from Picardy (pike men), in France.

Piccolo, Piccoli (*It.*) Descendant of Piccolo, a pet name for a small child; one of low stature.

Pick (*Eng., Cz.-Sl., Ger.*) Dweller near a pointed hill or on a highway; dweller at the sign of the pick (the bar-tailed godwit); dweller at the sign of the bull; a name sometimes adopted by people named Joseph because the Bible likened Joseph to a young bullock.

Pickell, Pickel, Pickle (*Eng.*) One who came from Pickhill (Pica's nook, or nook by the hills), in Yorkshire.

Pickens, Picken (*Eng., Scot.*) Descendant of little Pic, or Picon (pike).

Pickering (*Eng.*) One who came from Pickering (people at the edge of the hill), in Yorkshire.

Pickett (*Eng.*) Descendant of little Pic, or Picot (pike).

Pickford (*Eng.*) One who came from Pitchford (ford near where pitch is found), in Shropshire; dweller at a ford near a pointed hill.

Pidgeon, Pigeon (*Eng.*) Dweller at the sign of the pigeon; one thought to have some characteristic of a pigeon.

Piehl, Piehler (*Ger.*) Dweller at, or near, a hill.

Piekarz (*Pol.*) One who prepared bread, a baker.

Pieper (*Ger.*) One who whistled or played a pipe or fife, a piper.

Pierce, Piers (*Wel., Eng.*) Descendant of Pierce, or Piers, early English forms of Peter (rock).

Pierpont (*Fr.*) Dweller at, or near, the stone bridge.

Pierson (*Eng.*) The son of Piers, early English form of Peter (rock).

Pietrzak (*Pol.*) Descendant of Piotr (rock).

Pike, Pikes (*Eng.*) Dweller at, or on, a pointed hill; one who fought with a pike; dweller at the sign of the pike.

Pilch, Pilcher (*Ger., Eng.*) Dweller at the sign of the dormouse; one who made and sold fur garments.

Pilgrim, Pilgram (*Eng.*) One who visited a distant shrine.

Pill, Pilles (*Eng.*) Dweller near the pointed object, such as a pointed stake, post or hill, or at the creek.

Piller, Pillar, Pillers, Pillars (*Ger.*) Descendant of Bilihar (sword, army).

Pillsbury, Pilsbury (*Eng.*) One who came from Pilsbury (Pil's fort), in Derbyshire.

Pincus, Pinkus (*Heb.*) The dark-complexioned man.

Pine, Pines (*Eng.*) Dweller at, or near, a pine tree; dweller at the sign of the pine tree.

Pingree (*Fr.*) One who played the old French game of cockles.

Pink (*Eng.*) One with some quality of a chaffinch; dweller at the sign of the chaffinch.

Pinkerton (*Scot.*) One who came from the old barony of Pinkerton, in East Lothian.

Pinkham (*Eng.*) Dweller at a homestead where chaffinches are found.

Pinkney, Pinckney (*Eng., Fr.*) One who came from Pinkney, in Norfolk; one who came from Picquigny, in France.

Pinkston (*Eng.*) One who came from Pinxton (homestead by the end of the wood), in Derbyshire.

Pinsky, Pinsker, Pinski (*Rus., Ukr., Pol.*) One who came from Pinsk (foam), in Byelorussia.

Pinto (*Sp.*) One who painted; one who had a scar or blemish.

Pintozzi (*It.*) Descendant of the little, painted or colored one.

Piotrowski (*Pol.*) The son of Piotr (rock).

Piper (*Eng.*) One who played a pipe, especially a strolling musician.

Pirie, Pirrie (*Scot.*) Descendant of little Pierre (rock).

Pitcher, Picher (*Eng.*) One who covered or calked ships with pitch.

Pitchford (*Eng.*) One who came from Pitchford (river crossing near where pitch was found), in Shropshire.

Pitney (*Eng.*) One who came from Pitney (Pytta's island), in Somerset.

Pittman, Pitman, Pitmon (*Eng.*) Dweller at, or near, a pit or deep hollow.

Pitts, Pitt (*Eng.*) Dweller near a hole or steep hollow; one who came from Pitt (pit), in Hampshire.

Place, Plaice (*Eng., Fr.*) Dweller at a country mansion, near a market square or on a plot of land; one who came from Place (town, or fortress), in France; one who came from Plash or Plaish (marshy pool), the names of places in Somerset and Shropshire.

Placek (*Pol.*) Pancake, probably designating one who cooked them.

Plaisted (*Eng.*) Dweller near a playground, or place where sports are held.

Plant, Plante (*Eng.*) Dweller at the place where bushes and young trees were started for transplanting.

Platt (*Eng.*) One who lived on, or worked, a small piece of ground or patch; dweller near a small footbridge over a stream.

Player (*Eng.*) One who performed tricks to amuse others at fair and festival.

Pleasant (*Eng.*) An affable or agreeable person; descendant of Pleasant (pleasing).

Plimpton (*Eng.*) One who came from Plympton (homestead with plum trees), in Devonshire.

Plotke (*Ger.*) Dweller near a small fence; dweller near quicksand.

Plotkin (*Rus.*) Dweller at the sign of the plotka (kind of fish).

Plucinski (*Pol.*) One who came from Plucice (settlement of Plut's descendants), a village in Poland.

Plumer, Plomer (*Eng.*) A dealer in plumes or feathers; same as Plummer, q.v.

Plummer, Plumber (Eng.) One who worked, or dealt in, lead.

Plunkett, Plunket (*Eng.*) One who made and sold plunket, a coarse, white woolen cloth.

Pluta (*Pol.*) One who came from Pluty (settlement of the Pluty family), in Poland.

Pociask (*Pol.*) Cannon fire.

Pocius (*Pol.*) The powerful one, perhaps a noble.

Podgorski (*Pol.*) Dweller at the base of the mountain.

Podraza (*Pol.*) An agitator, one who excited others to action.

Poe, Powe, Pow (*Eng.*) Dweller at the sign of the peacock; a nickname given to a proud or gaudily dressed man.

Pohl, Poel, Pohle (*Ger., Du.*) The man who lived at, or near, the pool.

Poincare (*Fr.*) Square fist, referring to the strong man; dweller at the sign of the square fist.

Poindexter (*Eng.*) Dweller at the sign of the poindexter (right fist).

Pointer, Poynter (*Eng.*) One who made laces for fastening clothes.

Poirier (*Fr.*) One who grew and sold pears.

Poisson (*Fr.*) One who sold fish.

Poker (*Eng.*) One who made pokes, i.e., bags or small sacks.

Pokorny (*Cz.-Sl., Pol., Ukr.*) A humble or submissive man.

Polacek (*Cz.-Sl.*) The little man from Poland (level land).

Polak, Polack (*Cz.-Sl., Ukr., Rus., Ger.*) One who came from Poland (level land).

Poland, Polan, Polland (*Eng.*) Dweller at the homestead on which there was a pool, or through which a stream flowed; one who made and sold the long pointed shoes worn in the fourteenth century.

Polinski (*Pol.*) Dweller on, or owner of, a field.

Polischuk, Polishuck, Polishook (*Ukr.*) One who came from Polissia (woody and marshy land).

Polito (*It.*) Descendant of Polito, a pet form of Ippolito (he who sets horses free).

Polk (*Scot.*) One who came from the lands of Pollock (little pool), in Renfrewshire.

Polka (*Ukr., Rus.*) Descendant of the Polish woman.

Pollack, Pollak (*Ger., Fr.*) One who came from Poland (level land).

Pollard (*Eng.*) Dweller at, or near, the head or end of the pool; descendant of little Paul (small); one who had his hair cropped short.

Polley, Pollay, Polly, Polleys (*Fr., Eng.*) Descendant of little Paul (small); one who came from Poilley or Poilly, in France.

Pollock, Pollok (*Scot., Ger.*) One who came from the lands of Pollock (little pool), in Renfrewshire; variant of Pollack, q.v.

Polwhele (*Eng.*) One who lived in, or near, the field containing a pool.

Polzin (*Rus.*) One who engaged in transactions for profit, a merchant.

Pomeroy, Pomroy (*Eng., Ir., Fr.*) Dweller at, or near, an apple orchard; one who came from La Pommeraye, (apple orchard), in France.

Pond, Ponde (*Eng.*) Dweller near a small body of water; variant of Pound, q.v.

Poole, Pool (*Eng.*) Dweller near the deep place in a river or stream; one who came from Pool (pool), the name of several places in England.

Poor, Poore (*Eng.*) A poverty-stricken person; one who had taken a vow of poverty.

Pope (*Eng.*) One who played the part of the Pope in pageants and plays.

Popovich (*Yu.-Sl., Ukr.*) The son of the priest.

Popp, Poppe (*Ger.*) Descendant of Poppo, a pet form of Bodebert (messenger, bright), and Jakob (the supplanter).

Port, Porte (*Eng.*) Dweller near the entrance or gate; one who acted as a gatekeeper.

Porter (*Eng.*) One who carried goods; one who tended a gate, a gatekeeper.

Portnoy (*Rus.*) One who made outer garments, a tailor.

Posey (*Eng.*) One who came from Poce, in France; dweller near a post by the enclosure.

Posnanski (*Pol.*) One who came from Posen or Poznan, in Poland.

Posner, Posener (*Ger.*) One who came from Posen (now Poznan), a province in Poland.

Post, Poster (*Eng., Ger.*) Dweller at, or near, an important or unusual post, stake or marker; descendant of Post, a pet form of Pozdimir (backward); one who came from Post, in Germany.

Potempa (*Pol.*) One who played the part of a martyr in play or pageant; one who sacrificed something for the sake of principle.

Potocki (*Pol.*) Dweller near the brook.

Potter (*Eng.*) One who made utensils of earthenware or metal.

Pottle, Potel (*Eng.*) Descendant of little Pott, a pet form of Philip (lover of horses).

Potts, Pott (*Eng.*) Descendant of Pot or Pott, pet forms of Philpot (little lover of horses); one who made and sold pots; one who worked in the kitchen, cleaning utensils.

Poulos (*Gr.*) The son, a shortened form of a longer name.

Pounds, Pound, Pounder (*Eng.*) One who lived near, or had charge of, the pinfold or enclosure for animals.

Powell (*Wel.*) The son of Howell (eminent).

Powers, Power (*Eng., Ir.*) The poor man, a pauper; one who had taken a vow of poverty.

Prager (*Ger.*) One who came from Prague (the threshold).

Prather (*Wel.*) The son of Rhydderch or Rhudderch (the reddish-brown one).

Pratt, Prett, Prete (*Eng., Scot.*) Dweller on, or near, a meadow; one who employed wiles or stratagems in fighting; a cunning, astute person.

Pray (*Eng., Fr.*) Dweller at, or near, the grassy land or meadow.

Prazac (*Cz.-Sl.*) One who came from Prague (the threshold), in Czechoslovakia.

Preble, Prebble (*Eng.*) One who came from Prevelles, in France.

Prendergast (*Eng., Ir., Scot.*) Descendant of Pendegast (head stranger); one who came from Prendergast, a parish in Pembrokeshire; one who came from Prendergast (priest's deep glen), in Scotland.

Prentice, Prentiss (*Eng.*) One who was learning a craft, an apprentice.

Prescott (*Eng.*) One who came from Prescot (priest's cottage), the name of places in Lancashire and Oxfordshire; dweller near the priest's cottage.

Presley, Pressley (*Scot., Eng.*) One who came from Preslie or Presslie, both in Aberdeen; dweller in, or near, the priest's wood.

Press (*Eng., Wel., Scot.*) One who came from Prees (brushwood), in Shropshire or Preese (brushwood), in Lancashire; dweller at, or near, a thicket; the son of Rees (ardor, a rush); one who came from Press or Preas (thicket), in Scotland.

Prest, Prester, Priester (*Eng., Fr.*) One who performed sacerdotal functions; one whose function, behavior, spirit or appearance resembled that of a priest.

Preston (*Eng.*) One who came from Preston (priest's homestead), the name of many places in England.

Price, Preece (*Wel.*) The son of Rhys (ardor, a rush); one who came from Prees (brushwood), in Shropshire or from Preese, in Lancashire.

Pride, Pryde (*Eng.*) One who played the part of Pride in the early mystery plays or pageants; one who came from Priddy (earth or soil), in Somerset.

Priest, Priester, Priess, Pries (*Eng.*) One who performed sacerdotal functions; one whose function, behavior, spirit or appearance resembled that of a priest.

Priestley, Priestly (*Eng.*) Dweller in, or near, the priest's meadow or wood.

Prime, Prim, Primm (*Eng.*) The slender or small man.

Primmer (*Eng.*) The priest or official who read at prime, the first canonical hour.

Prince, Printz, Prinz (*Eng., Ger.*) Descendant of a prince or sovereign, or of one connected in some way with his household.

Prindiville, Prendiville, Prindeville (*Eng., Ir.*) One who came from Frendeville or Fermainville, in France.

Prindle (*Eng.*) Dweller in a small field or on a small farm.

Pringle (*Scot.*) One who came from the lands of Hoppringle (peg valley), near Stow in Roxburghshire.

Prior (*Eng.*) A member of a prior's entourage; one who was the head of a priory, a monastic official next in rank below an abbot; one who played the part of a prior in play or pageant.

Pritchard, Prichard (*Wel.*) The son of Richard (rule, hard).

Pritchett (*Eng.*) Dweller at the sign of the pricket, a buck in his second year; a variant of Pritchard, q.v.

Pritikin (*Rus.*) One who dwelt adjacent to another, a neighbor.

Prk, Prch (*Cz.-Sl.*) One with a goatish odor.

Probert (*Wel.*) The son of Robert (fame, bright).

Probst (*Ger.*) A provost, superintendent, or official head of an institution.

Prochaska (*Cz.-Sl.*) One who traveled by foot, a walker.

Proctor, Procter (*Eng.*) One who acted as an attorney in an ecclesiastical court.

Proffitt, Proffit (*Eng., Scot., Fr.*) One who enacted the part of the prophet in medieval pageants; one who was wealthy or in comfortable circumstances.

Prokop (*Pol., Ukr., Rus.*) Descendant of Prokop (progressive).

Prosser (*Wel.*) The son of Rosser (fame, spear).

Prost (*Eng.*) A variant of Priest, q.v.

Prothero, Protheroe (*Wel.*) The son of Rhydderch (the reddish-brown one).

Proudfoot, Proudfit (*Eng.*) One who walked with a haughty step or arrogant gait.

Prout, Prouty, Proud (*Eng.*) The proud, arrogant man.

Provenzano, Provenzale (*It.*) One who came from Provence, an historical region of France.

Provost, Proust, Prevot (*Eng., Fr.*) A commander, the chief magistrate.

Pruitt, Pruett, Prewitt (*Eng.*) The little, gallant or valiant man.

Pruszynski (*Pol.*) One who came from Pruszyn (Pruch's settlement), in Poland.

Pryor (*Eng.*) A member of a prior's entourage; one who was the head of a priory, a monastic official next in rank below an abbot; one who played the part of a prior in play or pageant.

Przybylski (*Pol.*) One who had just arrived, a newcomer.

Ptacek (*Cz.-Sl.*) Dweller at the sign of the little bird; one with some characteristic of a small bird.

Ptak, Ptack (*Pol.*) Dweller at the sign of the bird; one with birdlike characteristics.

Pucci, Puccini, Puccio (*It.*) Descendant of Pucci, a pet form of Iacopucci (the supplanter).

Puckett (*Eng.*) Descendant of little Puca (goblin).

Puddister, Puddester (*Eng.*) One, especially a woman, who is very busy doing what is of little or no practical value.

Puffer (*Ger.*) Descendant of Bodefrit (messenger, peace).

Pugh (*Wel.*) The son of Hugh or Hu (spirit).

Pulaski (*Pol.*) One who came from Pulawy, in Poland.

Pulgram (*Ger.*) Descendant of the pilgrim.

Pulliam (*Wel.*) The son of William (resolution, helmet).

Pullman (*Eng.*) Dweller at, or near, a pool or lake.

Pumphrey (*Wel.*) The son of Humphrey (supporter of peace).

Punch, Punches (*Eng.*) Dweller at, or near, a bridge.

Purcell, Pursell (*Eng.*) Dweller at the sign of the young pig; one with some quality of a young pig.

Purdy, Purdie (*Eng.*) One given to blasphemy, from the French *par Dieu* ("by God").

Purinton, Purrington, Purington (*Eng.*) One who came from Puriton (pear-tree enclosure), in Somerset.

Purnell (*Eng.*) Descendant of Pernel or Parnel, a contraction of Petronella (little rock).

Purpura (*It.*) The red-haired or ruddy-complexioned man.

Purvis, Purves (*Scot., Eng.*) Dweller at, or frequenter at, or near, a porch (generally of a church).

Pusateri, Pusatera (*It.*) One who kept a public inn, an innkeeper.

Pusey (*Eng.*) One who came from Pusey (pea island), in Berkshire.

Putman (*Eng.*) Dweller near, or worker in, a pit.

Putnam (*Eng.*) One who came from Puttenham (Putta's homestead), the name of places in Hertfordshire and Surrey.

Puttkamer (*Ger.*) One who cleaned rooms.

Putz (*Ger.*) One who came from Putz, in Germany; dweller at, or near, a well or spring.

Pye (*Eng.*) Dweller at the sign of the magpie; one with some characteristic of a magpie.

Pyle, Pyles (*Eng.*) One who came from Pylle (creek), in Somerset; dweller at a creek or small castle.

Pyne (*Eng.*) Dweller at, or near, the pine tree; dweller at the sign of the pine tree.

Pyrrhos (*Gr.*) The red-haired or ruddy man.

Pytel, Pytell (*Eng.*) Dweller in a small field or enclosure.

Quackenbush (*Du.*) Dweller in, or near, the wood frequented by frogs.

Quaile, Quill, Quail, Quale (*Ir.*) Dweller near the hazel tree.

Qualters, Qualter (*Eng.*) Descendant of Walter (powerful warrior); one who made quilts.

Quarles, Qualls (*Eng.*) One who came from Quarles (circles), in Norfolk.

Quealy, Queally (*Ir.*) Grandson of Caollaidhe (origin obscure).

Queen (*Eng.*) One who played the part of the queen in a play or pageant; one connected in some way with the queen's household.

Queeney (*Ir.*) The son of Maonach (wealthy, or dumb).

Quick (*Du., Eng., Ir.*) The lively or bright person; dweller by an aspen tree; grandson of Corc (heart); one who came from Quickbury, formerly Cuwyk (cow farm), in Essex.

Quigg (*Ir.*) Variant of Quick, q.v.

Quigley, Quigly (*Ir.*) Grandson of the escort or companion.

Quill (*Ir.*) Grandson of Coll (hazel, or head).

Quilligan (*Ir.*) The son of the bearded man.

Quilty (*Ir.*) Grandson of Caoilte (hardness).

Quimby, Quinby (*Eng.*) One who came from Quenby (queen's manor), in Leicestershire.

Quincy, Quinci, Quinsey (*Eng., Scot.*) One who came from Quincay, formerly Quinci (Quintus' estate), in Maine, France.

Quindry, Quintrie (*Fr.*) One who held land, a fifth of the produce of which went to the lord.

Quinlan (*Ir.*) Grandson of Caoindealbhan (gracefully shaped).

Quinn, Quin (*Ir.*) Grandson of Conn (reason, or a freeman).

Quirk, Quirke (*Ir.*) Descendant of the bushy-haired man; grandson of Corc (heart).

Quist (*Sw.*) Twig.

Rabin (*Fr.*) Descendant of the rabbi, or teacher.

Rabinowitz, Rabinovitz (*Cz.-Sl., Yu.-Sl., Pol., Ukr., Rus.*) The son of the rabbi, or Jewish teacher.

Racine (*Fr.*) One who grew root vegetables, a gardener.

Radcliffe, Radcliff (*Eng.*) One who came from Radcliffe (red cliff), in Lancashire.

Raddatz (*Yu.-Sl.*) Descendant of Radac, a pet form of Rad (happy).

Radermacher (*Ger.*) One who made wheels.

Radford (*Eng.*) One who came from Radford (red ford), the name of several places in England.

Radley (*Eng.*) One who came from Radley (red wood), in Berkshire.

Radtke, Radke (*Ger.*) Descendant of little Rado (counsel); descendant of little Rad, a pet form of Konrad (bold, counsel).

Rae, Ree (*Scot., Eng.*) Variants of Ray, q.v.

Raff, Raffe (*Eng.*) Descendant of Raff, a variant of Ralph (shield, wolf).

Raffel, Raffle, Raffles, Raffl (*Eng.*) Descendant of Raphael (God has healed).

Rafferty (*Ir.*) Grandson of Robhartach (origin obscure).

Ragan, Ragen, Ragin (*Ger.*) Descendant of Ragin, a short form of names beginning with Ragin (counsel), as Raganfrid, Ragingar and Raginald.

Rago (*It.*) One thought to possess some of the qualities of a frog, such as a croaking voice or a short, fat body; dweller at the sign of the green frog.

Rahn (*Ger.*) The slender, or thin, man.

Rainbird (*Eng.*) A corruption of Rambert (raven, bright).

Rainbow (*Eng.*) Descendant of Reginbald (might, bold).

Raines, Raine, Raynes, Rains, Reyns (*Eng.*) Descendant of Rain, a pet form of one of the old names beginning with Regen, or Ragin (counsel), or of Rayner (might, army); dweller at a boundary line; dweller at the sign of the frog; one with froglike characteristics.

Rainey, Raining (*Scot.*) Descendant of little Ren, a pet form of Reginald (counsel, judgment).

Rainsford (*Eng.*) One who came from Rainford (Regna's ford), in Lancashire.

Rak (*Pol., Ukr.*) One who fished for and sold crabs.

Rakowski (*Pol.*) Dweller at the sign of the crab; one who fished for crabs.

Raleigh, Raley, Ralley (*Eng.*) One who came from Raleigh (red meadow), in Devonshire.

Ralph (*Eng.*) Descendant of Ralph (shield, wolf).

Ralston, Rolston, Rolleston (*Eng.,* Scot.) One who came from Rolleston (Hrolf's homestead), the name of several places in England; one who came from the lands of Ralston, in Renfrewshire.

Ramage, Rammage (*Scot.*) The wild one who lived in the forest.

Ramey (*Fr.*) Dweller in a wooded area; a pilgrim who returned from Jerusalem with palm branches; descendant of Remy or Remigius (protector), a French saint of the fifth century.

Ramirez (*Sp.*) The son of Ramon (wise protector).

Ramsay, Ramsey (*Scot., Eng.*) One who came from Ramsay (ram's isle), in Scotland, or from Ramsey (wild garlic island), the name of places in Essex and Huntingdonshire.

Ramsdell, Ramsdill (*Eng.*) One who came from Ramsdale (ram valley), in Hampshire.

Ramsden (*Eng.*) One who came from Ramsden (ram valley), the name of several places in England.

Rand (*Eng., Ger.*) Descendant of Rand, a pet form of Randal or Randolph (shield, wolf), or of German names beginning with Rand (shield), as Ranthar and Randulf; one who came from Rand (marshy edge), the name of places in Lincolnshire and Yorkshire; dweller near the rim or edge.

Randall, Randle, Randale, Randel, Randell (*Eng.*) Descendant of Randal or Randwulf (shield, wolf).

Randazzo (*It.*) One who came from Randazzo, in Italy.

Randolph (*Eng.*) Descendant of Randwulf (shield, wolf).

Raney, Ranney (*Scot.*) Variants of Rainey, q.v.

Ranieri, Raniere (*It.*) Descendant of Ranieri (counsel, army).

Rank, Ranke (*Ger.*) Descendant of little Randolf (shield, wolf).

Rankin, Rankine, Ranken (*Eng.*) Descendant of little Rand, pet form of Randal or Randolph (shield, wolf).

Ransom, Ranson, Ransome (*Eng.*) The son of Rand, pet form of Randolph or Randal (shield, wolf).

Raphael (*Eng.*) Descendant of Raphael (healed by God).

Rappaport, Rapoport, Rappeport, Rapaport, Rappoport (*It.*) The physician who came from Porto (gate), in Italy.

Rasch, Rascher (*Ger.*) The quick, lively person; one who came from Rasch, in Germany.

Raschke (*Ger.*) Descendant of little Rado (counsel).

Raske, Rask (*Sw.*) Daring, a soldier name.

Raskin (*Rus., Pol.*) Descendant, or son, of Rashe, a pet form of Rachel (the ewe).

Rasmussen, Rasmusson, Rasmusen, Rasmuson (*Dan., Nor.*) The son of Rasmus, a variant of Erasmus (amiable).

Ratcliff, Ratcliffe (*Eng.*) One who came from Ratcliff (red cliff), the name of several places in England.

Rath, Rathe (*Ger., Ir.*) One who came from Rath (advice), in Rheinland; descendant of Rath, a form of Rado, a pet form of names beginning with Rat (advice), as Radulf, Ratward and Radoald; one who gave advice; one who came from Rath (fort), in Ireland.

Rathbun, Rathbone, Rathburn (*Eng., Wel.*) One who came from Radbourn (stream where reeds grew), in Warwickshire, or from Radbourne, with the same meaning, in Derbyshire; dweller in a stumpy clearing.

Rathmann, Rathman (*Ger.*) A city officer or alderman.

Ratliff, Ratliffe (*Eng.*) A variant of Ratcliff, q.v.

Ratner, Rattner (*Eng.*) One who caught rats.

Rattray (*Scot.*) One who came from Rattray (fort or mound dwelling), in Perthshire.

Rau, Rauh (*Nor., Ger.*) One who carried himself in a graceful manner; one with unusual body hair; a rough, boorish person.

Rauch, Raucher (*Ger.*) One who smoked meats; the hairy man.

Rauen, Rauh, Rauhe (*Ger.*) The hairy man, one with unusual body hair.

Raup, Raupp (*Ger.*) Descendant of Ruppo, a pet form of names beginning with Hrod (fame), as Hrotbald, Hrodobert and Rotbrand.

Rausch (*Ger.*) The excitable, or hurried, man; dweller near rushes.

Rawleigh, Rawley (*Eng.*) One who came from Rayleigh (meadow where rye was grown), in Essex, or from Rowley (rough wood), the name of several places in England.

Rawlings, Rawlins, Rawlinson (*Eng.*) Descendant of little Raoul or little Raw, pet forms of Ralph (shield, wolf).

Rawson (*Eng.*) The son of Raw, a pet form of Ralph (shield, wolf).

Ray, Raye (*Eng.*) Descendant of Ray, a pet form of Raymond (wise, protector); dweller at the sign of the roe deer; one with some of the qualities of the roe deer; one who played the part of the king in play or pageant; one who was connected in some way with a king's household.

Rayburn, Raybourn, Raybourne, Rayborn, Raeburn, Reyburn (*Eng., Scot.*) One who came from Ripponden, early form, Ryburn (fierce stream), in Yorkshire; one who came from the old lands of Ryburn, in Ayrshire.

Rayfield (*Eng.*) Dweller at, or near, the river field.

Rayford (*Eng.*) Dweller at, or near, the ford of the river.

Raymond, Reymond (*Eng.*) Descendant of Raymond (counsel, protection).

Rayner, Raynor, Rainer (*Eng.*) Descendant of Rayner (counsel, army).

Rea (*Eng.*) Dweller at, or near, the Rea (river), the name of several rivers in England.

Read, Reade (*Eng.*) The ruddy or red-haired man; one who came from Read (roe headland), in Lancashire.

Reader (*Eng.*) A variant of Reeder, q.v.

Reading (*Eng.*) One who came from Reading (the people of Read, red), in Berkshire.

Ready, Readey, Readdy, Readie (*Eng., Scot.*) Descendant of little Read (red), a nickname given to one with red hair; descendant of little Read or Red, pet forms of Redmond (counsel, protection); one who came from Reedie, in Angus.

Reagan, Reagen, Reagin (*Ir.*) Grandson of Riagan (little king).

Reardon, Rearden (*Ir.*) Grandson of Rioghbhardan (royal poet).

Reaves, Reavis (*Eng.*) Variant of Reeves, q.v.

Rector (*Eng.*) The official who had charge of a church or parish.

Redd (*Eng.*) The red-haired or ruddy person.

Redden (*Scot.*) One who came from Redden (raven dell), in Roxburghshire.

Reddick, Riddick, Reddicks (*Eng.*) One who came from Redditch (red or reedy ditch), in Worcestershire.

Redding (*Scot., Eng.*) One who came from Redding (clearing), the name of several places in Scotland; dweller in, or near, a clearing, or in, or near, a red meadow; one who came from Reading (Read's people), in Berkshire.

Reddington, Redington (*Eng.*) Dweller at the homestead in the clearing, that is, place cleared of trees; one who came from Rodington (homestead on the Roden River), in Shropshire.

Reddish (*Eng.*) One who came from Reddish (reed ditch), in Lancashire.

Reddy (*Scot., Eng.*) One who came from Reedy, in Angus. *See also* Ready.

Reder (*Eng.*) One who covered roofs with reeds, a thatcher.

Redfern, Redfearn (*Eng.*) Dweller at, or near, a place where red ferns grew.

Redfield (*Eng.*) One who lived on, or by, the cleared land.

Redman, Redmon (*Eng.*) The red-haired or ruddy man; descendant of Redmond (counsel, protection).

Redmond (*Eng.*) Descendant of Redmond (counsel, protection).

Reece (*Wel.*) The son of Rhys (ardor, a rush).

Reed, Reid (*Eng.*) The red-haired or ruddy person; one who came from Reed (reedy or rough growth), in Hertfordshire.

Reeder (*Eng.*) One who covered roofs with reeds, a thatcher.

Reedy (*Eng., Scot.*) A variant of Ready, q.v. Reed was an early spelling of red.

Reese, Rees (*Wel.*) The son of Rhys (ardor, a rush).

Reeves, Reeve (*Eng.*) A minor official appointed by the lord of the manor to supervise his tenants' work.

Regan (*Ir.*) Descendant of the impulsive man; grandson of Riagan.

Regnier, Regner (*Fr.*) Descendant of Raginhari (counsel, army).

Rehm (*Ger.*) Descendant of Raimo, a pet form of Reginmund (counsel, protection); one who came from Rehm, in Schleswig.

Reich (*Ger.*) Descendant of Rico, a pet form of Riculf (powerful, wolf).

Reichel (*Ger.*) Descendant of little Rico, a pet form of Riculf (powerful, wolf).

Reichert, Reichard, Reichardt, Reichart (*Ger.*) Descendant of Ricohard (rule, hard).

Reichman, Reichmann (*Ger.*) Descendant of Ricman (powerful, man).

Reidy (*Eng., Scot.*) A variant of Ready, q.v. Reid was an early spelling of red.

Reif, Reiff, Riff (*Ger.*) Descendant of Rifo, a pet form of Ricfrid (rule, peace).

Reimer, Reimers (*Ger.*) Descendant of Raginmar (counsel, famous) or of Ricmer (rich, famous) or of Rimher (mature, army).

Rein (*Ger.*) Descendant of Ragino, a pet form of names beginning with Ragin (counsel), as Raganfrid, Ragingar and Raginhart.

Reinecke, Reinicke, Reineck, Reinick (*Ger.*) Descendant of little Ragino, a pet form of names beginning with Ragin (counsel), as Raganrich, Raginscalc and Raginulf.

Reiner (*Ger.*) Descendant of Raginhari (counsel, army).

Reinert (*Ger.*) Descendant of Raginhart (counsel, strong).

Reinhardt, Reinhart, Reinhard (*Ger.*) Descendant of Reinhardt or Raginhart (counsel, hard).

Reinhold, Reinholtz (*Ger.*) Descendant of Reinold (counsel, force).

Reinke (*Ger.*) Descendant of little Ragino, a pet form of Raginulf (counsel, wolf).

Reinwald, Reinwall (*Ger.*) Descendant of Reinwald (counsel, force).

Reiser, Reisser (*Ger.*) One who left to go to war; one who came from Reiser, in Germany.

Reisman, Reismann (*Ger.*) One who went to war, a warrior.

Reiss, Reis (*Ger.*) Descendant of Riso (giant).

Reiter (*Ger.*) One who rode a horse, a cavalryman; one who cleared land for tilling.

Reitz (*Ger.*) Descendant of Ragizo, a pet form of names beginning with Ragan (counsel), as Raginhari and Reginmund; one who came from Ragizo, in Germany.

Remington (*Eng.*) One who came from Rimington (homestead on the rim or border), in Yorkshire.

Rempert (*Eng.*) Descendant of Reimbert (power, bright).

Remus (*Eng.*) Descendant of Remus (protector).

Renaud, Renault, Regnaud (*Fr.*) One who came from Renaix, in Belgium; descendant of Renaud (counsel, judgment).

Renfro, Renfroe, Renfrow, Rentfro, Rentfrew (*Scot.*) One who came from Renfrew (flowing brook), in Renfrewshire.

Renner (*Eng., Du.*) One who carried messages on foot or horseback, a runner.

Rennie (*Scot.*) Variant of Rainey, q.v.

Reno (*Sp.*) Dweller at the sign of the reindeer.

Rentz, Renz, Rentsch (*Ger.*) Descendant of Renz, a pet form of Laurentius (laurel, symbol of victory).

Renwick (*Eng.*) One who came from Renwick (farm frequented by ravens), in Cumberland.

Rescigno (*It*). One who came from Rescigno, in Italy.

Resnick, Reznick (*Pol., Rus., Ukr.*) One who sold meat, a butcher; one who slaughtered animals for meat according to Jewish ritual.

Reuss (*Ger.*) One who repaired shoes; one who came from Russia.

Reuter, Reuther (*Ger.*) One who cleared land for tilling.

Revere (*Eng., Fr.*) The robber; dweller on, or near, the bank or shore; one who came from Riviere, a village in Belgium.

Rex (*Eng.*) Latin for King, q.v.; the son of Rick, a pet form of Richard (rule, hard).

Rexford (*Eng.*) Dweller at the king's river crossing.

Reyes, Rey (*Eng.*) One who played the part of the king in a play or pageant; one connected in some way with the king's household; a variant of Ray, q.v.

Reynolds (*Eng.*) Descendant of Reginald or Regenweald (counsel, force).

Reznick, Reznik (*Cz.-Sl.*) One who cut and sold meat, a butcher.

Rhea, Rhay (*Wel.*) Dweller near the rapids; dweller near the river Rea (river), in Wales.

Rhodes, Rhode, Rhoades, Rhoads (*Eng.*) Dweller at a clearing; one who lived at the roadside.

Rhys (*Wel.*) Descendant of Rhys, (ardor, a rush).

Ricardo (*Sp., Port.*) Descendant of Ricardo (rule, hard).

Ricci, Ricca (*It.*) Descendant of Ricci, a pet form of Enrico (home ruler).

Riccio (*It.*) One who had wavy or curly hair.

Rice (*Wel.*) Descendant of Rhys (ardor, a rush).

Rich, Riche (*Eng.*) Descendant of Rich, a pet form of Richard (rule, hard); dweller near a ditch or small stream.

Richardson, Richards, Richard (*Eng., Wel.*) The son of Richard (rule, hard).

Richie, Richey (*Eng., Scot.*) Descendant of little Rich, a pet form of Richard (rule, hard).

Richman (*Eng.*) The servant of Rich, a pet form of Richard (rule, hard); variant of Richmond, q.v.

Richmond (*Eng.*) One who came from Richemont (lofty mountain), in Normandy, or from Richmond, in Yorkshire, which was named after one of the Richemonts in France.

Richter, Richters (*Ger.*) One who held the office of judge or magistrate.

Rickard, Rickards, Rickart (*Eng.*) Descendant of Rickard or Ricard, variants of Richard (rule, hard).

Ricker, Rickerson (*Eng.*) Descendant of Richere (mighty, army).

Rickert (*Eng.*) An Anglicization of the Dutch Rijkert, a variant of Richard (rule, hard).

Ricketts, Rickett (*Eng.*) Descendant of little Rick, a pet form of Richard (rule, hard).

Riddle, Riddell, Riddel, Ridell, Riddles (*Eng.*) Descendant of little Rada (counsel); dweller on, or near, a red hill; one who came from Rydal or Ryedale (valley where rye was grown), in Westmorland and Yorkshire respectively.

Rideout (*Fr.*) Descendant of Ridwulf (horseman, wolf), or possibly of Ridald (horseman, bold).

Rider (*Eng.*) The rider or trooper; a mounted guardian of a forest.

Ridge, Ridges (*Eng.*) One who came from Ridge, in Hertfordshire; dweller at, or near, a range of hills.

Ridgway, Ridgeway (*Eng.*) Dweller at the way, or road, along a ridge.

Ridley (*Eng.*) One who came from Ridley (cleared, or reedy, meadow), the name of several places in England.

Rieck, Riecke (*Ger.*) Descendant of Rieck, a pet form of Rieckert (rule, hard).

Riedel, Riedl, Riedle, Riedell (*Ger.*) Descendant of Riedel, a pet form of names beginning with Hrod (fame), as Hrotfrid, Rothhari and Hrodmar.

Rieger (*Ger.*) Descendant of Hrodgaer (fame, spear); the magistrate who censored people.

Riemer (*Ger.*) One who made and sold harness; descendant of Rimher (mature, army).

Ries, Riess, Riese (*Ger.*) The large man; descendant of Riso (giant); one who came from Riess, in Germany.

Rifkin (*Rus., Ukr.*) The son of Rifka (a snare).

Rigas (*Gr.*) One who played the part of a king in play or pageant.

Rigby (*Eng.*) One who came from Ribby (formerly Rigbi, homestead on a ridge), in Lancashire.

Riggio (*It.*) One who came from Reggio, in Italy.

Riggs, Rigg (*Eng., Scot.*) Dweller at a ridge or range of hills; one who came from the lands of Rigg, in East Lothian.

Rigoni (*It.*) Descendant of big Rigo, a pet form of Arrigo or Enrico (home ruler).

Rigsby, Rigsbey (*Eng.*) One who came from Rigsby (settlement on a ridge), in Lincolnshire.

Riha (*Cz.-Sl.*) The belching, vomiting person.

Riley, Reilly, Reilley (*Ir.*) Grandson of Raghallach (sportive).

Rill (*Ger.*) Descendant of Rido, a pet form of names beginning with Reiten (rider), as Ridperht, Ridhart and Ridher.

Rimkus (*Lith.*) Descendant of Rimkus, a pet form of Rimkantas (peaceful, suffer).

Rinella (*It.*) Descendant of little Rina, a pet form of Catrina, or Caterina (pure).

Ring, Ringe (*Eng.*) Dweller at a stone circle or circular entrenchment; descendant of Ring, a pet form of Hringwulf or Ringulfus (ring, wolf).

Ringer (*Eng.*) A bell or change ringer; one whose business it was to ring a church or town bell at stated times.

Rio, Rios (*Sp.*) Dweller near the river.

Riordan (*Ir.*) Grandson of Rioghbhardan (royal poet).

Ripley (*Eng.*) One who came from Ripley (long, narrow wood or meadow), the name of several places in England.

Ritchie, Ritchey (*Scot., Eng.*) Descendant of little Rich, a pet form of Richard (rule, hard).

Ritter (*Ger.*) A military servant, a knight.

Rivera (*Sp.*) Dweller near a brook or stream.

Rivers, River (*Eng.*) One who came from River (river), in Kent, or from River (brow of a hill), in Sussex; dweller by the river; one who came from Rivieres (shore), in France.

Rix, Rixe (*Eng.*) The son of Rick, a pet form of Richard (rule, hard); dweller near, or in, the rushes.

Rizzo, Rizza, Rizzi (*It.*) One who had wavy or curly hair.

Roach, Roache (*Ir.*) Dweller at, or near, a rock. *See also* Roche.

Roback, Robeck (*Ger.*) One who worked for another, without pay, a servant.

Robb (*Eng.*) Descendant of Rob, a pet form of Robert (fame, bright).

Robbie, Robie (*Scot.*) Descendant of little Rob, a pet form of Robert (fame, bright).

Robbins, Robins (*Eng.*) The son of little Rob, a pet form of Robert (fame, bright).

Roberson (*Eng.*) The son of Robert (fame, bright).

Roberts, Robertson, Robert, Robart (*Wel., Scot., Eng.*) The son of Robert (fame, bright).

Robey, Roby (*Eng.*) One who came from Robey or Roby (homestead near a boundary mark), in Derbyshire and Lancashire respectively; variants of Robbie, q.v.

Robin, Robyn (*Eng.*) Descendant of little Rob, a pet form of Robert (fame, bright).

Robinson, Robison (*Eng., Scot.*) The son of little Rob, a pet form of Robert (fame, bright).

Robles (*Sp.*) One who came from Robles (oak tree grove), in Spain.

Robson, Robeson (*Eng., Scot.*) The son of Rob, a pet form of Robert (fame, bright).

Rocca (*It.*) Dweller near a cliff, or near a fortress.

Rocco (*It.*) Descendant of Rocco (to crow or roar).

Roche, Roch, Rocher, Rochet, Roque (*Fr., Eng.*) Dweller near a rock; one who came from Roche (rock), in Cornwall.

Rochford (*Eng.*) One who came from Rochford (hunting dog's ford), the name of places in Essex and Worcestershire.

Rock, Rocke (*Eng.*) Dweller near some prominent boulder; probably a boundary marker; one who came from Rock (rock), in Northumberland, or from Rock (the oak), in Worcestershire.

Rockefeller, Rockenfeller (*Du.*) Dweller in, or near, the rye field.

Rockett (*Eng.*) One who came from La Roquette (the little rock), in Normandy.

Rockwell (*Eng.*) Dweller at, or near, the stony spring or stream.

Rockwood (*Eng.*) Dweller in, or near, a rocky wood or grove.

Rode, Rodd, Rodde, Rod (*Eng.*) Dweller in the clearing or place where the trees have been removed; descendant of Rod, a pet form of Roderick (famous, ruler).

Roderick, Rodrick (*Eng.*) Descendant of Roderick (famous, ruler).

Rodin (*Fr.*) Descendant of little Rod, a pet form of Girard (spear, firm).

Rodriguez (*Sp.*) Son of Rodrigo (famous, ruler).

Rodwell (*Eng.*) Dweller at the spring, or well, by the road, or cross; one who came from Rodwell (red spring, or stream), the name of places in Bedfordshire and Hertfordshire.

Roe (*Eng.*) Dweller at the sign of the roe deer; dweller at the row or hedgerow.

Roebuck, Robuck (*Eng.*) Dweller at the sign of the male roe deer.

Roeder, Roedder, Roeters (*Ger.*) Descendant of Rothari (fame, army); dweller on land recently cleared for tilling.

Roelandts, Roeland, Roelant (*Du., Bel.*) Descendant of Roeland (fame, land).

Rogalski (*Pol.*) Dweller near the Rogalskie (place frequented by animals with horns), a lake in Poland; a betrayed husband.

Rogers, Rodgers, Rodger, Roger, Rogerson (*Wel., Eng.*) The son of Roger (fame, spear).

Rogowski (*Pol.*) One who came from Rogow(o) (horn), in Poland.

Rohde (*Ger.*) Descendant of Hrodo, a pet form of names beginning with Hrod (fame), as Hrodulf, Hrodric and Hrodowald.

Rohr (*Ger.*) Dweller at a place where reeds grew.

Rohrbacher, Rohrbach, Rohrback, Rohrbacker (*Ger.*) One who came from Rohrbach (reedy stream), the name of places in Austria and Germany; dweller near the Rohrbach, the name of thirteen rivers in Germany.

Rohrer (*Ger.*) One who came from Rohr (spring), in Germany, or from Rohrau (reedy place), in Austria.

Roland, Rolland (*Eng.*) Descendant of Roland (fame, land).

Rolfe, Rolf (*Eng.*) Descendant of Rolf (fame, wolf).

Roller (*Eng.*) One who made and sold parchment rolls for manuscripts.

Rollins (*Eng., Fr.*) The son of little Roll, a pet form of Raoul or Ralph (shield, wolf); descendant of Roland (fame, land).

Roman, Romans (*Eng., Scot.*) One who had made a pilgrimage to Rome (four crossroads); one who came from Rome, a Roman; one who came from Romanno (circle of the monk), in Peeblesshire.

Romano, Romani (*It.*) One who came from Rome (four crossroads), or from within Rome's political sphere; one who has visited Rome.

Romanowski (*Pol.*) The son of Roman (one from Rome).

Rome (*Eng.*) One who had made a pilgrimage to Rome (four crossroads); one who came from Rome.

Romero (*Sp.*) One who has visited a shrine, a pilgrim.

Rommel (*Ger., Du.*) Descendant of Ruhm, a pet form of names beginning with Ruhm (fame), as Hrumheri, Rumerich and Rumuald; the messy or untidy man.

Ronan, Ronayne (*Ir.*) Grandson of Ronan (little seal).

Roney (*Ir.*) Grandson of Ruanaidh (hero).

Rood, Roode (*Eng.*) Dweller near a roadside cross. *See also* Rode.

Rook, Rooks, Rooke (*Eng.*) Dweller at the sign of the rook; nickname given to one with black hair and dark complexion.

Rooney (*Ir.*) Grandson of Ruanaidh (hero).

Roos, Roose (*Eng.*) A variant of Rose, q.v.

Roosevelt (*Du.*) One who lived at, or near, the rose farm or field.

Root, Rote, Rot (*Eng.*) The gay or cheerful man.

Roper (*Eng.*) One who made and sold rope.

Roscoe (*Eng.*) Dweller in, or near, a wood frequented by roes; one who came from Roscoe, in Yorkshire.

Rose (*Eng., Scot., Ger.*) Dweller at the sign of the rose, a not uncommon inn sign; dweller at the sign of the horse.

Roseman (*Ger., Eng.*) Rose man; descendant of Rosmund (horse or rose, protection).

Rosen (*Ger.*) Roses; descendant of Rose (horse or rose).

Rosenbach, Rosenbacher (*Ger.*) One who came from Rosenbach (rose brook), in southern Austria.

Rosenbaum (*Ger.*) Rose tree.

Rosenberg, Rosenberger (*Ger., Sw.*) One who came from Rosenberg (rose mountain), in Germany; rose mountain.

Rosenblatt, Rosenblat (*Ger.*) Rose leaf.

Rosenblum, Rosenbloom (*Ger., Sw.*) Rose flower.

Rosenfeld, Rosenfield, Rosenfelder, Rosenfelt (*Ger.*) One who came from Rosenfeld (rose field), in Germany.

Rosenkranz, Rosenkrantz, Rosenkrans (*Ger.*) One who came from Rosenkrantz (rose wreath), in Germany.

Rosenquist (*Sw.*) Rose twig.

Rosenschmidt (*Ger.*) The smith at the sign of the rose.

Rosenstein (*Ger.*) Rose stone.

Rosenthal (*Ger.*) One who came from Rosenthal (rose valley), in West Germany).

Rosenwald, Rosewald, Rosewall (*Ger.*) One who came from Rosenwald (rose forest), in Germany.

Rosenzweig (*Ger.*) Rose branch.

Rosin (*Fr., Ger.*) Descendant of little Rose; one who came from Rosien, in Germany.

Rosinski (*Pol.*) One who came from Rosiho (dew), in Poland, or Rosinski, in Byelorussia.

Rosner, Rossner (*Ger.*) One who rode a horse; one who came from Rosna, Rossen or Roessen, in Germany; descendant of Rozzo, a pet form of names beginning with Hrod (famous), as Hrodmund, Rothari and Hrotfrid.

Ross (*Scot.*) Dweller at the promontory or peninsula; one who came from Ross (promontory), in Scotland.

Rosser (*Wel.*) Descendant of Rosser (fame, spear).

Rossetti, Rossetto (*It.*) One who had ruddy cheeks or red hair.

Rossi, Rossini, Rossa, Rosso (*It.*) The red-haired or ruddy-complexioned man.

Rossman (*Eng.*) Dweller at a promontory or peninsula.

Rossow, Rosso (*Pol.*) One who came from Russia (derived from the Rossi, a tribe of Norsemen flourishing in the ninth century).

Roth, Rothe (*Ger.*) The red-haired or ruddy-complexioned man; one who came from Roth (red), the name of several places in Germany; descendant of Ruodo, a pet form of names beginning with Hrod (fame), as Hrodric, Hrodulf and Hrodowin.

Rothenberg, Rottenberg, Rottenberk, Rothenberger (*Ger.*) One who came from Rothenberg (red fortress), the name of several places in Germany.

Rothman, Rothmann (*Ger.*) One who had red hair; descendant of Hrodman (fame, man).

Rothschild (*Ger.*) The great banking family drew its name from the red shield which swung before the shop door in Frankfurt.

Rothstein (*Ger.*) Dweller at, or near, a red stone.

Rothwell (*Eng.*) One who came from Rothwell (spring or stream by a clearing), the name of several places in England; dweller near a red spring or stream.

Rotter, Roter (*Eng., Ger.*) One who played a rote, a musical instrument of the violin class; one with red hair or a ruddy complexion; one who came from Roth (red), the name of several places in Germany.

Rounds, Round (*Eng.*) The rotund or plump man; a variant of Rowan, q.v.

Rountree, Roundtree, Rowantree, Rowntree (*Eng., Scot.*) Dweller at, or near, a rowan tree (mountain ash); one who came from Rowantree, in Scotland.

Rouse, Roux, Rous (*Fr., Eng.*) The red-haired man, or one with a ruddy complexion.

Rousseau (*Fr.*) One with a ruddy complexion or with red hair.

Rowan, Rowen (*Eng., Ir.*) Dweller at, or near, a rowan tree (mountain ash); the little, red-haired man.

Rowe, Row (*Eng.*) Dweller at the rough or uncultivated land; one who lived at the hedgerow.

Rowell, Rowells, Rowels, Rowel (*Eng.*) One who came from Rowell (roe stream), in Gloucestershire; dweller at a spring frequented by roes; descendant of little Rowland (fame, land).

Rowland, Rowlands (*Wel., Eng.*) Descendant of Roland (fame, land).

Rowley, Rowlee (*Eng.*) One who came from Rowley (rough meadow), the name of several places in England.

Roy, Roye (*Fr., Eng., Scot.*) One connected in some way with the king's household; one who played the part of of a king in tournaments; the red-haired or ruddy man.

Royce, Royse (*Eng.*) Dweller at the sign of the rose; one who lived at the sign of the horse.

Royster (*Eng.*) A blustering, swaggering person, a roisterer, a bully.

Royston (*Eng.*) One who came from Royston (homestead by Roese's cross), in Hertfordshire.

Rozanski (*Pol.*) One who came from Rozana, in Byelorussia.

Rubenstein, Rubinstein (*Ger.*) Ruby, or red precious stone; one who came from Rubenstein, in Germany.

Rubin, Ruben, Rubens, Rubins (*Ger.*) One who came from Rubyn or Ruben (ruby stone), in Germany; descendant of Ruben (behold, a son).

Rubincam, Rubicam, Rubenkamp (*Ger.*) Dweller in, or near, a turnip field.

Ruby, Rubey (*Eng.*) One who came from Roubaix, in France; descendant of Ruby, a pet form of Reuben (behold, a son); red precious stone.

Rucinski (*Pol.*) Dweller at a place where rue (a medicinal herb) grew.

Ruck (*Ger.*) Descendant of Rocco, a pet form of names beginning with Hrok (to crow), as Rochold and Hroculf.

Rucker (*Ger.*) Descendant of Hrodgaer (fame, spear).

Rudd, Ruud, Rude, Rud, Rudde (*Eng., Nor.*) One with a ruddy complexion; descendant of Rud, a pet form of Rudolf (fame, wolf); variant of Rood, q.v.; dweller in, or near, the clearing in the forest.

Ruddy, Ruddie (*Eng.*) One with a red, or ruddy complexion; variant of Rudy, q.v.

Rudnick, Rudnicki, Rudnik (*Pol.*) One who worked in a mine; dweller near a mine; one who came from Rudnik (red), the name of many places in Poland and Ukraine.

Rudnyckyj (*Ukr.*) One who came from Rudnyk, Rudnyky or Rudnyca (red), in Ukraine, or who was the owner of these places.

Rudolph, Rudolf (*Eng., Ger.*) Descendant of Rudolf (fame, wolf).

Rudy (*Eng., Ger.*) Descendant of little Rud, a pet form of Rudolf (fame, wolf).

Ruff, Ruf (*Eng.*) The red-haired or ruddy man.

Ruffin, Ruffing, Ruffins (*Eng.*) Descendant of Rufinus (red), the name of several saints.

Ruffolo, Ruffulo, Rufolo (*It.*) Descendant of Ruffuli (fame, wolf); one thought to possesss the qualities of a horned owl.

Ruge, Rugg, Rudge (*Eng.*) Dweller at, or on, the ridge or range of hills; one who came from Rudge (ridge), the name of places in Gloucestershire and Shropshire.

Ruggiero (*It.*) Descendant of Ruggiero (fame, spear).

Ruggles (*Eng.*) One who came from Rugley (woodcock glade), in Northumberland.

Ruiz (*Sp.*) The son of Ruy, a pet form of Rodrigo (famous, ruler).

Rumble (*Eng.*) Descendant of Rumbeald (fame, bold).

Rumsey (*Eng.*) One who came from Romsey (Rum's island), in Hampshire.

Rund, Runde (*Ger.*) The round or fat man.

Rundlett (*Fr.*) The little, rotund or fat man.

Runge, Rung (*Ger.*) Descendant of Runico (secret wisdom).

Runyon, Runyan (*Eng.*) A mangy, scurvy person.

Rupp (*Ger.*) Descendant of Ruppo (fame), a pet form of names beginning with Hrodb-, as Hrotbald.

Ruppert, Rupert (*Eng.*) Descendant of Rupert (fame, bright).

Rusch (*Ger., Swis.*) Dweller in, or near, rushes or bent grass; dweller near an elm tree; an excitable person.

Rush (*Eng., Ger., Swis.*) Dweller near a clump of rushes; dweller near an elm tree; an excitable person.

Rushford (*Eng.*) Dweller at the river crossing where rushes grew.

Rushforth, Rushworth (*Eng.*) One who came from Rushford (homestead overgrown with rushes), in Norfolk.

Rushton (*Eng.*) One who came from Rushton (homestead with rushes), the name of several places in England.

Rusin (*Pol.*) One who came from Rus, now Ukraine.

Ruskin (*Eng.*) Descendant of little Rous (red).

Rusnak (*Ukr.*) One who came from Rus, now Ukraine.

Russ (*Eng.*) The red-haired or ruddy-complexioned man; descendant of Russ, a pet form of Russell (dim. of red).

Russell (*Eng.*) The little, red-haired man.

Russo, Russow (*Pol.*) One who came from Russia (from Rossi, a tribe of Norsemen in the ninth century).

Rust (*Eng., Scot.*) Shortened form of Russet (red-haired).

Rutgers (*Du.*) The son of Rutger, Dutch form of Roger (fame, spear).

Ruth (*Ger.*) Descendant of Ruodo, a pet form of names beginning with Hrod (fame), as Hrotfrid, Rothhari and Hrodmar.

Rutherford (*Scot.*) One who came from Rutherford (river crossing used by cattle), in Scotland.

Rutkowski (*Pol.*) Dweller at a place where rue grew.

Rutledge, Routledge (*Eng.*) Dweller at, or near, a red lake or pool.

Rutsen (*Du.*) The son of Rut or Ruut (fame).

Ruttenberg (*Pol., Ger.*) One who came from Rothenberg (red mountain), also called Rostarzewo, in Poland. Probably not from Rothenberg in Germany.

Ruusu (*Finn.*) Dweller at the sign of the rose; one who resided near a rosebush.

Ruzicka (*Cz.-Sl.*) Dweller at the sign of the little rose.

Ryan (*Ir.*) Grandson of Rian (little king).

Ryba (*Cz.-Sl., Pol.*) Dweller at the sign of the fish; one who sold fish.

Rybak, Ryback (*Pol.*) One who caught and sold fish, a fisherman.

Rybarczyk (*Pol.*) The son of the fisherman.

Rybicki (*Pol.*) Dweller at, or near, a fishpond.

Ryder (*Wel., Eng.*) The rider or trooper; a mounted guardian of a forest.

Ryerson, Ryersen (*Du.*) The son of Reyer or Reijer (rider).

Rynne, Rynn (*Eng.*) Dweller at a large drain or channel on the moor.

Rzepka (*Pol.*) One who grew turnips; dweller where turnips grew.

Saari (*Finn.*) Dweller on an island; dweller on, or near, a ridge.

Sabath, Sabbath (*Heb.*) Descendant of Sabath or Sabbatai, names given to boys born on the Sabbath; dweller near, or worker at, a Saturday market.

Sabatino, Sabatini (*It.*) Descendant of Sabbatino (name given to a child born on the Sabbath). *See also* Sabath.

Sabin, Sabine (*Eng.*) Descendant of Sabin, a name from the ancient Italian tribe of the Sabines.

Sabo (*Hun.*) One who made outer garments, a tailor.

Sacco (*It., Ger.*) Descendant of Sacco, a pet form of Isacco or Isaak (he who laughs); descendant of Sacco, a pet form of names beginning with Sache (legal action), such as Sacbert and Saghart; one who made and sold sackcloth.

Sachs (*Ger.*) One who came from Saxony (now Holstein); a name taken by the Jewish refugees from Stendal, in memory of the martyrdom of their companions, from the Hebrew initials for "The Holy Seed of Stendal."

Sackett, Sacket (*Eng.*) Descendant of little Sacq (adversary).

Sacks, Sack (*Fr.*) One who made, or sold, sackcloth or bags; descendant of Sack, a pet form of Isaac (he who laughs); one who came from Sacq, in France.

Sadler, Saddler (*Eng.*) One who made, or dealt in, saddles.

Sadowski (*Pol.*) Dweller at, or near, an orchard.

Sage (*Eng.*) The wise or learned person.

Sager (*Eng.*) Descendant of Sagar (sea, spear); one who sawed timber into boards.

St. Clair, St. Claire (*Eng.*) One who came from St. Clair (bright), the name of several villages in France.

Saint-Gaudens (*Fr.*) Descendant of Gaudentius (rejoicing), the name of five different saints revered by the Catholic church.

St. John (*Eng.*) One who came from St. Jean, a common French place name.

Saks (*Eng.*) A variant of Sax, q.v.

Sale, Salle (*Eng., Fr.*) Dweller in, or near, the manor house; servant in the principal room of the manor house; one who came from Sale (sallow), in Cheshire.

Salemi (*It.*) One who came from Salemi, in Sicily.

Salerno (*It.*) One who came from Salerno, a province and city in Italy.

Salisbury (*Eng.*) One who came from Salisbury (Searu's stronghold), in Wiltshire.

Salk (*Ger.*) Dweller near a willow tree.

Salmon, Salomon (*Eng.*) Descendant of Solomon (peaceful).

Salter, Saltman, Salzer (*Eng.*) One who processed, or sold, salt; one who came from Salter (salt hut), in Cumberland.

Saltonstall (*Eng.*) One who came from Salternstall (saltworks place), in Kent.

Saltzberg, Saltsberg, Salzberg (*Ger.*) One who came from Saltzberg (salt fortress), in Germany.

Salzman, Saltzman, Salzmann, Saltzmann (*Ger.*) One who processed, or sold, salt.

Sammons, Sammon, Samonds (*Eng.*) Descendant of Solomon (peaceful).

Samp (*Eng.*) A contraction of Sampson, q.v.

Sample, Samples (*Fr.*) One who came from St. Paul (small), the name of several places in France.

Sampson, Samson (*Eng.*) The son of Sam, a pet form of Samuel (God hath heard); descendant of Samson (splendid sun).

Samuels, Samuelson, Samuel (*Eng.*) The son of Samuel (God hath heard).

Sanborn (*Eng.*) One who came from Sambourn (sandy stream), in Warwickshire.

Sanchez (*Sp.*) The son of Sancho (sanctified).

Sandberg, Sandburg (*Sw.*) Sandy mountain, or fortified place.

Sanders, Sander (*Scot., Eng.*) The son of Sander, an abbreviation of Alexander (helper of mankind).

Sanderson (*Scot., Eng.*) The son of Sander, a pet form of Alexander (helper of mankind).

Sandler (*Eng., Heb.*) One who carts sand or gravel; one who repaired shoes, a cobbler.

Sandquist (*Sw.*) Sand twig.

Sands, Sand, Sande (*Eng.*) One who came from Send (sandy place), in Surrey.

Sandstrom (*Sw.*) Sand stream.

San Filippo, Sanfilippo, Sanfillippo (*It.*) Descendant of San Filippo (St. Philip, lover of horses).

Sanford, Sandford (*Eng.*) One who came from Sandford (sandy ford), the name of several places in England.

Sanger, Sangster (*Eng.*) One who sang in church.

Sankey (*Eng.*) One who came from Sankey (holy), in Lancashire; dweller near the Sankey, a brook in Lancashire.

Sansone (*It.*) Descendant of Sansone (splendid sun).

Santangelo (*It.*) One who came from Sant' Angelo (saint angel), in Italy.

Santiago (*Sp.*) One who came from Santiago (St. James), in Spain.

Santoro, Santore, Santori, Santora (*It.*) One who made saintly images.

Santos (*Port., Sp.*) One who came from Dos Santos or Los Santos (of the saints), the names of places in Portugal and Spain.

Santucci, Santelli, Santilli, Santillo (*It.*) The saintly or devout person; descendant of little Santo (saint).

Sargent, Sargeant, Sergeant (*Eng.*) One who worked as a servant; a tenant by military service under the rank of a knight, or a court officer.

Sargis (*Lith.*) The guard or watchman.

Sarna (*Pol.*) Dweller at the sign of the roe deer; one thought to possess some of the qualities of a roe deer; one who came from Sarnay (place where deer were found), in Poland.

Saroyan (*Arm.*) A corruption of the Armenian *Saro Khan* (mountain prince).

Sass, Sasse, Sasser (*Eng.*) Dweller at, or near, a willow tree, or at a lock in a river.

Sather (*Nor.*) Dweller on the mountain pasture.

Sato (*Jap.*) A village, one's home town, or the country.

Sattelmacher (*Ger.*) One who made saddles.

Satterlee, Satterley (*Eng.*) One who came from Satterleigh (robbers' wood), in Devonshire.

Satterthwaite, Satterwhite (*Eng.*) One who came from Satterthwaite (clearing by a hut), in Lancashire.

Sattler (*Ger.*) One who made and sold saddles.

Saucier, Saucer, Sauser, Sausser (*Fr., Eng.*) One who made and sold sauces, mustard, etc.; one in charge of that department of the kitchen where sauces were made in large households.

Sauer (*Ger.*) The sour or morose person; the sower.

Saul (*Eng.*) Descendant of Saul (desire); one who came from Saul (sallow wood), in Gloucestershire, or from Sall (sallow wood), in Norfolk.

Saulnier (*Fr.*) One who gathered, or sold, salt.

Saunders, Saunder (*Scot., Eng.*) The son of Saunder, an abbreviation of Alexander (helper of mankind).

Savage, Salvage (*Eng.*) The wild or fierce man.

Saville, Savill (*Eng.*) One who came from Saville or Sauville (willow estate), in France.

Savoy, Savoye (*Fr.*) One who came from Savoy or Savoie, in France.

Sawa (*Pol.*) Descendant of Sawa (desire).

Sawicki (*Pol., Ukr.*) The son of Sawa (desire).

Sawin, Sawinski (*Pol., Ukr., Rus.*) Descendant of Sawa (desire).

Sawyer, Sawier (*Eng.*) One who cut timber into boards.

Sax, Saxon, Saxe (*Eng.*) One who came from Saxony (now Holstein); descendant of Saxa, Saxo or Seaxa (short sword).

Saxton (*Eng.*) One who came from Saxton (village of the Saxons), the name of several places in England.

Sayce, Sayse (*Wel.*) The foreigner; the Englishman.

Sayers, Sayre, Sayres, Sayer (*Eng.*) One who sold silk or serge; one who assayed or tested metals, or tasted food; descendant of Saer or Sayer (victory, people).

Sayles, Sales, Sayle, Sale (*Eng.*) Dweller in, or near, a hall; one who worked in the dining hall; one who came from Sale (sallow), in Cheshire.

Saylor, Sailor, Sailer, Saylors (*Eng.*) One who danced at fair and festival; one who worked on a ship, a seaman.

Sayward (*Eng.*) The sea warden or coast guard; descendant of Saeward (sea, protection).

Sbarbaro, Sbarboro (*It.*) Descendant of Barbaro (the stranger); the foreigner, one in a rude, uncivilized state.

Scales (*Eng.*) One who came from Scales (hut or temporary shelter), the name of several places in England; dweller in the hut or shed.

Scaletta (*It.*) Descendant of little Scala, a pet form of Pasquale (Passover).

Scalzitti (*It.*) One who was in the habit of going barefoot.

Scanlan, Scanlon (*Ir.*) Grandson of little Scannal (scandal).

Scannell, Scannel (*Ir.*) Grandson of Scannal (scandal).

Scarborough, Scarbrough (*Eng.*) One who came from Scarborough (Skarthi's fort), in Yorkshire.

Scardina, Scardino, Scardine (*It.*) Descendant of Cardo, a pet form of Riccardo (rule, hard).

Scarpelli (*It.*) One who made and sold shoes; one with an unusual foot; one who chiseled stone.

Schaaf (*Du.*) Dweller at the sign of the carpenter's plane, probably a carpenter.

Schacht (*Ger., Du.*) Dweller at, or near, a mine; dweller on a ridge or tongue of land.

Schachter (*Heb.*) One who slaughtered animals, and cut and sold meat, a butcher.

Schaefer, Schafer, Schaffer, Schaeffer (*Ger.*) One who took care of sheep, a shepherd.

Schaffner (*Ger.*) The manager, or steward, of a household.

Schalk (*Ger.*) One who worked as a servant.

Schall (*Ger.*) Dweller near a stone slab; one who worked for another, a servant.

Schaller (*Ger.*) A talkative or garrulous person.

Scharf, Scharff (*Ger.*) An acute, keen-witted or sharp person.

Schatz, Shatz (*Ger., Heb.*) The dear or beloved person; contraction of Sheliah Tzibbur (minister of the congregation).

Schatzmann (*Ger.*) One who had charge of the treasury.

Schauer (*Ger.*) One who came from Schauen, in Germany; descendant of Scuro (storm of battle); one related in some way to a storm or bad weather.

Schechter, Schecter (*Ger.*) One who cut and sold meat, a butcher.

Scheck (*Ger.*) Dweller at the sign of the roan horse; one who made and sold certain quilted, tight-fitting coats.

Scheel, Scheele (*Ger., Du.*) One who was crooked or bent, a cripple; one who was cross-eyed; one who came from Scheel (bend), in Germany.

Scheer (*Ger., Du.*) Dweller at the sign of the shears, probably a tailor; one who cut hair or cloth.

Scheffler (*Ger.*) One who made casks and barrels, a cooper.

Schell, Schelle (*Ger.*) Dweller at the sign of the stallion; one with the qualities of a steed or stallion.

Schenk, Schenck (*Du., Ger.*) One who sold wine; a cupbearer or butler.

Scher (*Ger.*) One who caught moles; a contraction of Scherer, q.v.

Scherer, Scherrer (*Ger.*) One who cut hair, a barber.

Schiavone, Schiavoni, Schiavon (*It.*) Guard of the Doge of Venice who was armed with a schiavone, a broadsword; one who came from a Slavic country.

Schick (*Ger.*) The smart, stylish, well-dressed person; descendant of Schiko (order).

Schiff, Schiffman, Schiffmann (*Ger.*) One who worked on a ship, a sailor; dweller at the sign of the ship.

Schild (*Ger.*) Descendant of Schild, a pet form of names beginning with Schild (shield), as Scildfrid and Scildwald; dweller at the sign of the shield.

Schiller, Schieler (*Ger., Du.*) One having the habit of squinting his eyes, a squinter; one who prepared skins.

Schilling (*Ger.*) A serf who had paid money to his lord for his freedom; descendant of Schilling, a pet form of Scildwin (shield, friend).

Schimmel, Schimel (*Ger., Du.*) Dweller at the sign of the gray, or white, horse.

Schindler (*Ger.*) One who made shingles.

Schlegel, Schlegl (*Ger.*) One who was a guard or watchman in a prison; one who came from Schlegel (smith's shop, or slaughterhouse), the name of several places in Germany.

Schlesinger (*Ger.*) One who came from Schleusingen, in Thuringia.

Schlosser, Schloss, Slosser (*Ger.*) One who made locks, a locksmith; dweller in, or near, the manor house or castle.

Schlueter, Schluter (*Ger.*) One who worked as doorkeeper of a prison, a turnkey; one who came from Schluete, in Germany.

Schmalz, Schmaltz (*Ger.*) One who had a fat stomach; one who rendered lard; an old-fashioned, sloppy, sentimental person.

Schmidt, Schmitt, Schmid, Schmit, Schmitz (*Ger.*) The worker in metals, a smith.

Schmidtke (*Ger.*) Descendant of the little smith.

Schneeberger, Schneberger, Schneberg (*Ger.*) One who came from Schneeberg (snow mountain), the name of several places in Germany.

Schneider, Schnieder (*Ger.*) One who made outer garments, a tailor.

Schneiderman (*Ger.*) The servant of the one who made outer garments, i.e., a tailor.

Schnell (*Ger.*) The quick, lively person.

Schober (*Ger.*) Dweller at, or near, a haystack.

Schoen, Schon (*Ger.*) Beautiful, the handsome person; one who came from Schön (beautiful), in Germany.

Schoenfeld, Schoenfeldt, Schoenfelder (*Ger.*) One who came from Schönfeld (beautiful field), the name of more than fifty places in Germany.

Schofield, Scofield (*Eng.*) Dweller at the hut or shed in the field.

Scholl, Scholle (*Ger.*) One who is indebted to another, a debtor.

Scholz, Scholtz, Scholtes (*Ger.*) Variants of Schultz, q.v.

Schott, Schotte (*Ger., Du.*) One who carried goods for sale, a peddler; dweller near a sluice or floodgate; one who came from Scotland.

Schrader, Schraeder (*Ger.*) One who made garments, a tailor.

Schram, Schramm (*Ger.*) One deformed in body, a cripple; dweller near a rock cleft.

Schranz, Schrantz (*Ger.*) One in attendance at the court of a prince; a hanger-on at a court.

Schreiber (*Ger.*) An official, or public, writer, a clerk.

Schreiner (*Ger.*) One who worked with wood, a cabinetmaker.

Schroeder, Schroder, Schroter (*Ger.*) One who made garments, a tailor; one who drove a dray, a drayman.

Schubert, Schuberth (*Ger.*) One who made shoes.

Schuch, Schuh, Schuck, Schug (*Ger.*) Dweller at the sign of the shoe; one who sold shoes.

Schuessler, Schussler (*Ger.*) One who made wooden dishes.

Schuetz, Schutz, Schuetze, Schutze (*Ger.*) One who hunted and killed game; a watchman; one who came from Schutz, in Germany; one who fought with bow and arrow, an archer.

Schuler, Schuller, Schueler, Schueller (*Ger.*) One who taught school, a schoolmaster; a man who studied, a scholar.

Schulman, Schoolman (*Ger., Pol.*) One who taught in a school, a schoolmaster; an important functionary of the synagogue in the early Jewish communities of Poland.

Schultz, Schulz, Schulze, Schulte, Schultze (*Ger.*) The magistrate or sheriff; a steward or overseer.

Schumacker, Schumaker (*Ger.*) One who made shoes.

Schuman, Schumann (*Ger.*) One who made and sold shoes.

Schuster, Shuster (*Ger.*) One who made and repaired shoes, a cobbler.

Schutt, Schuett, Schuette (*Du.*) Dweller at, or near, the fence or hedge.

Schuyler (*Du.*) One who taught school, a schoolmaster; one who protected refugees.

Schwab, Schwabe (*Ger.*) One who came from Swabia (freemen), a duchy in medieval Germany.

Schwan, Schwaan (*Ger.*) Dweller at the sign of the swan; one with the characteristics of a swan.

Schwartz, Schwarz (*Ger.*) One with a dark or swarthy complexion, black.

Schwarzkopf, Schwartzkopf (*Ger.*) The dark or black-haired man.

Schwarzschild (*Ger.*) Dweller at the sign of the black shield.

Schweiger (*Ger.*) One who tended cows.

Schweitzer, Schweizer (*Ger.*) One who came from Switzerland, a Swiss.

Scimeca (*It.*) One who came from Scimeca, in Italy.

Scotland (*Scot.*) One who came from Scotland (cut place), a village in Scotland.

Scott, Scotch (*Eng.*) One who came from Scotland; originally, the word also included the Irish, i.e., one who came from Ireland.

Scottsmith (*Eng.*) One who made and sold darts or small javelins.

Scoville, Scovill, Scovil (*Eng.*) One who came from Escoville (Scot's estate), in Normandy.

Scribner, Scriber (*Eng.*) One who copied books and manuscripts.

Scruggs (*Eng.*) The thin, scraggy person; dweller by, or among, stunted bushes.

Scudder (*Eng., Du.*) One who fought with bow and arrow, an archer; one who constantly shook or trembled, from disease.

Scully, Scally, Sculley (*Ir.*) Descendant of the scholar or schoolman.

Seaberg, Seeberg, Seabergh (*Sw.*) Sea mountain.

Seabury, Seaberry (*Eng.*) One who came from Seaborough (seven hills), in Dorset.

Seals, Seale, Seales, Seal (*Eng.*) Dweller in, or near, a hall; one who came from Seal (hall, or small wood), the name of places in Kent and Derbyshire, or from Seale (hall), in Surrey.

Seaman, Seamans, Seamon (*Eng.*) One who worked on a ship, a sailor; descendant of Siemond (victory, protector), or of Saemann (victory, man).

Searcy, Searcie (*Eng.*) One who came from Cerisy or Cercy, in France.

Searles, Searls, Searle (*Eng.*) Descendant of Serle (armor).

Sears, Sear (*Eng., Ir.*) Descendant of Segar (sea, warrior), or of Sigehere (victorious, army).

Seaton (*Eng.*) One who came from Seaton (farm by the sea or lake), the name of several places in England.

Seaver, Sever, Seavers (*Eng.*) One with a grave and austere demeanor.

Seaverns, Severns (*Eng.*) Dweller by the Severn (origin obscure), a river in Britain.

Seavey (*Eng.*) Descendant of Saewig (sea, war).

Seaward (*Eng.*) Descendant of Sigeweard (victory, protection), or of Saeweard (sea, protection).

Seay, Say, Saye (*Eng.*) Dweller near the sea; one who came from Sai, in Normandy; the wise or prudent man.

Sebastian, Sebastiano (*Sp.*) Descendant of Sebastian (venerable).

Secord (*Fr.*) Descendant of Sicard (victory, hard).

Sedgwick (*Eng.*) One who came from Sedgwick (Siggi's dwelling), in Westmorland.

Sedivy, Sediwy (*Cz.-Sl.*) The old or gray-haired man.

Sedlacek, Sedlak, Sedlack (*Cz.-Sl.*) One who tilled the soil, a farmer.

See, Sea (*Eng.*) Dweller by the seacoast; dweller by a lake or pool.

Seeley, Sealey, Sealy, Seely (*Eng.*) The happy or prosperous person; the good, simple man.

Seelig, Seeliger (*Ger.*) One who came from Seelig (prosperous place), in Germany; the happy, lucky or fortunate man.

Seeman, Seemann (*Ger.*) One who worked on a ship, a sailor; descendant of Simon (gracious hearing), or of Sigiman (victory, man).

Segal, Segall, Segel, Segale, Seegall (*Fr., Ger.*) One who cultivated rye; contraction of *segan leviyyah,* literally assistant priest or rabbi, a name often adopted by Levites.

Seibert (*Ger.*) Descendant of Sigiperaht (victory, bright).

Seidel, Seidl (*Ger.*) Descendant of Sitto, a pet form of Sigebert (victory, bright); one who came from Seidel, in Germany.

Seidelmann, Seidelman (*Ger.*) One who worked with, or dealt in, silks; one who came from Seidel, in Germany.

Seidman, Seidmon, Seideman, Seidemann (*Ger.*) Descendant of Sitto, a pet form of Sigebert (victory, bright). *See also* Seidelmann.

Seifert, Seiferth, Seiffert, Seifferth (*Ger.*) Descendant of Sigifrith (victory, peace).

Seiler, Seyler (*Ger.*) One who made and sold rope.

Seitz (*Ger.*) Descendant of Sigizo, a pet form of names beginning with Sieg (victory), as Sigibald, Sigiheri and Sigismund.

Selby (*Eng.*) One who came from Selby (sallow copse), in Yorkshire.

Selden, Seldon, Seldom (*Eng.*) Dweller in a valley where willow trees grew; one who came from Salden (hill with a ledge), in Buckinghamshire; one who tended a booth or shop.

Self (*Eng.*) Dweller near a rock, or ledge, such as a riverbank.

Selfridge (*Eng.*) Dweller on, or near, the rocky ridge.

Seligman, Seligmann (*Ger.*) The happy, lucky or fortunate man; a variant of Salomon (peaceful).

Sell, Selle (*Eng.*) Dweller at the shelter for animals or in the herdsman's hut.

Sellers, Seller (*Eng.*) One who made saddles; one who had charge of the cellar or storeroom; one who dealt in commodities, a merchant.

Sellinger (*Eng., Ger.*) One who came from St. Leger, in France; one who came from Soellingen, in Germany.

Selzer, Seltzer (*Ger.*) One who salted or pickled foods.

Semper (*Eng.*) One who came from St. Pierre (rock), the name of many places in France.

Semple (*Eng.*) One who came from St. Paul (small), the name of many places in France.

Sender, Sendor (*Ger., Eng.*) Descendant of Sender, a shortened form of Alexander (helper of mankind); one who came from Sende, in Germany.

Sener (*Swis.*) One who tended a flock, a herdsman.

Senese (*It.*) One who came from Senise, in Lucania.

Senn, Senner (*Swis.*) The head man of an Alpine dairy farm.

Sennott, Sennett, Sennet (*Eng., Fr.*) The old, wise or sage person; descendant of Senet, a pet form of Sene (sensible); variants of Sinnett, q.v.

Seppanen (*Finn.*) One who worked in metals, a smith.

Serafin (*It.*) Descendant of Serafino (highest order of angels).

Serio (*It.*) The serious or solemn person.

Serlin (*Eng.*) Descendant of little Serle (armor).

Serritella, Serritelli, Serritello (*It.*) Dweller in, or by, a narrow valley or ravine.

Serrurier, Serruel (*Fr.*) One who made locks, a locksmith.

Sessions, Session (*Eng.*) One who came from Soissons, a district in France.

Settles, Settle (*Eng.*) One who came from Settle (dwelling), in Yorkshire; one who lived in a dwelling in the manor, but had no rights in the cultivated fields.

Severance (*Fr.*) Descendant of Severian (severe), the name of several saints.

Severin, Seurin (*Fr.*) Descendant of Severian (severe), the name of several saints.

Seward (*Eng.*) Descendant of Siward or Sigeweard (victory, protection).

Sewell, Sewall (*Eng.*) Descendant of Sewal (victory, strength); one who came from Sewell (seven wells), the name of places in Bedfordshire and Oxfordshire.

Sexauer, Sexaur (*Ger.*) One who came from Sexau, in Germany.

Sexton (*Eng.*) One who acted as an underofficer of a church and who had charge of the sacristy and its contents; variant of Saxton, q.v.

Seymour, Seymore (*Eng.*) Descendant of Seamer (sea, famous); one who came from Seamer (lake, sea), in Yorkshire; one who came from St. Maur (black), in France.

Seys (*Wel.*) The foreigner; the Englishman.

Shackelford, Shackleford (*Eng.*) One who came from Shackleford (Shackel's ford), in Surrey.

Shackford (*Eng.*) One who came from Shadforth (shallow ford), in Durham; a contraction of Shackelford, q.v.

Shackley (*Eng.*) One who came from Shackerley (wood of the robbers), in Lancashire.

Shaffer, Shafer, Shaeffer (*Ger.*) One who took care of sheep, a shepherd.

Shain, Shaine, Shaines (*Ger.*) The beautiful or handsome person.

Shakespeare, Shakespere (*Eng.*) One who lived on the peasant's farm; nickname for a soldier, one who wielded a spear.

Shanahan (*Ir.*) Grandson of little Seanach (old or wise).

Shand, Shands (*Eng., Scot.*) One who came from Chandai, in France.

Shane (*Ir.*) The son of Eoin or Seon (gracious gift of Jehovah).

Shank, Shanks, Shanke (*Eng., Scot.*) A nickname given because of some peculiarity of the legs; one who came from the lands of Shank, in Midlothian.

Shanklin (*Eng.*) One who came from Shanklin (leg hill), in Wight.

Shanley (*Ir.*) The son of Seanlaoch (old hero).

Shannon (*Ir.*) Grandson of little Seanach (old or wise).

Shapiro, Shapira, Shapero, Shapera (*Ger.*) One who came from Speyer (in the Middle Ages, spelled Spira, and by Jews spelled Shapira), in Bavaria.

Shapley, Shapleigh (*Eng.*) One who came from Shipley (pasture for sheep), the name of several places in England.

Sharkey (*Ir.*) Grandson of Searcach (loving).

Sharp, Sharpe (*Eng.*) An acute, keen-witted or quick person.

Sharples, Sharpless (*Eng.*) One who came from Sharples (steep place), in Lancashire.

Shattuck, Shaddick, Shattock (*Eng.*) Dweller at the sign of the little shad (fish); one who caught and sold shad.

Shaughnessy, Shannessy, Shaunnessey, Shanesy (*Ir.*) Grandson of Seachnasach; descendant of the elusive person.

Shaver, Shavers (*Ger.*) An Anglicization of Shaffer, q.v.

Shaw, Shawe (*Scot., Eng.*) Dweller at the small wood or thicket; descendant of Sithech (wolf); one who came from Shaw (small wood), the name of several places in England.

Shay (*Ir.*) A variant of Shea, q.v.

Shea (*Ir.*) Grandson of Seaghdha (majestic, or learned).

Shearer, Sheerer (*Eng.*) One who reaped standing crops; one who removed the fleece from animals.

Shedd, Shed, Shedis (*Eng.*) Dweller at the ridge or division separating lands sloping in different directions; dweller at, or near, a hut or shed.

Sheedy (*Ir.*) Grandson of Sioda (silk).

Sheehan, Sheahan, Sheen (*Ir.*) Grandson of little Siodhach (peaceful).

Sheehy, Sheehey (*Ir.*) The son of Sitheach (peaceful).

Sheeran, Sheerin, Sheeren (*Ir.*) Grandson of Sirin (origin obscure).

Sheets, Sheetz (*Eng.*) Dweller at, or near, a corner or projection, or on or near a steep hill; one who came from Sheat or Sheet (park), in Wight and Hampshire respectively.

Sheffield (*Eng.*) One who came from Sheffield (sheep field), the name of several towns in England.

Shelby (*Eng.*) One who came from Selby (village where willows grew), in Yorkshire.

Sheldon, Shelden (*Eng.*) One who came from Sheldon (valley with steep sides, or hill with a flat top), the name of three places in England.

Shell (*Eng.*) One who came from Shell (bank), in Worcestershire; dweller near a bank or ridge.

Shelley, Shelly (*Eng.*) One who came from Shelley (wood on a slope), in Essex.

Shelton (*Eng.*) One who came from Shelton (homestead on a bank or ledge), the name of several places in England.

Shepard, Shepherd, Sheppard, Shephard (*Eng.*) One who tended sheep.

Sher, Sherr (*Ger.*) Variants of Scher, q.v.

Sherbourne, Sherburne, Sherborne (*Eng.*) One who came from Sherborne (bright stream), the name of several places in England.

Shere (*Eng.*) One who came from Shere (bright), in Surrey.

Sheridan (*Ir.*) Grandson of Siridean (peaceful).

Sherlock (*Eng.*) One who had white hair; dweller at the bright, or clear, stream or pool.

Sherman (*Eng.*) The shearman or cutter of wool or cloth.

Sherrick (*Scot.*) One who came from Sherraig (clear bay), in Scotland.

Sherrill, Shirrell (*Eng.*) One who came from Shirwell (clear spring), in Devonshire.

Sherrod, Sherrard, Sherred (*Eng.*) Descendant of Scirheard (bright, hard); variants of Sherwood, q.v.

Sherry (*Ir.*) The son of Searrach (colt, flighty).

Sherwin (*Eng.*) Descendant of Scirwine (bright, friend); a nickname for a fast runner, "shear wind."

Sherwood (*Eng.*) One who came from Sherwood (the wood belonging to the shire or county), in Nottinghamshire.

Shields (*Eng.*) One who came from Shields (shepherd's summer hut), the name of places in Durham and Northumberland.

Shiffman, Schiff (*Ger.*) One who worked on a ship, a sailor or mariner; dweller at the sign of the ship.

Shimkus (*Lith.*) Descendant of Shimko, a pet form of Szymon (gracious hearing).

Shinnick (*Ir.*) Grandson of Seanach (wise, old).

Shipley (*Eng.*) One who came from Shipley (pasture for sheep), the name of several places in England.

Shipman (*Eng.*) One who worked on a ship, seaman or sailor; one who had the care of sheep, a shepherd.

Shipp, Shipman (*Eng.*) Dweller at the sign of the ship; one who worked on a ship, a sailor.

Shirley (*Eng.*) One who came from Shirley (wood belonging to the shire), the name of several places in England.

Shivers, Shiver, Shivver (*Fr.*) One who tended goats, a goatherd.

Shockett, Shocket, Shochet (*Fr.*) One who collected taxes on wine; dweller at, or on, cleared land with stumps.

Shoemaker (*Eng.*) One who made shoes.

Shoesmith, Shewsmith, Shoowsmith, Shughsmith (*Eng.*) One who made horseshoes.

Shore, Shor, Shorr, Shores (*Eng., Heb., Ger.*) Dweller at the shore; dweller at the sign of the bullock; a name possibly adopted by people named Joseph in response to Deut. 33:17 where Joseph is likened to a young bullock.

Shorey (*Eng.*) Dweller on the island near the shore.

Short (*Eng.*) One of low stature, a little man.

Shortall, Shortell (*Eng.*) Dweller at the small nook or corner.

Shott (*Eng.*) Dweller at, or near, the shot, an area designation, the same as Furlong, q.v.

Shrader (*Ger.*) A variant of Schrader, q.v.

Shreve, Sheriff (*Eng.*) The shire reeve, the chief civil officer of the crown in the county, a sheriff.

Shriner, Shreiner (*Ger.*) Variants of Schreiner, q.v.

Shriver, Shriber (*Ger.*) An official, or public, writer, a scribe.

Shubert, Shubart, Shubat (*Ger.*) One who made shoes.

Shulman (*Ger.*) A variant of Schulman, q.v.

Shuman, Shumaker, Shumacher (*Ger.*) One who made and sold shoes, a shoemaker.

Shure, Shur (*Ger.*) One who sheared sheep; the cunning or crafty man; variants of Schauer, q.v.

Shurtleff (*Eng.*) Dweller near the short cliff, or the bright or white cliff.

Shute (*Eng.*) One who came from Shute (park), in Devonshire; dweller at a narrow lane.

Shuttleworth (*Eng.*) One who came from Shuttleworth (enclosure made of bars), the name of several places in England.

Sibley (*Eng.*) Descendant of Sibley, an English pet form of Sibyl (prophetess).

Siciliano (*It.*) One who came from Sicily or Sicilia (tribe of the Siculi), an island in the Mediterranean Sea.

Sidebotham, Sidebottom (*Eng.*) Dweller in, or near, the wide valley.

Sidney, Sydney (*Eng.*) One who came from St. Denis (belonging to Dionysius, the Grecian god of wine), the name of several villages in France.

Sidor, Sider (*Pol., Cz.-Sl., Ukr.*) Descendant of Sidor or Sydor (gift of Isis).

Siebert, Sibert, Seebert (*Eng.*) Descendant of Sigibert (victory, bright).

Siegel, Siegal, Siegl, Siegle (*Ger.*) Descendant of little Sigo, a pet form of names beginning with Sieg (victory), as Sigivald, Sigiwart and Sigiwolf; variants of Segal, q.v.

Sienkiewicz (*Pol., Rus.*) The son of Sienko, a pet form of Szymon (gracious hearing).

Sievers, Siever (*Ger.*) Descendant of Sigiwart (victory, worthy).

Sievert, Siewert, Siewerth (*Ger.*) Descendant of Sigiwart (victory, worthy).

Sikora (*Pol., Ukr.*) One with some real or fancied resemblance to a titmouse; one who came from Sikora or Sikory (titmouse), in Poland.

Sikorski (*Pol., Ukr.*) One who came from Sikora or Sikory (titmouse), in Poland.

Silas (*Eng.*) Descendant of Silas, a contraction of Silvanus, the god of trees.

Silber, Silbert (*Ger.*) Descendant of Silber, a pet form of Sigilbert (victory, bright); one who came from Silber (silver), the name of various places in Germany; one with gray or silvery hair.

Silberman, Silbermann (*Ger.*) One who made and sold silver articles, a silversmith.

Silk, Silkes (*Eng.*) One who dealt in silk; variants of Sills, q.v.

Sills, Sill (*Eng.*) Descendant of Sill, a pet form of Silvester (forest dweller), of Silvanus (woods) and of Cecil (blind).

Silva (*Sp., Port.*) One who came from Silva (thicket of briers, or woods), the name of several places in Spain; dweller in, or by, the woods.

Silveira (*Port.*) Dweller in, or near, a wood, especially a wood of brier trees.

Silver (*Eng., Ger.*) One who came from a locality of that name; dweller near one of various streams in England with that name because of their clear and sparkling water; an Anglicization of Silber, q.v.

Silverberg (*Ger.*) One who came from Silberberg (silver mountain), in Germany.

Silverman (*Ger.*) An Anglicization of Silberman, q.v.

Silverstein, Silverstone, Silverstine (*Ger.*) Silver stone.

Silvester, Silvestre (*Eng., Fr.*) Descendant of Silvester (forest dweller).

Silvestri (*It.*) Descendant of Silvestro (forest dweller).

Silvey (*Fr.*) Descendant of Silvius (forest).

Sima (*Sp.*) Dweller near a hole or pit in the ground, or at the top of the hill.

Simcock, Simcox (*Eng.*) Descendant of little Sim, a pet form of Simon or Simeon (gracious hearing); the son of Sim.

Simek (*Pol.*) Descendant of little Sim, a pet form of Szymon (gracious hearing).

Simmons, Simmonds (*Eng.*) The son of Simon or Simeon (gracious hearing).

Simon, Simons (*Eng.*) Descendant of Simon (gracious hearing).

Simonds, Simond, Simund (*Eng.*) Descendant of Simon (gracious hearing).

Simonsen, Simonson (*Dan., Sw., Nor.*) The son of Simon (gracious hearing).

Simpkins, Simkins (*Eng.*) Descendant of little Sim, a pet form of Simon or Simeon (gracious hearing).

Simpson, Simson (*Eng.*) The son of Sim, pet form of Simon or Simeon (gracious hearing); one who came from Simpson (Sigewine's homestead), in Buckinghamshire.

Sims, Simms (*Eng.*) Descendant of Sim, a pet form of Simon or Simeon (gracious hearing).

Sinclair (*Scot., Eng.*) One who came from St. Clair (bright), the name of several places in Normandy; follower of St. Clare.

Sindelar (*Cz.-Sl.*) One who made shingles.

Singer (*Eng.*) One who sang, especially a church singer; the soloist in the synagogue.

Singleton (*Eng.*) One who came from Singleton (homestead with shingled roof, or on shingly soil), the name of places in Lancashire and Sussex.

Sinnett, Sinnott (*Eng.*) Dweller at the sign of the little swan; variants of Sennott, q.v.

Siskin, Siskind (*Ger.*) Sweet child.

Sisson, Sison, Sissons (*Eng.*) The son of Siss, a pet form of Cecil (blind).

Siwek (*Pol.*) Dweller at the sign of the gray horse; one who rode a gray horse.

Sixsmith, Sexsmith (*Eng.*) The smith who made small swords or daggers.

Skala (*Pol., Ger.*) Dweller near a rock; one who came from Skala (rock), in Germany.

Skelly, Skelley (*Ir.*) The son of Scalaighe (crier).

Skelton (*Eng.*) One who came from Skelton (the hill, or bank, manor), the name of parishes in Yorkshire and Cumberland.

Skene, Skeen, Skeene (*Scot.*) One who came from the lands of Skene (bush), in Aberdeenshire.

Skerry (*Eng.*) Dweller on a rocky isle.

Skiba (*Pol., Ukr.*) Single strip of soil thrown up by a plow, probably designating a plowman.

Skidmore (*Eng.*) Dweller at, or near, the dirty wasteland, or Skyti's wasteland.

Skiffington, Skeffington (*Eng.*) One who came from Skeffington (homestead of Sceaft's people), in Leicestershire.

Skillings, Skilling (*Eng.*) Descendant of Scilling (sonorous or shrill).

Skinner, Skynner (*Eng.*) One who prepared skins.

Sklar, Sklare (*Cz.-Sl., Ukr.*) One who made and sold glass and glassware, a glazier.

Skoglund, Skooglund (*Sw.*) Forest grove.

Skogsberg, Skogsbergh (*Sw.*) Forest mountain.

Skolnik, Skolnick (*Cz.-Sl., Ukr.*) The student, or one connected in some way with a school; an important functionary of the synagogue in the early Jewish communities.

Skoog, Skog, Skogh (*Sw.*) Dweller in, or near, a forest; forest.

Skora (*Pol.*) One who prepared skins, a skinner.

Skowronski, Skowron (*Pol.*) Dweller at the sign of the lark; one with the qualities of a lark.

Skyles, Skiles, Skeeles, Skeels (*Dan., Ice.*) Descendant of Skyli (protector, king).

Slack (*Eng.*) Dweller at a hollow or pass between hills.

Slade (*Eng.*) Dweller in the valley or dell.

Sladek (*Pol.*) Footprint, possibly one who made a large footprint.

Slager (*Ger., Du.*) One who chopped wood and cleared land; one who cut meat, a butcher.

Slater, Slayter (*Eng.*) One who roofed buildings with flat rock or slate.

Slattery (*Ir.*) Grandson of Slatra (bold or strong).

Slaughter (*Eng.*) Dweller at, or near, a slough or muddy place; one who came from Slaughter (muddy place), in Gloucestershire; one who killed animals, a butcher.

Slavin (*Rus.*) The son of Slav, a pet form of Jaroslav (strong, glorious).

Sleeper (*Eng.*) One who made scabbards for swords; one who polished or sharpened swords.

Sleigh, Slye, Sly (*Eng.*) One who was dexterous or skilled.

Slezak (*Cz.-Sl.*) One who came from Silesia (the bad land), for centuries a part of Poland.

Sliwa (*Pol., Ukr.*) Dweller near a plum tree.

Sloan, Sloane, Slown, Sloyne (*Ir.*) Grandson of Sluaghan (soldier or warrior).

Slocum, Slocomb, Slocombe, Slocumb (*Eng.*) Dweller in a valley where blackthorn or sloe trees flourished.

Slowik (*Pol.*) Dweller at the sign of the nightingale; one with some quality of a nightingale.

Slowinski (*Pol.*) One who came from Slovenia, a country now in Yugoslavia.

Slutsky (*Rus.*) One who came from Slutsk, in Byelorussia.

Slyne (*Eng.*) One who came from Slyne (slope), in Lancashire.

Smail (*Scot.*) A variant of Small, q.v.

Small, Smale (*Eng.*) The little or slender person.

Smalley (*Eng.*) One who came from Smalley (narrow wood), in Derbyshire.

Smart, Smert (*Eng.*) The quick, sharp person.

Smedley (*Eng.*) Dweller at the smooth or flat meadow.

Smetana (*Cz.-Sl., Pol., Ukr.*) Sour cream, a nickname given to one in recognition of some quality, probably mental.

Smiddy (*Eng.*) Dweller at, or near, the smithy.

Smiley, Smylie, Smyly, Smilie, Smillie (*Eng., Scot.*) One who came from Semilly or Semily, in France; variants of Smalley, q.v.

Smit, Smid, Smidt (*Du.*) The worker in metals.

Smith, Smithe (*Eng., Scot., Ir.*) The worker in metals.

Smither, Smithers (*Eng.*) One who plys the trade of a smith, or worker in metals; dweller near the workshop of a smith.

Smithke, Smithkey, Smithka (*Ger.*) The little smith.

Smithson, Smithsonne, Smithsome (*Eng.*) The son of the smith.

Smoker (*Eng.*) One who made or sold smocks, formerly a woman's undergarment; one who cured fish or meat by means of smoke.

Smolinski (*Pol.*) One who came from Smolensk (pitch), in Russia.

Smollett (*Eng., Scot.*) One who had a small head.

Smutny, Smutney (*Cz.-Sl.*) The moody or sorrowful man.

Smyth, Smythe (*Eng.*) The worker in metals. This is the old spelling of the name.

Sneed, Snead, Sneyd (*Eng.*) Dweller at a clearing or piece of woodland; one who came from Snaith (piece of land), in Yorkshire.

Snell (*Eng., Scot.*) The quick, agile person; descendant of Snell (strong, smart).

Snite (*Eng.*) Dweller at the sign of the snipe; one with some characteristic of a snipe.

Snodgrass (*Eng., Scot.*) Dweller at the smooth, trim, grassy place; one who came from Snodgrasse, in Ayrshire.

Snooks, Snook (*Eng.*) One who came from Sevenoaks (seven oaks), in Kent; dweller on, or near, a projecting point or piece of land.

Snow (*Eng.*) Descendant of Snow, a name given to one born in the time of snow; a white-haired or very light-complexioned person.

Snowden, Snowdon (*Eng.*) Dweller near a snow hill; one who came from Snowden (snow hill), the name of several small places in England.

Snowman (*Ger.*) One who had snow-white hair.

Snyder, Snider, Sneider (*Du.*) One who made outer garments, a tailor.

Sobczak (*Pol.*) The son of the egotist.

Sobel, Sobol (*Pol., Rus.*) Dweller at the sign of the sable; one who trapped and sold sables.

Sobieski (*Pol.*) One who came from Sobieski, Sobieszki or Sobieszyn (Sobiech's settlement), the names of villages in Poland.

Socha (*Pol., Rus., Ukr., Cz.-Sl.*) One who used the wooden plow.

Soderberg (*Sw.*) South mountain.

Soderlund (*Sw.*) South grove.

Soderstrom (*Sw.*) South stream.

Sohn (*Ger.*) The son, a shortened form of names with this termination.

Sokol, Sokolowski, Sokolski (*Cz.-Sl., Pol.*) One with the qualities of a falcon or hawk; dweller at the sign of the falcon.

Sola (*Finn.*) Dweller at the pass or gorge.

Solberg, Sohlberg (*Nor., Sw.*) Sun mountain.

Solomon, Soloman (*Eng.*) Descendant of Solomon (peaceful).

Soltis, Soltys (*Pol.*) The official who performed the duties of a magistrate or mayor of a village.

Somerville, Sommerville (*Eng.*) One who came from Sommerville (Sumar's estate), in Normandy.

Sommer, Sommers, Somers (*Eng.*) Descendant of Sumer or Somer (summer); variants of Summers, q.v.

Sommerfeld, Sommerfield (*Ger.*) One who came from Sommerfeld (summer field), the name of several places in Germany; dweller at, or near, the place used in summer.

Sonnenschein (*Ger.*) Sunshine.

Sonntag (*Ger.*) Descendant of Sonntag, a name sometimes given to one born on Sunday.

Soper, Sopster (*Eng.*) One who made or sold soap.

Sorensen, Sorenson (*Dan.*) The son of Soren (severe or strict), from Severinus, the name of several saints. Soren has also been used as a term for the devil.

Sorkin (*Rus.*) Descendant of Sorkeh, a pet form of Sarah (princess).

Sorrell, Sorrells, Sorrels (*Eng.*) The man with the reddish-brown complexion.

Sorrentino, Sorrento, Sorrenti (*It.*) One who came from Sorrento, in Napoli.

Sosa (*Sp.*) Spanish form of Sousa, q.v.

Sosnowski (*Pol.*) Dweller in, or near, a forest of pine trees.

Soto (*Sp.*) One who came from Soto (wooded place on the bank of a river), the name of numerous places in Spain.

Soukup (*Pol.*) One who was a business partner of another.

Soule, Soul, Soules (*Eng.*) Dweller at, or near, a muddy pond.

Sousa, Souza (*Port.*) One who came from Sousa or Souza (salty place), the names of several places in Portugal; dweller near the Sousa, a river in Portugal.

Southard (*Eng.*) Dweller at the south wood; one who came from Southworth (southern homestead), in Lancashire.

Southern, Souther (*Eng.*) One who came from the south.

Southwick (*Eng.*) One who came from Southwick (southern dwelling), the name of several places in England.

Southworth (*Eng.*) One who came from Southworth (southern homestead), in Lancashire.

Sowa (*Pol.*) One with owlish qualities; dweller at the sign of the owl.

Sowinski (*Pol.*) One who came from Sowa or Sowin (owl), the name of places in Ukraine and Byelorussia.

Spain (*Eng., Scot.*) One who came from Spain, or who returned after having resided in Spain.

Spangler (*Ger.*) One who mended pots and kettles, a tinker; one who worked with, or dealt in, lead.

Spanier, Spanjer (*Ger.*) One who came from Spain, a Spaniard.

Sparks, Sparkes, Spark, Sparhawk (*Eng.*) Dweller at the sign of the sparrowhawk; one with some characteristic of a sparrowhawk.

Sparling, Sparr (*Eng.*) One with some characteristic of a little sparrow.

Sparrow (*Eng.*) One thought to possess some quality of a sparrow, such as a homey, chirpy disposition; dweller at the sign of the sparrow.

Spatz (*Ger.*) One with some characteristic of a little sparrow.

Spaulding, Spalding (*Eng.*) One who came from Spalding (tribe of Spaldas), in Lincolnshire.

Speaker, Speakman (*Eng.*) One who acted as a spokesman for others.

Spearman (*Eng.*) A soldier or warrior armed with a spear.

Spears, Spear, Spiers, Speirs (*Eng.*) The watchman or lookout man.

Specht (*Ger.*) Dweller at the sign of the woodpecker; one with the qualities of a woodpecker.

Speck, Speight (*Eng.*) One who came from Speke (brushwood), in Lancashire; one thought to possess some characteristic of a woodpecker; dweller at the sign of the woodpecker.

Spector (*Rus.*) A title meaning "inspector," used by Hebrew teachers in old Russia, which, when registered with the police, enabled them to live in areas forbidden to Jews.

Speer (*Eng.*) The watchman or lookout man.

Spellman, Spelman (*Ir., Eng.*) A preacher or orator; one who entertained by stories, songs, buffoonery or juggling.

Spence, Spens (*Eng., Scot.*) Custodian of a storage room for provisions; dweller near the place where provisions were stored.

Spencer, Spenser (*Eng.*) One who dispensed, or had charge of, the provisions in a household.

Spengler (*Ger.*) One who worked with tin, a tinsmith.

Sperling (*Ger.*) One with some characteristic of a sparrow; dweller at the sign of the sparrow.

Spero, Spiro, Spira, Spera (*Ger.*) One who came from Spira, now spelled Speyer, in Bavaria.

Sperry (*Eng.*) Descendant of Sperri (spear).

Speyer (*Ger.*) One who came from Speyer, in Bavaria.

Spicer (*Eng.*) One who dealt in spices, a druggist or apothecary.

Spiegel, Spiegl (*Ger.*) Dweller at, or near, a watchtower; one who made and sold tools.

Spielman, Spielmann (*Ger.*) One who manned a watchtower, a watchman; one who made and sold toys; a player.

Spies, Spiess, Spietz (*Ger.*) One who fashioned objects on a lathe, a turner; one who came from Spies, in Germany.

Spiewak (*Pol.*) The singer.

Spikes, Spiker, Spike (*Eng.*) One who made and sold spikes or nails.

Spillane (*Ir.*) Grandson of Spealan (little scythe).

Spiller (*Eng.*) One who preached, a preacher; one who entertained others.

Spindler, Spindell, Spindel (*Eng., Ger.*) One who made spindles for use in spinning.

Spinner (*Eng.*) One who spun wool or yarn.

Spinney (*Eng.*) One who came from Spinney (thicket), in Cambridgeshire.

Spittal, Spital, Spittle, Spitale (*Eng., Scot.*) Dweller in, or near, a hospital, a house for travelers, generally a religious house, later a home for the needy and infirm; one who came from Spittal (house), the name of many places in Scotland.

Spitzer, Spitz (*Ger.*) Dweller on, or near, a peak or pointed hill; one who came from Spitzen or Spitz (pointed hill), the names of places in Germany.

Spofford (*Eng.*) One who came from Spofforth (plot of land by a ford), in Yorkshire.

Sponner, Sponder, Spooner (*Eng.*) One who made shingles or spoons.

Spraggins, Spracklin, Spracklen (*Eng.*) The little, lively, talkative person.

Sprague, Spragg (*Eng.*) The alert, lively, intelligent man.

Spratt, Sprott, Sprotte, Spratte (*Eng.*) Descendant of Sprot (twig or small branch); one thought to possess some characteristic of a sprat (fish); dweller at the sign of the sprat.

Spriggs, Sprigg (*Eng.*) A small, slender person, one so called from some resemblance to a stick or twig.

Springer, Springs, Spring (*Eng.*) Dweller at, or near, the spring or well; dweller near a thicket or group of young trees.

Sproul, Sproule, Sprowl, Sprowles (*Eng.*) One who spoke in a slow, drawling voice.

Spry, Spray (*Eng.*) The lively, alert person.

Spurr, Spurlin, Spurling (*Eng.*) One with some characteristic of a sparrow; dweller near a beam or pole; dweller at the sign of the sparrow.

Squibb, Squibbs (*Eng.*) Nickname applied to a mean, insignificant or paltry fellow.

Squires, Squire, Squier (*Eng.*) A young man of gentle birth attendant upon a knight.

Sroka (*Pol.*) One who had some characteristic of a magpie; dweller at the sign of the magpie.

Stacey, Stacy (*Eng.*) Descendant of Stacy, a pet form of Anastasius (one who shall rise again), and of Eustace (steadfast); descendant of Stacius (stability).

Stach (*Pol.*) Descendant of big Stanislaw (camp, glorious).

Stachnik (*Pol.*) Descendant of Stachnik, a pet form of Stanislaw (camp, glorious).

Stack (*Eng., Scot.*) Dweller at a cliff or steep rock; one who came from Stack (cliff, isolated rock), in Caithness.

Stackhouse (*Eng.*) One who came from Stackhouse (habitation by a steep rock or hill), a hamlet in Yorkshire.

Stackpole, Stackpool (*Wel., Eng.*) One who came from Stackpole (pool by a cliff), in Pembrokeshire; dweller near a pool by a steep hill or cliff.

Stadler, Statler (*Eng., Ger.*) Dweller near a barn; one who came from Stadel (barn), in Germany.

Stafford (*Eng.*) One who came from Stafford (stony ford, or ford by a landing place), the name of several places, besides the county with that name, in England.

Stahl, Staehle (*Ger.*) One who worked with steel.

Staley (*Eng.*) One who came from Staveley (wood where staves were obtained), the name of several places in England.

Stalin (*Rus.*) Steel (an adopted name).

Stallings, Stalling (*Eng.*) One who came from Stalling (stallion), in Yorkshire.

Stallworth, Stallsworth (*Eng.*) The strong, stalwart man.

Stamm (*Ger.*) Dweller near an unusual tree trunk.

Stamps (*Eng.*) One who came from Estampes, in Normandy.

Standish (*Eng.*) One who came from Standish (stony pasture), the name of places in Gloucestershire and Lancashire.

Stanek (*Pol.*) Descendant of Stanek, a pet form of Stanislaw (camp, glorious).

Stanfield, Stanfel, Stanfill (*Eng.*) One who came from Stanfield (stony field), in Norfolk; dweller on, or near, stony land.

Stanford, Stamford, Stanforth (*Eng.*) One who came from Stanford (stony ford), the name of several places in England.

Stange, Stang, Stanger (*Eng., Ger.*) Dweller at, or near, a stagnant pool; dweller near a pole; a tall or thin man.

Stanhope (*Eng.*) One who came from Stanhope (stony valley), in Durham.

Stankiewicz (*Pol., Rus.*) The son of Stanko, a pet form of Stanislaw (camp, glorious).

Stanko (*Pol., Yu.-Sl.*) Descendant of Stanko, a pet form of Stanislaw (camp, glorious).

Stankus (*Pol.*) Descendant of Stankus, a pet form of Stanislaw (camp, glorious).

Stanlake (*Eng.*) One who came from Standlake (stony stream), in Oxfordshire.

Stanley, Standley (*Eng.*) One who came from Stanley (stony meadow), the name of several places in England; dweller at a rocky meadow.

Stannard, Stankard (*Eng.*) Descendant of Stanard (stone, firm).

Stansbury, Stansberry (*Eng.*) One who came from Stanbury (stone fort), in Yorkshire.

Stansfield (*Eng.*) One who came from Stansfield (stony field), the name of places in Suffolk and Yorkshire.

Stanton (*Eng.*) One who came from Stanton (homestead on stony ground), the name of many places in England.

Stanwood (*Eng.*) Dweller in, or near, a stony wood.

Staples, Staple (*Eng.*) One who came from Staple (post or pillar), in Kent; dweller at a post.

Stapleton (*Eng.*) One who came from Stapleton (homestead by a post), the name of several places in England.

Starbird (*Eng.*) Descendant of Storbeorht (strong, bright).

Starbuck, Starbeck (*Eng.*) One who came from Starbeck (brook near where sedge grew), in Yorkshire; dweller at, or near, a stream where sedge or swamp grass grew.

Starck, Stark, Starke, Starch (*Ger.*) Descendant of Starco, a pet form of Starculf (strong, wolf).

Stark, Starks, Starke, Starkman (*Eng.*) The strong, severe man.

Starkey, Starkie (*Eng., Ir.*) Descendant of Starkie, a pet form of names beginning with Starc (strong), such as Starcbeorht, Starcfrith or Starcwulf; the little, strong man.

Starkweather (*Eng.*) One who worked in severe weather.

Starnes (*Eng.*) The severe, austere man; dweller at the sign of the stars.

Starr, Star (*Eng.*) Dweller at the sign of the star; descendant of Sterre (star).

Starrett, Starratt (*Scot., Ir.*) One who came from Stairaird, now Stirie (path over a bog), in Ayrshire; variant of Stewart, q.v.

Starzyk (*Pol.*) The gray-haired man.

Stassen (*Nor.*) The son of Stass, a pet form of Anastasius (resurrection).

Staszak (*Pol.*) Descendant of Staszek, a pet form of Stanislaw (camp, glorious).

Statura (*Sp.*) The tall man.

Staudenmaier, Staudenmayer, Staudenmeyer (*Ger.*) One who took care of the shrubs or bushes, a horticulturist or forester.

Stauffer, Staufer (*Ger.*) One who came from Staufen (goblet), in Germany; dweller at the top of the mountain; dweller at the sign of the goblet or cup, a tavern sign.

Stead (*Eng., Wel.*) Dweller at a dairy farm.

Stearns (*Eng.*) A variant of Starnes, q.v.

Stebbins, Stebbing (*Eng.*) One who came from Stebbing (clearing), in Essex.

Stec (*Ukr.*) Descendant of Stecko, a pet form of Stepan (crown or garland).

Steck (*Ger.*) Dweller on, or near, a steep incline.

Stedman, Steadman (*Eng.*) One who had charge of horses; one who tilled the soil, a farmer.

Steege, Steeg (*Du.*) Dweller on the alley or lane.

Steele, Steel (*Eng.*) One who came from Steel (stile, or place where one has to climb), the name of places in Northumberland and Shropshire.

Steen (*Du., Scot.*) Dweller near a stone; descendant of Stephen (crown or garland).

Steere, Steer (*Eng.*) Dweller at the sign of the ox; one with oxlike qualities.

Steeves, Steeve (*Eng.*) Descendant of Steeve, a pet form of Stephen (crown or garland).

Stefan, Stefani, Stefanski (*Pol.*) Descendant of Stefan (crown or garland).

Stefansson (*Ice.*) The son of Stefan (crown or garland).

Steffens, Steffen, Steffan (*Eng.*) Descendant of Steffen, a variant of Stephen (crown or garland).

Steger (*Ger.*) Dweller near a narrow bridge; one who came from Stegen, in Germany.

Steiger, Stiger (*Du.*) Dweller on, or near, the pier or boat-landing place.

Stein, Steiner, Steen (*Ger., Du., Swis.*) Dweller near a stone or rock, often a boundary mark; one who came from Stein, the name of several villages in Switzerland; descendant of Staino or Stein, pet forms of names beginning with Stein (stone), as Steinher and Stainold.

Steinbach, Steinback (*Ger.*) One who came from Steinbach (stony brook), the name of many places in Germany.

Steinbeck (*Ger.*) Dweller near the stony stream.

Steinberg, Steinberger (*Ger.*) One who came from Steinberg (stone mountain), the name of many places in Germany.

Steinfeld, Steinfeldt (*Ger.*) Dweller in, or near, a stony field.

Steinhaus, Steinhauser (*Ger.*) One who came from Steinhaus (stone homestead or castle), the name of many places in Germany.

Steinhoff (*Ger.*) One who came from Steinhofel (stone hill), in Germany; dweller near a stone courtyard.

Steinke, Steinicke, Steinken (*Ger.*) Descendant of little Staino, a pet form of names beginning with Stein (stone), such as Stenulf, Stainold and Steinwart.

Steinman, Steinmann (*Ger.*) One who worked with stone, a mason.

Steinmetz (*Ger.*) The stonecutter, or builder with stone.

Steinweg, Steinway (*Ger.*) Dweller near the stony path or road.

Stella, Stello (*It., Eng.*) Dweller at the sign of the star; descendant of Stella (child of fate); descendant of Stella, a pet form of Battisstella; one who came from Stella (pasture with a cattle shed), in Durham.

Stelzer, Stelzner (*Ger.*) One who walked on stilts, to entertain, as at a carnival;

one who came from Stelzen, in Germany; dweller in a narrow field.

Stengel, Stengele (*Ger.*) Dweller near a small pole or stake.

Stenson (*Eng.*) One who came from Stenson (Stein's homestead), in Derbyshire; the son of Stean (stone).

Stepan (*Ukr.*) Descendant of Stepan (crown or garland).

Stepanek (*Pol.*) Descendant of little Stefan (crown or garland).

Stephan, Stephen (*Ger., Eng.*) Descendant of Stephen (crown or garland).

Stephens, Stephenson (*Wel., Eng.*) The son of Stephen (crown or garland).

Sterling (*Scot.*) One who came from Stirling (dwelling of Velyn), in Scotland.

Stern, Sterne (*Eng., Ger.*) The severe, austere man; dweller at the sign of the star.

Sternberg, Sternberger (*Ger.*) One who came from Sternberg (star mountain), the name of ten places in Germany.

Sterritt (*Scot.*) Variant of Starrett, q.v.

Stetson, Stutson (*Eng.*) The son of the stupid, clumsy fellow; the son of Stedda or Stith; descendant of the stepson.

Stetter, Stettner, Stettin, Stettinius (*Ger.*) One who came from Stetten (place of green grain), the name of many small places in Germany.

Stevens, Stevenson, Steven (*Eng.*) The son of Stephen (crown or garland).

Stewart, Steward (*Eng., Scot.*) Keeper of the sty, pen or hall, later manager of a household or estate; one who had charge of a king's, or important noble's, household.

Stickney (*Eng.*) One who came from Stickney (stick island), in Lincolnshire.

Stiles (*Eng.*) Dweller at the steps leading over a fence or wall, or at a steep path up a hill.

Stille, Still, Stiller (*Eng.*) Dweller at a place where fish were caught; the still, quiet person; variants of Stiles, q.v.

Stillings, Stilling, Stelling (*Eng.*) One who came from Stelling (Stealla's people), in Kent.

Stillman (*Eng.*) Dweller at the stile, or steep path up a hill.

Stillwell, Stilwell (*Eng.*) Dweller at the spring where the water flowed continuously.

Stine, Stiner (*Ger.*) An Anglicization of Stein, q.v.

Stinson, Stimpson, Stimson (*Eng.*) The son of Stin, a pet form of Stephen (crown or garland).

Stirling (*Scot.*) One who came from Stirling (dwelling of Velyn), in Stirlingshire.

Stitt, Stith, Stitts (*Eng.*) The strong, hard man.

Stock, Stocker (*Eng.*) Dweller near a tree stump; dweller near a footbridge; one employed in grubbing up trees.

Stockbridge (*Eng.*) One who came from Stockbridge (monastery cell at the bridge), in Hampshire.

Stocking (*Scot.*) One who came from Stocking (enclosed), in Scotland.

Stocks (*Eng.*) Dweller near a monastery or holy place.

Stockton (*Eng.*) One who came from Stockton (village belonging to a monastery, or some outlying place), the name of various places in England.

Stockwell (*Eng.*) One who came from Stockwell (stream with a footbridge), in Surrey.

Stockwood (*Eng.*) One who came from Stockwood (monastery by a wood), in Dorset.

Stoddard, Stoddart (*Eng.*) One who had the care of the horses or oxen.

Stokes, Stoker (*Eng.*) One who came from Stoke or Stokes (monastery, cell, place or outlying farm), a very common place name in England.

Stoll, Stoller, Stolle (*Ger.*) Dweller near a post or pole; dweller near a mine shaft.

Stone, Stoner (*Eng.*) Dweller near some remarkable stone or rock, often a boundary mark; one who came from Stone (the stone or stones), the name of various places in England.

Stopka (*Pol., Rus., Ukr.*) One who drank large glasses of vodka.

Storer (*Eng.*) The keeper, or overseer, of the provisions for a large household.

Storey, Story, Storie (*Eng.*) Descendant of little Store or Stori (strong, powerful).

Storm, Storms (*Eng.*) Descendant of Storm (storm); variants of Sturm, q.v.

Stott, Stotts (*Eng.*) Dweller at the sign of the stot (horse or ox); the fat or stout person.

Stoudemire, Stoudenmire, Stoudmire (*Ger.*) One who took care of the shrubs or bushes, a horticulturist or forester.

Stout, Stoute (*Eng.*) The bold, strong and valiant man; the proud man.

Stovall (*Eng.*) One who came from Esteville (east settlement), in France.

Stover (*Ger.*) One who came from Stove, in Mecklenburg; one who conducted a public bathhouse; variant of Stauffer, q.v.

Stowe, Stow (*Eng.*) Dweller near a holy place, probably a monastery or church; one who came from Stow (holy place), the name of many places in England.

Stowell (*Eng.*) One who came from Stowell (stony stream), in Gloucestershire.

Strand, Strande (*Eng.*) Dweller on the bank of a river.

Strandberg (*Sw.*) Shore mountain.

Strang, Stranger (*Ger., Eng., Scot.*) One with great physical power, a strong man; one who came from a distance, a stranger.

Strange, Strangeman, Stranger (*Eng.*) The stranger, one who came from a distance.

Strassburger, Strassberger (*Ger.*) One who came from Strassburg (fortified place on a road), a German city now within the French border.

Strasser (*Ger.*) Dweller on, or near, a country road.

Stratford (*Eng.*) One who came from Stratford (ford at a Roman road), the name of various places in England.

Stratton (*Eng.*) One who came from Stratton (homestead on a Roman road), the name of various places in England.

Straub, Straube (*Ger.*) One with bushy or bristly hair; one who came from Straube, in Germany; descendant of Strubo, a pet form of names beginning with Strud (destroy, rob), as Strudbalt and Strudolf.

Straubinger (*Ger.*) One who came from Straubing (place of Strubo's people), in Bavaria.

Strauch (*Ger.*) Dweller near a bush, underbrush or copse; one who came from Strauchau (swamp with low bushes), in Germany.

Strauss, Straus (*Ger.*) Dweller at the sign of the ostrich; one with ostrich-like characteristics; bouquet of flowers.

Streadbeck (*Sw.*) Dweller near a violent, or rapid, brook.

Streeter, Street, Streets (*Eng.*) Dweller on a paved road, especially an ancient Roman road; one who came from Street or Strete (Roman road), the names of several places in England.

Streich (*Ger.*) Descendant of Stregus (refuge, protection).

Streit (*Ger.*) Descendant of Streit (battle), a short form of names beginning with Streit, as Stridbert, Striter and Stritmar.

Streng, Strenge (*Ger.*) One with great physical power, a strong man; the brave man.

Stricker, Strickler (*Eng., Ger.*) One who stretched, or smoothed, fabrics; one who poached, or killed game unlawfully; one who came from Streich, in Germany.

Strickland (*Eng.*) One who came from Strickland (pasture for cattle), the name of several places in England.

Stringer (*Eng.*) One who made strings for bows.

Stritch (*Ir.*) Dweller at the street or paved road.

Strobel, Strobl (*Ger.*) One with bushy or bristly hair; descendant of Strubo, a pet form of names beginning with Strud (destroy, rob), as Strudbalt and Strudolf; one who came from Strobel, in Germany.

Strode, Stroder (*Eng.*) Dweller at, or near, a marshy place overgrown with brushwood.

Strohm (*Ger.*) Dweller at, or near, a stream; one who came from Strohm (stream), in Germany.

Strom (*Sw.*) Stream.

Stromberg (*Sw.*) Stream mountain.

Stromquist (*Sw.*) Stream twig.

Strong, Strongs (*Eng.*) One with great physical power, a strong man.

Strother, Strothers, Stroter, Strotter, Strothman (*Eng.*) Dweller on, or near, marshy land overgrown with brushwood; one who came from Strother (marshy meadow), in Northumberland.

Stroud, Strode, Strout (*Eng., Ger.*) Dweller at a marshy place overgrown with brushwood; one who came from Stroud (marshy land), in Gloucestershire; descendant of Strut, a pet form of Strudmar (ravage, famous), or Strudolf (ravage, wolf).

Strube, Strub, Strubbe (*Ger.*) One who had bristled or tousled hair.

Struck (*Ger.*) Dweller near a bush, underbrush or copse.

Struthers (*Scot.*) Dweller in, or near, a marsh or swamp; one who came from Struthers (marsh), in Fife.

Stuart (*Eng., Scot.*) Keeper of the sty, pen or hall, later manager of a household.

Stubblefield (*Eng.*) Dweller in a recently cleared field where the stumps of the trees were still evident.

Stubbs, Stubbe (*Eng.*) Dweller near a tree stump, or on recently cleared land where the stumps were still evident; nickname given to one of a short, stumpy stature; one who came from Stubbs (tree stumps), in Yorkshire.

Stuck (*Ger.*) One who came from Stuck (plot of land), in Mecklenburg; dweller on a piece of land.

Stucker, Stucke (*Ger.*) Dweller near a tree stump. *See also* Stuck.

Stuckey, Stockey, Stocky (*Eng.*) The short, thick or stocky man.

Studley (*Eng.*) One who came from Studley (pasture for horses), the name of several places in England.

Stumpf, Stump (*Ger.*) Dweller near a tree stump; one who was short and fat.

Sturgis, Sturges (*Eng.*) Descendant of Turgis (hostage of Thor, god of thunder).

Sturm, Sturmer (*Ger.*) One who was stormy and excitable; one who engaged in combat.

Sturman (*Du.*) One who worked on a boat, a sailor or navigator.

Sturt (*Eng.*) Dweller on a promontory or tongue of land, or on the spur of a hill.

Sturtevant, Sturdivant (*Eng.*) A nickname given to a messenger or pursuivant, the surname literally meaning "start forward."

Stutz, Stutzke (*Ger.*) The short or little man.

Stuyvesant (*Du.*) One who came from Stuvesant (quicksand), in Zeeland.

Styles (*Eng.*) Dweller at the steps leading over a fence or wall, or at a steep path up a hill.

Sugar, Sugarman, Sugerman (*Eng.*) One who shoed horses; descendant of Sigar or Sigegar (victory, spear).

Suggs, Sugg (*Eng.*) Dweller at the sign of the sow; one with some characteristic of a female hog.

Sugrue, Sughrue (*Ir.*) Grandson of Siocfhraidh (victory, peace).

Sullivan (*Ir.*) Grandson of Suileabhan (black-eyed).

Summerfield, Summerfelt (*Eng., Ger.*) Dweller at, or near, a field used by sheep or cattle in the summer.

Summers, Sumner, Summer (*Eng.*) The summoner, i.e., the petty officer who warns people to appear in court. *See also* Sommers.

Summerville, Summerbell (*Eng.*) Variants of Somerville, q.v.

Sundberg (*Sw.*) Sound (i.e., a narrow watercourse) mountain.

Sunde, Sund (*Nor.*) Dweller near the narrow water passage; dweller near the ferry landing.

Sundstrom (*Sw.*) Sound (i.e., a narrow water course) stream.

Sunners (*Eng.*) A variant of Summers, q.v.

Supple, Supplee, Supplice (*Fr.*) Descendant of Sulpicius (red-spotted face).

Surette, Surrette (*Fr.*) Descendant of Suret, a pet form of Sureau (elder tree); one who was stable, steady or sure.

Suslov (*Rus.*) One with some resemblance to a gopher; dweller at the sign of the gopher.

Sussman, Susman (*Ger.*) Sweet man, an affectionate person.

Sutcliffe (*Eng.*) Dweller by the south cliff or slope.

Sutherland, Sutherlan (*Scot.*) One who came from the county of Sutherland (southern land), in Scotland.

Sutter (*Eng.*) One who made shoes, a shoemaker.

Sutton (*Eng.*) One who came from Sutton (southern village or homestead), the name of many places in England.

Svec, Sveck (*Cz.-Sl.*) One who made shoes, a shoemaker.

Svendsen, Svensen (*Dan.*) The son of Svend or Sven (young boy, or servant).

Svoboda (*Cz.-Sl., Pol., Ukr.*) Liberty or freedom.

Swain, Swaine, Swayne (*Eng.*) The man who acted as a servant or attendant; one who tended swine; descendant of Swain (young man, or boy servant).

Swallow (*Eng.*) One who came from Swallow (rushing river), in Lincolnshire; dweller at a deep hollow.

Swan, Swann, Swane (*Eng., Sw.*) Dweller at the sign of the swan; the swain, a servant; descendant of Sveinn or Swan (knight's attendant); one who kept swans.

Swanson, Swansen (*Sw.*) The son of Swan (servant).

Swanton (*Eng.*) One who came from Swanton (place of the swineherds), the name of several places in England.

Sward (*Sw.*) Sword, a soldier name.

Swartz, Swarts, Swart, Swarz (*Ger.*) One with a dark or swarthy complexion, black.

Swedberg (*Sw.*) Burned-over clearing mountain; contraction of Swedenborg, q.v.

Swedenborg, Swedenburg (*Sw.*) Sweden stronghold.

Sweney, Sweeny, Swiney (*Ir.*) The son of the peaceful or quiet one.

Sweet, Sweete (*Eng.*) The dear, or beloved, person; descendant of Swet (agreeable).

Sweetman, Sweetnam (*Eng.*) One who was pleasant and agreeable; the servant of Swet (sweet); one who came from Swettenham (Sweta's homestead), in Cheshire.

Sweetser, Sweetsir (*Eng.*) One who came from Switzerland; an agreeable, elderly person.

Sweitzer, Switzer (*Ger., Ir.*) One who came from Switzerland.

Swem, Swaim (*Du.*) Dweller at the sign of the swan.

Swenson, Swensen (*Sw., Dan.*) The son of Swen (young boy or servant).

Swett, Swetts, Swets, Swetz (*Eng., Rus., Du.*) Descendant of Swet (agreeable); the light-complexioned man; the son of Witte (white).

Swiatek (*Pol.*) One who came from the demimonde.

Swiatkowski (*Pol.*) One who came from Swiatkowka, a city, or from Swiatkowo, a village (both meaning world), in Poland.

Swiderski, Swider (*Pol.*) One who bored or drilled holes.

Swift (*Eng.*) One who was fleet of foot, probably a messenger.

Swindell, Swindells, Swindle, Swindall (*Eng.*) Dweller in the valley where swine were bred.

Swindlehurst (*Eng.*) Dweller in the wooded valley where swine were bred.

Swindler, Swingler (*Eng.*) One who beat and dressed flax.

Swinton (*Eng., Scot.*) One who came from Swinton (pig farm), the name of four places in England and one in Scotland.

Swope, Swopes (*Ger.*) Variant of Schwab, q.v.

Sydor (*Cz.-Sl., Ukr.*) Descendant of Sydor (gift of Isis).

Sydoruk (*Ukr.*) The son of Sydor (gift of Isis).

Sykes (*Eng.*) Dweller by a mountain stream or ditch.

Sylvester (*Eng.*) Descendant of Silvester (forest dweller).

Symington (*Scot.*) One who came from Symington (Symond's stone), the name of places in Ayrshire and Lanarkshire.

Symmes, Symms, Syms (*Eng.*) Descendant of Sim, a pet form of Simon or Simeon (gracious hearing).

Symons, Symmons, Symonds, Symon, Symond (*Eng.*) The son of Simon or Simeon (gracious hearing).

Sypniewski (*Pol.*) One who came from Sypniewo (Sypien's settlement), in Poland.

Szabo (*Hun.*) One who made outer garments, a tailor.

Szafranski (*Pol.*) Dweller at a place where saffron or crocus grew.

Szczepaniak (*Pol.*) The son of Szczepan (crown or garland).

Szczepanik, Szczepanek (*Pol.*) Descendant of little Szczepan (crown or garland).

Szczepanski (*Pol.*) The son of Szczepan (crown or garland).

Szewc (*Pol.*) One who made and repaired shoes, a shoemaker or cobbler.

Szewczyk (*Pol.*) The little man who made outer garments, a tailor.

Szymanski (*Pol.*) Descendant of Szymon (gracious hearing).

Szymczak (*Pol.*) The son of Szymon (gracious hearing).

Tabor, Taber (*Eng.*) One who performed on the tabor, a small drum.

Taft, Taff, Taffe (*Eng., Ir.*) Dweller at a toft, a yard enclosing a residence; descendant of Taff, a pet form of David (beloved), or of Theophilus (loved by God).

Taggart, Taggert (*Scot.*) The son of the priest.

Taglia (*It.*) One who cut, a cutter, often a short form of a longer name, such as Tagliaferro (cut iron).

Tagliaferro, Taliaferro (*It.*) One who cut, or otherwise worked with, iron.

Tague (*Ir.*) Grandson of Tadhg (poet).

Taillandier (*Fr.*) One who made or sold iron articles.

Tailleur (*Fr.*) One who made outer garments, a tailor.

Tait, Taitt (*Eng.*) One with a large or peculiar head; a gay or cheerful person; dweller at the top of the hill.

Talbot, Talbert, Talbott (*Eng.*) Descendant of Talbot (to cut fagots); the pillager or bandit.

Talcott (*Eng.*) Dweller in front of, or opposite, the cottage, or in the cottage in the dale.

Talley, Tally (*Ir.*) Grandson of Taithleach (quiet, peaceful).

Tallman, Talman (*Eng.*) The able, obedient servant.

Tamony, Tamney (*Ir.*) The son of the tympanist.

Tanaka (*Jap.*) Dweller in, or near, a rice swamp.

Tanis (*Lith.*) Descendant of Tanis, a pet form of Athanasius (immortal).

Tannenbaum (*Ger.*) Dweller at, or near, a fir tree.

Tanner (*Eng.*) One who made or sold leather.

Tansey (*Eng.*) One who came from Tansey (island in the branch of a river), in Somerset.

Tapley (*Eng.*) One who came from Tapeley (wood where pegs were cut), in Devonshire.

Tappan, Tappen (*Du.*) One who drew wine or beer.

Tapper (*Eng., Sw.*) One who tapped casks, or drew liquor, a tavernkeeper; brave.

Tarbell (*Fr.*) One who came from Tarabel (auger), in France.

Tarbox (*Eng.*) One who came from Tarbock (thorn brook), in Lancashire.

Tarkington, Turkington (*Eng.*) One who came from Torkington (homestead of Turec's people), in Cheshire.

Tarr, Tarre, Tar (*Eng.*) Dweller in, or near, a tower or near a tower-like rock or hill.

Tarrant (*Eng.*) One who came from Tarrant (trespasser), the name of several places in England, or who dwelt at the Tarrant River, in Dorset.

Tasker (*Eng.*) One who worked, or was paid, by the task or piece.

Tate (*Eng.*) One who had a large or peculiar head; a gay or cheerful person; dweller at the top of the hill.

Tatten (*Eng.*) One who came from Tatton (Tata's homestead), the name of places in Cheshire and Dorset.

Tatum, Tatham (*Eng.*) One who came from Tatham (Tata's homestead), in Lancashire.

Tauber, Taube, Taub (*Ger.*) Dweller at the sign of the dove; one with the qualities of a dove; descendant of Tabo, a pet form of names beginning with Diet, as Theudobald, Theudobert and Theudobrand.

Taussig, Tausig, Tauss (*Ger.*) One who came from Tauss, in Bohemia.

Tavenner (*Eng.*) One who sold ale and wine, a tavernkeeper.

Taylor, Tayler (*Eng.*) One who made outer garments, a tailor.

Taymore, Taymor (*Heb.*) Descendant of Tamar or Tawmawr (palm tree).

Tead (*Eng.*) Descendant of Tead, a pet form of names beginning with Theod (people), as Theodberht, Theodred and Theodric.

Teague, Tegge (*Wel., Ir., Eng.*) One with a fair complexion; grandson of Tadhg (poet); dweller in an enclosure or near a common pasture.

Tebbetts, Tebbets (*Eng.*) Descendant of little Tebb, a pet form of Theobald (people, bold).

Teed (*Eng.*) Descendant of Teed, a pet form of names beginning with Theod (people), such as Theodbald, Theodric and Theodred.

Teele, Teel, Teal (*Eng.*) Dweller at the sign of the teal (a small duck).

Tegtmeyer, Tegmeyer, Tegtmeier (*Ger.*) One who collected the farm rent equal to a tenth of the income.

Teich, Teicher (*Ger.*) One who came from Teich (low ground), in Germany.

Teichert (*Ger.*) Descendant of Tagahard (light, hard); descendant of Dihart (thrive, firm).

Teichman, Teichmann (*Ger.*) Dweller near a pond or depression in the ground; same as Teich, q.v.

Teitelbaum (*Hun.*) The date palm tree, a name selected from Psalm 92:12, where it is written, "The righteous shall flourish like the palm tree."

Teixeira (*Port.*) One who came from Teixeira (place of yew trees), the name of several places in Portugal.

Telfer, Telfair (*Eng.*) One who cut iron.

Teller (*Eng.*) One who made or sold linen cloth.

Temperley (*Eng.*) One who came from Timperleigh (timber wood), in Cheshire.

Temple (*Eng.*) Dweller in, or near, a religious house of the Knights Templars; descendant of Temple, a name sometimes given a foundling abandoned in a temple.

Templeton (*Eng.*) One who came from Templeton (manor belonging to the Knights Templars), the name of places in Berkshire and Devonshire.

Templin, Timblin (*Eng.*) Descendant of little Tim, a pet form of Timothy (honor God).

Ten Broeck, Ten Broek, Ten Brook (*Du.*) Dweller at, or near, the marsh.

Ten Eyck (*Du.*) One who lived near an oak tree.

Tennant (*Eng.*) One who rented land of another, a tenant.

Tenney, Tenny (*Eng.*) Descendant of Tenney, a pet form of Dennis (belonging to Dionysius, Grecian god of wine).

Tennyson, Tennison (*Eng.*) The son of Tenny, a pet form of Dennis (belonging to Dionysius, Grecian god of wine).

Tepper, Tipper (*Eng.*) One who furnished articles, particularly arrows, with metal tips.

Terrell, Terrill (*Eng.*) Descendant of Turold or Thorold (Thor, strong); one who came from Tirril (wooden hut), in Westmorland.

Terry (*Eng.*) Descendant of Terry (people, rule).

Terwilliger (*Du.*) One who came from Willige (Wille's settlement), in Holland.

Tesar (*Cz.-Sl.*) One who worked in wood, a carpenter.

Teske, Teska, Teschke (*Ger.*) Descendant of Tech (consolation).

Testa (*It.*) One who had a large or unusual head; descendant of Testa, a pet form of Battista (Baptist).

Tetzlaff (*Ger.*) Descendant of Tetzlaff (consolation, fame).

Teufel (*Ger.*) Descendant of Tiefel, a pet form of Theudobald (people, bold), and Theudofrid (people, peace); descendant of one nicknamed "the devil."

Tewksbury, Tewkesbury (*Eng.*) One who came from Tewkesbury (Teodec's fort), in Gloucestershire.

Thackeray, Thackery (*Eng.*) Dweller at the corner where the thatch was stored.

Thatcher, Thaxter, Thacker, Thacher (*Eng.*) One who covered roofs with straw, rushes, reeds or the like.

Thayer (*Eng.*) Descendant of Thaider (people, army).

Theis, Theiss, Theise (*Ger.*) Descendant of Theis, a pet form of Matthias (gift of Jehovah); descendant of Theis, a form of Dago, a pet form of names beginning with Dag (light), as Tagibod and Tagamar.

Thelen, Thelin (*Ger.*) Descendant of Thilo, a form of Tiuto, or Theuda, short forms of names beginning with Thiud (people), as Theudobald, Theudoricus and Theudoald.

Theobald, Theobold (*Eng.*) Descendant of Theobald (people, bold).

Theodore (*Eng.*) Descendant of Theodoric (people, rule); rarely of Theodore (gift of God).

Thibault, Thibeault, Thibeau (*Fr.*) Descendant of Theudbald, Thibaut or Thibaud (people, bold).

Thibodeau, Thibedeau, Thibideau (*Fr.*) Descendant of Theudbald, Thibaut or Thibaud (people, bold).

Thiel, Thiele, Thielen, Thiell (*Ger.*) Same as Thelen, q.v.

Thigpen (*Ger.*) Descendant of Thigfuns (thrive, swift); one who begged for coins.

Thistle (*Eng.*) Dweller near thistles or prickly plants.

Thoma (*Eng.*) Descendant of Thoma, a German form of Thomas (a twin).

Thomas (*Wel.*) Descendant of Thomas (a twin).

Thome, Thom (*Eng.*) Descendant of Thome, a pet form of Thomas (a twin).

Thompkins (*Eng.*) The son of little Thom, a pet form of Thomas (a twin).

Thompson, Thomson (*Eng., Scot.*) The son of Thom, a pet form of Thomas (a twin); one who came from Thompson (Tumi's homestead), in Norfolk.

Thomsen, Thompsen (*Dan.*) The son of Thom, a pet form of Thomas (a twin).

Thoresen (*Nor.*) The son of Thor (the old Norse god of thunder).

Thorley (*Eng.*) One who came from Thorley (thorny wood), the name of places in Hertfordshire and Wight.

Thornburn (*Eng., Scot.*) Dweller near a stream where thornbushes grew.

Thorndike, Thorndyke (*Eng.*) Dweller on, or near, a dike where thornbushes grew.

Thorne, Thorn (*Eng.*) Dweller near a thornbush.

Thornehill, Thornell (*Eng.*) One who came from Thornhill (hill overgrown with thornbushes), the name of several places in England.

Thorner (*Eng.*) Dweller at, or near, a thornbush.

Thornley (*Eng.*) One who came from Thornley (thorny glade), the name of places in Durham and Lancashire.

Thornton (*Eng.*) One who came from Thornton (place where thornbushes grew), the name of many places in England.

Thorpe, Thorp (*Eng.*) One who came from Thorpe (farm), the name of many places in England; dweller at a farmstead.

Thorsen, Thorson (*Nor.*) The son of Thor (the old Norse god of Thunder).

Thresher, Thrasher (*Eng.*) One who beat out grain by striking with a flail.

Thulin, Thullen, Thull (*Ger.*) Same as Thelin, q.v.

Thurber (*Eng.*) Descendant of Thurgar or Thorgeirr (Thor's spear); dweller at Thor's grove.

Thurlow (*Eng.*) One who came from Thurlow (assembly hill), in Suffolk.

Thurman, Thurmond (*Eng.*) Descendant of Thurmund (Thor's protection).

Thurston (*Eng.*) Descendant of Thurstan (the stone of Thor, Norse god of thunder); one who came from Thurston (Thori's homestead), in Suffolk.

Tibbetts, Tibbits, Tibbitts (*Eng.*) Descendant of little Tibb, a pet form of Theobald (people, bold).

Tibbs, Tebbe (*Eng.*) Descendant of Tibb or Tebb, a pet form of Theobald (people, bold).

Tibon (*Sp.*) The son of Tibbon (generous, noble or wolf), from the Arabic *ibn Tibbon.*

Ticknor, Tichnor, Tickner (*Eng.*) One who came from Tichnor (Tyca's shore), in Kent.

Tidwell (*Eng.*) One who came from Tideswell (Tidi's stream), in Derbyshire.

Tierney (*Ir.*) Grandson of Tighearnach (lordly).

Tietz, Tietze (*Ger.*) Descendant of Teuzo (people).

Tiffany, Tiffin (*Eng.*) Descendant of Tiffany (name given to child born on Epiphany Day, January 6), or a pet form of Theophania (manifestation of God).

Tighe, Tigue, Tige (*Ir.*) Grandson of Tadhg (poet).

Tilden (*Eng.*) One who came from Tillingdown (Tilmund's hill), in Surrey.

Tildsley (*Eng.*) One who came from Tyldesley (Tilwald's meadow), in Lancashire.

Tilford (*Eng.*) One who came from Tilford (convenient ford), in Surrey.

Till (*Eng.*) Descendant of Tilla, Tilli or Tila (good, brave); dweller near the Till (stream), a river in Lincolnshire.

Tilley, Tilly (*Eng.*) One who came from Tilley (branch or bough), in Shropshire; one who came from Tilly (lime tree), the name of two places in France.

Tillinghast (*Eng.*) Dweller near a place where auctions were held.

Tillman (*Eng.*) One who was employed in tilling the soil; the brave man.

Tillotson (*Eng.*) The son of little Till, a pet form of names so beginning, as Tilli, Tilbeorht and Tilfrid, as well as of Mathilda.

Tilson, Tillson (*Eng.*) The son of Til or Till. *See* Tillotson.

Tilton (*Eng.*) One who came from Tilton (Tila's homestead), in Leicestershire.

Tim, Timms, Tims, Timme (*Ger., Eng.*) Descendant of Thim or Tim, pet forms of Thiemo, a short form of Theudemar (people, famous); descendant of Tim, a pet form of Timothy or Timotheus (honoring God).

Timmerman, Timmermann (*Ger., Du.*) One who worked in wood, a carpenter.

Timmons, Timmins (*Eng.*) Descendant of little Timm, a pet form of Timothy (honoring God).

Timson (*Eng.*) The son of Tim, a pet form of Timothy (honoring God).

Tindall, Tindal, Tindill, Tindle (*Eng., Scot.*) One who came from Tindale (fort in fertile upland region), in Cumberland.

Tingley, Tingle (*Eng.*) Dweller at, or near, the meeting place or court.

Tinker, Tinkler (*Eng.*) One who mended pots and kettles.

Tinkham (*Eng.*) One who came from Tyneham (homestead where goats were bred), in Dorset.

Tinsley (*Eng.*) One who came from Tinsley (Tynne's hill), in Yorkshire.

Tippett, Tippet, Tippetts, Tippitt (*Eng.*) Descendant of little Tibb, a pet form of Theobald (people, bold).

Tipping (*Eng.*) The son of Tibba, pet forms of Theobald (people bold); the son of Tippa (to tap).

Tipton (*Eng.*) One who came from Tipton (Tibba's homestead), in Staffordshire.

Tirrell (*Eng.*) One who came from Tirril (wooden hut), in Westmorland; descendant of Tirrell, a variant of Turold or Thorold (Thor, strong).

Tisdale, Tisdell, Teasdale (*Eng.*) One who came from Teesdale (surging river valley), in Durham.

Titcomb (*Eng.*) One who came from Tidcombe (Titta's valley), in Wiltshire.

Tittle, Tittel (*Eng.*) One who came from Titley (Titta's wood), in Herefordshire.

Titus (*Eng.*) Descendant of Titus (safe).

Tobias, Toby, Tobey, Tobie, Tobiason (*Eng.*) Descendant of Tobias, or Toby the pet form (Jehovah is good).

Tobin (*Eng.*) Descendant of little Tob, a pet form of Tobias (Jehovah is good).

Todd (*Eng.*) Dweller at the sign of the fox; one with some of the qualities of a fox.

Todhunter (*Eng.*) One who hunted foxes.

Toft, Toff (*Eng.*) Dweller at a toft, a yard enclosing a residence; one who came from Toft, the name of several places in England.

Tokarz (*Pol.*) One who fashioned objects on a lathe, a turner.

Toland, Tolland (*Eng.*) One who came from Tolland (land on Tone River), in Somerset.

Tolbert, Tolbart (*Eng.*) Variants of Talbot, q.v.

Toler, Toller (*Eng.*) One who collected tolls at a tollgate, a tax collector.

Toliver, Tolliver (*It.*) One who cut iron, or a worker in iron.

Toll, Tolson (*Eng.*) Descendant of Toll, a pet form of Bartholomew (son of Talmai, furrow); dweller, or collector, at a tollhouse.

Tolman, Tollman (*Eng.*) The man who collected tolls, the keeper of a tollgate.

Toman (*Cz.-Sl.*) Descendant of Thomas (a twin).

Tomaszewski (*Pol.*) The son of Tomasz (a twin); one who came from Tomaszow (twin), in Poland.

Tomczak (*Pol.*) The son of Tom, a pet form of Tomasz (a twin).

Tomlinson, Tomlin (*Eng.*) The son of little Tom, a pet form of Thomas (a twin).

Tompkins, Tomkins, Tomkin (*Eng.*) Descendant of little Tom, a pet form of Thomas (a twin).

Tooley (*Eng., Ir.*) One who came from Tooley (lookout hill), in Leicestershire; descendant of Tuathal (people, mighty).

Toombs, Tomb (*Eng.*) Descendant of Tom, a pet form of Thomas (a twin).

Toomey, Tomey (*Ir.*) Grandson of Tuaim (a sound).

Toothaker (*Eng.*) Dweller at, or in, the lookout field.

Topel, Toppel (*Ger., Pol.*) Dweller near a poplar tree.

Topham (*Eng.*) Dweller at the upper, or highest, homestead.

Topol, Topolski (*Pol.*) Dweller near a poplar tree.

Topping (*Eng.*) Dweller at the upper meadow.

Torrence, Torrance (*Scot.*) One who came from Torrance (little hills), the name of places in Lanarkshire and Stirlingshire.

Torres (*Sp.*) Dweller at, or near, a tower or spire.

Torrey, Torry (*Scot., Eng.*) One who came from Torrie (hill), the name of places in Kincardineshire and Fife, or from Torry, in Aberdeen; descendant of Torry, a pet form of Theodoric (gift of God).

Toth (*Hun.*) The small one or tot.

Touhy, Toohey, Tuohy, Touhey, Tooey, Twohey (*Ir.*) Descendant of the sturdy man; grandson of Tuathach (rustic, or a lord).

Toussaint (*Fr.*) Descendant of Toussaint (all saints).

Tovar (*Sp.*) One who came from Tovar (quarry of soft, sandy stone), in Spain.

Tower, Towers (*Eng.*) Dweller in, or near, a high building; one who processed leather.

Towle, Towles (*Eng.*) A variant of Toll, q.v.

Towne, Towner, Town, Towns (*Eng.*) Dweller at the enclosure, homestead or manor.

Townsend (*Eng.*) Dweller at the outskirts of the village.

Toynbee (*Eng.*) Dweller at Teoda's homestead.

Tracy, Tracey, Treacy (*Eng.*) One who came from Tracy (terrace), in France.

Trainor, Treanor, Trainer (*Ir.*) The son of Treanfhear (strong man or champion).

Trapp, Trappe (*Eng.*) The short, stocky man; dweller near a footbridge.

Trask, Traske (*Eng.*) Dweller on, or near, a bog or marsh.

Traub, Traube (*Ger.*) Dweller near where grapes are grown; descendant of Trubo, a pet form of names beginning with Drud (power), as Drudbald and Drudpraht.

Trautman, Traut, Trautmann (*Ger.*) The dear, beloved servant.

Travers, Traver, Traverse (*Eng., Fr.*) Dweller at a crossroad.

Travis, Travise, Traviss (*Eng., Fr.*) Variants of Travers, q.v.

Traxler, Trachsler (*Ger.*) One who fashioned objects on a lathe, a turner.

Traynor (*Ir.*) The son of Treanfhear (strong man or champion).

Treadwell, Tredwell (*Eng.*) Dweller at a path, or road, by a spring or stream.

Treat (*Eng.*) The dear, beloved person.

Tremblay, Trembly, Trembley (*Eng.*) One who came from Trimley (Trymma's wood), in Suffolk.

Trent (*Eng.*) One who came from Trent (trespasser), in Dorset; one who lived on, or near, the Trent River in England.

Trevelyan (*Eng.*) Dweller at the mill homestead.

Tribble (*Eng.*) Descendant of Thrythbald (might, bold).

Trice, Triche (*Ger.*) One who made and sold little bells; dweller on, or near, a fallow field.

Trickett (*Fr.*) Descendant of little Trigg (true); one who carried a little cudgel.

Trimarco, Trimarchi (*It.*) One who came from Trimarco, in Italy.

Trimble, Tremble (*Eng.*) Dweller near an aspen tree.

Triplett, Triplet, Triplette (*Eng.*) One of three born at one birth, a triplet.

Tripp, Trippe (*Eng.*) One who took care of a flock of sheep or a herd of swine or goats.

Trojan (*Ger., Bel., Pol.*) Descendant of Trojan (from Troy, the settlement of the Tricasses); one who came from Trojan, in Germany; descendant of Trojan (one of three sons).

Trojanowski (*Pol.*) One who came from Trojano(w) (settlement of three brothers), in Poland.

Trombley, Trombly, Tromblay (*Eng.*) Variants of Tremblay, q.v.

Trost (*Ger.*) Descendant of Traostilo (helper).

Trott (*Eng.*) Descendant of Trott (defiance).

Trotter, Trottier, Troter, Trotier (*Eng., Scot., Fr.*) One who acted as a runner or messenger.

Trowbridge (*Eng.*) One who came from Trowbridge (wooden bridge), in Wiltshire.

Troy (*Eng.*) One who came from Troyes (from Gaulish tribe, the Tricassii), in France.

Trudeau (*Fr.*) Descendant of Trudeau, a pet form of Thorvald (Thor's power), also a pet form of Gertrude (spear, maiden).

True (*Eng.*) The faithful, loyal man.

Trueblood (*Eng.*) The true or loyal man.

Truesdale, Truesdell, Trusdell (*Eng.*) One who came from Trouts Dale (earlier spelling Trucedale, trout pool), in Yorkshire.

Truhlar (*Cz.-Sl.*) One who worked in wood, a carpenter.

Trujillo, Trujilo (*Sp.*) One who came from Trujillo (citadel of Julian), in Spain.

Truman, Trueman (*Eng.*) The faithful or loyal servant.

Trumbull, Trumble (*Eng.*) Descendant of Trumbald (strong, bold).

Trump, Trumpp (*Eng.*) Descendant of Trum (strong), a pet form of names beginning with Trum, such as Trumbald, Trumbeorht and Trumwine.

Trussell, Trusselle (*Eng.*) One who came from Trusley (wood with fallen leaves), in Derbyshire.

Tryder (*Eng., Du.*) Dweller in the oak hamlet; one who traveled.

Tschaikowsky, Tchaikovsky (*Rus.*) One who came from Czajkow(o), the name of many places in Poland and Russia.

Tschudi (*Swis.*) One who sat in judgment, a judge.

Tubbs (*Eng.*) One who made tubs, a cooper.

Tubelis (*Lith.*) Descendant of little Tobiosius or Tobijas (goodness of Jehovah).

Tuck (*Eng.*) Descendant of Tucca (to draw), or of Toke (people).

Tucker (*Eng.*) One who cleaned and thickened cloth.

Tuckerman, Tuckman (*Eng.*) One who assisted in cleaning and thickening cloth, the tucker's servant.

Tudor, Tudyr, Tewdwr (*Wel.*) Descendant of Tudor (gift of God) or Tudyr (country, tribe).

Tufo (*It.*) Dweller on, or near, soft, sandy stone.

Tufts, Tuff, Tuffs, Tuft, Tufte (*Eng.*) Dweller at a toft, a yard enclosing a residence.

Tuggle, Tuggles (*Eng.*) One who came from Tughall (Tucga's corner), in Northumberland.

Tully, Tulley (*Scot., Ir.*) One who came from Tullo, in Scotland, or Tully (small hill), in Ireland.

Tumas, Tumasonis (*Lith.*) Descendant of Tumas (a twin).

Tumulty, Tumelty (*Ir.*) The son, or grandson, of Tomaltach (large, bulky).

Tunney, Tunny (*Ir.*) Grandson of Tonnach (glittering).

Tupper (*Eng.*) One who bred tups or rams; one who made and sold tubs.

Turek (*Pol., Cz.-Sl.*) One who came from Turkey.

Turnbull, Trumble, Trumbull (*Scot.*) Descendant of Trumbald (strong, bold).

Turk (*Eng., Cz.-Sl., Yu.-Sl.*) One who came from Turkmen, now a Soviet Socialist Republic; one who came from Turkey.

Turner (*Eng.*) One who fashioned objects on a lathe.

Turney (*Ir., Eng.*) Grandson of Torna (a lord); one who came from Tournai, Tournay or Tourny (Tornus' estate), the names of places in Normandy.

Turtle (*Eng.*) One with some characteristic of the European wild dove, such as an affectionate disposition; the deformed or crippled man; descendant of Torquil (Thor's kettle).

Tuttle, Tuthill, Tutle, Toothill (*Eng.*) Dweller at a toot-hill, i.e., a hill with a good outlook to detect an enemy's approach; one who came from Tothill (lookout hill), the name of places in Lincolnshire and Middlesex.

Twaddle, Twaddell, Twadell (*Eng.*) Variants of Tweedale, q.v.

Tweedale, Tweeddle, Tweedle (*Scot.*) One who lived in, or near, the pasture dale; dweller in the valley of the Tweed (swelling), a British river; one who came from Tweedle (pasture dale), in Scotland.

Tweedie, Tweedy (*Scot.*) One who came from the lands of Tweedie (hemming in), in the parish of Stonehouse, Lanarkshire.

Twelvetrees (*Eng.*) Dweller in, or near, a clump of trees.

Twigg, Twiggs (*Eng.*) Descendant of Twicga (twig).

Twitchell, Twichell (*Eng.*) Dweller at an alley, or narrow passage, between houses; dweller at a bend in the road.

Twohig (*Ir.*) Grandson of Tuathach (rustic, or a lord).

Twombly (*Eng.*) One who came from Twemlow (by the two hills), in Cheshire.

Twomey, Tuomey (*Ir.*) Grandson of Tuaim (a sound).

Tye (*Eng.*) Dweller near the large common pasture or enclosure.

Tyler (*Eng.*) One who made or sold tiles, or who covered buildings with tiles.

Tyrrell, Tyrell (*Eng.*) Variants of Terrell, q.v.

Tyson (*Eng., Du.*) The son of Ty, a variant of Dye, a pet form of Dionysius (the Grecian god of wine); the son of Tys, a pet form of Matthias (gift of Jehovah); one who kindles strife or mischief.

Uberti (*It.*) The son of Hubert (spirit, bright).

Udell (*Eng.*) One who came from Yewdale (yew valley), in Lancashire.

Ullman, Ullmann, Ulman (*Ger.*) One who owned land in fee, i.e., without paying rent or acknowledging any superior; one who came from Ulm (place of elm trees), in Germany.

Ullrich, Ulrich, Ulreich, Ullrick (*Ger., Eng.*) Descendant of Ulrich (wolf, rule).

Umansky (*Rus., Ukr.*) One who came from Uman (the wise one's settlement), in Ukraine.

Umnov (*Rus.*) The son of the wise man.

Underhill (*Eng.*) Dweller under, or at the foot of, the hill.

Underwood (*Eng.*) One who came from Underwood (within a forest), the name of places in Derbyshire and Nottinghamshire; dweller within a wood.

Unger, Ungar (*Ger.*) One who came from Hungary (country of the Huns).

Unsworth (*Eng.*) One who came from Unsworth (Hund's homestead), in Lancashire.

Unthank (*Eng., Scot.*) One who came from Unthank (place settled without leave of the lord), the name of several places in England; one who came from Unthank (barren soil), a common farm name in Scotland.

Upchurch (*Eng.*) One who came from Upchurch (the higher or farther inland church), in Kent.

Updyke, Updike, Updyck (*Du.*) Dweller on the dike.

Upham (*Eng.*) Dweller at the homestead which was higher than another neighboring one.

Upjohn (*Wel.*) The son of John (gracious gift of Jehovah).

Upshaw (*Eng.*) Dweller at a grove or thicket above another, or up a stream.

Upton (*Eng.*) One who came from Upton (higher homestead or village), the name of many places in England.

Urba (*Cz.-Sl.*) Dweller at, or near, a willow tree.

Urban, Urbain (*Eng.*) Descendant of Urban (of the town).

Urbanek (*Pol.*) Descendant of little Urban (city).

Urbanski (*Pol.*) The son of Urban (city).

Urey, Urie (*Scot.*) One who came from Urie (abounding in yews), in Scotland.

Urquhart (*Scot.*) One who came from Urquhart (on a wood), the name of several places in Scotland.

Urso (*It.*) Dweller at the sign of the bear; one thought to possess some of the qualities of a bear, such as uncouthness, surliness, hirsuteness and dullness.

Usher (*Eng., Scot.*) A doorkeeper, one who kept the door of the king's apartment.

Utley (*Eng.*) One who came from Utley (outer wood or meadow), in Yorkshire; dweller at the outer meadow or wood.

Utter (*Sw.*) Otter.

Vaccaro, Vaccari, Vaccarello (*It.*) One who tended cows.

Vail, Vale (*Eng., Scot.*) Dweller in the valley.

Vaillant (*Fr.*) The courageous man.

Valente, Valenti (*It.*) The valiant or brave man.

Valentine, Vallentyne (*Eng.*) Descendant of Valentine (vigorous or healthy).

Valentino, Valentini (*It.*) Descendant of Valentino (vigorous or healthy).

Valkoinen (*Finn.*) The son of the light-complexioned man.

Valle, Vallee, Valley (*Fr.*) Dweller in a depression between ranges of hills or mountains.

Vana (*Rus.*) Descendant of Vanya, a pet form of Ivan (gracious gift of Jehovah).

van Brugge, Vanbrugh (*Du.*) One who lived at, or near, the bridge.

Van Buren (*Du.*) One who came from the neighborhood.

Van Camp (*Du.*) Dweller at, or in, the field.

Vance (*Eng., Du.*) Dweller near a small hill or burial mound; the son of Van.

Van Cleave, Van Cleve, Van Cleef, Van Clief (*Du.*) One who came from the city or duchy of Cleve (cliff), in West Germany; dweller near the cliff.

van Cortlandt (*Du.*) One who came from Cortlandt, a local district in Holland.

Van Dam, Van Damm, Van Damme (*Du.*) Dweller on, or near, the dam or dike.

Vanderbilt (*Du.*) Dweller at, or near, the heap or mound.

Vandermeer (*Du.*) Dweller at, or near, the lake.

Vanderploeg, Vanderplow (*Du.*) One who was formerly a plowman.

Vanderpool, Vanderpoel (*Du.*) Dweller near a pond.

Vandersteen (*Du.*) Dweller at, or near, the rock or stone, usually a boundary marker.

Vanderveen (*Du.*) Dweller near the peat bog.

Vanderveer (*Du.*) Dweller near the ferry; one who operated a ferry.

Vanderwoude (*Du.*) Dweller in, or near, a wood.

Van Devanter (*Du.*) One who came from Deventer, in Holland.

Van Dyke, Vandyck (*Du.*) Dweller on, or near, the dike.

Vanek (*Cz.-Sl.*) Descendant of Vanek, or little Van, pet forms of Ivan (gracious gift of Jehovah).

Van Gelder (*Du.*) One who came from the county of Gelder, in Holland.

van Hoek (*Du.*) Dweller in, or near, the spur, river bend or corner, referring to some natural feature.

Van Horn, Van Horne (*Du.*) One who came from Hoorn (the promontory), in Holland.

Vann, Van (*Eng.*) Dweller near the place where grain was threshed.

VanNess, VanNes, Van Ess (*Bel., Du.*) Dweller near, or on, the cape or headland; one who came from Nes (headland), the name of several villages in Holland; dweller near an ash tree.

van Patten (*Du.*) One who came from Putten (well or pool), in Holland.

Van Pelt (*Du.*) One who came from Pelt (the marshy place), in Holland.

van Rensselaer (*Du.*) One who came from Renselaer in Gelderland; dweller near a place frequented by deer.

Vansittart (*Du.*) The man from Sittard, a town in Holland.

Van Winkle, Van Winkel (*Du.*) One who worked, or lived, in a shop or store.

Vapaa (*Finn.*) The free man, i.e., one not owing allegiance to a lord.

Varg (*Sw.*) Wolf, a soldier name.

Varga (*Hun.*) One who made shoes, a shoemaker.

Vargas (*Sp., Port.*) One who came from Vargas (steep hill), the name of several places in Spain and Portugal.

Varley, Verley (*Eng., Ir.*) One who came from Verly, in France; the son of the sharp-eyed man.

Varney, Verney (*Eng.*) One who came from Vernay or Verney (alder grove), in France.

Vasquez (*Sp.*) One who came from the Basque country; one who tended ewes, a shepherd.

Vaughn, Vaughan (*Wel.*) Descendant of Vaughan (little).

Vedder (*Ger.*) The father's brother; one related to another, later, a male cousin.

Vega (*Sp.*) Dweller in the meadow.

Velasquez (*Sp.*) The sluggish, slow or weak person.

Venables, Venable (*Wel.*) One who came from Venables or Vignoles (vineyard), in France.

Ventura, Venturini (*It.*) Descendant of Ventura, a pet form of Buonaventura (good luck), or of Ventura, a name sometimes given to a deserted baby.

Verbrugge, Verbrughe, Verbrugghen, Verbruggen (*Du.*) Dweller at, or near, the bridge.

Verdier (*Fr.*) One who had charge of the forest for the lord, a gamekeeper.

Vergara (*It.*) One who tended animals, a herdsman.

Verge (*Eng., Fr.*) One who tilled a verge or yardland (from fifteen to thirty acres); one who had sworn fealty to his lord; dweller near a boundary.

Verner, Vernier, Verniere (*Fr., Eng.*) Descendant of Warinhari (protection, army).

Vernon (*Fr., Eng.*) One who came from Vernon (the alder grove), the name of several places in France.

Verry, Very, Verrey (*Eng.*) One who came from Verrey, Very or Verry (glassworks), the names of several places in France.

Vesely, Vessely, Vesley (*Eng., Rus., Ukr., Pol.*) Descendant of Vasily, a pet form of Basil (kingly); one who came from Vesly or Vezelay, in France; a joyous or happy fellow.

Vesey, Vessey, Veasey, Veazey (*Eng.*) One who came from Vessey (estate of Vitius), the name of places in Normandy and Burgundy.

Vetter (*Ger.*) The father's brother; one related to another, later, a male cousin.

Vick, Vicks (*Eng.*) One who came from Vicq (village), the name of various places in France.

Vickers (*Eng.*) Descendant of the vicar, an incumbent of a parish. *See* Vickery.

Vickery (*Eng.*) The priest of a parish who receives only the smaller tithes or a salary.

Victor (*Eng., Fr.*) Descendant of Victor (conqueror).

Viles (*Eng.*) Variant of Files, q.v.; the old man.

Villa (*Sp.*) Dweller on a large estate.

Villanueva (*Sp.*) One who came from Villanueva (the recently founded settlement), the name of several places in Spain.

Villarreal, Villareal (*Sp.*) One who came from Villareal (the royal estate), the name of several places in Spain.

Vincent (*Eng.*) Descendant of Vincent (conquering).

Vinci (*It.*) One who came from Vinci (enclosed place), in Italy.

Vines, Vine (*Eng.*) Dweller at a vine, or in, or near, a vineyard.

Vining, Vinning (*Eng.*) The son of Wine (friend); descendant of Wynning (pleasure).

Vinson, Vincson (*Eng., Fr.*) The son of Vin, a pet form of Vincent (conquering); descendant of Vincent.

Vinton (*Eng.*) One who came from Feniton (village by a boundary stream), in Devonshire.

Viola (*It.*) Descendant of Viola (violet); one who played a viol.

Virgin (*Eng.*) Dweller at, or near, a medieval image of the Virgin Mary; one who played the part of the Virgin in a play or pageant.

Visser, Vischer (*Du.*) One who caught, or sold, fish.

Vitale, Vitalo (*It.*) Descendant of Vitalis (relative to life), the name of ten martyrs in the early church.

Vivian (*Eng.*) Descendant of Vivian (animated).

Vlach, Vlachos (*Cz.-Sl.*) One who came from Italy (land of cattle).

Vlk (*Cz.-Sl.*) Dweller at the sign of the wolf; one with the qualities of a wolf.

Vogel, Vogl (*Ger., Du.*) Dweller at the sign of the bird; one with birdlike characteristics.

Vogler (*Ger.*) The birdcatcher or fowler.

Vogt, Voight, Voigt, Voit, Voigts (*Ger.*) The overseer or manager of a household, a steward.

Voisin (*Fr.*) One who came from an adjoining area.

Voke, Vokey (*Eng.*) Descendant of Foulk or Fulko (people).

Volk, Volke (*Ger.*) Descendant of Volk, a short form of names commencing with Volk (people), as Volkold, Folcmar and Fulculf.

Volkman, Volkmann (*Ger.*) Descendant of Folcman (people, servant).

Vollmer, Vollmar, Volmar, Volkmar (*Ger.*) Descendant of Folcmar (people, famous).

Volpe, Volpi (*It.*) Dweller at the sign of the fox; a cunning person; one with foxlike characteristics.

von der Tann (*Ger.*) Dweller near a pine tree.

von Feilitzen (*Ger.*) One who came from Feilitzsch, in Bavaria.

Voorhees, Voorhies, Voorheis (*Du.*) One who lived in front of Hess, a town in Gelderland.

Voros (*Hun.*) The red-haired or ruddy man.

Voroshilov (*Rus.*) One who stirs or tosses, a restless person.

Vose (*Eng.*) Dweller at, or near, a ditch.

Voss, Vos (*Du., Ger.*) One with foxlike characteristics; dweller at the sign of the fox.

Vrooman, Vroom, Vroman, Vromans (*Du.*) The pious, or wise, man.

Wachowski (*Pol.*) One who came from Wachow(e) (guard), in Poland.

Wachter (*Ger., Du.*) The watchman or guard.

Wacker (*Ger., Eng.*) Descendant of Wacar (vigilant); the active and energetic man.

Waddell, Waddle (*Scot., Eng.*) Dweller in the valley where woad grew; one who came from the parish of Waddel (valley where woad grows), in Midlothian; one who came from Wadley (Wada's wood or meadow), in Berkshire.

Waddington, Waddleton (*Eng.*) One who came from Waddington (homestead of Wada's people), in Yorkshire, or from Waddington (wheat hill), in Surrey.

Wade, Waide, Waid (*Eng.*) Dweller at the shallow river crossing or ford; descendant of Wada (to advance).

Wadley, Wadleigh (*Eng.*) One who came from Wadley (Wada's meadow), in Berkshire.

Wadsworth (*Eng.*) One who came from Wadsworth (Wada's homestead), in Yorkshire.

Wagg, Wagge (*Eng.*) Dweller near the quaking bog or marsh.

Wagner, Waggoner, Wagoner (*Eng., Ger.*) Driver of a wagon; one who made wagons, a cartwright.

Wagstaff (*Eng.*) Nickname given to an official who carried a wand or staff, such as the parish beadle.

Wahl (*Ger., Sw., Eng.*) Dweller at, or near, a wall; one who lived at, or near, a well or spring; one who lived at, or near, the pool or bog; dweller in a field.

Wahlgren, Walgren, Wallgren, Walgreen (*Sw.*) Field branch.

Wahlstrom (*Sw.*) Field stream.

Wainer, Wayner (*Eng.*) One who drove a wagon or cart, a carter.

Wainhouse (*Eng.*) Dweller at the house where wagons were made or stored.

Wainwright (*Eng.*) One who made wagons and carts.

Waite, Wait, Wayt (*Eng.*) The watchman or lookout, especially a watchman in a castle or fortified place.

Wakefield (*Eng.*) One who came from Wakefield (field where the festival plays were held), the name of several places in England.

Wakeman (*Eng.*) The watchman for a village, castle or fortified place.

Walcott (*Eng.*) One who came from Walcot (cottage of the serfs), the name of various places in England.

Walczak (*Pol.*) The son of Walek, a pet form of Walenty (valorous).

Wald, Walder (*Ger.*) Dweller near, or in, a forest; one who came from Wald (forest), in Germany.

Walden, Waldon (*Eng.*) One who came from Walden (the valley of the Britons), the name of several places in England; dweller in a forested valley; descendant of Walden (power, little).

Waldman, Waldmann (*Ger.*) One who took care of a forest for the lord; a gamekeeper.

Waldo (*Ger., Eng.*) Descendant of Waldo, a pet form of names beginning with Wald (forest), as Waldomar and Waldorad; descendant of Waldo, a pet form of Waltheof (power, thief).

Waldron (*Eng.*) One who came from Waldron (house in a wood), in Sussex.

Wales (*Eng.*) One who came from Wales (the Welsh), the country, or from Wales, a village in Yorkshire.

Walk, Walke (*Ger., Pol.*) Dweller at the sign of the wolf; one with the characteristics of a wolf; descendant of Walek, a pet form of Walerian (healthy).

Walker (*Eng.*) One who cleaned and thickened cloth, a fuller; one who came from Walker (marsh by the Roman wall), in Northumberland.

Walkowiak (*Pol.*) One who came from Walkow (battle place), in Poland.

Wall, Walls, Walle (*Eng.*) Dweller at, or near, a wall such as the old Roman wall; dweller at, or near, a spring or stream; one who came from Wall (on the Roman wall, or near a stream), the name of several places in England; dweller at, or near, a pool or bog.

Wallace, Wallis (*Scot.*) The foreigner or stranger; one who came from Wales (foreign).

Wallach, Wallack (*Ger.*) One who came from Wallach, in Germany; the stranger or foreigner.

Waller (*Eng.*) One who built walls; dweller at, or near, a wall, such as the old Roman wall.

Walley (*Eng.*) A variant of Whaley, q.v.

Wallin, Wallen, Wallins (*Sw.*) Dweller on, or near, a fallow field.

Walling (*Eng.*) The son of Wealh (foreigner).

Wallingford (*Eng.*) One who came from Wallingford (ford of Wealh's people), in Berkshire.

Wallner (*Ger.*) One who came from Wallen (forest), in Germany.

Walmsley (*Eng.*) One who came from Walmesley (lake by the wood), in Lancashire.

Walpole (*Eng.*) One who came from Walpole (pool by the wall, or pool of the Welsh), the name of places in Norfolk and Suffolk.

Walsh, Walshe (*Eng., Ir.*) One who came from Wales (foreign), a Welshman.

Walters, Walter (*Wel.*) Descendant of Walter (rule, army).

Walther, Walthers (*Ger.*) Descendant of Walthari (rule, army).

Walton (*Eng.*) One who came from Walton (homestead by a wall, homestead in a wood, or the serf's homestead), the name of many places in England.

Walz, Waltz (*Ger.*) Descendant of Walzo (to rule or manage).

Wanamaker, Wannamaker, Wannemacher (*Du.*) One who made baskets, particularly certain broad, shallow baskets.

Wang (*Chin.*) The prince; yellow.

Wantenaer (*Du.*) One who made and sold gloves.

Warburton (*Eng.*) One who came from Warburton (Waerburg's homestead), in Cheshire.

Ward, Warden, Warder (*Eng.*) The guard, keeper or watchman; dweller near a marsh.

Wardell (*Eng.*) One who came from Wardle (watch hill), the name of places in Cheshire and Lancashire.

Wardlow (*Eng.*) One who came from Wardlow (watch hill or slope), in Derbyshire.

Wardwell (*Eng.*) One who came from Wordwell (winding brook), in Suffolk.

Ware (*Eng.*) One who came from Ware (dam or fish trap), in Hertfordshire; dweller near the dam.

Wareham (*Eng.*) One who came from Wareham (homestead by a dam or fish trap), in Dorset.

Warfield (*Eng.*) One who came from Warfield (cleared land on the Wearne River), in Berkshire.

Waring, Wareing (*Eng.*) Descendant of Warin or Guarin (protection).

Wark (*Eng.*) One who came from Wark (fort), in Northumberland.

Warneke, Warnecke, Warneck, Warnicke (*Ger.*) Descendant of little Waro (protection), a pet form of names beginning with Warin, as Warinbold, Warengar and Werinhart.

Warner (*Eng.*) Descendant of Warner (protecting warrior); an officer employed to watch over the game in a park.

Warnock (*Eng.*) Descendant of little Warn or Warin (protection).

Warren, Warrin (*Eng.*) Dweller at, or keeper of, a game preserve; descendant of Warren, from Old French, Warin (protection).

Warrick (*Eng.*) A variant of Warwick, q.v.

Warrington (*Eng.*) One who came from Warrington (homestead at a dam or fish trap), in Lancashire.

Warsaw, Warshaw, Warshauer, Warshawer (*Pol.*) One who came from Warsaw (the fortified place).

Warshawsky, Warsawsky (*Rus., Pol.*) One who came from Warszawa (the fortified place), the capital of Poland.

Warwick (*Eng.*) One who came from Warwick (farm by a dam or fish trap, or on the bank), the name of places in Warwickshire and Cumberland.

Washburn, Washburne (*Eng.*) One who came from Washburn (fuller's stream), in Yorkshire, or from Washbourne (stream where washing was done, or the Wash River), in Devonshire and Gloucestershire.

Washer, Wascher (*Eng., Ger.*) One who washed, especially one who washed or bleached flax and wool fibers, and finished cloth.

Washington (*Eng.*) One who came from Washington (the homestead of Wassa's people, or the manor of the Wessyng family), the name of places in Durham and Sussex. The name has been adopted by many Negroes.

Wasielewski (*Pol.*) The son of Basyl or Wasyl (kingly).

Wasik (*Pol.*) One who had a small mustache.

Waskey (*Ukr.*) The heavy or fat man.

Wass, Was (*Eng., Ger.*) One who came from Wass (swamp), in Yorkshire; dweller in, or near, a swamp; descendant of Was (sharp), or of Vad (strife).

Wasserman, Wassermann (*Ger.*) One who worked on the water, a seaman.

Wasson, Wason (*Eng., Sw., Ger.*) Descendant of little Waso or Wasso (sharp), or of little Wace (watchful); the son of Waso or Wace; the son of one who came from Wasa, a province in Finland; descendant of Waso, a pet form of names commencing with Was (sharp), as Hwasmot.

Waterbury (*Eng.*) One who came from Waterperry (pear tree by a stream), in Oxfordshire.

Waterford (*Eng.*) One who came from Watford (ford where woad grew), the name of places in Hertfordshire and Northamptonshire.

Waterhouse (*Eng.*) Dweller in the house by the lake or stream.

Waterloo (*Bel.*) One who came from Waterloo (settlement near water), in Belgium.

Waterman (*Eng.*) One who operated a boat, especially a ferryman.

Waters, Watters, Watterson (*Wel., Eng.*) Descendant of Walter (rule, folk), the early pronunciation of the name; dweller near the stream or lake.

Watkins, Watkin (*Wel., Eng.*) Descendant of little Wat, a pet form of Walter (rule, folk).

Watland (*Nor.*) Dweller on land near the water.

Watman (*Eng.*) Descendant of Whatman (behold, man).

Watmough (*Eng.*) The brother-in-law of Wat, pet form of Walter (rule, folk).

Watson (*Eng.*) The son of Wat, a pet form of Walter (rule, folk).

Watts, Watt, Watte (*Eng.*) Descendant of Wat, a pet form of Walter (rule, folk).

Waugh (*Scot.*) Dweller at, or near, the wall.

Wavell (*Eng.*) One who came from Vauville, in France.

Wawrzyniak (*Pol.*) The son of Wawrzyn or Wawrzyniec (laurel, symbol of victory).

Wax, Wacks, Wachs (*Ger.*) One who dealt with wax; descendant of Waccho, a pet form of names beginning with

Wachen (watch), as Wachari and Wacold; descendant of Waso (sharp).

Waxman (*Eng.*) One who gathered and sold wax.

Way, Weyer (*Eng.*) Dweller at the path or road.

Wayne, Wain, Waine (*Eng.*) Dweller at the sign of the wagon.

Weakley, Weakly (*Eng.*) Variants of Weekley, q.v.

Weatherall (*Eng.*) One who came from Wetheral (enclosure where sheep were kept), in Cumberland.

Weatherby, Weathersby, Weatherbee (*Eng.*) One who came from Wetherby (sheep farm), in Yorkshire.

Weatherford (*Eng.*) Dweller at, or near, a stream crossing used by wethers, i.e., castrated rams or sheep.

Weatherley (*Eng.*) Dweller near the meadow, or wood, where sheep were kept.

Weathers, Wethers (*Eng.*) One who tended wethers or sheep, a shepherd.

Weatherspoon, Wetherspoon, Wedderspoon (*Scot., Eng.*) Dweller at, or near, the wether or sheep enclosure.

Weaver (*Eng.*) One who wove cloth; dweller near the Weaver (winding river), a river in Cheshire.

Webb, Webbe (*Eng.*) One who wove cloth, either a male or a female.

Weber, Webster, Webber (*Eng., Ger.*) One who wove cloth.

Weddington (*Eng.*) One who came from Weddington (wet homestead), in Warwickshire.

Weddleton (*Eng.*) One who came from Widdington (homestead by the wood), in Yorkshire.

Wedel, Wedell, Weddle (*Eng.*) Descendant of Wedel (to move); dweller at Wada's hill; one who came from Wadley (Wada's wood or meadow), in Berkshire.

Wedge (*Eng.*) One who acted as pledge or surety for another.

Wedgewood (*Eng.*) One who came from Wedgwood (guarded wood), in Staffordshire.

Wedlock, Wedlake (*Eng.*) One who gave a gift in pledge of marriage.

Weed (*Ger., Eng.*) Descendant of Wido, a pet form of names beginning with Wid (forest), as Widwalt and Widulf; dweller in, or near, a weedy place.

Weeden, Weedon (*Eng.*) One who came from Weedon (temple on a hill), in Buckinghamshire.

Weekley (*Eng.*) One who came from Weekley (wych-elm wood), in Northamptonshire.

Weeks, Weaks, Weekes, Weeke (*Eng.*) Dweller at the dairy farm; one who came from Week (dairy farm), the name of several places in England.

Weems (*Scot.*) One who came from the lands of Wemyss (caves), pronounced Weems, in Fifeshire.

Weglarz (*Pol.*) One who dealt with coal.

Wegner, Wegener (*Ger.*) One who made wagons, a cartwright; dweller near a path.

Wegrzyn (*Pol.*) One who came from Wegry, i.e., a Hungarian.

Weidman, Weidmann, Weidemann, Weideman (*Ger.*) One who hunted game, a huntsman.

Weidner (*Ger.*) One who hunted game, a huntsman; dweller on, or near, a pasture; one who came from Weidenau (pasture land), in Germany.

Weil, Weiler, Weill, Weiller (*Ger.*) One who came from Weil (house), in Wurttemberg.

Weiland (*Ger., Du.*) One who came from Weilen (hamlet), in Germany; a variant of Wieland, q.v.; dweller in the meadow.

Weimer, Weimar (*Ger.*) One who came from Weimar (soft swamp), in Thuringia; descendant of Wigmar (fight or sanctify, famous); dweller on, or near, church property.

Wein (*Ger.*) One who made and sold wine.

Weinberg, Weinberger (*Ger., Swis.*) One who came from Weinberg or Weinberge (grape mountain), the name of many places in Germany and Switzerland; dweller at, or near, a vineyard.

Weiner (*Ger.*) Descendant of Winiheri (friend, army); one who made and sold wine; one who came from Weine or Weiner, in Germany; one who made and sold wagons or carts.

Weinert (*Ger.*) Descendant of Winihart (friend, strong); one who made and sold wagons or carts.

Weingart, Weingarten, Weingartner (*Ger.*) One who came from Weingarten (vineyard), the name of many places in Germany; one who lived in, or near, a vineyard.

Weinman, Weinmann (*Ger.*) One who sold or dispensed wine; one who made and sold wagons or carts.

Weinstein (*Ger.*) Wine stone.

Weinstock (*Ger.*) Dweller near a large or unusual grapevine.

Weintraub, Weintrob, Weintroub (*Ger.*) One who grew, or handled, grapes.

Weir (*Eng.*) Dweller near a dam or fish trap.

Weisberg, Weissberg, Weisberger (*Ger., Cz.-Sl.*) One who came from Weisserberg (white mountain), the name of places in Germany and Czechoslovakia; dweller on, or near, a white hill.

Weise (*Ger.*) Descendant of Weise (wisdom); the learned person; one who had no parents, an orphan; descendant of Wizo (see Weitz).

Weiser (*Ger.*) One who came from Weis (white), in Germany; descendant of Wisheri (wise, army); a learned man; one who whitewashed walls.

Weishaar, Weishar (*Ger.*) One who had white hair.

Weiskopf, Weisskopf, Weishaupt (*Ger.*) One with a white head, i.e., white hair.

Weisman, Weismann, Weiseman (*Ger.*) The wise or learned man; descendant of Wisman (wise, man).

Weiss, Weis (*Ger.*) One who came from Weis (white), in Germany; the light-complexioned or white-haired man; variants of Weitz, q.v.

Weissman, Weissmann (*Ger.*) The light-complexioned or white-haired man.

Weitz, Weitzel (*Ger.*) Descendant of Wizo, a pet form of names beginning with Wid (forest), as Witbald and Wittimar, or with Wig (fight or sanctify), as Wigibald and Wigbrand.

Weitzman, Weitzmann (*Ger.*) Same as Weitz, q.v.

Welby (*Eng.*) One who came from Welby (village by a stream), in Lincolnshire.

Welch (*Eng.*) One who came from Wales (foreign), a Welshman.

Welcome (*Eng.*) One who came from Welcombe (valley with a stream), in Devonshire.

Weld (*Eng.*) One who came from Weald (woodland), the name of several places in England; dweller at a woodland.

Weldon, Weldin (*Eng.*) One who came from Weldon (hill by a stream), in Northamptonshire.

Weller (*Eng.*) One who boils, probably a saltboiler, or one who casts metal; dweller at the spring or well.

Wellington (*Eng.*) One who came from Wellington (village of the heathen temple in a glade), the name of several places in England.

Wellman (*Eng.*) Dweller at the spring or well.

Wells, Well, Welle (*Eng.*) Dweller at, or near, the spring or stream; one who came from Well (spring or stream), the name of several places in England.

Welsh, Welsch (*Eng.*) One who came from Wales (foreign), a Welshman.

Welter, Welther (*Ger.*) Variants of Walter, q.v.; one who came from Welte (border), in Germany.

Welton (*Eng.*) One who came from Welton (homestead by a stream or on the Welve River), the name of various places in England.

Wendell, Wendel (*Ger.*) Descendant of little Wendimar (wander, famous).

Wendorf, Wendorff (*Ger.*) One who came from Wendorf (village of the Wends), in Germany.

Wendt (*Ger.*) One who came from the Wends, a Slavic tribe of eastern Germany.

Wenig, Weniger (*Ger.*) The short or small man.

Wentworth (*Eng.*) One who came from Wentworth (Wintra's homestead), the name of places in Cambridgeshire and Yorkshire.

Wenzel (*Ger.*) Descendant of Wenceslaw (wreath, fame).

Werckmeister (*Ger.*) One who supervises the work of others, a foreman.

Werkman (*Eng.*) One who worked so many days a week for the lord of the manor in return for the land he held.

Werner (*Ger.*) Descendant of Warinhari (protection, army).

Wernick, Wernicke, Wernecke (*Ger.*) Variants of Warneke, q.v.

Werth, Wert (*Ger.*) Descendant of Wirth, a pet form of names beginning with Wert (worth), as Werdheri or Werdmann.

Wertheimer, Wertheim, Werthimer (*Ger.*) One who came from Wertheim (river island place), the name of several towns in Germany.

Wesebaum (*Ger.*) Dweller at, or near, the meadow tree.

Weslager, Wellslager (*Ger.*) Corruption of Wollschlager, one who prepared wool for manufacture into cloth.

Wesley (*Eng.*) One who came from Westleigh or Westley (western glade), the name of several places in England.

Wesolowski (*Pol.*) One who came from Wesolow (gay), in Poland.

Wessel, Wessels, Wessells, Wessell (*Ger.*) One who came from Wesel, in Germany; descendant of little Varin, a pet form of names beginning with Warin (protector), as Warinbert and Warinhari.

West (*Eng.*) One who came from the west, a west countryman.

Westberg (*Eng.*) One who came from Westborough (western fort), in Lincolnshire.

Westbrook (*Eng.*) One who came from Westbrook (western brook), the name of several places in England.

Westcott, Wescott, Westcot (*Eng.*) One who came from Westcot (western cottage), the name of several places in England; dweller at the western cottage.

Westerberg (*Sw.*) Western mountain.

Westervelt (*Du.*) Dweller in, or near, the west field.

Westgate (*Eng.*) One who came from Westgate (west gate), the name of several places in England.

Westlake (*Eng.*) Dweller at, or near, the west stream or pool.

Westlund (*Sw.*) West grove.

Westman, Westerman (*Eng.*) The man who came from the west.

Weston (*Eng.*) One who lived in the western homestead.

Westphal, Westfall, Westfal, Westphalen (*Ger.*) One who came from Westphalen (western plain), in Germany.

Wetherby, Wetherbee (*Eng.*) One who came from Wetherby (sheep farm), in Yorkshire.

Wetherell, Wetherill, Wetherall, Wetherald (*Eng.*) One who came from Wetheral (enclosure where sheep were kept), in Cumberland; dweller near an enclosure where sheep were kept.

Wetmore (*Eng.*) One who came from Wetmoor (lake by a river bend), in Staffordshire.

Wetzel, Wetzell (*Ger.*) Descendant of little Varin, a pet form of names beginning with Warin (protector), as Warinbert and Warinhari.

Wexler, Wechsler (*Ger.*) One who was a banker or money changer.

Whalen, Whalin, Whalon (*Ir.*) Grandson of Faolan (little wolf).

Whaley, Whalley (*Eng.*) One who came from Whaley (meadow by a road or hill), the name of places in Cheshire and Derbyshire.

Wham, Whan (*Eng., Scot.*) Dweller at a corner or at a morass; one who came from Wham (cave), in Scotland.

Wharton (*Eng.*) One who came from Wharton (homestead on Weaver River, or on an embankment), the name of several places in England.

Wheat (*Eng.*) The light-complexioned or white-haired man; a variant of Waite, q.v.

Wheatley (*Eng.*) One who came from Wheatley (open place where wheat was grown), the name of several places in England.

Wheaton (*Eng.*) One who came from Wheaton (homestead where wheat was grown), in Staffordshire.

Whedon (*Eng.*) One who came from Wheddon (wheat hill or valley), in Somerset.

Wheeler, Wheler (*Eng.*) One who made wheels and wheeled vehicles.

Wheelock (*Eng.*) One who came from Wheelock (winding), in Cheshire; dweller near the Wheelock River.

Wheelwright (*Eng.*) One who made wheels and wheeled vehicles.

Whelan, Wheland (*Ir.*) Grandson of Faolan (little wolf).

Whelpley (*Eng.*) The wood frequented by cubs or young animals.

Whelton (*Eng.*) One who came from Wheelton (homestead with a water wheel), in Lancashire.

Whidden, Whiddon (*Eng.*) One who came from Wheddon (wheat hill or valley), in Somerset.

Whipple (*Eng.*) One who came from Whimple (white stream), in Devonshire.

Whistler (*Eng.*) One who whistled or blew a pipe.

Whiston (*Eng.*) One who came from Whiston (white stone, or Hwit's homestead), the name of several places in England.

Whitacre (*Eng.*) One who came from Whitacre (white field), in Warwickshire; dweller at the white field.

Whitaker, Whittaker (*Eng.*) Dweller at, or in, the white field.

Whitcher (*Eng.*) One who made whitches, i.e., chests and coffers.

Whitcomb (*Eng.*) One who came from Whitcombe (wide valley), the name of places in Dorset and Wiltshire.

White (*Eng.*) The light or fair-complexioned person, or one with white hair; descendant of Hwita (white).

Whitehead (*Eng.*) One with a white head, i.e., white hair.

Whitehouse (*Eng.*) Dweller in, or near, a white house.

Whiteside (*Eng.*) Dweller on the white side (of a hill, valley, etc.).

Whitfield (*Eng.*) One who came from Whitfield (white field), the name of several places in England.

Whitford (*Eng.*) One who came from Whitford (white ford), in Devonshire.

Whitham (*Eng.*) Dweller at the white homestead; one who came from Whitwham (white valley or corner), in Northumberland.

Whiting (*Eng.*) Descendant of Whiting (Hwita's son); dweller at the white meadow.

Whitley, Whitely (*Eng.*) One who came from Whitleigh (white wood), the name of several places in England.

Whitlock, Whitelock (*Eng.*) One who had white hair; dweller at, or near, the white enclosure.

Whitman, Whiteman (*Eng.*) The light-complexioned or white-haired man.

Whitmarsh (*Eng.*) Dweller in, or near, the white marsh or bog.

Whitmore, Whittemore (*Eng.*) One who came from Whitmore (white moor), in Staffordshire.

Whitney (*Eng.*) One who came from Whitney (Hwita's island or white island), in Herefordshire.

Whitten, Whitton (*Eng.*) One who came from Whitton (Hwita's homestead or white homestead), the name of several places in England.

Whittier (*Eng.*) One who prepared white leather; one who came from

Whitacre (white field), in Warwickshire.

Whittington (*Eng.*) One who came from Whittington (homestead of Hwita's people), the name of several places in England.

Whittle (*Eng.*) One who came from Whittle (white hill), the name of several places in England.

Whitton (*Eng.*) One who came from Whitton (Hwita's homestead or the white homestead), the name of various places in England.

Whittredge, Whittridge (*Eng.*) Dweller at, or near, a white ridge or range of hills.

Whitty, Whitey (*Eng.*) Dweller at the white enclosure.

Whitworth (*Eng.*) One who came from Whitworth (Hwita's homestead), the name of places in Durham and Lancashire.

Wholley, Wholly, Whooley (*Ir.*) Grandson of Uallac (proud).

Whynot, Whynott, Whynaught (*Fr.*) Descendant of little Guyon (little wood).

Whyte (*Eng.*) Variant of White, q.v.

Wich, Wiche (*Eng.*) Dweller by the wych-elm tree; dweller at, or near, a salt spring.

Wick, Wicker, Wicke (*Eng.*) Dweller at the dairy farm; one who came from Wick (dairy farm), the name of several places in England.

Wickham, Wickum, Wickhem (*Eng.*) One who came from Wickham (manor or dwelling place, or homestead with a dairy farm), the name of various places in England.

Wicklund (*Sw.*) Bay grove.

Wickman (*Eng.*) One who worked on a dairy farm.

Wicks, Wickes, Wix (*Eng.*) The son of little Wilk, a pet form of William (resolution, helmet); variants of Wick, q.v.; one who came from Wix (dairy farms), in Essex.

Wickstrom, Wikstrom (*Sw.*) Bay stream.

Widdicomb, Widdicombe (*Eng.*) One who came from Widdicombe (willow valley), in Devonshire.

Wideman, Widman, Widmann (*Ger.*) Descendant of Widiman (forest, man); one who took care of church property.

Widen, Widden (*Eng.*) Dweller in the broad valley; one who came from Weedon (hill with a temple), the name of several places in England.

Widmeyer, Widmer, Witmeyer (*Ger.*) One who worked a farm, the products of which went to the support of a church.

Wieczorek (*Pol.*) One who engaged in some activity in the early evening.

Wiegel, Wiegele (*Ger.*) Descendant of Wigilo, a pet form of names beginning with Wig (fight or sancitfy), as Wigold, Wigland and Wigheri.

Wieland (*Ger.*) Descendant of Wieland or Wayland (work by hand), the fabled smith.

Wielgus (*Pol.*) The large, husky man.

Wiencek (*Pol.*) Descendant of Wiencek, a pet form of Wiencyslaw (more glorious than his parents).

Wiener (*Ger.*) One who came from Wien (Vienna), in Austria.

Wierzbicki (*Pol.*) Dweller near a willow tree.

Wiese (*Ger.*) Dweller in, or near, a meadow.

Wiggins, Wiggin (*Eng.*) Descendant of little Wicga (warrior), or of Wigan or Wygan (warrior); one who came from Wigan (Wigan's homestead), in Lancashire; dweller by a mountain ash.

Wigginton (*Eng.*) One who came from Wigginton (Wicga's village), the name of several places in England.

Wigglesworth (*Eng.*) One who came from Wigglesworth (Wincel's homestead), in Yorkshire.

Wight (*Eng.*) One who came from the Isle of Wight (that which has been raised), part of the former county of Hampshire.

Wightman (*Scot., Eng.*) The agile or strong man; the man from Wight, q.v.

Wigmore (*Eng.*) One who came from Wigmore (Wicga's waste land), in Herefordshire.

Wilbur, Wilber (*Eng.*) Descendant of Wilburh or Wilburg (beloved, stronghold), a woman's name.

Wilburn, Wilborn, Wilbourn, Wilborne (*Eng.*) One who came from Welborne (brook coming from a spring), the name of several places in England.

Wilcox, Willcox (*Eng.*) Descendant of little Will, a pet form of William (resolution, helmet).

Wilczak, Wilczek (*Pol.*) Dweller at the sign of the little wolf; one thought to have some characteristic of a little wolf.

Wilde, Wild (*Eng.*) One who came from Wild or Wyld (trick), in Berkshire; dweller on a wasteland.

Wilder (*Eng.*) Dweller in a forest; descendant of Wealdhere (powerful, army).

Wildsmith, Waldsmith, Walsmith (*Ger.*) The smith, the worker in metals, who lived and worked in the forest.

Wiley (*Eng.*) Dweller near a trap or mill; dweller near the Wylye or Wiley (tricky river), a river in Wiltshire; one who came from Wylye, in Wiltshire.

Wilhelm (*Ger.*) Descendant of Wilhelm (resolution, helmet).

Wilke, Wilk, Wilkes, Wilks (*Eng.*) Shortened forms of Wilkins, q.v.

Wilkie, Wilkey (*Scot., Eng.*) Descendant of little Wilk, a shortened form of Wilkins, q.v.

Wilkins, Wilkinson, Wilkerson, Wilkens, Wilkin, Wilken (*Eng.*) The son of little Will, a pet form of William (resolution, helmet).

Will (*Eng.*) Descendant of Will, a pet form of William (resolution, helmet), or of Willa (will); dweller at, or near, a spring or stream.

Willard (*Eng.*) Descendant of Wilhead (resolute, brave).

Wille (*Ger., Eng.*) Descendant of Wille (resolution), or of Willo, a pet form of names beginning with Wille, as Willifrid, Willibrand and Willimod.

Willeke, Willecke (*Ger.*) Descendant of little Willo, a pet form of names beginning with Wille (resolution), as Willifrid, Williger and Willamar.

Willer (*Eng., Ger.*) Descendant of Wilhere (desire, army), or of Williheri (resolution, army); dweller at, or near, a spring or stream.

Willett, Willet, Willette (*Eng.*) Descendant of little Will, a pet form of William (resolution, helmet); dweller near the Willett (stream), a river in

Somerset; one who came from Willet, a village in Somerset.

William (*Eng.*) Descendant of William (resolution, helmet).

Williams, Williamson (*Wel., Eng.*) The son of William (resolution, helmet).

Willie, Willey (*Eng.*) Descendant of little Will, a pet form of William (resolution, helmet).

Willing, Willin, Willings (*Eng.*) Descendant of little Will, a pet form of William (resolution, helmet).

Willis, Willison (*Eng.*) The son of Will, a pet form of William (resolution, helmet).

Williston (*Eng.*) One who came from Willaston (Wiglaf's homestead), in Cheshire.

Willoughby (*Eng.*) One who came from Willoughby (homestead among willows), the name of various places in England.

Wills (*Eng.*) The son of Will, a pet form of William (resolution, helmet).

Wilmot, Wilmoth (*Fr.*) Descendant of little Will, a pet form of Guillaume (resolution, helmet).

Wilson, Willson (*Eng., Scot.*) The son of Will, pet form of William (resolution, helmet).

Wilt, Wiltz (*Ger.*) Descendant of Willihard (resolution, brave).

Wilton (*Eng.*) One who came from Wilton (homestead among willows, or by a well), the name of several places in England.

Wimberly, Wimberley, Wimbley (*Eng.*) One who came from Wimboldsley (Wynbald's wood), in Cheshire.

Wimmer (*Ger.*) One who tended the vines in a vineyard; one who took care of church property; descendant of Winimar (friend, famous).

Winandy, Winand (*Ger., Du.*) Descendant of Wignand (combat, venture).

Winchell, Winchel (*Eng.*) Descendant of Wincel (child); dweller by a corner or nook.

Winchester (*Eng.*) One who came from Winchester (Roman fort of Wintan), in Hampshire.

Wind, Winde (*Eng.*) Dweller on the narrow street or passage turning off from the main thoroughfare.

Windham (*Eng.*) One who came from Wenham (meadow homestead), in Suffolk.

Windmiller, Windmueller (*Ger.*) One who owned, or dwelt by, a windmill.

Windsor, Winsor (*Eng.*) One who came from Windsor or Winsor (landing place with a windlass), the names of several places in England.

Winer (*Ger.*) One who came from Wien, in Austria; one who dealt in wines.

Winfield (*Eng.*) One who came from Wingfield (grazing ground), in Derbyshire.

Wing, Winge (*Chin., Eng.*) Warm; one who came from Wing (Weohthun's people, or field), the name of places in Buckinghamshire and Rutland; descendant of Winge (protector).

Wingard (*Eng.*) Dweller at, or near, a vineyard.

Wingate (*Eng.*) One who came from Wingate (pass where wind rushes through), in Durham.

Wingfield (*Eng.*) One who came from Wingfield (grazing ground, or field of Wiga's people), the name of various places in England.

Winkler, Winkelman, Winkel, Winkle, Winkelmann, Winkleman (*Ger., Du.*) Dweller on land enclosed by mountains or woods; one who came from Winkel (corner); one who operated a small shop.

Winn (*Eng.*) Dweller at a meadow or pasture.

Winship (*Eng.*) One who played the part of Friendship in the medieval pageants; dweller in a wine valley.

Winslow, Winsloe (*Eng.*) One who came from Winslow (Wine's burial mound), in Buckinghamshire.

Winston (*Eng.*) One who came from Winston (Wine's or Winec's homestead), the name of several places in England.

Winter, Winters (*Eng., Ger.*) Descendant of Winter (name given to one born during the winter); dweller at the white water; descendant of Winidhari (wind, army); one who dealt in wine.

Winterbottom, Winterbotham (*Eng.*) Dweller at the valley or hollow used by shepherds for shelter in the winter.

Winthrop (*Eng.*) One who came from Winthorpe (Wina's, or Wigmund's, dairy farm), the name of places in Lincolnshire and Nottinghamshire.

Winton (*Eng.*) One who came from Winton (grazing farm, Wina's homestead, or homestead with willows), the name of several places in England.

Wirth (*Eng., Ger.*) One who came from Worth (enclosure), the name of several places in England; one who acted as host in a tavern or inn.

Wirtz, Wirt, Wirz (*Ger.*) One who acted as host in a tavern or inn.

Wise (*Eng., Scot., Ger.*) The sage or learned man; dweller by a stream or marshy meadow.

Wiseman, Wisman (*Eng., Scot.*) A learned man; one who practiced magic arts; one who played the part of one of the Wise Men of the East in the Candlemas pageant.

Wish, Wisher (*Eng.*) Dweller at, or near, a marsh.

Wisner, Wissner (*Ger.*) One who came from Wissen (white sand), in Germany; dweller on, or near, a meadow.

Wisniewski (*Pol.*) One who came from Wisznia (cherry tree), in Poland.

Wiswall, Wiswell (*Eng.*) One who came from Wiswell (Wissey River), in Lancashire.

Witcher, Wicher (*Eng.*) Dweller by the wych-elm tree; dweller at, or near, a salt spring.

Witek (*Pol.*) Descendant of Witek, a pet form of Witosz or Witold (with rule).

Witham (*Eng.*) One who came from Witham (Wita's homestead), the name of several places in England; dweller near the Witham (forest river), a river in England.

Withee, Withey (*Eng.*) Dweller at a willow tree.

Witherell (*Eng.*) A variant of Wetherell, q.v.

Withers (*Eng.*) Dweller at the sign of the ram.

Witherspoon (*Eng.*) A variant of Weatherspoon, q.v.

Withington (*Eng.*) One who came from Withington (homestead among willows), the name of several places in England.

Withrow, Witherow (*Eng.*) Dweller at a lane through the willow trees.

Withycombe (*Eng.*) One who came from Withycombe (willow valley), the name of places in Devonshire and Somerset.

Witkowski (*Pol.*) The son of Witek, a pet form of Witold (with rule).

Witt, Witte, Witty (*Du., Ger.*) The light-haired or light-complexioned man.

Witten, Witton (*Eng.*) One who came from Witton (homestead by a village, or wood), the name of many places in England.

Wittenberg, Wittenberger (*Ger.*) One who came from Wittenberg (white mountain), in Germany.

Witz, Witzel (*Ger.*) Variants of Weitz, q.v.

Wnek (*Cz.-Sl.*) Grandson, probably a shortened form of a longer name; one associated with his grandfather.

Wodrich, Wodrick (*Ger.*) Descendant of Wodrich or Wodaricus (battle rage, king).

Wojciech (*Pol.*) Descendant of Wojciech (noble, bright). The name is common due to Voitech, a popular Czech missionary who converted Poland to Christianity.

Wojciechowicz (*Pol.*) The son of Wojciech, q.v.

Wojceichowski (*Pol.*) One who came from Wojciechow, in Poland. *See* Wojceich.

Wojcik (*Pol.*) Descendant of little Wojciech (noble, bright).

Wojtas (*Pol., Lith.*) Descendant of large Wojciech (noble, bright).

Wojtowicz (*Pol., Ukr.*) The son of the mayor (of a village).

Wolcott (*Eng.*) One who came from Woolscott (Wulfsige's cottage), in Warwickshire.

Wold (*Eng.*) Dweller at, or in, the wold or forest.

Wolf, Wolff, Wolfe (*Eng., Ger.*) Dweller at the sign of the wolf; one with the characteristics of a wolf; descendant of Vulf, a pet form of names beginning with Wolf (wolf), as Wolfbrand, Wolfgang and Wolfgard.

Wolfeschlegelsteinhausenbergerdorff (*Ger.*) Descendant of Wolfeschlegelstein (one who prepared wool for manufacture on a stone), of the house of Bergerdorf (mountain village). (Found in the Philadelphia telephone directory.)

Wolford (*Eng.*) One who came from Wolford (enclosure protected from wolves), in Warwickshire.

Wolfson, Wolfsohn (*Eng., Ger.*) The son of Wolf (wolf), or of Wolf, a pet form of one of the many names beginning with Wolf.

Wolin (*Pol.*) One who came from Volhynia (the plain), in Poland.

Wolk, Wolke (*Ger.*) Dweller at the sign of the wolf; one with the characteristics of a wolf.

Woll, Woller (*Eng.*) Dweller at, or near, a wall.

Wollack, Wollak (*Rom.*) One who came from Wallachia (the stranger's land), a district in Romania.

Wolski (*Pol.*) One who came from Wola (liberty), in Poland.

Wolter, Wolters (*Eng.*) Descendant of Walter (rule, folk).

Wong (*Chin., Eng.*) Wide (sea or ocean); a variant of Wang, q.v.; dweller in, or near, a field or meadow.

Wood, Woods (*Eng.*) Dweller in, or near, a grove or dense growth of trees.

Woodall (*Eng.*) One who came from Woodale (wolves' valley), in Yorkshire; dweller at the hall by the wood.

Woodard (*Eng.*) Variant of Woodward, q.v.; descendant of Wodard (wood, hard).

Woodbridge (*Eng.*) One who came from Woodbridge (wooden bridge), in Suffolk; dweller at, or near, a wooden bridge.

Woodbury, Woodberry (*Eng.*) One who came from Woodbury or Woodborough (fort built of wood, or in a wood), the names of several places in England.

Wooden (*Eng.*) Dweller at the end of the wood.

Woodfall (*Eng.*) One who came from Woodfall (wood where trees are down), in Lancashire.

Woodford (*Eng.*) One who came from Woodford (ford by a wood), the name of various places in England.

Woodfork, Woodforks (*Eng.*) Variants of Woodford, q.v.

Woodhouse (*Eng.*) Dweller in the house in, or by, a wood.

Wooding, Woodin (*Eng.*) Dweller at a clearing or place where wood has been cut.

Woodland (*Eng.*) One who came from Woodland (wooded land), the name of several places in England.

Woodley, Woodle (*Eng.*) One who came from Woodleigh (glade in a wood), in Devonshire.

Woodlock (*Eng.*) Dweller at the enclosure in, or by, the wood.

Woodman (*Eng.*) One who cut and sold timber, in a wood or forest; one who hunted game in a wood; one who dyed with woad; descendant of Wudeman (woodman).

Woodrick, Woodrich, Woodridge (*Eng.*) Dweller in, or near, the wood on a ridge or range of hills.

Woodrow (*Eng.*) One who came from Woodrow (row of trees), the name of places in Wiltshire and Worcestershire.

Woodruff, Woodroffe, Woodroofe (*Eng.*) A wood or forest keeper for the lord of the manor.

Woodside (*Eng., Scot.*) Dweller at the side of the wood; one who came from Woodside (side of the wood), in Ayrshire.

Woodson, Woodsum, Woodsome (*Eng.*) One who came from Woodsome (houses in a wood), in Yorkshire; the son of Wuda (wood).

Woodward (*Eng.*) The officer who had charge of the wood, a forester.

Woodworth (*Eng.*) Dweller at the homestead in, or by, a wood.

Wool (*Eng.*) One who came from Wool (springs), in Dorset.

Wooldridge, Wooldredge (*Eng.*) Descendant of Wulfric (wolf, rule).

Wooley, Woolley (*Eng.*) One who came from Wooley (wolves' meadow), in Yorkshire.

Woolf (*Ger.*) Same as Wolf, q.v.

Woolner (*Ger.*) One who prepared wool for manufacture.

Woolridge, Woolrich (*Eng.*) Descendant of Ulrich (wolf, rule).

Woolsey, Wolsey (*Eng.*) Descendant of Wulfsige (wolf, victory).

Wooten, Wootton, Wootten (*Eng.*) One who came from Wootton (homestead in, or by, a wood), the name of many places in England.

Worcester, Wooster, Wurster, Worster (*Eng.*) One who came from Worcester (Roman fort of the Wigoran tribe), in Worcestershire.

Word (*Eng., Ger.*) Dweller near a thicket or a winding brook; descendant of Werdo, a pet form of names commencing with Wert (worthy), as Werdheri and Werdmann; dweller at an open place in a village.

Worden, Werden (*Eng.*) One who came from Worden (valley with a weir or dam), in Lancashire.

Work, Worker (*Eng.*) Dweller near the fortification; variant of Wark, q.v.

Workman (*Eng.*) One who worked so many days a week for the lord of the manor in return for the land he held.

Worley (*Eng.*) One who came from Worle (woodgrouse wood), in Somerset.

Wormley (*Eng.*) One who came from Wormley or Warmley (wood infested by reptiles), in Hertfordshire and Gloucestershire.

Worrell (*Eng.*) One who came from Worrall (bog mytrle on a river lowland), in Yorkshire.

Worrick (*Eng.*) One who came from Warwick (village by a dam or shore), the name of places in Cumberland and Warwickshire.

Worth, Werth (*Eng.*) Dweller in, or near, an enclosure or on a dependent farm; one who came from Worth (enclosure), the name of several places in England.

Wortham, Worthem (*Eng.*) One who came from Wortham (enclosed homestead), in Suffolk.

Worthington (*Eng.*) One who came from Worthington (village of the Wurthingas'), in Lancashire.

Worthy, Worthey (*Eng.*) One who came from Worthy (enclosed homestead), in Hampshire.

Wotten (*Eng.*) One who came from Wootton (homestead in, or by, a wood), the name of many places in England.

Wozniak (*Pol., Ukr.*) The son of the messenger.

Wozny (*Pol.*) One who summoned people to a court of law.

Wraight (*Eng.*) Variant of Wright, q.v.

Wray (*Eng.*) One who came from Wray (isolated place), the name of several places in England.

Wren, Wrenn (*Eng., Ir.*) One with some characteristic of the wren; grandson of Reann (spear).

Wright (*Eng.*) One who worked in wood, or other hard material, a carpenter.

Wrightson (*Eng.*) The son of the worker in wood.

Wrigley (*Eng.*) Dweller at the ridge meadow.

Wrobel (*Pol.*) One with some real or fancied quality of a sparrow; dweller at the sign of the sparrow.

Wroblewski (*Pol.*) One who came from Wroblewsk (sparrow village), in Poland.

Wrona (*Pol.*) Dweller at the sign of the crow; one with the qualities of a crow.

Wulf, Wulff (*Ger.*) Descendant of Vulf, a pet form of names beginning with Wolf (wolf), as Wolfbrand, Wolfgang and Wolfgard; dweller at the sign of the wolf; one with the qualities of a wolf.

Wunderlich, Wunder (*Ger.*) The odd, or moody, man; one who was curious or nosy.

Wuori (*Finn.*) Dweller on a mountain.

Wurster (*Ger.*) One who made and sold sausage. *See also* Worcester.

Wyant, Wyand, Wyands (*Eng.*) Descendant of Weigand or Wygan (warrior).

Wyatt, Wyott (*Eng.*) Descendant of little Guy (wood).

Wyche, Wych (*Eng.*) Dweller by the wych-elm tree; dweller at, or near, a salt spring.

Wydra (*Pol.*) Dweller at the sign of the otter; one with some quality of an otter.

Wye (*Eng.*) One who came from Wye (heathen temple), in Kent; dweller at, or near, the Wye (running water) or Wey, the names of several British rivers.

Wyer (*Eng.*) Dweller at, or near, a dam or fish trap; dweller near one of the rivers Wye (running water), in England.

Wyeth, Wythe (*Wel., Scot.*) The brave man; dweller near a ford or wood; dweller near a willow tree.

Wylie (*Eng.*) A variant of Wiley, q.v.

Wyman (*Eng.*) The warrior or soldier.

Wyndham (*Eng.*) Dweller at a homestead approached by a winding ascent or path; one who came from Wyndham, in Sussex.

Wynkoop, Wynekoop (*Du.*) One who sold wine, a wine merchant; one who came from Wijnkoop (place where wine was sold), a small local district in Holland.

Wynn, Wynne (*Scot., Wel.*) Dweller on a wynd, a narrow street in a town; descendant of Gwynn (fair).

Wynot, Wynott (*Fr.*) Descendant of little Guyon (little wood).

Wysocki (*Pol.*) One who came from Wysock (high), in Poland.

Xanthos (*Ger.*) The golden or yellow-haired man.

Xaverius (*Ger.*) Descendant of Xaverius (brilliant).

Xavier (*Sp.*) One who came from Xaberri or Xaverri, abbreviated forms of Etchaberri (new house), the name of numerous places in Spain.

Xenophon (*Eng.*) Descendant of Xenophon (strange voice).

Xenos (*Gr.*) The stranger.

Ximena (*Sp.*) One who came from Ximena (place of Jimena or Simon), in Spain.

Yaeger, Yager (*Ger.*) One who hunted game, a huntsman.

Yaffe (*Heb.*) Descendant of Yaffe, a pet form of Japheth (increase).

Yale (*Eng.*) Dweller at a corner, nook or secret place, or at the side of a hill.

Yalowitz (*Ukr.*) Dweller near a green bush or juniper tree.

Yamamoto (*Jap.*) Dweller at the base of a mountian.

Yancey, Yancy (*Fr.*) One who came from England, an Englishman.

Yanke, Yankee (*Du.*) Descendant of little Jan (gracious gift of Jehovah); one who came from Holland; a name sometimes applied to a stranger.

Yarbrough, Yarborough (*Eng.*) One who came from Yarborough or Yarburgh (earth fortification), in Lincolnshire.

Yard, Yarde (*Eng.*) One who tilled a yard or yardland (about thirty acres).

Yardley (*Eng.*) One who came from Yardley (wood where spars were obtained), the name of several places in England.

Yarnell, Yarnall (*Eng.*) Dweller at the slope where eagles were seen; descendant of Arnold (eagle, rule).

Yates, Yeates (*Eng.*) One who lived in, or near, the gate or gap in a chain of hills.

Yeager (*Ger.*) One who hunted game, a huntsman.

Yeaton (*Eng.*) One who came from Yeaton (homestead on the river), in Shropshire.

Yee (*Chin.*) First person singular pronoun, I.

Yell (*Scot.*) One who came from Yell (barren), an island in the Shetland group.

Yeomans, Yeoman (*Eng.*) One owning a small landed property, a freeholder; one who acted as a retainer or gentleman attendant in a royal or noble household.

Yerkes, Yerke (*Ger.*) Descendant of Jorg (farmer).

Yocum, Yocom, Yokum, Yoakum (*Du.*) Descendant of Jojakim (Yah makes to stand still).

Yohanan, Yohanna, Yohana (*Ger., Heb.*) Descendant of Johannes (gracious gift of Jehovah); descendant of Yohanan, the Hebrew form of John.

Yonan (*Ger.*) Descendant of Johann (gracious gift of Jehovah).

Yonker, Yonkers, Younker (*Du.*) The young nobleman or squire.

Yore (*Eng.*) Dweller near the Yare (babbling river), a river in Norfolk, or near the Yar or Yare (of obscure origin), a river in Wight.

York, Yorke, Yorks (*Eng.*) One who came from York (place of yew trees), in Yorkshire.

Yost (*Ger.*) Descendant of Jodocus (fighter).

Youmans, Youman, Yomans (*Eng.*) Variants of Yeomans, q.v.

Young, Younger, Younge, Yung, Yunger (*Eng., Ger.*) One younger than another with whom he was associated, or of two bearing the same Christian name; the younger son.

Youngberg (*Sw.*) Heather mountain.

Youngblood (*Sw., Ger.*) Heather leaf; a translation of German Jungblut, q.v.

Youngdahl (*Sw.*) Heather valley.

Younghusband (*Eng.*) The farmer who was younger than another with whom he was associated.

Younglove (*Sw.*) Heather leaf.

Youngman, Youngmann, Youngerman (*Ger.*) Variants of Jungmann, q.v.

Youngquist (*Sw.*) Heather twig.

Yule, Yuill, Youle (*Eng.*) Dweller near a yew tree; descendant of Yule (Christmas).

Yunker (*Du.*) Variant of Yonker, q.v.

Yust (*Du.*) Descendant of Joost (the just).

Zabel (*Pol., Cz.-Sl.*) Dweller at the sign of the sable; one with the qualities of a sable; one who trapped and sold sables.

Zacharias, Zachary (*Eng.*) Descendant of Zacharias or Zachary (whom Jehovah remembers).

Zack, Zach (*Ger.*) Descendant of Zacco or Zach, pet forms of Zacharias (whom Jehovah remembers).

Zagar, Zager (*Du.*) One who cut timber into boards, a sawyer.

Zagorski (*Pol.*) Dweller behind, or beyond, the hill.

Zahara (*Sp.*) One who came from Zahara (desert), a town in Spain.

Zaharias (*Gr.*) Descendant of Zaharias (whom Jehovah remembers).

Zahn (*Ger.*) Dweller near a pointed rock; one who had a prominent tooth.

Zajac, Zajic (*Pol., Ukr.*) One with some characteristic of a rabbit; dweller at the sign of the rabbit.

Zajicka, Zajic (*Cz.-Sl.*) One with some characteristic of a rabbit; dweller at the sign of the rabbit.

Zak (*Cz.-Sl.*) One who attended school, a schoolboy.

Zaleski (*Pol.*) Dweller beyond the forest.

Zalewski (*Pol.*) Dweller near a flooded place.

Zander (*Ger.*) Descendant of Zander, a pet form of Alexander (helper of mankind); one who came from Zandt, the name of several places in Germany.

Zaremba (*Pol.*) A warrior who fought with a sword.

Zawacki (*Pol.*) One who came from Zawada (troublemaker), a village in Poland.

Zeigler (*Ger.*) A variant of Ziegler, q.v.

Zelenka (*Cz.-Sl.*) The little, green one; one not acquainted with the ways of man, a greenhorn.

Zeleny (*Cz.-Sl.*) One who wore green garments.

Zeller, Zell (*Ger.*) One who came from Zell (church), a village in Switzerland.

Zeman (*Cz.-Sl.*) One who acted as a gentleman; one who aped the manner of a gentleman.

Zender (*Ger.*) One who collected rents; descendant of Zender, a pet form of Alexander (helper of mankind).

Zenner (*Ger.*) One who worked in pewter; an officer of a hundred, a district in the Middle Ages chiefly important for its court of justice.

Zeno (*It.*) Descendant of Zeno (of Zeus).

Zhukov (*Rus.*) The son of the beetle or scarab.

Zick (*Ger.*) Descendant of Sigo, a pet form of names beginning with Sieg (victory), as Sigimar, Sigibrand and Sigivald.

Zidek (*Pol.*) The little Jew, a contemptuous term.

Ziebell, Zibell (*Ger.*) One who raised and sold onions; one who came from Zibelle (place where onions grew), in Germany.

Ziegler (*Ger.*) One who built with, or made, bricks or roof tiles.

Zielinski (*Pol., Ukr.*) One who came from Zielinsk or Zielen (green place), the names of places in Poland and Ukraine.

Zielke, Ziehlke (*Ger.*) One who raised and sold cabbages.

Ziemann, Zieman (*Ger.*) Descendant of Sigiman (victory, man).

Ziemba (*Pol.*) Dweller at the sign of the bullfinch or grosbeak; one thought to possess the characteristics of a bullfinch.

Ziemer (*Ger.*) Descendant of Sigimar (victory, famous).

Ziff, Zipf (*Ger.*) Dweller near the point or corner.

Zilch, Zillich, Zillig (*Ger.*) Descendant of Ziv (alive).

Zima (*Cz.-Sl., Pol., Ger.*) One who worked in the winter.

Zimmerman, Zimmer, Zimmermann (*Ger.*) One who worked in wood, a carpenter.

Zink, Zinke (*Ger.*) One with a large or prominent nose; one who played the medieval cornet, the zinke.

Ziolko (*Pol.*) One who grew and sold herbs; dweller at a place where herbs grew; in figurative speech, a smart man.

Ziolkowski (*Pol.*) One who came from Ziolkow(o) (herbs), in Poland.

Zion (*Heb.*) One who came from Zion (monument raised up), a hill in Jerusalem; one who had made a pilgrimage to Zion, a religious name for the Holy Land of Palestine.

Zisook (*Pol.*) Descendant of Isaac (he who laughs).

Zito (*Cz.-Sl.*) Dweller near the rye field.

Ziv, Zivin, Ziven (*Pol., Cz.-Sl., Rus.*) The vigorous, alive person.

Zizzo, Zizza (*It.*) One who gave undue attention to dress, a dandy.

Zlaty (*Cz.-Sl.*) One who had a golden complexion.

Zmich (*Ukr.*) The pleasant, smiling person.

Zmuda (*Pol.*) The inactive or lazy person.

Zobel (*Ger.*) Dweller at the sign of the sable; one who trapped and sold sables.

Zola, Zolla (*It.*) Dweller on, or near, a hill or mound; descendant of Zola, a pet form of names so ending, as Franzola, Renzola and Anzola.

Zoll (*Ger.*) Descendant of Zollo; a variant of Zoller, q.v.

Zoller, Zollner (*Ger.*) One who collected duty on goods coming into the country, perhaps one who had purchased the concession.

Zona (*It.*) Descendant of Zona, a pet form of Franzona (the free).

Zook (*Pol., Ukr., Rus.*) Descendant of Zuk (beetle).

Zorich (*Ukr.*) The son of Zorya (star).

Zorn, Zorner (*Ger.*) One who came from Zorn (anger), in Germany.

Zuber (*Ger., Swis.*) Dweller by the little stream.

Zuckerman, Zucker (*Ger.*) The robber; one who dealt in sugar.

Zuelke (*Pol.*) One who gathered herbs; the smart or clever man.

Zug (*Swis., Ger.*) One who came from Zug (from the tribe of the Tugeni), a canton in Switzerland.

Zukerman, Zuker (*Ger.*) The robber; one who dealt in sugar.

Zukor, Zuker (*Hun.*) Sugar.

Zukowski (*Pol.*) One who came from Zukow(o) (place infested by beetles), in Poland.

Zullo (*It.*) Descendant of Zullo, a pet form of Ignazio (fiery).

Zurawski (*Pol.*) One who came from Zuraw (place where cranes abound), in Poland.

Zurek (*Pol.*) One who made sour meal pap.

Zweig (*Ger.*) Branch (of a plant).

Zweigler (*Ger.*) Dweller on the side road, or branch of the stream.

Zwick (*Ger.*) One who dwelt on a wedge-shaped piece of land; one who dealt in nails; descendant of Cvik (crafty man).

Zwicker (*Ger.*) One who came from Zwickau, a city and district in Saxony; one who made and sold nails; descendant of Swidiger (strong, spear).

Zych (*Pol.*) Descendant of Zych, a pet form of Zyla (vein).

Zylstra (*Du.*) Dweller near a drainage sluice.